African American Rhetoric(s)

African American Rhetoric(s)

Interdisciplinary Perspectives

Edited by
Elaine B. Richardson
and
Ronald L. Jackson II

With a Foreword by Jacqueline Jones Royster
With an Introduction by Keith Gilyard

Southern Illinois University Press • *Carbondale*

Chapter 2, "From Panther to Monster: Representations of Resistance from the Black
Power Movement of the 1960s to the *Boyz in the Hood* and Beyond," copyright © by
Kalí Tal 2002. Chapter 6, "The Multiple Dimensions of Nubian/Egyptian Rhetoric
and Its Implications for Contemporary Classroom Instructions," copyright © 2003 by
Clinton Crawford.

Publication partially funded by the Africana Research Center of the Pennsylvania State
University.

Library of Congress Cataloging-in-Publication Data

African American rhetoric(s) : interdisciplinary perspectives / edited by Elaine B.
Richardson, Ronald L. Jackson II.
        p. cm.
    Includes bibliographical references (p.   ) and index.
        1. American prose literature—African American authors—History and criticism.
2. Speeches, addresses, etc., American—African American authors—History and
criticism. 3. English language—Rhetoric—Study and teaching—United States. 4.
Rhetoric—Political aspects—United States. 5. English language—United States—
Rhetoric. 6. Politics and literature—United States. 7. African Americans—Communication. 8. African Americans—Language. 9. Black English. I. Title: African American
rhetoric. II. Richardson, Elaine B., date. III. Jackson, Ronald L., date.
    PS153.N5 A69 2004
    808'.0089'6073—dc22
    ISBN 0-8093-2565-9 (alk. paper)   2003019272

Printed on recycled paper. ♻

The paper used in this publication meets the minimum requirements of American
National Standard for Information Sciences—Permanence of Paper for Printed Library
Materials, ANSI Z39.48-1992. ♾

Contents

Part Two: Visions for Pedagogy of African American Rhetoric

Part Three: Visions for Research in African American Rhetoric(s)

Foreword

Jacqueline Jones Royster

AFRICAN AMERICAN RHETORIC(S) IS A COLLECTION THAT RESPONDS
to the question: What parameters can we use to begin a more thoughtful and useful consideration of African Americans in rhetorical space?
Elaine B. Richardson and Ronald L. Jackson II frame their views as "the
study of culturally and discursively developed knowledge-forms, communicative practices and persuasive strategies rooted in freedom struggles
by people of African ancestry in America." This viewpoint is quite provocative in the sense that they bring into focus several points that are
actually quite contentious in scholarly endeavors. They centralize the use
of cultural frameworks in rhetorical analysis as they emphasize the importance of the practices that they are showcasing having emerged from
people with a particular ancestry—African. They focus on discursive
forms, which underscores the importance of verbality and rationality,
rather than just orality and literacy. They acknowledge persuasion as the
abiding purpose of interactive engagement within and across communities, and they make clear that the mandate that is quite compelling in these
discursive forms is tied unequivocally to struggles for freedom among this
group. What's more, they present this view as part of knowledge-making processes, rather than as simply expressive traditions, suggesting that
there are consequences for language use in terms of the ways that we
think, act, and consider ourselves in the world. All of these points help
to make a place for this collection amid some of the most intellectually
challenging spaces of our times in interdisciplinary fields of rhetoric.

Richardson and Jackson divide the essays into three sections, highlighting the range of work that researchers and scholars are currently doing
in response to the rising tide of interests in underrepresented communities in dominant scholarly areas. The focus of part one is "Historicizing
and Analyzing African American Rhetoric(s)"; part two, "Visions for
Pedagogy of African American Rhetoric"; and part three, "Visions for

Research in African American Rhetoric(s)." These divisions indicate the considerable variety of work from which the collection draws and signal critical points of concern specifically relevant to African American rhetorical practices. Clearly, there is a call in this collection for a recovery of achievements and legacies, a call to pull forth for contemporary critical inquiry the practices and performances that constitute the contours of a rhetorical landscape that remains relatively unknown in mainstream scholarly discourses. There is also a call for us to address directly and specifically complex pedagogical problems and to use a more richly endowed and inclusive knowledge base to help contemporary students use their literate resources more effectively. Most certainly, there is the challenge of generating more powerful interpretive frames within an interdisciplinary discipline. The call is for analytical and interpretive models capable of helping us to incorporate well into theories and practices what we are coming to know about these rhetorical legacies and ongoing achievements, in terms of sites for engagement; the media by which rhetors are meeting their persuasive mandates; and the focal points that allow us to understand their contexts, purposes, and actions.

In order to appreciate this perspective more fully, it follows that as readers we should pay attention to some striking concepts. Among such ideas, I find compelling the notions listed below:

1. a view of culture, as influenced by African ancestral traditions, as an appropriate factor in analyzing performance.

2. a critical exploration of the ways in which strategies and practices participate dynamically in knowledge-making enterprises.

3. closer attention to the specific material conditions out of which practices come—in this case, the activist agenda of a historically and consistently oppressed people who continue to struggle for freedom, as evidenced by their rhetorical performances.

So, why is this approach important, and particularly, why is it important now? As we enter a new century of scholarship in interdisciplinary fields, many of us have finally come to appreciate and to understand critical advantages in having theoretical frames that take into account achievements that may and may not resonate with European cultural traditions. In broadening our horizons with experiences and information from different geographical and cultural spaces, we extend our horizons and enrich our understanding, not just of peripheral people in knowledge-making arenas but of human potential. The challenge, however, remains one of actually building a base that is indeed capable of informing us, and also one of finding productive ways to use that newly formed information base to re-create and reconstitute theories and practices. This collection, therefore, serves critical purposes. It helps us to see a wider range of experiences and to learn more about rhetorical practices and performances that are not well known in academic arenas. The collection helps us to see that those practices are deserving of both respect and critical eyes. My expectation is that *African American Rhetoric(s)* will go quite far in helping us to chart new pathways to understanding. This collection encourages us to notice the inventions and refinements in rhetorical practices that have emerged from the cultural fusions of this particular group, but more generally it encourages us to be informed by what human beings, in all of our variety, have the capacity to do in the interest of rhetorical exigency.

I am grateful to these scholars, the editors, and the contributors for bringing to our attention with such insightful articulation, a rhetorical landscape that deserves attention. This collection will indeed be in a vanguard of publications that can cast our gaze on both continuities and change in rhetorical scholarship and keep our scholarly dialogues well invigorated and meaningfully engaged.

Preface

Elaine B. Richardson
Ronald L. Jackson II

AFRICAN AMERICAN RHETORIC(S) IS AN INTRODUCTION TO
fundamental concepts as well as a systematic integration of historical and
contemporary lines of inquiry in the study of African American rhetoric(s).
African American rhetoric(s) is the name we prefer for the study of culturally and discursively developed knowledge-forms, communicative practices and persuasive strategies rooted in freedom struggles by people of
African ancestry in America. Each chapter in the collection raises issues
concerning the practicality of Black rhetoric(s) in order to explore them
more deeply; to consider how they influence our work in the study of
cultural rhetorics; and to think about how these rhetorics might be suited
to better accommodate the development of empowering rhetorics, ideologies, and rhetorical strategies. This text has strong theoretically oriented
pieces that push thinking in the discipline in new directions or that revisit,
recontextualize, and revise more traditional lines of inquiry. Another focus of this collection is on oral/written intertextuality, so that the analysis of orations by African Americans is not the focus; rather, African American discourse, written or spoken, is viewed as always already polyphonous.
The collection also has a strong pedagogical and practical bent, as well
as empirically oriented pieces that examine theories and social literacies
in practice. This text treats literary, cultural, discursive, and linguistic aspects of African American rhetorics such as womanist, Reconstructionist,
Ancient Egyptian, and Afrocentric rhetorics as indivorceable components
of a larger study of the universe of Black discourse. From this perspective, African Americans and other diasporic Africans have developed communicative behaviors, ideas, and persuasive techniques to advance and
protect themselves while counteracting injustice.

In these essays, we seek a broader conceptionalization of African
American rhetoric(s) by exploring the roots of African American cultural

understandings and practices found in diverse places as literary texts, barbershops, historical documents, and cultural practices, to name a few, and the articulation of these in their connection to current persuasive and negotiation strategies. Another unique focus of these essays is their persistent effort to delineate debates within the fields of rhetoric and composition, (African) American literature and criticism, and African American studies in general. Furthermore, the connection of linguistic and cultural variation to rhetoric is emphasized. The essays contained here are an attempt to explore the development, meaning, themes, strategies, and arguments of African American rhetoric(s), as well as the connections of these to culture, rhetoric, poetics, composition, and literacy and among the same. In this text, we use the terms *Black, African American, Afro-American,* and *people of African descent* synonymously. We realize that there are semantic differences between the terms. For example, for some people, *Black* implies a political edge that the term *African American* or *Afro-American* does not. Conversely, for some people, *African American* and *Afro-American* signal a neutral designation in a way that *Black* does not. For others, *Black* and *Afro-American* refer to people of African descent located throughout the Diaspora, including the Americas, the Caribbean, the African continent, and throughout Europe. However, for this volume, we impose no uniformity of usage upon the authors. We trust the reader won't find this too much of a hindrance.

Keith Gilyard's introduction maps the historical terrain of the field, identifying some of the earliest dissertations written on the rhetoric of Frederick Douglass through studies of Black Power rhetoric to the rhetoric of the jeremiad (the fall of America), up through contemporary, as his title reflects, Aspects of African American Rhetoric as a Field.

Part one, "Historicizing and Analyzing African American Rhetoric(s)," contains five essays concerning aspects of the history of Black Power rhetoric, new ways of theorizing African American rhetoric(s), theories pertaining to appeals and rhetorical strategies employed by historical and contemporary African American rhetors, rhetorical analysis of literature, as well as analysis of the work of two pioneering African American female linguistic anthropologists.

The chapter by Shirley Wilson Logan, "Black Speakers, White Representations: Frances Ellen Watkins Harper and the Construction of a Public Persona," explores African American rhetors' creation of ethical appeals. Logan's analysis of Frances Ellen Watkins Harper's construction of a public persona attributes much of Harper's training to her womanist consciousness, composed of a vernacular sensibility informed by life experiences and cultural orientation as well as formal elocutionary training. In fact, Harper grew up observing the strategic freedom and education practices of her uncle and his colleagues who fought against racist laws and the enslavement of free Blacks in Maryland. Specifically, Logan analyzes White audiences' responses to articulate Black speakers (bodies), something that was unfamiliar to White American audiences during the nineteenth century.

The essays of both Kalí Tal and Gwendolyn D. Pough offer critical examinations of conflicting strategies within and among the political rhetoric of the Black Panthers and various other rhetorics in African American communities both historically and contemporarily.

Kalí Tal's "From Panther to Monster" treats the development and dialogue between dominant racist rhetorics and African American and other unofficial rhetorics in its exploration of 1960s African American rhetorics of revolution and their incorporation of Marxist, Socialist, and other Black freedom rhetorics such as those that influenced the great Afro-French psychologist and scholar, Frantz Fanon. According to Tal, the book *Monster* and a host of Black cultural productions are created in isolation from such African American counterpublic discourse texts. Tal's analysis is valuable, for it brings to light very important questions: Where are texts such as *Monster* located in the continuum of African American rhetorics? What is the value of films such as *Boyz in the Hood* and *Posse* when their ideological value has to translate into market value? How can African American artists exploit media to develop critical consciousness in audiences?

Gwendolyn D. Pough's study "Rhetoric that Should Have Moved the People," focusing on the Black Panther Party and its rhetoric, traces the impact of this rhetoric on its Black audiences, where it intersected with issues of class, homosexual rights, women's rights, Black religious beliefs, and alliances with Whites. In doing so, Pough reveals rhetorical problems that occurred, which contributed to the Panthers' alienation from many segments of the Black community in general, while illuminating strategies that may be applicable to the contemporary struggle for human rights.

Jacqueline K. Bryant mines the Afrocentric freedom rhetoric of "The Literary Foremother." The rhetorical strategies and power of Black women, whether orators (as explored by Logan), writers, scholars, or astronauts, for that matter, have been woefully undertheorized. As Bryant points out, this is even more so in the case of the everyday Black mother (whether she was blood mother or community mother) who stood up under the weight of the Black and White communities in slavery. This motif is apparent in the "discursive practice of early Black women writers [which] results in the construction of the foremother figure—a figure that clearly opposes and subverts the mammy figure . . . needed to create and perpetuate [Western culture]."

Kimmika L. H. Williams in "Ties that Bind" presents a study of two African American women linguistic anthropologists in her comparative analysis of Geneva Smitherman's and Zora Neale Hurston's work on African American Language, discussing the important contributions these women made despite societal and academic constraints.

Within part two, "Visions for Pedagogy of African American Rhetoric," are four essays, which are all concerned with the teaching of composition and rhetoric. We see this part as a necessary resource for educators and educational researchers who often offer compelling cases for the inclusion of a multicultural curriculum that embraces innovation and have been frustrated by the lack of classroom research and models in this area.

In his discussion of ancient African texts and thought and their influence on classical Greek traditions, "The Multiple Dimensions of Nubian/Egyptian Rhetoric and Its Implications for Contemporary Classroom Instructions," Clinton Crawford argues that we must recast Nile Valley rhetoric and its history accurately, as they inform the creation of modern Black cultural rhetorics and could help in the rhetorical education of today's youth.

Lena Ampadu's "Modeling Orality" presents cutting-edge scholarship while it reports on a study wherein college students of multicultural backgrounds (including European American) imitated the rhetorical strategies of African American oral texts as a means of improving their writing. Specifically, the students imitated the repetition schemes of anaphora, antithesis, chiasmus, and parallelism. In so doing, Ampadu's work draws on both the Greek classical rhetorical tradition and African American rhetorical traditions.

In her chapter, "Coming from the Heart," Elaine B. Richardson presents an ethnomethodological study of two students (as presented in interviews and analysis of pieces of their writing) and their struggle to develop academic personas. The value of the chapter is that it outlines some of the struggles African American students from middle-class as well as lower economic backgrounds face in college writing courses (as well as throughout educational institutions). Further, Richardson discusses African American literacy and epistemological practices and how they may be connected to instruction in composition and rhetoric.

Using methodology of deconstruction and African American significa-tion, Victoria Cliett's essay "The Rhetoric of Democracy: Contracts, Dec-larations, and Bills of Sales" explores the dialectical structure of African American discourse and traces the genealogical systems of power that produce artificial notions of truth as embedded in documents such as the Declaration of Independence and the Constitution. This "playful" exami-nation of political discourse and its influence on the writing classroom yields a serious critique of the notion of the "democratic" and "liberatory" writing classroom and its effects on African American students.

Part three, "Visions for Research in African American Rhetoric(s)," contains state of the art discussions concerning the interface of technol-ogy and African American rhetoric(s); new theorizations of African American rhetoric(s) and rhetoric in general; pedagogy of race, gender, culture, and writing in the academy; and the centrality of understand-ing the African American Vernacular English (AAVE) oral tradition as it informs the written word in the works of African American writers and cultural performers.

Adam J. Banks's "Looking Forward to Look Back: Technology Ac-cess and Transformation in African American Rhetoric" argues that the study of the impact of technology on African American rhetoric(s) is just as central an organizing scheme as the study of "the word" in under-standing development and manipulation in African American rhetoric(s).

Kermit Campbell's essay "We Is Who We Was: The African/Ameri-can Rhetoric of *Amistad*" uses critical rhetorical analysis as well as criti-cal race theory to analyze certain aspects of the film *Amistad* and John Q. Adams's historical role in the trial. Campbell argues for the notion of cultural hybridity in the study of rhetoric and rhetorical traditions.

In "From the Harbor to Da Academic Hood: Hush Harbors and an African American Rhetorical Tradition," Vorris L. Nunley locates an aspect of the vernacularity of African American cultural production, by uncovering camouflaged sites, or hush harbors, wherein African Ameri-can rhetorics flourish, demonstrating that African American rhetorics can be theorized in their distinctive forms. Nunley argues that these hush harbors are locations within African American rhetorical traditions with a distinctive relationship to audience and to the rhetorical commonplace, a relationship mediated through material and discursive space. In so doing, Nunley demonstrates that rhetorical scholarship has undertheo-rized how the politics and poetics of geography and space mediate rhetorical performances. After anchoring hush harbors historically and establishing linkages to contemporary versions of hush harbors, this essay provides examples to illustrate the implications of hush harbor rhetorics for the classroom.

In "'Both Print and Oral' and 'Talking About Race': Transforming Toni Morrison's Language Issues into Teaching Issues," Joyce Irene Middleton uses Morrison's nonfiction (including her Nobel lecture), to analyze her language issues as teaching issues, exploring the usefulness of theories of orality to student discussions about personal and cultural language use. Middleton examines Morrison's theories of language in a racialized society, locating them in dialectical relations with literary studies, language and literacy studies, and rhetorical education for social justice. In this way, Middleton's essay reflects a new vision for research in African American rhetoric(s).

Finally, William W. Cook's essay "Found Not Founded" guides us from West Africa to the New World and to America as he connects the West African background of African American cultural productions as varied as poetry, dance, religion, literature, and Hip Hop lyricism. For Cook, these art forms are connected by the force of the cultural use of language, the masking function and effect of Black discourse, which seeks to resist oppression and domination. Cook's essay is in direct conversation with Tal's. While Tal's work evokes the question, where are Black popular culture productions located in African American rhetorics of struggle? Cook's discussion locates them on the continuum of subversive art forms in the vernacular tradition.

Arguments such as those by Cook, Tal, Banks, and others in *African American Rhetoric(s): Interdisciplinary Perspectives* support one of the reasons that we chose to identify the study of persuasive language use by African Americans as rhetoric(s), rather than rhetoric. There is a continuum of African American rhetorics within the universe of Black discourse. Putting a twist on the words of Adam J. Banks, not only must we "look back as we look forward" but we must emphasize the scope of diversity within African American(s) and how these are themselves always already intertextual.

Introduction: Aspects of African American Rhetoric as a Field

Keith Gilyard

TO ENCAPSULATE ALL THE VARIOUS EFFORTS IN THE SCHOLARLY study of African American rhetoric would be a task virtually as daunting as if the object were to summarize all reportage and analysis of the Black experience overall. Voluminous attention has been devoted to Black discourses because such discourses have been the major means by which people of African descent in the American colonies and subsequent republic have asserted their collective humanity in the face of an enduring White supremacy and tried to persuade, cajole, and gain acceptance for ideas relative to Black survival and Black liberation. So immediately one recognizes the impracticality of trying to write definitively about such a vast network of activities in such limited space. What I attempt, therefore, is a meaningful historical sketch of a particular body of rhetorical scholarship, a choice that necessarily implies certain critical sacrifices. For example, I will forgo formal discussion of linguistics and the creative arts, although I possess impressive arguments why such truncation of rhetorical inquiry should not be carried too far. The very existence of African American Vernacular English (AAVE) inscribes a significant rhetorical situation, and the prevailing functional character of African American artistic expression renders problematic any move to divorce its production and any criticism thereof from the realm of rhetorical inquiry. Nonetheless, I maintain that it is useful, in order to actually get through one essay, to focus on what there is to say about Black persuasive or associative verbal practices beyond the specific linguistic items of AAVE, or Standard English for that matter, or on what is left to say of public discourse if one agrees to bracket texts that are literary or musical. What is left to say of strategy and method? The answer comprises the terrain that this essay explores. The focus is on what scholars working taxonomically and employing rhetorical perspectives ranging from Aristotelian principles to Afrocentric conceptions have made of oratory by those of African descent in the United States. Of course, this approach also ignores what normally would be regarded as interpersonal communication. I am aware, too, how ultimately indefensible that decision is in the long run given that even one-on-one verbal interaction designed to elicit cooperation is surely rhetoric as well. However, some of the collections I mention, such as *Language, Communication, and Rhetoric in Black America* (A. Smith, 1972), do include such work that extends beyond the scope of this project. In addition, I recommend Thomas Kochman's *Rappin' and Stylin' Out* (1972) and Michael Hecht's *African American Communication* (1993).

Serious analysis of African American oratory dates back to the nineteenth century. In the 1850s and 1860s, speeches by the likes of Frederick Douglass and Charles Langston were published and commented on in publications such as the *Liberator* and the *Anglo American Magazine*. By 1890, anthologies such as E. M. Brawley's *The Negro Baptist Pulpit* were being produced. However, the first standard reference work on African American rhetoric, *Negro Orators and Their Orations,* was compiled by Carter G. Woodson in 1925. Woodson reveals himself to be of a classical bent methodologically. He liberally invokes such authorities as Demosthenes, Quintillian, and Cicero. He employs Aristotelian classifications, categorizing speeches as judicial, deliberative, or epideictic. Nonetheless, Woodson does move beyond the classical by positing Christian pulpit oratory as a fourth major category. Of course, Black orators did not get much practice with speeches of the judicial type, or the deliberative when *deliberative* is narrowly defined as being before legislative bodies. But by Woodson's reckoning, Blacks excelled at the epideictic, or the occasional speech, and in the pulpit.

By use of chapter headings, Woodson traces a movement from "The First Protest" to "Progressive Oratory," with stops along the way that signal "More Forceful Attacks," "Further Efforts for a Hearing," "The Oratory of the Crisis," "The Oratory of Defiance," "Deliberative Oratory—Speeches of Negro Congressmen," "Speeches of Negro Congressman Outside of Congress," "Oratory in the Solution of the Race Problem," "The Panegyric," "Optimistic Oratory," and "Occasional Oratory." He cites as first examples of public protest against enslavement two speeches: one titled "Negro Slavery" by "Othello," which was subsequently printed in 1787, and a second titled "Slavery," which was signed "By a Free Negro" and printed in 1788. For more forceful appeals, he offers such examples as Peter Williams's 1808 "Oration on the Abolition of the Slave Trade" and James Forten's 1813 "A Late Bill Before the State of Pennsylvania," in which Forten argued against a proposed bill to bar free people of color from entering the state. The chapter "Further Efforts" includes James McCune Smith's 1838 "The Abolition of Slavery and the Slave Trade in the French and British Colonies," which was celebratory of the political event and designed to spur hope and further the cause of abolition in the United States. As abolitionist activity gathered force, Charles Lenox Remond and then Frederick Douglass became the most famous Black orators, and a dozen or so speeches by the two between 1841 and 1863 are Woodson's main examples of those who spoke to the "crisis" and to the issue of "defiance." Speeches by congressmen during the Reconstruction era include, in session, John Willis Menard's 1868 "The Negro's First Speech in Congress, Made by John Willis Menard in Defense of His Election to Congress when His Seat Was Contested and Won by His Political Opponent" and, out of session, James Mercer Langston's 1874 "Equality before the Law." Douglass's 1879 "The Negro Exodus from the Gulf States" is noted as an example of "solution" rhetoric; Bishop Reverdy Ransom's 1905 centennial oration in appreciation of William Lloyd Garrison is included among examples of the panegyric. Optimistic oratory is most closely associated with Booker T. Washington. C. V. Roman at various times delivered "A Knowledge of History Conducive to Racial Solidarity," which is presented as an excellent example of the occasional address. Progressive oratory, to Woodson, is symbolized by the likes of Ida B. Wells-Barnett, William Monroe Trotter, James Weldon Johnson, Mordecai Johnson, Archibald Grimké, Francis Grimké, and William Pickens, who delivered at several venues the notable address "The Kind of Democracy the Negro Race Expects."

Woodson was a historian by training; thus, he attempts little in the way of technical or structural analysis of the speeches themselves. His emphasis is on documenting and cataloging, a tendency that is again evident in *The Mind of the Negro* (1926), which includes more than 250 letters, most of which had been published in the *Journal of Negro History,* of which Woodson was editor. The letters, in Woodson's view, help to round out a conception of the Black mindset. But he views the letters as shapers of perspective, not merely as reflective. Authors include several who were known for their oratory as well, such as Richard Allen, Absalom Jones, Douglass, Remond, Henry Highland Garnet, and William Wells Brown.

Religious oratory, as Woodson affirms, has been central to the African American rhetorical tradition from the outset and was the primary channel by which millions of Blacks came to comprehend and speculate about the social world of which they were part. Richard Allen, Absalom Jones, Henry Highland Garnet, and Francis Grimké, for example, were all preachers. Therefore, the study of Black pulpit oratory as well as scholarly treatment of the Black church in general are necessary components of research in African American public discourse. As early as 1890, anthologies like E. M. Brawley's *The Negro Baptist Pulpit* were published, and W. E. B. Du Bois wrote about Black religious practices in *The Negro Church* (1903) and *The Souls of Black Folk* (1903/1989). James Weldon Johnson's 1927 *God's Trombones* is based on the "stereotyped sermon" he identified that moves formulaically from creation to judgment day. However, the first thorough treatment of Black preaching is William Pipes's *Say Amen, Brother! Old-Time Negro Preaching: A Study in American Frustration* (1951/1992). In this work, based on seven sermons recorded in Macon County, Georgia, Pipes classifies such preaching according to the following scheme derived from classical rhetoric:

Invention

A. Purposes

To persuade the sinner to "take up the new life" according to the Bible, the real world of God.

To impress the audience, so that there will be an outburst (escape) of emotion in shouting and frenzy.

To give religious instruction, according to the Bible.

B. Subject Matter

The Bible is the source of all ideas, information, and truths: God is good; "the more we suffer in this world, the greater will be our reward after death"; morality, social obligations, and religious fidelity are to be emphasized; there are evidences of fear and superstition.

C. Modes of Persuasion

Personal Appeal: the minister is uneducated but is "called" by God; his word is the word of God; the preacher is usually an impressive person, has a dramatic bearing and a melodious voice.

Emotional Appeal: by means of rhythm, sensationalism, rhetorical figures, imagery, suggestion, etc., the minister puts the audience into a mood to accept his ideas; this is the greatest appeal.

Logical Argument: not as important as emotional appeal; the best argument is that "it's true because the Bible said so."

Disposition
There is no logical organization because there is little preparation. The emotions determine everything.

Style
Familiar, concrete, narrative, ungrammatical language; Biblical; humor; deals with *things* rather than with *ideas.*

Delivery
Awkward, spectacular, dramatic, bombastic; musical voice; rhythmical and emotional; enthusiastic; sincere. (p. 72)

Pipes's work remains significant for the rigor with which he treats Black sermons and for his insights about the continuing importance of old-time preachers to the African American struggle for equality. However, he bases much of his analysis of Black religious practices on an acceptance of stereotypes about "primitive" Africans who, restricted to the "jungles of Africa," lacked opportunities to develop sophistication. Given his perspective, Pipes sees early Black religion as primarily an escapist adaptation to servitude. He ignores its rebellious, in some cases multilayered, meanings. Other scholars avoid this mistake, most notably Henry H. Mitchell, whose *Black Preaching* (1970) now arguably stands as the best book on Black religious oratory.

General historical treatments of Black oratory include Lowell Moseberry's *An Historical Study of Negro Oratory in the United States to 1915* (1955) and Marcus Boulware's *The Oratory of Negro Leaders: 1900–1968* (1969). Moseberry, trained in a department of speech, brings a broader array of rhetorical methods to his task than does Woodson. Like Woodson, he regards his primary objective to be "a historical report on the platform activities of the Negro" (p. iv). However, differing in method, he seeks to "discover areas in the eloquence of the Negro that seemed to deviate from standard oratorical practice" (p. iv). After painting the familiar social, political, and economic backdrop against which African American oratory up until the death of Booker T. Washington took place, he turns his attention to what he perceives to be a Black expressive and signifying difference. He argues that while Black orators used the same degree of induction, deduction, and causal reasoning employed by White rhetors of similar training and educational levels, they made a distinct departure from Anglo-Saxon patterns of oratory in terms of pathetic proof and style (p. 147). Black orators relied on keen invective, humor, and distinct—what Moseberry was willing to call African—brands of rhythmic phrasing. These observations are similar to those made by Pipes about Black sermons—evidence that sacred and secular African American rhetorical practices are interpenetrating. According to Moseberry, the most striking display of Black form is what we may call a jubilee rhetoric. As he explains:

> A stylistic device of the Negro orators that, perhaps, was contrived as much for its appeal to the emotions as for its rhetorical value was an antithetical refrain that strongly resembles the "jubilee" tones of the Negro spirituals. This "jubilee" consists of a series of ideas containing a major undertone of tragedy, alternating with a contrasting jubilant response. The pathetic appeal of the "jubilee" builds in emotional intensity until it explodes climactically in an exultant "shout" of challenge. (1955, p. 150)

As Moseberry further indicates, Douglass's 1852 "Fifth of July Oration" is a clear example, one in which the optimistic notes precede the tragic:

Jubilee
The sunlight that brought life and healing to you

Tragic Undertone
Has brought stripes and death to me.

Jubilee
The Fourth of July is yours,

Tragic Undertone
Not mine.

Jubilee
You may rejoice

Tragic Undertone
I must mourn. To drag a man in fetters into the grand illumined temple of liberty and call upon him to join you in joyous anthems, were inhuman mockery and sacrilegious irony. (p. 151–152)

The same technique, in reverse pattern, is demonstrated by Francis Grimké:

Tragic Undertone
The way is certainly very dark. There are many things to discourage us.

Jubilee
But there is a brighter side to the picture, and it is of this side that I desire especially to speak.

Tragic Undertone
Before doing so, however, it may be well for us to notice in passing some of the things which seem to indicate the approach of a still deeper darkness . . . and first, lawlessness is increasing in the South.

Jubilee
After thirty-three years of freedom.

Tragic Undertone
Our civil and political rights are still denied us. The Fourteenth and Fifteenth Amendments to the Constitution are still a dead letter. The spirit of opposition, of oppression, of injustice is not diminishing but increasing. (Moseberry, 1955, p. 152)

Boulware's study is the first major historical treatment of African American rhetoric devoted exclusively to texts of the twentieth century. He takes as his major tasks a chronicling of Black oratorical output and the creation of classification schemes. For Boulware, the mission of the Black orator invariably revolved around six goals: (1) to protest grievances, (2) to state complaints, (3) to demand rights, (4) to advocate racial cooperation, (5) to mold racial consciousness, and (6) to stimulate racial pride. He sets the pursuit of this mission in the twentieth century against the backdrop of, in his view, the century's six great American presidents—Theodore Roosevelt, Woodrow Wilson, Franklin D. Roosevelt, Harry Truman, John F. Kennedy, and Lyndon B. Johnson—and their presidencies as popularly labeled, that is, the Rooseveltian Era, 1901–1909; the New Freedom Period, 1913–1921; the New Deal, 1933–1945; the Fair Deal, 1945–1953; the New Frontier, 1961–1965;[1] and the Great Society, 1965–1969. Guided by his typologies, Boulware spins a history of African American oratory that begins in 1900, when Booker T. Washington was the dominant African American figure and orator in the country, up until the summer of 1968. He traces or alludes to such public careers as those of Washington, Mary Church Terrell, W. E. B. Du Bois, Mordecai Johnson, Marcus Garvey, Sadie Mossell Alexander, James Weldon Johnson, Nannie Helen Burroughs, Langston Hughes, Charlotte Hawkins Brown, Paul Robeson, Mary McLeod Bethune, A. Philip Randolph, Zora Neale Hurston, Adam Clayton Powell Jr., Benjamin Mays, Gardner Taylor, Walter White, Roy Wilkins, Father Divine, Daddy Grace, Roy Wilkins, Malcolm X, James Baldwin, and Martin Luther King Jr.

By the time Boulware's study appeared, African American political and cultural expressions had reached a high point in terms of their impact on the national consciousness. Major civil rights protests had been featured prominently for more than a decade on television, as were, more recently, the inner-city rebellions and Black Power pronouncements. It was also evident that civil progress, ongoing demands, and violent civil unrest by African Americans were driven largely by passions and rhetoric little known or understood by the nation at large. Of course, some folks never cared to know or understand, but public and academic gatherings relative to African American issues, including artistic and overall communication issues, attracted significant audiences. From this context stemmed a large wave of books on the Black experience. Among that wave were several major works of rhetorical scholarship such as Haig Bosmajian and Hamida Bosmajian's *The Rhetoric of the Civil Rights Movement* (1969), Robert Scott and Wayne Brockriede's *The Rhetoric of Black Power* (1969), Arthur Smith's *Rhetoric of Black Revolution* (1969), and James Golden and Richard Rieke's *The Rhetoric of Black Americans* (1971).

The Bosmajians' work is intended for use as a textbook; they refrain from offering rhetorical analyses of the individual pieces in the collection because they planned to leave those tasks to prospective students. However, they impressively frame their volume with rhetorical and historical commentary. In particular, they describe how African Americans and their allies mounted a massive persuasion campaign aimed at securing equality and justice on the heels of the Supreme Court desegregation decision and the Montgomery bus boycott. Actions themselves were decidedly rhetorical in that campaign; the sit-ins, freedom rides, picketing, marches, wade-ins, read-ins, and jail-ins were perhaps the more effective forms of persuasion. Yet the speeches, songs, and pamphlets were indispensable in terms of, as the Bosmajians term it, "a rhetorical or suasory function" (1969, p. 5). The authors also indicate a continual situation with which the activists were confronted:

The civil-rights leaders faced a formidable rhetorical problem; several questions about their persuasion had to be answered: To whom was their persuasion to be directed? Segregationists? Moderate whites? Negroes? What form should the protest take? What effect would the persuasion have on the audience? For example, on one hand the Montgomery bus boycott was directed against city authorities and the bus company with their segregation policies; yet, on the other hand, the boycott, with the accompanying mass meetings, speeches, songs, and demonstrations, had a persuasive effect upon the thousands of Negroes who had to become united participants in the boycott; unless the Negroes of Montgomery could be persuaded to stop riding the buses, the boycott was doomed to failure. Further, because the nation and the entire world had their attention focused on Montgomery and the actions of the civil-rights leaders, this larger audience also had to be considered, for they too were watching and being persuaded. (p. 5)

The Bosmajians highlight the words of Martin Luther King Jr., James Farmer, and Roy Wilkins as examples of the mainstream, integrationist civil rights campaign. But because the editors' view of the Civil Rights Movement allows for a certain indeterminacy, they show how those speakers were in dialogue with competing and challenging rhetorics, that of conservative Alabama clergy on the one hand and Black power advocates on the other. Thus King's April 16, 1963, "Letter from Birmingham Jail" is reprinted as is the April 12, 1963, "Public Statement by Eight Alabama Clergymen." Also included are the transcript of the debate between Farmer and Malcolm X that took place at Cornell University on March 7, 1962; Wilkins's July 5, 1966, "Keynote Address to the NAACP Annual Convention," in which he condemned the idea of Black power; and Floyd McKissick's July 1967 "Speech at the National Conference on Black Power," in which he advocated the concept.

Two selections by Stokely Carmichael are presented: a pamphlet, *Power and Racism*, which was distributed by the Student Nonviolent Coordinating Committee, and his January 16, 1967, "Speech at Morgan State College." Carmichael is the person most associated perhaps with both the Student Nonviolent Coordinating Committee (SNCC) and the slogan "Black Power." *Newsweek* reported in its May 15, 1967, issue that he was speaking at various campuses and "soaking whites $1,000 for a rather tame exposition of black power, charging Negro colleges $500 for the gloves-off treatment" ("Which Way for the Negro?" 1967, p. 28). The pamphlet is intended to illustrate the former approach; the speech at Morgan State College is meant to indicate the latter.

Scott and Brockriede also present civil rights and Black power discourses as integrally connected. Just as the statements of Black power advocates constitute much of the Bosmajians's "civil rights" book, the arguments of King, and even Hubert Humphrey, and accompanying critical perspectives by the editors constitute a sizable portion of the "Black power" book. In particular, the editors/authors detail Humphrey's technique as he denounced Black power at the NAACP Annual Convention in 1966 one day after Roy Wilkins had done so. But they feel that while Humphrey managed to establish great ethos with the 1,500 delegates, mainly by parroting Wilkins's address, in doing so he missed an opportunity to complicate and enrich a discussion of Black power. It is an opportunity that King himself never missed. Although he never embraced the slogan, he was never simplistically antagonistic toward it and always considered carefully its rhetorical effects and the premises behind it. This is illustrated by the selection "Martin Luther King, Jr. Writes about the Birth of the Black Power Slogan," which is a reprint of the second chapter of his *Where Do We Go from Here: Chaos or Community?* (1968). The complexity of King's thinking and the influence of Black power proponents upon him is also evident in his last speech to the Southern Christian Leadership Conference (SCLC) on August 16, 1967, "The President's Address to the Tenth Anniversary Convention of the Southern Christian Leadership Conference."

Contrasting speeches by Carmichael are included in the text; in this case they represent a talk given before an African American audience in Detroit and one given before a White audience in Whitewater, Wisconsin. Background essays on Black power are provided by James Comer and Charles V. Hamilton.

Smith's book, along with two subsequent works, *The Voice of Black Rhetoric* (1971), edited with Stephen Robb, and *Language, Communication, and Rhetoric in Black America* (1972), represent some of the most in-depth work in the area of African American rhetoric. Smith, now known as Molefi Asante, developed a specialty in agitational rhetoric as part of his doctoral studies at UCLA. He was well equipped and positioned, as a theorist and a witness, to assess the agitational Black rhetoric of the 1960s. He sees Black nationalist and Black power rhetorics to be essentially aggressive (toward Whites) and unifying (toward African

Americans). To move the Black masses, the Black rhetor must, as Boulware suggests, posit grievances. Of course, given America's treatment of Black folks, that is the easiest part of the job. The harder task is to fulfill the requirement that the rhetoric be consistent with or overcome an audience's mythology. King, for example, could always count on a large audience, particularly in the South, to hear an appeal based on Christian love. Malcolm X, on the other hand, had to overcome Christian beliefs to attract disciples to the Nation of Islam.

Smith employs several classification schemes regarding strategies, themes, and audiences to enhance his descriptions. Particularly useful is the four-part strategic structure that appears as part of all long-term agitation campaigns: (1) vilification, (2) objectification, (3) mythication, and (4) legitimation. *Vilification* is to create an antihero by attacking the ideas, actions, and being of a conspicuous member of the opposition, mainly by charging that the person is a key agent of domination. *Objectification* is to blame a specific but ill-defined group, such as the White power structure or, simply, Whitey for the audience's suffering. This gives the rhetor more flexibility to denounce, tap into his or her audience's mythology, and arouse them. *Mythication* is the suggestion that "suprarational" forces support the audience's struggle; this often means using religious symbolism to convey a sense that triumph has been ordained. This is exemplified by King speaking of the "coming of the Lord"; Malcolm asserting that the government, that which oppresses, is against God; or numerous speakers' likening the Black struggle to the story of Exodus. *Legitimation* is the attempt to justify one's own actions or those of fellow activists, usually by reversing blame and citing the oppressor's "original sin." It is generally the only defensive strategy employed by revolutionists, who characteristically remain on the offensive.

Smith also identifies a four-part thematic structure that is basic to Black secular, agitational rhetors: (1) all Blacks face a common enemy, (2) there is a conspiracy to violate Black manhood, (3) there is pervasive American hypocrisy, and (4) Black unity is requisite for Black liberation. With respect to the nature of the Black audience, Smith (1969, p. 67) proposes the following table:

AUDIENCE COMPOSITION

Characteristics	Type of Audience
Age	
Adults	Religious
Youth	Secular

Sex
Female	Religious
Male	Secular

Education
Less	Religious
More	Secular

Adult audiences, then, are seen to favor and be more apt to respond to religious oratory than would Black youth. Females are seen as more religious than males, and those less formally educated are seen as more religious than those with more education. Broad tendencies, of course, can always be complicated. There have always been old, secular, informally educated radicals around in the 'hood, some of them women. Smith, however, feels that the table is an accurate indicator of where audible support is likely to emanate from during a speech.

In *The Voice of Black Rhetoric*, Smith and Robb describe the general characteristics of African American rhetoric considered historically. Twenty speakers are offered as exemplary, ranging from David Walker, who keynoted a meeting of the First General Colored Association in Boston in 1828, to H. Rap Brown, who spoke on colonialism and revolution in Detroit in 1967. An interesting methodological development involved the editors' discussion of Nommo, the African belief in the pervasive, mystical, transformative, even life-giving power of the Word. As they articulate:

> It is a cardinal mistake of our society to operate on the basis that language functions of whites are everywhere reproducible in black societies in terms of influences and ends. With an African heritage steeped in oral traditions and the acceptance of transforming vocal communication, the Afro-American developed, consciously or subconsciously, a consummate skill in using language to produce his own alternate communication patterns to those employed by whites in the American situation. Communication between different ethnic and linguistic groups was difficult, but the almost universal African regard for the power of the spoken word contributed to the development of alternate communication patterns in the work songs, Black English, sermons, and Spirituals, with their dual meanings, one for the body and one for the soul. It is precisely the power of the word in today's black society that authentically speaks of an African past. Thus, to omit

black rhetoric as manifest in speeches and songs from any investigation of black history is to ignore the essential ingredient in the making of black drama. (1972, p. 2)

The concern with African influences would become a more prominent component of Smith's evolving rhetorical theory. Among the twenty-nine essays in *Language, Communication, and Rhetoric in Black America,* which were on by that time predictable topics or subjects, Smith includes six of his own, including "Markings of an African Concept of Rhetoric." As the title suggests, he begins to rely more heavily on Afrocentric concepts of rhetoric, posing Nommo, for example, as opposite Western persuasive technique:

> The public discourse convinces not through attention to logical substance but through the power to fascinate. Yet this does not preclude the materials of composition or the arrangement and structure of those materials; it simply expresses a belief that when images are arranged according to their power and chosen because of their power, the speaker's ability to convince is greater than if he attempted to employ syllogisms. The syllogism is a Western concept; *Nommo* is an African concept. . . . Perhaps that is drawing the choices too clearly, inasmuch as few neo-Aristotelians would argue for a dichotomy of emotion and logic. However, it is necessary to state the polar positions to illustrate the emphasis of the traditional African speaker. (1972, pp. 371–372)

Of course, the African concept of rhetoric is to be used to explicate oratory in the United States as well. In fact, Smith's essay addresses in a sense the peculiar qualities of African American oratory noted by the likes of Moseberry. Elaboration of Smith's ideas can be found in subsequent works, most notably the numerous passages on rhetoric in *The Afrocentric Idea* (Asante, 1998).

Golden and Rieke's anthology is fairly duplicative, including texts by speakers such as Walker, Remond, Douglass, Garvey, King, and Malcolm X. The distinguishing and lasting quality of the collection is the lengthy introduction, which is an insightful discussion of various political goals and rhetorical issues, and which culminates in figure 1. The figure is self-explanatory except for the arrow pointing from separation to assimilation. However, as Golden and Rieke explain, they are suggesting that "some of the separatist rhetoric includes the possibility that once black men have gotten together and established some political, economic and cultural identity and power, they might be able to join other ethnic groups forming a kind of assimilated United States society" (1971, p. 44).

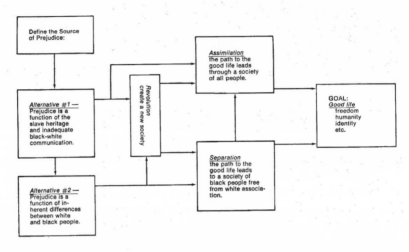

Fig. 1. Rhetorical Strategies of Black Americans (Golden & Rieke, 1971, p. 40) Reprinted by permission of R. D. Rieke.

An additional issue addressed by Golden and Rieke is the very worth of large-scale rhetorical intervention. Are the problems faced by the nation with respect to racialized inequality open to amelioration through what we generally regard as persuasive means? Or, given some of the deep-rootedness of racism, are coercive means, such as the physical force that ended enslavement or influenced legislation in the 1960s, more appropriate? These questions point to a possible "crisis of faith," particularly for Black rhetors and scholars, and are queries that must be confronted seriously.

Geneva Smitherman's widely acclaimed book, *Talkin and Testifyin: The Language of Black America* (1977/1986) also was conceived in the late 1960s. Although primarily considered a linguist, Smitherman is perhaps most responsible for popularizing the "Black Modes of Discourse," vernacular conceptions that are invaluable with respect to rhetorical analysis. The modes are (1) call-response, a series of spontaneous interactions between speaker and listener; (2) signification, the art of humorous put downs, usually through verbal indirection; (3) tonal semantics, the conveying of meanings in Black discourse through specifically ethnic kinds of voice rhythms and vocal inflections; and (4) narrative sequencing, the habitual use of stories to explain and/or persuade. Smitherman (1995) alternately conceptualizes an African American Verbal Tradition (AAVT) that encompasses (1) signification, (2) personalization, (3) tonal semantics, and (4) sermonic tone. The latter framework enables her to make sense of Black discourse that is not generally regarded as AAVE. She theorizes, for example, that the use of AAVT made Clarence Thomas a more sympathetic figure than Anita Hill in the African American community. While the syntax they both used during the confirmation hearings was unquestionably standard, Thomas made the matter personal and emotional, signifying along the way. Hill, on the other hand, seemed without passion or anger, emotions she had a right to feel and if displayed would have cast her inside AAVT and probably garnered her more support, particularly among African American women. Smitherman, therefore, seemingly in response to Golden and Rieke, points clearly to the value of rhetorical study as a mode of activist intervention. Because Hill did not resolve her rhetorical dilemma in the most socially productive way, she missed, according to Smitherman, an important moment to deliver more incisive and powerful commentary on sexual harassment, which is certainly a Black as well as larger issue. Smitherman concludes that Black women seeking to develop effective voices as part of the freedom struggle need a "head and heart rhetoric" to provide leadership for African Americans and the nation (2000, p. 265).

Significant post-1970s treatments of African American rhetoric include David Howard-Pitney's *The Afro-American Jeremiad: Appeals for Justice in America* (1990); Keith Miller's *Voice of Deliverance: The Language of Martin Luther King, Jr., and Its Sources* (1992); Shirley Wilson Logan's *With Pen and Voice: A Critical Anthology of Nineteenth-Century African-American Women* (1995) and *"We Are Coming": The Persuasive Discourse of Nineteenth-Century Black Women* (1999); Bradford Stull's *Amid the Fall, Dreaming of Eden: Du Bois, King, Malcolm X, and Emancipatory Composition* (1999); and Jacqueline Jones Royster's *Traces of a Stream: Literacy and Social Change among African American Women* (2000).

Howard-Pitney identifies the African American jeremiad to be an appropriation of the American jeremiad, which itself consists of statements of or references to the popular doctrine of America's divine promise, chastisement because of present moral decline, and prophecy that the nation will soon overcome its faults and emerge transcendent. The African American version posits Blacks as a chosen people within the parameters of the nation's archetypal civil myth. Howard-Pitney describes and discusses thoroughly the successes and failures of six leaders—Douglass, Washington, Wells, Du Bois, Bethune, and King—who utilized the form extensively. King and Du Bois, along with Malcolm X, are the subjects of Stull's study; Stull suggests that their composing processes, broadly and deeply construed, could serve as a model for liberatory composition classrooms. And King is obviously the sole subject of Miller's book, which locates King firmly within the tradition of Black religious oratory while exploring his borrowings from the writings of Whites.

Logan's first book, an important anthology that represents the frequently neglected tradition of Black woman rhetors, mainly features speeches by seven women—Maria Stewart, Sojourner Truth, Frances Ellen Watkins Harper, Anna Julia Haywood Cooper, Ida B. Wells, Fannie Barrier Williams, and Victoria Earle Matthews. Her second is an in-depth study in which most of these women are seen in the context of a particular trope—Maria Stewart in connection with the idea of "Ethiopa Rising," for example, or Ida B. Wells in relation to the "Presence of Lynching." Directly connected to Logan's project is Royster's book, which focuses on the essays of elite nineteenth-century African American women such as Stewart, Cooper, and Wells. Royster also posits an Afrafeminist ideology and argues its relevance for rhetorical studies.

Despite the recent impressive work in the field, which includes, by the way, Philip Foner and Robert James Branham's compilation of older speeches, *Lift Every Voice: African American Oratory, 1787–1900* (1998), many of the earlier volumes have gone out of print. In 1995, citing the lack of a sufficiently comprehensive text as well as a decline in African American rhetoric course offerings, Lyndrey Niles edited *African American Rhetoric: A Reader.* Approximately half the volume consists of reprinted material (mentioned above) by Asante, Golden, and Rieke. The most interesting additions for these purposes are Melbourne Cummings and Jack L. Daniel's "A Comprehensive Assessment of Scholarly Writings in Black Rhetoric" and Ronald Jackson's "Toward an Afrocentric Methodology for the Critical Assessment of Rhetoric." These scholars, affirming work by the likes of Asante and Smitherman, consider traditional academic models and limited notions such as "persuasion" to be too static to account for the richness, dynamism, and cultural content relative to speaker-audience interactions in African-derived contexts. As Cummings and Daniel assert, "Black rhetoric, with its concentration on Nommo, rhythmical patterns, audience assertiveness, and so on, cannot be dealt with by simply applying the conventional Euro-

American tools of rhetorical criticism" (p. 100). In line with this think-ing, Jackson proffers an Afrocentric model in which Nommo is graphi-cally posited as the center around which eight elements—rhythm, soundin', stylin', improvisation, storytelling, lyrical code, image mak-ing, and call and response—revolve (see fig. 2; R. Jackson, 1995, p. 154). As Jackson elaborates:

> Rhythm is similar to polyrhythm in that it suggests that the energy of the rhetor must be one with the energy of the au-dience. . . . The rhythm must coincide with the mystical and magical power of the word, so that the speaker, the word, and audience are all on one accord. . . . Soundin' is the idea of wolfin' or signifyin' within the African American tradition. . . . Stylin' is the notion that a speaker has combined rhythm, excitement, and enthusiasm which propel a message and the audience. . . . Improvisation is a stylistic device which is a verbal interplay, and strategic catharsis often resulting from the hostility and frustration of a white-dominated society. It is spontaneity. . . . Storytelling . . . is often used by a rhetor to arouse epic memory. . . . Lyrical Code is the preservation of the word through a highly codified system of lexicality. It is the very dynamic lyrical quality which provides youth to the community usage of standard and Black English. It is often used by speakers to appear communalistic, common-place, and not so convoluted in diction. . . . Image making is the element which considers legends, myths, and heroes in a given culture. . . . Call and response is the final element which offers a culmination of all these elements into an interactive discourse atypical of European communities. It is the idea that one should affirm by clapping, saying "amen," or re-sponding in some way. (p. 154)

At this point, I hope to have amply demonstrated the richness of African American rhetoric as a field of inquiry while indicating, if only implicitly, what future work needs to be done. Numerous studies are required that will allow us to understand the import of current and emerg-ing Black discourses. This is not to project an insular sense but to suggest that an understanding of continued Black articulations for a better soci-ety form a central question to be confronted by all if we are to bring a better society into existence. Nor do I mean to imply, by emphasizing contemporary subject matter, that we halt historical investigations. In

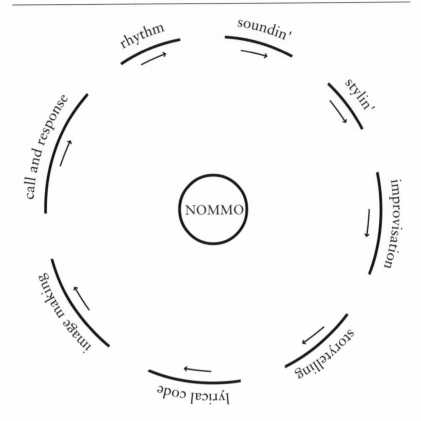

Fig. 2. Representation of Nommo

fact, it is crucial that we uncover and remain aware of some of the questions our forerunners posed because some of them remain unanswered. Will optimists, which all rhetoricians are at heart, remain prone, as both Woodson and Boulware suggest, to losing whatever hold they have on the public because of the inability to deliver tangible results? Will Black leadership that emerges from the working classes become more important, as Pipes envisions it might, than that which stems from the academy? There is yet much to witness.

Note

1. Although Kennedy was assassinated in 1963, I have used the dates of his elected term as the period of the New Frontier.

Part One

Historicizing and Analyzing African American Rhetoric(s)

1

Black Speakers, White Representations: Frances Ellen Watkins Harper and the Construction of a Public Persona

Shirley Wilson Logan

IN LANGSTON HUGHES'S SHORT STORY "THE BLUES I'M PLAYING," Oceola, the main character, ultimately resists the attempts of her patron, Mrs. Ellsworth, to mold her into a classical pianist, choosing instead to play the blues. Her patron never attempted to understand Oceola, her preferred lifestyle, or her mode of creative expression (1934). Frances Ellen Watkins Harper, poet, novelist, social activist, and public speaker, addressed audiences for over half a century. Yet she left little in the way of personal reflections on her career, no indication of her intentions, or, to paraphrase the title of Hughes' short story, no notes from the blues she was playing. Although she consistently received glowing comments on her performances, we know little about the extent to which Harper was an agent in the construction of this public persona. Reporters at various events had a tendency to record audience reactions to nineteenth-century Black speakers as if those reactions originated solely within a group of self-regulated hearers responding to passive subjects. Two frequent objects of this White gaze were Sojourner Truth and Frederick Douglass. Both left lasting impressions on the woman's rights and anti-slavery audiences who heard them. But these speaker-focused impressions revealed limited expectations and tinges of exoticism. Consider, for example, Frances Gage's "remembered" reactions to Truth's "Ain't I a Woman" speech, written in 1863:

> She had taken us up in her strong arms and carried us safely over the slough of difficulty, turning the whole tide in our favor. I have never in my life seen anything like the magical

influence that subdued the mobbish spirit of the day. (qtd. in Truth, 1988, p. 135)

Harriet Beecher Stowe's 1863 essay "Sojourner Truth, the Libyan Sibyl" provides another example:

> I do not recollect ever to have been conversant with anyone who had more of that silent and subtle power which we call personal presence than this woman. In the modern, spiritualistic phraseology, she would be described as having a strong sphere. (qtd. in Truth, 1988, p. 151)

In both instances, a White woman recalls or constructs an impression of Truth in terms of the effect she had on those in her presence. Both women claimed to be remembering statements and events that had unfolded a decade or more earlier.[1] Both describe how Truth made them feel, how she drew them into her "strong sphere" through her "magical influence." She is described in terms that evoke an exotic othered protectress.[2]

Comments about Douglass center on his forceful articulation and magnetic physical presence. In a June 1858 article to her German readers, journalist Ottilie Assing, extolling the power of Douglass's oratory, revealed more about her own attraction to the speaker than about the speaker himself:

> This excellent speaker knows how to electrify and captivate his audience. Something like a personal relationship develops between him and the listeners and elicits their undivided sympathy, letting them experience the magic of amiability that wins the heart of everyone who is fortunate enough to meet this vibrant and noble man. (qtd. in Diedrich, 1999, p. 161).

Assing had traveled to Rochester, New York, in 1856 to interview Douglass for a journal article and subsequently developed a twenty-eight-year relationship with him. As with Gage in her description of Truth, she wrote here of the effect of Douglass's performance rather than of its unique characteristics.

An American who observed Douglass giving an 1845 speech in Cork, Ireland, recalled the following:

> He was more than six feet in height, and his majestic form, as he rose to speak, straight as an arrow, muscular, yet lithe and graceful, his flashing eye, and more than all, his voice, that rivaled Webster's in its richness, and in the depth and

sonorousness of its cadences, made up such an ideal of an orator as the listeners never forgot. (qtd. in McFeely, 1991, pp. 124–125).

Note the initial attention to Douglass's physical attributes—his height, his posture, his size, his eyes, and finally his voice. All this made him an orator "listeners never forgot." It is not clear whether they remembered what he said, but they did remember him.

A speech at London's Finsbury Chapel in May 1846, delivered by Douglass during the same trip abroad, prompted the following exhortation from a Reverend Campbell:

> He must for a season make England his home. He must send for his wife. He must send for his children. *I want to see the sons and daughters of such a sire.* We, too, must do something for him and them worthy of the English name. I do not like the ideas of *a man with such mental dimensions, such moral courage, and all but incompatible talent* having his own small wants, and the wants of a distant wife and children, supplied by the poor profits of his publication, the sketch of his life [the *Narrative*]. Let the pamphlet be brought by tens of thousands. But we will do something more for him, shall we not? (qtd. in Douglass, 1855/1969, p. 420; italics added)

Here the Reverend Campbell's remarks express a curiosity about the kind of children a man of Douglass's physical appearance would produce as well as regrets that such persons with "incompatible talent," in their own country, were considered slaves. This notion of merit-based freedom resonates in comments discussed below on Harper's exceptional ability some ten years later. Fully endorsed by the crowd, it is a response to Douglass rather than to his message. Douglass had been in Great Britain for nine months and had won over the people by the time he delivered the Finsbury Chapel speech. He had embraced the political cause "Send Back the Money," a response to the Free Church of Scotland's decision to accept the financial support of Southern slaveholders. But it appeared that in some respects, Douglass's campaign against slavery in the United States became a campaign against the enslavement of Douglass alone. All accounts of his delivery concentrate on his fine appearance. He was, according to European standards, handsome. Some even expressed the wish that he were blacker. Others commented on the extent to which English women were attracted to him. Harper herself acknowledged Douglass's appeal in a letter to a friend, anticipating that he would speak "with his lips freighted with eloquence and utterance clothed with power" (1860, n.p.). But included in Harper's praise of delivery is praise for the substance, the power of "utterance," as well.

A review of an 1862 speech published in the African Methodist Episcopal Church's *Christian Recorder* lamented that words could not capture the force of Douglass's delivery. The transcript, wrote the reviewer, represented a "fair view of the ideas, but no printed sentences can convey any adequate idea of the manner, the tone of voice, the gesticulation, the action, the round, soft, swelling pronunciation with which Frederick Douglass spoke, and which no orator we have ever heard can use with such grace, eloquence and effect as he" (qtd. in McFeely, 1991, p. 213). After a passing reference to the "ideas," the writer moved quickly to what to him was most salient, if difficult to describe, in this performance—the speaker himself.

This representation of speaker as passive object of the White gaze is especially applicable to Frances Harper, who, unlike Douglass and Truth, left no autobiography and wrote very little about herself except in letters to her friend, prominent Philadelphia Underground Railroad agent William Still. It is primarily from these letters and her speeches themselves, that we acquire a glimpse of Harper's own awareness of and reactions to these characterizations.

This essay will examine some of these reactions to Harper's public rhetorical performances and to the performances of several of her contemporaries, discussing their embedded racialized and gendered presumptions. I then consider what Harper herself said about those reactions, highlighting speech passages that demonstrate her ongoing construction of a womanist ethos. Throughout this essay, I use the term *womanist,* coined by Alice Walker, to suggest Harper's consistent identification with and articulation of the ways in which Black women's experiences were different from those of their White contemporaries. Like most nineteenth-century Black women speakers, Harper believed that race, class, and gender constructions had to be taken into account in any deliberations about woman's rights and that arguments in support of those rights needed to be tempered in the purple heat of racial oppression. Although Harper did not identify herself as a womanist, the attribution is not anachronistic. Nineteenth-century Black women speakers like Harper were womanist foremothers, in much the same way, perhaps, that in Jacqueline Bryant's essay in this collection Aunt Nancy and Aunt Marthy served as Harriet Jacobs's liberatory foremothers. One salient example of this womanist rhetorical stance is Harper's 1866 speech to the Eleventh National Woman's Rights Convention, "We Are All Bound up Together," in which she dissociates herself from her auditors, stating, "You white women speak here of rights. I speak of wrongs" (Foster, 1990, p. 218). She continued by describing discrimination she had experienced on public transportation, discrimination suffered not because she was a woman, but because she was Black. The final section will offer some tentative conclusions as to what these observations suggest about the African American rhetor's sources of appeal.

Many reports on Frances Ellen Watkins Harper's public performances offered details representing exceptions to the general practice of reporting on what a speaker said rather than how the speaker looked or how the speech was delivered. These reports invariably included comments on her tone of voice, her general demeanor, and her overall delivery, giving support to the claim that nineteenth-century audiences were fascinated with the articulate Black body. These reports came from both Black and White, male and female observers, to include William Wells Brown, Grace Greenwood, Monroe Majors, Mary Ann Shadd Cary, and Phoebe Hanaford. They often moved from summary of her speeches to personal characterization and incorporated such phrases as "eloquent," "quiet," projecting "feminine modesty," with "gestures few and fitting," "never assuming, never theatrical," with language "pure," and "chaste." I quote Greenwood's remarks on a series of lectures Harper gave in Philadelphia at length because they are particularly telling:[3]

> Next of the course was Mrs. Harper, a colored woman, about as colored as some of the Cuban belles I have met with at Saratoga. She has a noble head, this bronze muse, a strong face, with a shadowed glow upon it indicative of thought and of a nature most femininely sensitive, but not in the least morbid. Her form is delicate, her hands daintily small. She stands quietly beside her desk and speaks without notes, with gestures few and fitting. Her manner is marked by dignity and composure. She is never assuming never theatrical. In the first part of her lecture she was most impressive in her pleading for the race with whom her lot is cast. . . . The woe of two hundred years sighed through her tones. (qtd. in Still, 1872, p. 779)

William Still was apparently struck by Greenwood's description because he used it to close his biographical sketch of Harper, published in *The Underground Rail Road*. Hallie Quinn Brown in *Homespun Hero-*

ines and Other Women of Distinction also quotes Greenwood's description in full. Restraint, from Greenwood's perspective, was Harper's most salient attribute. Greenwood identified features, gestures, tone, and manner, attributes that were all under control—moderated, composed, quiet, ennobled, dignified. It was almost as if Greenwood, who knew and had heard many abolitionist lecturers, was expecting something else, perhaps a high-strung, ranting, angry, confrontational speaker. Otherwise, what would have made Harper's delivery so remarkable? She provides a possible answer in her closing comment:

> As I listened to her, there swept over me, in a chill wave of horror, the realization that this noble woman, had she not been rescued from her mother's condition [it is not clear that Harper's mother was ever enslaved], might have been sold on the auction-block, to the highest bidder—her intellect, fancy eloquence, the flashing wit, that might make the delight of a Parisian saloon, and her pure, Christian character all thrown in—the recollection that women like her could be dragged out of public conveyances in our own city, or frowned out of fashionable churches by Anglo-Saxon saints. (qtd. in Still, 1872, p. 780).

Harper, who hardly looked the imagined part of slave, could have been one, and there she stood. Thus, Harper's performance, as much as her ideas, argued against slavery, at least for some.

To be sure, Harper suited her audiences' rhetorical tastes. In response to a speech she delivered in the Reconstruction South, the editor of the Alabama *Mobile* wrote the following:

> The lecturer was then introduced as Mrs. F. E. W. Harper, from Maryland. Without a moment's hesitation she started off in the flow of her discourse, which rolled smoothly and uninterruptedly on for nearly two hours. It was very apparent that it was not a cut and dried speech, for she was as fluent and as felicitous in her allusions to circumstances immediately around her as she was when she rose to a more exalted pitch of laudation of the "Union," or of execration of the old slavery system. Her voice was remarkable—as sweet as any woman's voice we ever heard, and so clear and distinct as to pass every syllable to the most distant ear in the house. . . . We confess that we began to wonder, and we asked a fine-

looking man before us, "What is her color? Is she dark or light?" He answered, "She is mulatto; what they call a red mulatto." (qtd. in Still, 1872, p. 775)

A reporter from the *Portland (Maine) Daily Press* described Harper as having "splendid articulation," using "chaste, pure language," having "a pleasant voice," and allowing "no one to tire of hearing her" (qtd. in Still, 1872, p. 760). Carla Peterson suggests that such descriptions represent attempts to "decorporealize Watkins Harper by emphasizing the quietness of her body, the chastity of her language, and the purity of her voice," adding that the resulting effect is "to eliminate the public presence of the Black female body perceived as sexualized or grotesque, and to promote the voice as pure melody, insubstantial sound, a negation of presence" (1995, pp. 122, 124). Peterson here bases her critique not only on reviews of Harper but also those of Elizabeth Taylor Greenfield, a famous Black antebellum singer, who was often referred to as the "Black Swan," suggestive of Harper's appellation, the "bronze muse." In the case of both women, audiences needed to reconcile an apparent contradiction between speaker and speech, singer and song, performer and performance. One solution was to deny the excellence of the performance, apparently the solution adopted by many who heard Elizabeth Greenfield. Another solution was to praise the performance as the exception that proved the rule of inferiority, applied both to Greenfield and Harper. Still a third way out of this dilemma was to call into question the identity of the performer. This resolution worked well with respect to Harper ("She is not colored, she is painted."), but because Greenfield was "coloured as dark as Ethiopia," it probably was not applied to her (qtd. in Peterson, 1995, p. 124).

Further, these comments resonate also with gendered assumptions about women. A review reprinted in the May 21, 1864, *Christian Recorder* praised Harper's deviation from societal gender limitations in a lecture she gave at a local A.M.E. church: "Seldom have we heard a more cogent, forcible, and eloquent lecture upon any subject, *especially from a woman.* Her subject was: 'The Mission of the War,' and its treatment discovered an amount of accurate thought, close investigation, extensive reading, and withal a comprehension of liberty and Republicanism remarkable *in any woman*" (Harper, 1864, n.p.; italics added). Although revealing low expectations for women speakers, this response, unlike many others, does speak to the logic of Harper's arguments rather than to her physical appearance or delivery.

Reprinted reports on Harper's rhetorical performances at various abolitionist gatherings all provide further evidence of focused attention to aspects of sex, gender roles, and race:

> Miss W. is slightly tinged with African blood, but considering her humane mission in behalf of her oppressed race, . . . the color only serves to add a charm to the occasion which nothing else could give, while at the same time it disarms the fastidious of that so common prejudice which denies to white ladies the right to give public lectures. (*Portland Advertiser,* March 15, 1856)

> Wherever she has spoken, thus far, she has given the most decided satisfaction. The lady like case [sic] and modesty of her deportment and the poetic beauty and pathos of her speaking alike delight and surprise her hearers. ([National] *Anti-Slavery,* December 27, 1856)

> Miss Watkins the colored woman who delivered lectures in the Lyceum in this Town, on Friday and Saturday evenings last, on the subject of Slavery, without exception, the best female speaker we ever heard. She has a fine voice, uses the choicest language, and is very fluent. We are not willing to adopt her views, yet we will accord to her an unusual amount of ability in the discussion of her favorite topic. (*New Jersey Mirror,* March 7, 1857)

> [S]he rose to a dignity of style as a public speaker, surpassed by no woman who has been in our midst, it was really beautiful in parts, and modest withal, giving offence to none, melting her audience into sympathy and tears for the poor slave. (*Noristown Republic,* July 11, 1857)[4]

Although these comments originally appeared in the White press, they were subsequently reprinted in the *Provincial Freeman* (Chatham, Canada West), a Black newspaper edited by Mary Ann Shadd Cary. Regardless of how we may react to them today, antebellum Black political activists understandably found encouragement in such favorable responses.

The following description from Phoebe Hanaford's *Daughters of America* (1882) points to Harper's eloquence as an argument against slavery and recalls Grace Greenwood's shock that such a woman might have been enslaved.[5]

> Francis [*sic*] E. W. Harper is one of the most eloquent women lecturers in the country. As one listens to her clear, plaintive, melodious voice, and follows the flow of her musical speech in her logical presentation of truth, he can but be charmed with her oratory and rhetoric, and forgets that she is of the race once enslaved in our land. She is one of the colored women of whom white women may be proud, and to whom the abolitionists can point and declare that a race which could show such women never ought to have been held in bondage. She lectures on temperance, equal rights, and religious themes, and has shown herself able in the use of the pen. (qtd. in Majors, 1893, p. 26)

One troublesome aspect of such praise is that it carries with it the assumption that freedom, rather than being a natural right, depended, as mentioned above in the case of Douglass, on exceptional ability. The auditors found it difficult to believe that someone with such intelligence and rhetorical ability could have lived under the threat of slavery. Their descriptions of these speakers reveal a shock of self-recognition. Of course, an audience's identification of a sense of oneness with the rhetor can be a compelling source of persuasion. The image of Blacks as sub-human served to justify their enslavement. Being brought face to face with a different image, an image of humanity oppressed, audiences often rationalized this contradiction as an anomaly, rather than incorporating this new image into a broader conception of what it represented. Thus, after hearing Douglass at Finsbury Chapel, the audience wanted to purchase his freedom. As the Reverend Campbell proclaimed, "He that was covered with chains, and that is now being covered with glory, and whom we will send back a gentleman" (Douglass, 1855/1969, p. 420). The Reverend Campbell echoed here Phoebe Hanaford's sentiment that Harper was "one of the colored women of whom White women may be proud," quoted above.

These delivery-focused remarks were not entirely atypical. Such attributions as "with gestures few and fitting" bring to mind Edwin Black's essay on the aesthetics of rhetoric. He attributes to the nineteenth-century elocutionary movement the principle that people are persuaded by that which is aesthetically pleasing, aesthetics being an influential component of a rhetorical encounter. The elocutionary movement, with its focus on delivery, incorporated rules governing facial expressions, posture, stance, quality of voice, and pronunciation. Among the factors influencing its popularity were an increase in systematic training in oral address among ministers, lawyers, and politicians, the revival of interest in the theater and in staged performance, and the belief that persuasive power was linked to ability in public speaking (B. G. Brown, 1996, p. 214). Collective and private training in elocution, at all levels, was common. Hallie Quinn Brown, Harper's younger contemporary, was a practicing elocutionist and professor of elocution at Wilberforce College. In one of several treatises on the subject, Brown wrote that elocution was a source of empowerment for women: "Thanks to elocution, the sickly, young lady with her puny form and wasp waist, is being supplanted by the strong, vigorous woman, who is to preside in the home and to move to and fro over the land as a queen among men" (qtd. in Donawerth, 1997, p. 344). It is not surprising then that audiences paid attention to particular features of oral performances, especially from women. Press reviews frequently rated delivery and elocutionary techniques along with the strength of arguments. Thus, these descriptions of gesture, tone of voice, emphasis, and timing were not unusual. In fact, as E. Black suggests, it would be difficult to separate delivery from other aspects of a rhetorical performance in evaluating its persuasiveness. The difference with many descriptions of nineteenth-century Black public speakers, however, is in the almost exclusive attention to delivery.

Nineteenth-century audiences generally had difficulty separating how women spoke from what they had to say, in the context of prohibitions against their speaking publicly and promiscuously. And this tendency persists. In her September 1999 *New York Times* op-ed piece, Maureen Dowd comments on an *Esquire* article in which the writer describes Hillary Clinton during a New York "listening tour" with such seductive descriptors as "a sexy mouth" whose "lips extend their reach into her cheeks and carve out a wolfish, carnal line. . . . Her laugh is the sexist thing about her. . . . The most interesting sexual persona of our time." As Dowd notes, such characterizations "yank us back to judging women on looks and desirability," where they "have been through history" (p. 19). Nineteenth-century White women speakers were subjected to the same kind of scrutiny. Angelina Grimké, a well-known abolitionist lecturer during the 1830s, prompted one reporter to observe of "the graceful chestnut-ringleted, blue-eyed daughter of the South" that "in propriety of manner and gesture, beauty of elocution, and excellence of arrangement and conclusiveness of reasoning, [she] satisfied even the most fastidious." Another wrote of her "unaffected pathos, the sound and comprehensive intelligence, the magnanimous and meek spirit, [and] the sweet eloquence" (qtd. in Yoakam, 1943, pp. 160–161). The previously mentioned Black journalist, Mary Ann Shadd Cary, was a year older than Harper and promoted the emigration of Blacks to Canada. She was often described condescendingly. In August 1853, Cary and her father, Abraham Shadd, were featured speakers at a meeting in West Chester, Pennsylvania, organized in opposition to African colonization. As Jane Rhodes observes, published reports concentrated on Cary's delivery rather than her arguments: "She appears quite young, but has a fine spirit, a noble independence; and expresses herself with astonishing facility. Her ideas, indeed, crowd upon her too fast for expression, as a consequence she is too rapid in her elocution" (qtd. in Rhodes, 1998, p. 79). These observations contrast sharply with those describing her father's performance and suggest some discomfort with Mary Ann Shadd Cary's age and sex. Although new to antislavery lecturing, Cary had had considerable experience as a speaker. Twenty-nine years old when these patronizing remarks were made, Cary had gained a reputation as a forthright speaker who at times could be abrasive.

It has always been the case that women who speak forthrightly are often the most heavily criticized. Attempting to understand why many of Zora Neale Hurston's male contemporaries disliked her, Henry Louis Gates quotes the comment made about Virginia Woolf that "the unlovable woman was always the woman who used words to effect" (Gates, 1985, p. 43). Hurston was certainly outspoken and frequently characterized unfavorably by her Black male peers. The label "unlovable woman" attaches itself more easily, however, to Harper's younger contemporary Ida B. Wells, whose unflinching manner of expressing her opinions won her few friends. "[T]here is nothing in this speech to indicate that it was given by a woman," writes Campbell, referring to the text of Wells's 1892 "Southern Horrors" lecture (1986, p. 441). Of course, that was just the impression Wells wanted to cultivate. For Wells, crying was "woman's weakness," and she criticized her own performance of that speech because she at one point gave in to that emotion, asserting, "Whatever my feelings, I am not given to public demonstrations" (Wells, 1970, p. 80). Added to this difficulty was general amazement that Black women and men could speak at all. The numerous authenticating documents prefaced to the slave narratives of such writers as Frederick

Douglass, William Wells Brown, Sojourner Truth, and Harriet Jacobs all represent responses to the curiosity people had about the origins of literacy for Black speakers and writers.

The prevailing view was that Black women had to project an ethos of respectability when addressing members of the alleged cult of true womanhood. I suspect that too much credence is given to this notion that Black women, in order to appear more acceptable to their White sisters, appeared to subscribe to the tenets of this cult, in other words, that they were "acting White." Foster (1997) cautions against the tendency to "attribute gentility to mindless imitation of the dominant culture or to blind acceptance of Puritanism and classism, when concern for decorum and ritual may just as well stem from African traditions of respect and honor" (p. 51). Harper was not merely performing for her White auditors, but to be sure, she was aware of the impression she was making. She wrote to Still in 1870 concerning reactions to lectures given in postbellum Georgia, "I don't know but that you would laugh if you were to hear some of the remarks which my lectures call forth: 'She is a man.' Again 'She is not colored, she is painted.'" Harper was amused with such characterizations but did not dwell on them. She was more concerned about audiences' responses to her message. In another letter, she wrote, "I don't know what the papers will say to-day; perhaps they will think that I dwelt upon the past too much. . . . I . . . gave them more gospel truth than perhaps some of them have heard for some time" (Still, 1872, pp. 772, 775).

Carson (1995), in a compelling essay "The Gender of Sound," surveys the many ways in which our presumptions about gender affect the way we hear the human voice. She observes that "[e]very sound we make is a bit of autobiography. It has a totally private interior yet its trajectory is public. A piece of inside projected to the outside" (p. 130). She writes of those who control censorship of these projections, but of particular relevance here is the notion of sound as autobiography. These responses to Harper's performance represent attempts to dissociate inside from outside and suggest that many auditors were simultaneously composing Harper's biography, based on voice and other aspects of delivery, as they listened to her. This is, of course, a natural tendency. We all construct biography from voice, especially from disembodied voice and are often surprised when our constructions prove wrong. Those constructing Black biographies in the nineteenth century had to resolve the conflict between what they heard and what they saw. The oxymoronic articulate Black body presented a unique challenge.

What in Harper's rhetorical training may have enabled such responses to her public speaking? She attended her uncle William Watkins's Academy for Negro Youth in Baltimore until she was thirteen. The Reverend Watkins taught grammar from Samuel Kirkham's *English Grammar in Familiar Lessons,* a popular nineteenth-century textbook. In his classroom, Watkins emphasized elocution and precise composition. One former student, who matriculated ten years after Harper, recalled William Watkins as a strict teacher, "demanding an exact inflection of a pupil's voice" and adding that "every example in etymology, syntax and prosody had to be given as correctly as sound upon a key-board . . . pupils were compelled to be correct both in speaking and writing" (J. H. A. Johnson, 1886, pp. 11–12). But we need not look solely to the formal training prescribed in textbooks at the time to account for Harper's rhetorical skills. Foster (1997) points out that we do not hesitate to "applaud the verbal agility of the trickster in folktales and extol the improvisational dexterity of the spirituals and the blues but, when it comes to the published literature, [we] assume that a desire to be published by or read by White people necessitated abandoning such strategies and copying the conventions and convictions of others" (p. 51). Reverend Watkins was a prominent member of a progressive community of intellectuals and free thinkers. They established schools such as the African Academy on Sharp Street, under the leadership of Daniel Coker, as early as 1802. They organized churches and literary societies. The Galbreath Lyceum, led by Hiram Revels, delivered lectures and wrote articles against slavery and colonization for such newspapers as the *Liberator* and the *Genius of Universal Emancipation.* They petitioned against such inflammatory legislation as the 1859 Jacobs Bill proposing the enslavement of free Blacks in Maryland. Coming from this antebellum Black Baltimore tradition valuing education and political activism, Harper had the opportunity to consume and produce discourse directed toward multiple audiences. She was not merely imitating the dominant discourse nor speaking solely to dominant society. Speakers like Harper, Foster adds, had "read the texts by Eurocentric writers, White liberals, and Black reactionaries, but they had also listened to their ancestors, to their kinsfolk, and to their hearts" (Foster, 1997, p. 52).

Harper as Agent

Harper addressed Black Southerners in the Reconstruction South, for she writes to Still about standing at the door of a crowded Darlington, South Carolina, church so that she could be heard by those outside and about meeting with women in their homes. But no one was taking notes. Thus, we have no recorded reactions to these talks. To what extent might Harper have helped to shape these perceptions and consciously constructed ethos, particularly with respect to womanist issues? She was careful to include women as agents in her public discourse. In an 1857 speech to the New York Anti-Slavery Society, Harper, discussing the dangers of the Fugitive Slave Law, creates this scene: "A man comes with his affidavits from the South and hurries me before a commission; upon that evidence *ex parte* and alone he hitches me to the car of slavery and trails my womanhood in the dust" (Foster, 1990, p. 102). Here, the rhetorical persona is gendered female; a standard rhetorical strategy of Harper's, pointed out by Sale (1992), "in which she used the word "womanhood" or makes other references to women in a discussion that is otherwise not gender specific in order to make women's presence and participation explicit" (p. 706). Other examples of this tactic can be found in "Our Greatest Want," an 1859 essay Harper published in the *Anglo-African Magazine* in which she calls for "not gold or silver, talent or genius, but *true men and true women*," and acknowledged a "need to build up a *true manhood and womanhood* for ourselves" (Foster, 1990, pp. 103, 104; italics added). Three times Harper reminded the audience at the 1858 meeting of the American Anti-Slavery Society that the suffering "slave mother who clasps her child to her heaving breast does not own it by right of possession" (Harper, 1858, p. 1).

Her postbellum speeches include women in all cataloging of progress. In "Duty to Dependent Races," she was careful to include women (e.g., "Colored men and women have gone into journalism"), in reference to race accomplishments (Logan, 1995, p. 38). Harper's postbellum speeches to White women's groups were presented within a carefully worded frame of progress through increased influence. But her Burkean move toward identification also brought with it a necessary womanist division, and she often found herself identifying with and then separating herself from them at the same time, as if to say, "Yes, we are all women, but I have additional concerns as a Black woman."

Speaking of the common problems all women share, using the example of what happened after her husband died and her property was taken, she said: "[Had] I died instead of my husband, how different would have been the result! By this time he would have had another wife, it is likely; and no administrator would have gone into his house, broken up his home and sold his bed, and taken away his means of support." Here she is aligning herself with all women. But later in the same speech she admits that White women have not always been supportive: "I do not believe that giving the woman the ballot is immediately going to cure all the ills of life. I do not believe that White women are dew-drops just exhaled from the skies. I think that like men they may be divided into three classes, the good, the bad, and the indifferent." In the same speech, she describes an incident on a Philadelphia streetcar, where she was asked to ride on the platform with the driver and asks the question: "Have women nothing to do with this?" (Foster, 1990, pp. 217, 218). Finally, Harper, in her 1893 speech, "Woman's Political Future," delivered at the Columbian Exposition, makes the following dissociative move: "I am not sure that women are naturally so much better than men that they will clear the stream by the virtue of their womanhood; it is not through sex but through character that the best influence of women upon the life of the nation must be exerted" (Logan, 1995, p. 45).

We have here then the influence of race, gender, and oratorical conventions on the way audiences responded to Harper, but we also have the agency of Frances Harper to take into account. As we reconsider Harper, other Black women rhetors, and by extension all women speakers generally—and I think it is important to be specific without being exclusive—we need to consider them as agents in their own performances, agents who were engaging a range of rhetorical practices to reach their audiences.

Conclusions

I am aware that these quoted reactions to Harper, Douglass, Truth, and other nineteenth-century speakers have all been critiqued out of their contexts, contexts that would be difficult if not impossible to reconstruct with accuracy. Of particular concern is the linguistic context. Word connotations change over time. Some disappear from our lexicon entirely; others take on new meanings. Another concern is the social context. What was the nature of the relationships among these various speakers and those who wrote about them? What could and could not be said? McDowell warns against the tendency to assume that "context can be retrieved as whole cloth," reminding us that "what we know of context we have made" (1995, p. 57). In the absence of such contexts, these reactions have, to some extent, been measured against current ideas about race, class, and gender. Still we must continue our efforts to understand the past. It may contain answers.

Another consideration is that attention to delivery can be a way of assessing character. Aristotle's *Rhetoric* points out that of the three methods of persuasion in oral discourse, the ethical, which draws on the personal character of the speaker, may well be the most effective. Before auditors weigh the validity of the arguments or respond to their own self-interests, they often must establish a tacit relationship with the speaker. If having a good opinion of the speaker makes his or her arguments more compelling, then attention to delivery facilitates the construction of this favorable ethos, especially in instances in which the rhetor is an unknown entity. For nineteenth-century audiences gazing perhaps for the first time at the articulate Black body, the foremost question was "Who is this?" The manifestation of this gaze is more than rhetorical depiction or ocular demonstration, creating a mental picture. The argument is not imagined; it is literally placed before the eyes of the audience as the body of the speaker. The performance becomes the argument. As is often the case, hearers respond to the man or woman rather than to the embedded meaning of his or her lyrics, the blues playing. In a society in which identity is so prominent an issue, it may be undesirable if not impossible to have a color-blind gaze. We need to ask what is gained and what is lost in the attempt to erase race. We may not like the resulting characterization, but would the silence be more satisfying?

Notes

1. Stowe's "Libyan Sibyl" describes Truth's 1853 visit to her home in Andover, Massachusetts. Gage's account of Truth's 1851 performance followed Stowe's in April 1863.

2. See Nell Irvin Painter's (1996) biography, *Sojourner Truth: A Life, a Symbol* (New York: W. W. Norton), in which she comments on the publication of Frances Gage's version of Truth's 1851 speech, some twelve years after the event. As Painter points out, it is quite likely that "Gage reached back to a different setting and invented 'and ar'n't I a woman?'" (p. 164).

3. Grace Greenwood was the pen name of Sara Jane Clarke Lippincott (1823–1904). She wrote poetry and short fiction and occasional pieces for such periodicals as *Godey's Lady's Book, the Saturday Evening Post,* and the *National Era.* A friend of John Greenleaf Whittier, she was active in the antislavery movement.

4. All quotes were taken from editions of Mary Ann Shadd Cary (Ed.) *Provincial Freeman* [On-line]. Accessed from Accessible Archives, Inc., *http://srch.accessible.com/.*

5. Phoebe Ann Coffin Hanaford (1829–1921), one of the first female ordained ministers in the United States, became a Universalist minister in 1868. Hanaford, cousin of Lucretia Mott, was also a writer and woman's suffragist.

2

From Panther to Monster: Representations of Resistance from the Black Power Movement of the 1960s to the *Boyz in the Hood* and Beyond

Kalí Tal

SEVERAL YEARS AGO, WHILE BROWSING THE "AFRICAN AMERICAN" section of a local bookstore, I picked up *Monster: The Autobiography of an L.A. Gang Member* (1994), by Sanyika Shakur, also known as Monster Kody Scott. I had been rereading *Blood in My Eye,* the last work of incarcerated Black Panther Party associate George Jackson, and a blurb on the back cover of *Monster* caught my eye. A reviewer claimed that, like George Jackson, Sanyika Shakur had made a "complete political and personal transformation . . . from Monster to Sanyika Shakur, Black nationalist, member of the New Afrikan Independence Movement and crusader against the causes of gangsterism." When I began to read the book, I had no idea that it was going to relate to my decade-long study of the narratives and myths of the Vietnam War or that my reading would result in a new understanding of the power and attractiveness of Vietnam War imagery to Black youth. This imagery, as my readings reveal, serves as a bridge between the consciously ideological and radical formulations of the Black Panther Party and the politically incoherent and image-obsessed world of mainstream contemporary Black youth culture.

In this essay, I examine the revision of the image of the Black Panther, refracted through the lens of the popular history of the Vietnam War. The erasure of explicit political ideology in much of mainstream contemporary Black popular culture is intimately connected to the way in which mythic narratives and iconography of the Vietnam War have replaced the critical economic and social analysis so prevalent in the 1960s.

The rehabilitation of the image of the (White) Vietnam veteran was begun with the dedication of the Vietnam Memorial wall in Washington, D.C., in 1982, and completely affected by the renewal of American "pride" and U.S. imperialism via the celebration and patriotic rhetoric surrounding the Gulf War.[1] In Black popular culture, the consciously political, often explicitly Marxist, rhetoric of the Black Panthers and other Black liberation workers has been worn away until almost all that is left is the image of the black clad, leather-jacketed, beret-wearing Black man with a gun, bereft of political or ideological coherence. *Monster* is the text in my hand, but as I hope to illustrate, it is representative of a much larger trend.

In 1960, George Jackson was convicted of stealing seventy dollars from a gas station and given a sentence of one year to life. In prison, he "met Marx, Lenin, Trotsky, Engels and Mao" and began to study economics and military history. It became Jackson's goal "to transform the Black criminal mentality into a Black revolutionary mentality" (G. Jackson, 1994, p. iii). Jackson didn't start off as a political prisoner, but he slowly became one as he was radicalized first by his reading and then through his growing connections to revolutionary organizations outside the prison walls and his own attempts to organize inside prison. Jackson was shot and killed by guards inside San Quentin on August 21, 1971, during an alleged escape attempt. He had several times voiced the conviction that there was a conspiracy against his life.

The literature of the Black Power Movement of the 1960s and early 1970s was self-consciously ideological. As Gwendolyn D. Pough describes in her essay "Rhetoric that Should Have Moved the People: Rethinking the Black Panther Party" in this volume, much Panther rhetoric was so explicitly Marxist that at times its dogmatism and employment of jargon alienated rather than attracted the Black public. As Pough points out, though, the Panthers' message and self-presentation was effective enough to draw a large number of African Americans to their cause, to strike sympathetic chords in White radicals, and to frighten the White establishment severely enough that the Panthers were awarded the title of "Public Enemy Number One" on FBI Director J. Edgar Hoover's infamous Most Wanted list.

Blood in My Eye begins with Jackson's description of the path of Black radicalism, from "the confused flight to national revolutionary Africa, through the riot stage of revolutionary Black Amerika." Jackson wrote,

"We have finally arrived at scientific revolutionary socialism with the rest of the colonial world." And he comments—with relief—to a fellow activist, "I was hoping that you wouldn't get trapped in the riot stage like a great many other very sincere brothers. I have to browbeat them every day down here. They think they don't need ideology, strategy or tactics. They think being a warrior is quite enough. And yet, without discipline or direction, they'll end up washing cars, or unclaimed bodies in the city-state's morgue." Jackson goes further, "The only independent African societies today are socialistic. Those which allowed capitalism to remain are still neo-colonies. Any Black who would defend an African military dictatorship is as much a fascist as Hoover" (1990, p. ii).

Jackson carefully separated "rioting" from armed struggle, which he called "the very heart of revolution." "I'm convinced," he said,

> that any serious organizing of people must carry with it from the start a potential threat of revolutionary violence. Without [the threat of violence], the establishment forces will succeed in isolating the political organizer and closing down his project before the people can feel its benefits. Self-determination requires a small, hidden, highly trained army equipped with the very best and most destructive of military weapons, and a bodyguard of counter-terrorists. (1990, p. ii)

I spend a great deal of my time immersed in the rhetoric of Black liberation. It's easy for me to forget that most Americans—Black or White—haven't heard this kind of clearly expressed radical political rage in almost a quarter of a century. But I am regularly reminded each time I teach a course on the 1960s and my students—Black and White—(almost all born after 1980)—express astonishment when exposed to it.

They are not astonished at the bold style of the Black Liberation Movement, for many of them are well acquainted with the equally bold posturing of the gangsta rappers who inhabit the urban airwaves. Black men posing with guns are either thrilling or intimidating (depending on their perspective) but certainly not new to my students. What does surprise them is the pervasiveness of political references in Panther texts—from Fanon to Ché to Memmi to Marx to Mao—and the authors' explicit identification as a socialist or communist, words that my students cannot, usually, even define.

Political scientist Michael Dawson argues that a venue for Black public discussion—what he calls a "counterpublic" because it provides a space for an alternative to the White public sphere—existed in the 1960s and early 1970s in the form of both church and secular organizations within the Black community where intense political debate and practice proliferated. Dawson claims:

> Black workers' caucuses . . . , community-based civil rights and Black power organizations all provided forums for debate over the direction of Black liberation, the relation of Black political action to political activity occurring throughout the polity, and created an environment that closely linked political debate to political action. These overlapping sets of discourse communities provided the foundation for many of the social movements of Blacks and whites during the height of the activism a generation ago. (1995, p. 211)

But Dawson believes that this counterpublic sphere was undermined by a combination of "state repression and internal dissension." COINTELPRO (the FBI and police counterintelligence program) activities instigated intergroup violence, legal fights drained organizational coffers, and a withdrawal into race-interest-specific cadres fragmented a unified movement of people of color.[2] Economic factors also weakened the Black counterpublic sphere as a "structural shift in the U.S. economy away from manufacturing and toward low-wage service industries eroded the institutional base of the Black counterpublic, and, in particular its points of contact with other oppositional forces." Finally, the Reagan presidential administration launched a "massive ideological attack on the fruits of the Civil Rights Movement, refusing to talk with the established leadership of the Black community, and working to systematically overturn Black victories in the areas of voting rights, antisegregation legislation, education, and economic advancement" (Dawson, 1995, p. 221).

What does the decline of the Black counterpublic have to do with Sanyika Shakur's *Monster*? First of all, it suggests that *Monster* is a text produced in isolation from other African American texts or, rather, in relation only to an idiosyncratic and limited number of other texts that are not representative of anything that might have, in the 1960s and early 1970s, comprised Black counterpublic discourse. It also means that *Monster* is heavily influenced by the White popular culture texts to which Sanyika Shakur has been exposed, and which—without a tradition of Black critical discourse—he is helpless to critique.

Whereas George Jackson uncovered a lost history of critical exchange between African American and Third World intellectuals that connected him to a political conversation dating back to the early nineteenth century, Sanyika Shakur's narrative is almost entirely based on personal references. He says he considered himself a communist for a while but changed his mind because communism is, in his words, a Eurocentric philosophy. He fell out with the political study group in San Quentin because he believed,

> We were making the same mistakes that the Black Panthers had made. We were importing revolutionary ideals, trying to apply them to our setting. In this light, those who could quote Marx, Mao, or Comrade George the most were the sharpest. It began to irritate the hell out of me. Nothing was corresponding with concrete conditions, and we had no mass appeal. On top of this, our troops sent back out into Babylon were falling prey to parochialism and tribalism. (1994, p. 349)

Rather than blaming the failure of the Panthers on state repression (unlike both Dawson and Pough who placed the blame on COINTELPRO), Shakur places the responsibility for failure on the Panthers' "imported revolutionary ideals." Shakur returns to a condition of alienation, embracing a traditional (White) American individualism that leads him, inevitably, into despair over his own powerlessness and a personal belief that the only solution is separation of the races. Back in jail for attacking a local drug dealer and "confiscating" his vehicle, at the conclusion of *Monster* Shakur is hopeless and defeated.

What struck me most forcefully in my reading of *Monster* was not any connection between Shakur's text and the writings of African American revolutionaries who preceded him but the similarity between *Monster* and popular culture narratives of the Vietnam War, such as Oliver Stone's *Platoon*. In fact, *Monster* concludes with a comparison of the Rodney King uprising to the Vietnam War:

> [The beating of Rodney King] brought the realization of my powerlessness crashing down upon me, and with it, my rage and appetite for destruction rose. It was while in this mindset that I clearly overstood the agitated rage meted out during the 1992 rebellion in Los Angeles, which was truly surprising to me. I wasn't surprised that it occurred—that was inevitable. But I was surprised by the swiftness with which it unfolded. Some people say that the participants burned their own neighborhoods, which seems as crazy as saying that

the Vietnamese destroyed their land to rout out the Americans. (Shakur, 1994, p. 342)

Here, Sanyika Shakur identifies with the Vietnamese, in opposition to the occupying army of Americans, and he contests the "official" version of the war by questioning those people who made statements equivalent to that of the apocryphal American officer who claimed "we had to destroy this village in order to save it." But in Shakur's version, the victory of the National Liberation Front is hardly conceivable, since he concludes that the United States' 130-year-old experiment with multiculturalism has failed, that the country is dividing like Bosnia and Herzegovina, and that separation is the only solution.

Despite his intermittent identification with the Vietnamese, Shakur's narrative is far from politically coherent. A mythologized "history" of the Vietnam War has replaced political ideology in his narrative, and this fictive "history" underlies much of African American contemporary popular culture. The demise of the Black counterpublic sphere has resulted in the substitution of a White-constructed, Black-reconstructed popular culture iconography—an iconography in which the Vietnam War is widely represented. Shakur refers to his neighborhood as "in-country" and "the war zone." He speaks of his participation "in the war" and uses Vietnam-era words such as *free fire zone* and *escalation* to describe it. Though he sometimes refers to his job responsibilities in the Crips gang in terms also adopted by the Black Panther Party (*minister of information, minister of defense*), he is more likely to use military language. Young Crips are "recruited." He describes an attack on a rival gang as "our own little Tet offensive." But whereas Huey Newton took the next step and equated the African American struggle for freedom with the Vietnamese war for liberation (actually offering to send a unit of Panthers over to assist Ho Chi Minh in his struggle) (1971, p. 78), Shakur simply moves on to another topic, either unable or unwilling to introduce ideological arguments into his text.

The Vietnam War had an enormous effect on the Black Liberation Movement of the 1960s and 1970s. Many members of Black radical organizations were veterans of the Vietnam War and put their military training to use organizing Black self-defense groups. The connections that Black activists were making with the war in those days were explicitly and entirely political—the Vietnam War was "a White man's war," an "imperialist war" waged by White capitalist America on a Third World nation whose people fought for political independence and self-determination. In *Monster*, the war has lost its historicity and been turned into a landscape in which "free fire zones" exist without political meaning, where the underlying "story" of the conflict goes without saying. Caught in a war without meaning, stripped of ideological tools for analysis, Shakur is doomed to impotence and failure, despite his struggle to change his life. Only ideology can provide the basis for structural change, and structural change is what it will take to end gang warfare.

In contemporary pop culture terms, the platform of the Black Panther Party and the Black Liberation Movement has been reduced to the image of the black-leather-jacketed, black-beret-wearing Black man with a gun. And the image of the Black Vietnam War veteran has become indistinguishable from the image of the Black liberation fighter. The key word here is *image,* which necessarily goes without saying. If ideology was the heart of the Black Liberation Movement, and image was used to underline ideology, then today's representations of that movement directly contradict its intent, entirely replacing ideology with image. As Angela Davis notes in *Black Popular Culture,* many producers of Black popular culture today "call upon a market-mediated historical memory of the Black movement of the sixties and seventies. The image of an armed Black man is considered the 'essence' of revolutionary commitment today" (1999, p. 325).

Though I do not have the space to fully explore the meaning of Vietnam War imagery in rap music, I would like to briefly discuss a few of the Panther/Vietnam War crossovers made in this medium, with particular focus on gangsta rap. Rap is one of the most widely disseminated contemporary Black popular culture productions, and the popularity of gangsta rap is evident well beyond the neighborhoods and the culture that spawned it. Because of its wide distribution, no discussion of Black popular culture can exclude these texts from its critique.

Carlos Morrison's article, "Death Narratives from the Killing Fields" (2003) details the war imagery in gangsta rap and explicitly links it to the rhetoric employed by Sanyika Shakur in *Monster.* Adopting Cornel West's description of inner city Black America as "the killing fields" (a phrase referencing the killing fields of Cambodia, via the Hollywood movie of the same name), Morrison accepts gangsta rappers' descriptions of themselves as soldiers "warring over territory or 'turf,' drugs or even gang colors." This image is, in fact, so ubiquitous that it appears self-evident. But there is a great deal of irony in this reading. While Shakur explicitly draws on the Vietnam War for his imagery, in *Monster* he is demonstrably unclear about the Black liberation fighter's position on imperialist wars. When Sanyika Shakur's Vietnam War references pass through Morrison's hands, they are further stripped of ideological meaning, dislocated to the point where they can be employed to describe a situation in which "Black men are 'at war' with other Black men." The end result of this slippage is the elision of the real enemy—the racist state.

"Soldier" imagery is so pervasive and so rarely critiqued that the militarization of images of Black youth now seems "natural" and it most often goes without saying. A weakened Black counterpublic cannot ensure that references to the Vietnam War are historicized or linked to antiracist, anticapitalist, anti-imperialist struggle, nor can it effectively counter the appropriation of the "Black soldier" image by White mainstream image producers in film, television, music, or literature.

Angela Davis warns us that "[w]here cultural representations do not reach out beyond themselves, there is the danger that they will function as surrogates for activism, that they will constitute both the beginning and end of political practice" (1999, p. 327). Gangsta rap seems to embody this dilemma perfectly—adopting the posture of the Black man with the gun without the ideologies that motivated Black liberationists. Furthermore, as Hazel Carby notes, "Black cultural texts have become fictional substitutes for the lack of any sustained social or political relationships with Black people in a society that has retained many of its historical practices of apartheid in housing and schooling" (1999, p. 249). Black gangsta rap may be largely perceived throughout mainstream and African American contemporary popular culture as the current extent of and reflection of Black activism, particularly since the limitations that Dawson described have cut away at the amount of available space for a Black counterpublic.

When I lecture to my classes about the Panthers, I often play a clip from a documentary film made in 1968, titled *No Vietnamese Ever Called Me Nigger.*[3] I queue it up to a segment of an interview with Akmed Lorence, a young Black Vietnam War veteran explaining to his White interviewer why he is so angry about the political and racial situation in the United States, and what he intends to do about it. Because the film is so hard to find today, it is worth quoting Lorence at length:

> You know this revolution is filled with so many ironies, really. First you tell us that it is manly to keep your word. . . . And now all that the Black people in this country are demanding, and even that the Black people in the whole world are demanding, is that you keep your word. And let us *see* the

justice and equality for all. Or else admit to us that you're not a man, you're a worm, you're afraid of us, you're afraid to give us equal standing. You're afraid that if you give us equal ground, that we will match you and override you. And if that's what you're afraid of, then tell us that's what you're afraid of. But don't keep hiding it from us and holding [welfare] up to us, and every time we ask you for something you give us a little bit of something, and it's all tokenism. . . . You're playing *games* with us. . . . Now, there are many Black veterans who are coming back and they're mad, they're angry. Do you think that they're going to sit down through this? . . . We know about Ché. We know about Fanon. We've read the books of revolution. We've listened to Mao and his quotations. We know where we stand. And we're not gonna sit for it. We're asking, and if we ask and we don't get, we're prepared to *take* it. . . .

All we're asking—no one wants to see blood, no one likes the smell of blood, no one wants war, anyone who has been in war doesn't want war. Every [vet] knows what it's like to see the inside of a man's gut hanging out, and see your friends die, see relatives die. No one wants to regress back to the state of mind where you think, "It's all for the cause, therefore my mother has to die, my wife has to die, my brothers and sisters have to die." No one wants that. But you're pushing us to it. You're leaving us no choice. We're asking. We're begging. The students up at Columbia, they asked. The brothers down south asked. The brothers in Latin America, the brothers in Africa, they're all asking. All they're doing is asking. Our fathers asked. Our grandfathers asked. . . . And yet, still, they asked and asked and asked and you refused to give them anything. And we're just about out of patience. We're not gonna ask any more. . . . And we're not going to take it. We're not going to take sitting in rotten parks and in places that just aren't fit for living. We're not going to take it. There's a limit to a man's patience and everyone knows that. . . . [W]hat we're asking for is humanity. We're asking to be allowed to live like human beings. And, God., you tell us that this is too much to ask. You're sick! You're definitely sick! How can you tell me that it's too much to ask to be a human being?

Lorence's rhetoric is remarkably convincing, and he has explicit politics. Throughout the film, he connects his ability to formulate revolutionary ideas with his connection to the ideas of other Third World radical intellectuals. He identifies with the Vietnamese and is ready to go to war with the United States. The other two veterans interviewed on the tape express similar sentiments. I'd like to note the difference between Lorence and all the Black Vietnam War veterans and soldiers that have since been portrayed on film (by Black or White directors).[4] Lorence has a program. He is, as they say in the military, a highly motivated individual. He has an agenda of his own and a plan to help his people. I play this segment because of the notable absence of such characters on the current popular culture scene, Black or White. Lorence and the other Black veterans interviewed in *No Vietnamese . . .* were hardly unique in that era. Geronimo Ji-Jaga Pratt earned eighteen combat decorations in Vietnam before his transformation from U.S. soldier to Black Panther Party leader (Churchill & Vander Wall, 1988, p. 77). The question is why men like this have been erased from history, why they are absent from both White and Black contemporary popular culture productions.

I often contrast Lorence's fiery speech with a clip from John Singleton's celebrated directorial debut, *Boyz in the Hood* (1991). *Boyz* features Laurence Fishburne as a Vietnam veteran, an advocate of armed self-defense, and a Black community activist. But Fishburne's character, tellingly named "Furious," is no revolutionary. Below is a transcript of the speech he gives when he takes his son, Tre, and Tre's young friend out to Compton and lectures them on the need for Black economic solidarity. He drives them out there to show them a billboard that reads "Seoul to Seoul Real Estate: Cash for your homes." As he talks, local gang members (who make his middle-class son and friend nervous) and an old man gather around to listen.

> *Furious:* It's the Nineties. We can't afford to be afraid of our own people anymore. I want y'all to take a look at that sign up there and see what it says. Cash for your home. Know what that is? What are y'all? Amos and Andy? You Steppin' and he's Fetchit? I'm talking about the message—what it stands for. It's called gentrification. It's what happens when the property value of a certain area is brought down. Huh, you listening? Bring the property value down, they can buy the land at a lower price. Then they move all the people out. Raise the property value, and sell it at a profit. Now, what we need to do is keep everything

in our neighborhood—everything—Black. Black owned with Black money, just like the Jews, the Italians, the Mexicans, and the Koreans do.

Old man: Ain't nobody from outside bringing down the property value. It's these folk [gestures at the gang members], shooting each other and selling that crack rock and shit.

Furious: How you think the crack rock gets into the country? We don't own any planes. We don't own no ships. We are not the people who are flying and floating that shit in here.[5] I know every time you turn on the TV that's what you see—Black people selling the rock, pushing the rock, pushing the rock. But that wasn't a problem as long as it was here. That wasn't a problem until it was in Iowa, and it showed up on Wall Street where there are hardly any Black people. And if you wanna talk about guns, why is it that there's a gun shop in almost every block in this community? For the same reason that there's a liquor store in almost every corner of the Black community. They want us to kill ourselves. You don't see that shit in Beverly Hills. But they want us to kill ourselves. Yeah, the best way you can kill a people is you take away their ability to reproduce themselves. Who is that dying out here in these streets every night? Young brothers like yourselves. . . .

Gang member: What am I supposed to do? Fool roll up and try to smoke me, I'm gonna shoot the motherfucker, he don't kill me first.

Furious: You doing exactly what they want you to do! You have to think, young brother, about your future.[6]

Playing off the "Seoul to Seoul" billboard, Furious launches into an argument for Black economic self-sufficiency, Black capitalists reinvesting in their own communities, and Black self-help programs, just as the "Jews and Orientals" have. Ideologically, Furious seems confused. On the one hand, he supports capitalism. On the other hand, he believes in a nationwide anti-Black conspiracy that encourages Black drug use in the ghetto,[7] presents media images of Blacks as drug dealers, seeds Black urban areas with liquor stores and gun shops, and prevents Black people from reproducing themselves—hardly a situation that can be resolved by adopting a particular economic strategy. Furious's rhetoric pushes lots of sympathetic buttons in Black and White-liberal audiences (including the button of anti-Asian racism, underlined by Furious's status as a Vietnam

War veteran). But in his strangely incoherent vision, there is little mention of the state apparatus—it is neither repressive nor supportive; it is,
in fact, barely there at all. *Boyz* pretty much treats the state as if it doesn't
exist; it appears mostly in the form of a self-hating Black cop who calls
other Black people "nigger" and tells Furious he should have shot an
intruder and kept more "garbage" off the streets.

It would be foolish to argue that Singleton's apparent political naiveté
is a result of his youth, since many dedicated Black Panther Party members his age or younger had well-formed political ideologies, or had already died for them. Singleton's 1970s counterpart, the young filmmaker
Melvin Van Peebles, embraced Marxist rhetoric to support his Black
Power ideology: "Black films should deal with images of our position
in the superstructure. They should all work toward the decolonization
of Black minds and the reclaiming of Black spirit" (qtd. in Lyne, 2000,
p. 43). Twenty years later, in the absence of a viable Black counterpublic,
it seems likely that Singleton ignores the state because his personal experience and the contemporary popular culture representations upon
which he drew to write and direct *Boyz* simply didn't provide him with
the tools for state-based political analysis. Instead, what was available
to him were the usual pop culture representations of Black communities, and the rhetoric of the Black Muslims—a well-publicized nationalist group with a focus on economic independence.

Singleton has doubtless matured in the decade since *Boyz* hit the big
screen, but his fascination with a depoliticized version of Black street
culture continued with his 2000 remake of the classic blaxploitation film
Shaft. "I wanted to grow up and be that guy," said Singleton in an interview in the *Manchester Guardian*. "I wanted to dress cool, and get
all the ladies. It was always like one day I would make a Shaft movie"
(Leigh, 2000, p. 2, 14). Singleton's remake made good use of Samuel
Jackson's incredible projection of cool but completely dropped the original *Shaft*'s explicitly political subplot. That the industry rewards Singleton (and other Black filmmakers) for avoiding explicitly ideological films
is clear given the box-office failure of his critically acclaimed *Rosewood*,
a historical fiction based on the historical massacre of a Black community by a mob in Florida in the 1920s.[8]

Boyz opened the door for a series of Black films featuring soldiers and
Vietnam veterans, culminating in the flood year of 1995, which saw the
release of Preston A. Whitmore II's Vietnam War film *Walking Dead*;
Mario Van Peebles's *Panther* (focusing on Huey Newton and Bobby Seale,

and the fictional character "Judge"); and the Hughes brothers' over-the-top ghetto/'Nam/Black liberation extravaganza, *Dead Presidents.*

The bumper crop of 1995 all reflect a similar incoherence and were all directed by very young Black men. (Youth in Black directors seems to be a quality that producers now prize.) Each of these films features soldier or Vietnam veteran antiheroes who benefit from the general post–Vietnam War Memorial wall and welcome-home-parade recuperation of the image of the Vietnam veteran in White popular culture while promoting a vision of Black liberation in uneasy tandem with the dream of economic self-sufficiency. Film critic Cynthia Fuchs notes:

> The question of legitimacy—how it is assigned and by whom, how it shapes notions of honor, loyalty and betrayal, and specifically, how it is shaped by race and racism in the United States—is at the center of Whitmore's film, which tracks the increasingly horrific experiences of a mostly Black Marine unit in South Vietnam in 1971. The question also informs *Panther,* written by Melvin Van Peebles and directed by Mario Van Peebles. A fictionalized account of the birth of the Black Panther Party in Oakland, 1968–1969. (1996, p. 108)

Walking Dead is Whitmore's attempt to pay tribute to Black American soldiers who fought in Vietnam. It is constructed on the model of the White-produced Vietnam War films that came before (*Platoon, Born on the Fourth of July, Apocalypse Now,* etc.) and utilizes the familiar device of flashbacks (complete with Motown soundtrack) to establish the history of each of the five main characters in the film. Like most other Vietnam War films, it focuses on relationships between soldiers in an environment strangely bereft of connection to the world outside the war. This particular platoon is sent out on a mission with the ostensible purpose of rescuing American POWs.

Dale Dye, Marine veteran and consultant for many of the most well-known Vietnam War films, was hired by Whitmore to ensure the "authenticity" of *Walking Dead,* and concern with visual realism replaces, in Whitmore's film as in others, any attention to the ideological basis of the war. (Not that Dye was doing his job. It seems unbelievable that an infantry platoon would be sent on such a rescue mission as late as 1972, at the height of Nixon's Vietnamization program, a time when U.S. infantry in South Vietnam was growing scarcer and scarcer.) Even the fine actors Joe Morton and Eddie Griffin are unable to lift this film out of the predictable Vietnam War film format. For a film about the experiences of Black soldiers in the Vietnam War, it is sadly lacking in historical content or analysis.

Unable to confront such issues as the racist nature of Robert McNamara's "Project 100,000" (a program that changed the standards for admission into the military and cast a wider net for Black and other minority soldiers), the conflict between Black and White soldiers in base camps, the inordinate number of Black soldiers sentenced to U.S. military prisons in Vietnam, sharply increasing drug use among soldiers, the politicization of Black soldiers and veterans, or the identification of Black soldiers with the Vietnamese, Whitmore settles for a string of clichés derived from existing White popular culture sources. Actor Joe Morton's comment on the film sums up its disconnection from history: "It's seldom that you see a movie with Blacks where we aren't killing each other" ("The Walking Dead," 1995, p. 36). The Black Panthers and other Black liberationists of the 1960s and 1970s could and did see that Blacks killing Vietnamese *was* equivalent to Blacks killing each other. Black identification with oppressed Third World peoples was clear and based on an anti-imperialist, racially egalitarian, socialist ideology summed up in the slogan: "No Vietnamese Ever Called Me Nigger." Akmed Lorence would have thought Morton desperately in need of some political education.

The twins Allen and Albert Hughes's film *Dead Presidents* received far more favorable reviews than Whitmore's *Walking Dead*. The twenty-three-year-old team had burst onto the scene in 1993 with *Menace II Society,* a boys-go-bad film that rode in on the wave of enthusiasm inspired by nineteen-year-old John Singleton's *Boyz in the Hood*. The Hughes brothers do a better job than Whitmore when it comes to dealing with the prewar adventures of protagonist Anthony Curtis (Lorenz Tate) but certainly succumb to the same clichéd representations of war that ruin *Walking Dead*. Riddled with absurdities (a four-year tour in Vietnam? in the bush?) and over-the-top insanity worthy of Gus Hasford, Michael Herr, or Stanley Kubrick (a Black soldier who carries around the head of a dead Vietnamese, a skinned-soldier staked out with his severed penis in his mouth) the central section of the film fails to work as a coherent bridge between Curtis's prewar and postwar life. Despite Albert Hughes's assertion that the Black *bildungsroman* of the Vietnam War had never been filmed before ("Hughes Brothers'," 1995, p. 60), *Dead President's* representation of the Black Vietnam "experience" is neither particularly Black nor particularly original.

The Hughes brothers loosely based part of the story on the most sensational (and overused) autobiography in Wallace Terry's oral history anthology *Bloods*. Their documentary research on the war does not appear to include much more than this single book (which they call a book of "short stories" in their interview), and perhaps the documentary film that was made based on the book.[9] Though Terry's book was written at least in part to counter normative White Vietnam War narratives, in *Dead Presidents* the influence of Terry is overshadowed by that of Michael Herr, the godfather of Vietnam War journalism. Herr's gonzo journalism best-seller *Dispatches* has been quoted or referenced in almost every blockbuster Vietnam War film from *Apocalypse Now* onward. The attempt to wed the perspectives of the two journalists results in the construction of a Frankenstein's monster of a film, lurching along and scaring everybody for all the wrong reasons. The film draws heavily on the same texts and movies that established the Vietnam War genre: *Apocalypse Now, Platoon,* and *Full-Metal Jacket.*

In an interview in *Film Scouts,* Albert Hughes is asked where the Vietnam War scenes in *Dead Presidents* were filmed. He laughs and says "Disneyworld! Actually two miles away from Orlando, with some backdrop stills shot in Thailand" (Béhar, 1995). The casual embrace of simulation, and the connection between Vietnam during wartime and the self-contained fantasy environment of Disneyworld are disturbing, especially when one considers that one phrase "soldiers in-country" used to refer to Vietnam was "The Brown Disneyland." I have written before about how popular culture shapes both experience and memory for soldiers in the Vietnam War. Young filmmakers such as the Hughes Brothers are bereft of any firsthand experience and, without a serious effort to do scholarly research, are left only with popular culture images and the war stories of now middle-aged and older veterans. Lorenz Tate's description of the "reality" on which the film was based shows this pop culture influence and is riddled with myths about the Vietnam War:

> There was more psychological warfare because Vietnam vets were so used to seeing different violent acts. They got used to it. That kind of messes with a person. And I'm glad I got a chance to speak with a lot of Vietnam vets and just kind of pick their brains to see where they were mentally. There are so many stories Vietnam vets can tell you. I think the Hughes brothers touched upon several in one story. ("Hughes Brothers'," 1995, p. 60)

Tate expresses an equally clichéd view of the Vietnam War veteran, based entirely on post-1982 popular culture representations:

> Coming home was the problem," he said. "When he's walking around with all these medals on him, nobody really cared. He put his life on the line for millions of Americans and when he gets back, people spit on his face. They didn't care. He couldn't find jobs. He couldn't provide for his family. ("Hughes Brothers'," 1995, p. 60)

This could be a description of most movies about White veterans, from *First Blood* to *Born on the 4th of July*. There's nothing specifically "Black" about it. When the Hughes brothers revised the Vietnam War story to include Black soldiers and veterans, they failed to reject White clichés. It was White veterans, not Black veterans, who were shocked at being ignored and unemployed when they came home. In contrast, many Black veterans had gone to fight in Vietnam because they couldn't get into college or get a job in the first place.

Most of the war stories on the set probably were told by writer Michael Henry Brown, whom the Hughes brothers had hired because he was "an ex-Marine, he knew the book." Brown's memory of his own experience would have been influenced by both popular culture and by his status of employee. Says Allen Hughes, "We told him what scenes we wanted, he just went and wrote them" (Béhar, 1995). Brown may have been reluctant to contradict the young directors, or their take on the war may have matched his own internal revisions. In the "back and forth" between Brown and the Hughes brothers, it is likely that many myths and apocryphal tales were shared. The problem with relying on the testimony of veterans twenty years after a war experience is that the memory of veterans grows more and more like popular culture representation of the war as time goes on. None of those vets apparently told Tate the old joke about war stories:

> Q: What's the difference between a fairy tale and a war story?
> A: A fairy tale opens with "once upon a time, . . ." and a war story begins with "this is no shit."[10]

Black veterans, unlike White veterans, came home from a war to a war at home and many of them responded like young Black activist Akmed Lorence and joined the struggle for Civil Rights and human dignity being waged by the Panthers and others. By embracing a White popular culture version of the "real" war (complete with vets being spat upon by antiwar activists)[11] and failing to accurately represent the responses Black soldiers and veterans of the late 1960s and early 1970s, the Hughes brothers are left with no coherent explanation for Anthony Curtis's decision to plan and carry out an armed robbery with a group of friends and strangers, some of whose attire and sloganeering is ostensibly "political" but whose agenda is totally obscure and unfathomable. Curtis's own motives seem bourgeois and overtly apolitical—he's attracted to robbery not because of his political convictions but because he is ashamed that he cannot support his family. Sentenced to life in prison after the spectacular failure of the group's plan, Curtis can stand for nothing but a general sense that Black people are oppressed by White institutions. He can represent nothing greater or more particular because the movie takes no ideological stance and offers no cogent analysis of U.S. racism. As Desson Howe notes, the film manages to be "intense (and very bloody), heartfelt and superficial all at the same time" (1995, C1).

Howe also compares Anthony Curtis of *Dead Presidents* to Kadeem Hardison in *Panther,* a character who "goes from saluting Uncle Sam to infiltrating the Panthers to, finally, joining the cause—all in one heavy-handed character arc" (1995, C1). Howe reviewed *Panther* for the *Washington Post* and describes it in these terms:

> Sorting fact from fiction is a thorny thing—unless you're something of a social historian. Clearly, the movie's about a significant period in American history, and filmmaker Mario Van Peebles (working with his father and scriptwriter Melvin) is more emotional than dispassionately dogged about the facts. "Panther" is a fictionalized account—an interpretation—of the stormy period (between 1966 and 1970) when the Black Panther Party for Self-Defense used weapons, retaliatory belligerency and empowerment training for their troops and people to mobilize against perpetual police harassment. (1995, C1)

Panther stars Vietnam War movie veteran Courtney B. Vance as Bobby Seale and Marcus Chong as Huey Newton. These "real life" figures are joined by the fictional character Judge, played by Kadeem Hardison. Judge is a Vietnam War veteran whose initially patriotic and conciliatory stance is shifted by exposure to radicals Newton and Seale. Newton anticipates that the police will approach Judge and ask him to spy on the Panthers, and he encourages Judge to agree, setting him up as a double agent. Judge agrees and winds up in an increasingly dangerous position. Reviews of *Panther* are rife with references to Oliver Stone's technique of merging documentary footage with fictional scenes, and Van Peebles certainly does seem to embrace this strategy to make his portrait of the Panthers more "real." The plot, however, is drawn more closely from his father's novel (Melvin Van Peebles also wrote the *Panther* screenplay) than from history itself.

Judge, a student on the GI Bill, is introduced to the Panthers on the UC Berkeley campus when he runs across a Black activist handing out copies of Mao's writings in Sproul Plaza. A cautious skeptic, Judge is not drawn into the organization until he sees the Panthers engaged in work that supports the Black community in Oakland. And this is one of the great flaws of the film: a fictionalized J. Edgar Hoover is after the Panthers because he thinks they are communists. Judge would like to protect the Panthers because he knows they are *not* communists but selfless, freedom-loving heroes of the Black community. Thus, a false contradiction is created to make the plot sensible to contemporary Americans at the cost of obscuring the roots of the movement. The real Panthers were most certainly socialists—many of them were avowed communists—but far from seeing a contradiction between their politics and the work they did for the Black community, they felt that community activism could and should be rooted in a clear political ideology. To erase this history—to portray the Panthers as larger-than-life heroes while stripping them of their politics—is typical of Van Peebles, whose project of constructing a mythic, heroic past for African Americans has already been described. The introduction of a subplot in which the mafia and the FBI are blamed for supplying drugs to the Black community with deliberate genocidal intent resonates nicely with the plots of classic blaxploitation films[12] (Fred Williamson's *Black Caesar* series, for example) but draws attention away from the real importance of the Panther organization. Van Peebles's preoccupation with male heroes also leads him to underplay the history and importance of women in the Panther Party. Elaine Brown and Angela Davis aren't even given a nod in *Panther,* and their absence in the film is sorely missed.

The film may have lacked a sound ideological basis, but that didn't prevent it from being the center of ideological struggle:

> A committee of Black entertainers and athletes, including Danny Glover, Spike Lee and Magic Johnson, took out ads in *Daily Variety* to support Van Peebles *pere et fils:* "We laud their efforts and their courage for making a movie that sends

a message of strength, dignity and empowerment to the African American community—especially to our youth." This was in response to an earlier ad, declaring Panther "a two-hour lie," that was placed in *Daily Variety* by David Horowitz's Center for the Study of Popular Culture, a neoconservative outfit in Los Angeles. Horowitz, a reformed leftie who worked for the Panthers in the '70s, now believes that "the overwhelming impact of the Panthers was negative." And he fears *Panther* will have a toxic effect: "I fully expect that there will be people who will die because of this film." (Corliss, 1995, p. 20)

Horowitz's dramatic rhetoric is indicative of how threatening conservatives (and many liberals) find the Panthers even when their ideology is stripped from their representation. But Horowitz's fear is no longer rooted in ideology either—it is rooted in the equally reactionary and incoherent fear of Black men with guns. And that is what representation of the Panthers has become—an argument between those who like to see Black men with guns, and those who do not.

In a capitalist state, every image becomes a product one can sell, and there is tremendous pressure to produce sellable images and equally tremendous pressure to reshape the context in which images are viewed so they do not represent ideas or historical facts that threaten the capitalist value system. Black filmmakers, however concerned they are with Black history and culture, are not immune from these pressures and are forced by the market to engage in competitive rather than supportive practices:

> "In part, Mario and his father have done a very good job of showing our history," says David Hilliard, former Panther chief of staff. "But the characterization of Bobby Seale being dominant over Huey Newton is certainly a reversal of history. Unfortunately, most of the people in the party leadership who could have helped are on my project." Hilliard, you see, is working with Seale on their own film for Warner Bros. These days Panther adversaries don't have shootouts, they have rival development deals with movie studios. (Corliss, 1995, p. 20)

Despite his complaints, Van Peebles did have a significant promotion budget and the help of a media giant, the Black Entertainment Television Network (BET). In May 1995, I spotted a half-page ad in *YSB* (the

Magazine for Young Brothers and Sisters), which is published by BET. As a promotion for Mario Van Peeble's film *Panther,* it advertised a contest in which the winner would receive a monetary award and "live the Panther dream."

The campaign had distorted the "dream" into a promise of financial gain for the lucky winner, whereas once it had been a belief in a society where all citizens could be assured of justice and equality. Presented entirely without irony, the contest promo underlined the complete commercialization and appropriation of Panther history. The Panther revolutionary agenda has been revised and repackaged to the point where it could be used to promote the very capitalist structures the Panthers sought to destroy. Ideology had, finally and completely, been subsumed by image. The trajectory from George Jackson to Monster Cody passed the peak of its arc.

Epilogue

In February 1996, Sanyika Shakur was pulled over by police officers, who allege that they discovered a gram of marijuana in his car. In March, Shakur fled when parole officers entered his home to search it and to test him for drugs. He avoided the law for almost three months. When he was finally captured, the police found him signing autographs on the front porch of a house in South-Central Los Angeles. There were about ten people lined up waiting (Corwin, 1996, p. 1). At the time Shakur jumped parole, he was working on a movie script for *Monster,* which had by then sold more than one hundred thousand copies in ten languages (Mitchell & Hodari, 1996, p. 1). While on the lam, he kept in close touch with his agent and in daily touch with Antoine Fuqua, who had been hired by Propaganda films to document Shakur's life (*Oregonian,* 1996, p. A30).

Sanyika Shakur gave an interview to journalist Susan Faludi in September 1999, a few days after being released from jail after serving a one-year sentence for a second parole violation. He explained to her, "I got all those ideas from watching movies and watching television. I was really just out there acting from what I saw on TV" (Faludi, 1999, p. 52).

> And he wasn't referring to *Superfly* or *Shaft.* "Growing up I didn't see one blaxploitation movie. Not one." His inspiration came from shows like *Mission Impossible* and *Rat Patrol* and films like *The Godfather.* "I would study the guys in those movies," he recalled, "how they moved, how they

stood, the way they dressed, that whole winning way of dress-
ing. Their tactics became my tactics. I went from watching
Rat Patrol to being it." His prime model was Arthur Penn's
1967 movie *Bonnie and Clyde.* "I watched how in *Bonnie
and Clyde* they'd walk in and say their whole names. They
were getting their reps. I took that and applied it to my situation. It's a thin line between criminality and celebrity. Someone has to be the star of the 'hood. Someone has to do the
advertising for the 'hood."(Faludi, 1999, p. 52)

Though Shakur doesn't explicitly mention it, this essay demonstrates that
he was also strongly influenced by the images in Vietnam War films and
perhaps also television shows such as *Tour of Duty* and *China Beach.*
The distance between George Jackson and Sanyika Shakur is the distance
between the 1960s and the 1990s, between a strong Black counterpublic
sphere and a weak one, between ideology and image, between the Black
liberation fighter and the "ghetto star." The revolution may not be tele-
vised, but we're all waiting for the next spin-off.

Notes

1. This process is fully explicated in Kalí Tal (1995), *Worlds of Hurt: Reading the Literatures of Trauma* (New York: Cambridge University Press).

2. For a full analysis of COINTELPRO's effect on the Black Panthers, see
Ward Churchill and Jim Vander Wall (1988).

3. Produced by David Loeb Weiss. Transcribed by the author.

4. The notable exception is Stan Shaw's remarkable character in *The Boys
in Company C.* Directed by Sidney J. Furie (1978). Shaw plays Tyrone Washington, who displays both political savvy and street savvy.

5. As it turns out, Singleton's Furious was quite right. See Gary Webb
(1998), *Dark Alliance: The CIA, the Contras, and the Crack Cocaine Explo-
sion* (New York: Seven Stories Press) for a detailed description of government
involvement in the importation of crack cocaine into U.S. ghettoes.

6. Transcribed by the author.

7. As noted before, this latter claim has been proven to be at least partially
true. See Webb (note 2).

8. A critical comparison of *Rosewood* and Mario Van Peebles's *Posse* simply begs to be written.

9. Although *Bloods* was welcomed by scholars because resources in the field
of Black autobiography from the Vietnam War are slim, it has also been strongly
critiqued because of Terry's admission that he reordered, smoothed out, and
rephrased his interviews to make them more readable.

10. Heard repeatedly from more infantrymen than I can count.

11. See Jerry Lembke's book-length study (2000), *The Spitting Image: Myth,
Memory and the Legacy of Vietnam* (New York: New York University Press).

12. This subplot is actually not at all far-fetched, as Gary Webb's reportage for the *San Jose Mercury* certainly made apparent in the late 1990s (see note 2). However, it draws our focus from the Panthers and their history without adding relevance or clarity to the historical analysis.

3

Rhetoric That Should Have Moved the People: Rethinking the Black Panther Party

Gwendolyn D. Pough

In terms of the search for Black selfhood, the Black Panthers and proponents of the Black Power Movement make an interesting case study. First, there was the attire: basic Black leather and shades, often accompanied by weapons. The physical intimidation factor alone led to outrageous Hooveresque estimates as to the number of Panthers inhabiting the nation. Second, here was a group of men and women who stood unified behind a race-based fight for equality. Third, this mission dedicated them to changing the world.

—A. B. White, "Fragmented Souls"

AS THE ABOVE EPIGRAPH INDICATES, THE BLACK PANTHER PARTY (BPP) had impacts on J. Edgar Hoover's FBI, the search for Black selfhood, and radical politics. The BPP's rhetoric and politics have essentially been ignored, however, despite the fact that the members' attire and pro-Black rhetoric inspired thousands of young Black people across the country to join them. The party formed alliances with other social groups, such as White radicals, gays, and women, and the rhetoric of its ten-point program inspired other groups in their fights for liberation. Kobena Mercer (1992) offers a discussion of the influence of the BPP in his article "'1968': Periodizing Postmodern Politics and Identity." He notes that the BPP's ten-point platform "formed a discursive framework through which the women's movement and the gay movement displaced the demand for reform and 'equality' in favor of the wider goal of revolution and 'liberation'" (p. 434). He argues that the BPP's slogans also influenced the women's and gay liberation movements' rhetoric as well.

Thus, "Gay Pride" could be linked to "Black Pride" and "notions of 'brotherhood' and 'community' in Black political discourse influenced assertions of 'global sisterhood' or 'sisterhood is strength'" (p. 434). The BPP's visual presence—which hinted at armed resistance and retaliation—changed the way Black people were perceived in the American imagination and gave America its first real glimpse at Black rage. The BPP members had an impact on Blacks and non-Blacks. They saw themselves as leaders in the struggle for Black liberation, and they felt that liberation was linked to other struggles for freedom.

In October 1966, Huey P. Newton and Bobby Seale founded the Black Panther Party in Oakland, California. Tired of police brutality and the lack of what they considered relevant Black political organizations, the two men developed what would become the BPP's "Ten-Point Platform and Program: What We Want, What We Believe." The ten-point platform called for Black self-determination, freedom, employment, decent housing, exemption from military service, and an end to police brutality and murder in Black communities. Seale and Newton, both students at Merritt Junior College in West Oakland, came up with the idea of "policing the police" as a method of combating rampant police brutality. The BPP's militant stance—its active use of the right to bear arms—gave the small group of original Panthers a significant amount of media coverage. However, it was the thirty Panthers who marched into the state capitol at Sacramento to protest the Mulford Act, a bill aimed at taking away the right to publicly display weapons, that catapulted the BPP further into the public eye. From that point on, the presence of the party in the American public sphere was very much a rhetoric of disruption; party members changed the way America looked at Black people, not only with their physical presence but also with their rhetorical presence. Very few could forget the image of Bobby Seale, with his gun at his side, reading the powerful words of protest that he and Huey had prepared.

The BPP opened chapters in New York, Chicago, Connecticut, Los Angeles, and Detroit, to name only a few cities. And these other chapters spawned equally charismatic and influential leaders, such as Fred Hampton in Chicago; Bunchy Carter and John Huggins in Los Angeles; and Assata Shakur, Afeni Shakur, and the Panther 21 in New York. They gathered such a tremendous following that, as the epigraph above states, they struck a cord of fear with Hoover in terms of exactly how many Panthers were in the country. The BPP had every hope the Black people for whose freedom and power they fought would stand behind it—the vanguard of the revolution. Of course, the party's rhetoric, intended to move the people toward revolution, did not accomplish its goal. However, the BPP did leave behind a sense of standing up for one-self and one's people. It became the legacy upon which other twentieth-century Black public spheres would build their foundations. Traces of the party's revolutionary residue can be seen in the political rap music of the 1980s and the bad brothers on the block that refuse to buckle down under police harassment.

Kalí Tal (chapter 2, this volume) addresses traces of revolutionary residue by looking at contemporary Black popular culture and its ties to the Black Power Movement. However, as Tal points out, the themes of death and dying from the era of Black Power were linked to a politi-cal agenda—a political agenda that is missing in contemporary Black popular culture. The images of death and war found in the writing of Black Vietnam War veterans and proponents of Black Power went hand in hand with a strong political ideology. Tal notes that the material rem-nants of the Black Power Movement that surface in contemporary films, autobiographies, and music are somewhat problematic. They have a tendency to make one yearn for the days of old when brothers were bad and did not take any shit from the police, when sisters wore big afros, gave guns to revolutionaries, and became the FBI's most wanted crimi-nals. In her article "Afro Images: Politics, Fashion, and Nostalgia" (1994), Angela Davis writes of the problems with this kind of nostalgia. She investigates the nostalgic mass marketing in popular culture today of her own 1960s image. She is remembered as a hairdo, much as the BPP is remembered as a group of gun-toting, leather-jacket-wearing bad boys. With the exception of a few catch phrases such as "Power to the People," "Off the Pigs," and "Black Power," the BPP's political ideologies are somewhat lost on younger generations, having become empty of their original power. Davis suggests "find[ing] ways of incorporating them [African American historical images] into social and political memory instead of using them as a substitute which encourages atrophy of such memory" (1994, p. 45).

Davis calls for the kind of "critical memory" Houston Baker (1995) describes in "Critical Memory and the Black Public Sphere." Baker sets up his article by making an important distinction between "critical memory" and "nostalgia." He describes nostalgia as a "homesickness" and a "purposive construction of a past filled with golden virtues, golden men and sterling events" (Baker, 1995, p. 7). In contrast, he describes critical memory as "always uncanny; it is always in crises. Critical memory judges severely, censures righteously, renders hard ethical evaluations of the past that never defines as well passed" (p. 7). He defines critical memory as "the very faculty of revolution. Its operation implies a continuous arrival at turning points. . . . To be critical is never to be safely housed or allegorically free of the illness, transgression and contamination of the past" (p. 7). Baker critiques Black conservative nostalgia as well as Habermas's description of the public sphere. Baker recognizes that there are multiple Black public spheres, such as the Black public sphere of incarceration and the urban Black public sphere.

Critical memory thus guards against nostalgia by asking hard questions. This essay uses critical memory to explore the BPP's position as a "counter-public sphere" to an already existing "counter-public sphere"— the Black community it was trying to reach.[1] The term *counter-public sphere* is taken from Nancy Fraser's (1993) definition of "subaltern counter publics." She defines *subaltern counter publics* as "parallel discursive arenas where members of subordinated social groups invent and circulate counter discourses, so as to formulate oppositional interpretations of their identities, interest and needs" (Fraser, 1993, p. 14). Thus, the BPP became a subordinated group within a subordinated group: it became a marginalized faction of a group already marginalized by the larger society.

In this essay, I analyze various BPP documents and examine some of the places where the BPP fell short of making the Black community follow them into revolution—the places where there were contradictions in its rhetoric. I analyze the rhetorical practices that led to the BPP's alienation from the very community it was trying to uplift and its members' attempts to change and transform their rhetoric to better appeal to the people. I also analyze other changes in their rhetoric. For example, how did the party move from being disrespectful to homosexuals and women in general to wanting to form an alliance with the gay liberation and women's liberation movements? How did the BPP move from making contradictory sexist comments about the role of women in the movement to having several women serving in key positions in the party? Did the BPP's call for a united struggle against oppression lead to their demise? And lastly, what can we learn from their rhetorics and struggles— specifically in terms of coalition building—that will help us to affect change today?

Although this essay is largely about the ways in which the Panthers failed to reach the community in the ways they'd hoped to, I by no means want to suggest that they did not have an impact on the hearts and minds of the people. Rather, this is an attempt to learn by analysis—to figure

out what did not work for the Panthers in order to develop better political strategies today. As Baker (1995) writes, "[T]he essence of critical memory's work is the cumulative, collective maintenance of a record
that draws into relationship significant instants of time past and the
always uprooted homelessness of now" (p. 7). This essay functions therefore as a template—a "case study," to use Artress Bethany White's (1998)
language—and a twentieth-century starting point for the study of the
rhetoric and Black public spheres that came after the BPP.

White People, Black Panthers, and Cultural Nationalism

The BPP worked diligently to form coalitions with other radical groups
and likeminded individuals. They formed alliances with such groups as
the Young Lords, a former Puerto Rican street gang turned political
group; the Brown Berets, a group of Chicano radicals; and White radical groups such as Students for a Democratic Society and the Patriot
Party. It was the BPP's attempts to form coalitions with others—specifically White radicals that caused the party the most trouble with the Black
community they sought to reach. Panther David Hilliard recalls in his
autobiography the trouble people had with the BPP's White allies. He
notes, "[L]ater, detractors of the Panthers criticize this [White] support,
claiming white allegiance, rather than our appeal to the Black community, causes the Party's rapid growth" (Hilliard & Cole, 1993, p. 144).
The BPP saw the struggle against oppression not only as a race struggle
but also as a class struggle. As the bitter remembrance by David Hilliard
suggests, the BPP took a lot of criticism for its alliances with Whites. Even
some members of the BPP who did not leave at the first sign of White
people resented working with Whites.

The BPP's alliances with Whites and unwillingness to change its belief, that they "could have a solidarity and friendship in a common
struggle without whites taking over;" (Hilliard & Cole, 1993, p. 172)
helped to fuel the ongoing war between the BPP and Ron Karenga's
United Slaves (US). Ron Karenga's US was a cultural nationalist group
based in Los Angeles. It struggled against the BPP for power and control in Los Angeles, specifically for control over Black community organizations and Black student groups. The groups had several public
confrontations, many of which were fueled by the U.S. government. After
two BPP leaders of the Los Angeles chapter, Bunchy Carter and John
Huggins, were murdered by members of Karenga's group (who were later
proven to be FBI informants), Fred Hampton, chairman of the Chicago
chapter, gave the following statement:

> You can see the pressures the Black Panther Party goes through by making a coalition with whites. You can see that we had a group in California who committed their first acts of violence on the Black Panther Party. Ron Karenga and US never shot nothing but dope until they shot them brothers. . . . When the Black Panther Party stood up and said we not going to fight racism with racism, US said "NO, we can't do that because it's a race question and if you make it a class question then the revolution might come sooner. (qtd. in Heath, 1976, p. 242)

Hampton teased US by implying that the group was not a "real revolutionary" group because it only wanted to focus on race issues. By stating that US did not want the revolution to come soon, Hampton painted the BPP as the real revolutionaries ready for revolution. Hampton criticized a Black group at the same time that he validated and commended the united struggle with Whites. This speech also called for the Black community to take the huge step of putting racism and race issues aside for the class struggle. He made fun of the newfound African pride and questioned vehemently the cultural nationalist's place in the revolution. Hampton's remarks about Black culture and Black cultural nationalists helped to sever the ties between the BPP and the Black community. The BPP was notorious for making degrading remarks about Black cultural nationalists. Remarks such as "porkchop-nationalism" can be found in many Panther speeches. One such example occurred in David Hilliard's account of a speech given by Bobby Seale. "We don't care about changing what we wear; we want power—later for what we wear. Dashikis don't free nobody and porkchops don't oppress nobody" (Hilliard & Cole, 1993, p. 122). The porkchop insult can be likened to the BPP's pig epitaph for the police in that neither was seen to be in the best interest of Black people.

The cultural nationalists were counterrevolutionary as far as the BPP was concerned. Newton sums up the BPP's feeling best when he said,

> The cultural nationalists are concerned with returning to old African culture and thereby regaining their identity and freedom. In other words, they feel that assuming the African culture is enough to bring political freedom. . . . We have to realize our Black heritage in order to give us strength to move on and progress. But as far as returning to old African culture, it's unnecessary and in many respects unadvantagous. (Heath, 1976, p. 45)

The Panthers were concerned with the state of Black people *in* America. They did not see the need to "return to African culture." They did not see how it would help end oppression. And ending oppression was their ultimate goal—not looking for their African roots.

However, at a time when Black Americans were just beginning to exhibit self-pride and search for their African roots, the thought of dismissing cultural nationalism did not go over well, at least not with the other elements of the Black Power Movement.[2] With Jim Crow laws, riding in the back of the bus, and the struggle to use their right to vote still fresh in their minds, Black Americans were not inclined to believe in a united front. Even though many Whites participated in the Civil Rights Movement, it was that very participation and the notion that they took over the running of the movement that caused a lot of skepticism.[3] White people marched side by side with Blacks during the Civil Rights Movement, but racial tensions still existed, and those tensions led to more mistrust and resentment. Martin Luther King was dead. Malcolm was dead. And Black people were weary, to say the least, of Whites and those who held alliances with Whites. Yet despite this weariness, the BPP continued to build alliances with Whites.

It was the alliance with one White French writer in particular that helped to change the once homophobic rhetoric used by many BPP members. That man was Jean Genet.

The relationship between the BPP and French, White, gay playwright Jean Genet was, at first glance, a highly unlikely one. But probing deeper, it's clear that the BPP sought and openly accepted Genet because he could help gather funds during a time of financial desperation. The BPP did not really have a choice. They needed money to pay the numerous court fees incurred from the various arrests of BPP members. Genet was willing to come to America and help them in their fund-raising efforts.

Of his closeness with Blacks in general, Genet commented, "What makes me feel so close to them is the hatred they bear for the white world that scorned me because I was a bastard, with no father and no mother. Perhaps I am a Black man who happens to have white or pink skin. I don't know my family" (qtd. in Savona, 1984, p. 97). The Panthers, who already had built into their discourse a willingness to work with anyone who was willing to "unite against a common enemy," did not have a problem working with Genet.

Genet's writings often discredited Whites, homosexuals, and revolutionaries—the very identities he held himself. His life and work offers an example of self-critique. His play *The Blacks: A Clown Show* was a cynical piece that made a mockery of the White established power structure and even militant Black uprising. The performance of this play in America led to protest against Genet, and in turn the BPP. One such protest written by playwright Ed Bullins, a one-time BPP member, appeared in the magazine *Black Theater*.

> Jean Genet is a white, self-confessed homosexual with dead white western ideas—faggoty ideas about Black Art, revolution, and people. His empty masochistic activities on behalf of the Black Panther Party should not con Black people. Genet, in his writing, had admitted to seeing himself as a so-called "nigger." Black people cannot allow white perversion to enter their communities, even if it rides in on the Black of a panther. . . . Black people, in this stage of the struggle have no use for self-elected "niggers." (qtd. in E. White, 1993, p. 441)

Bullins urged the Black community to be suspicious of Genet for several reasons. First, he was a White man, and his brothers and fathers figuratively were oppressors. Second, he was a homosexual, and Bullins's homophobia played on the homophobia that existed in the Black community. And third, Genet claimed to be Black. Bullins used this claim to play on the resentment that many Blacks felt toward people claiming to understand and identify with their struggles as Black in racist America. In other words—"everybody wanna sing our blues, nobody wanna live our blues."

Fortunately, the BPP did not buy into the criticism. The Panthers continued to work with Genet. And he in turn had a large impact on the group and its rhetoric. Edmund White (1993) writes of Genet and the BPP, "he was sufficiently irritated by the Panthers' repeated references to their white male enemies (especially Nixon) as 'faggots' or 'punks' that he made strong objections, which resulted in the publication of a position paper by Newton" (p. 527). That paper was titled "The Women's Liberation and Gay Liberation Movements." Newton writes, "[W]e should be careful about using those terms that might turn our friends off. The terms 'faggot' and 'punk' should be deleted from our vocabulary." (1995, p. 154). Newton made a strong demand of his party members to respect gays: "They may be the most oppressed people in society" (1995, p. 153). Newton's position paper showed a commitment by BPP leadership to change the homophobic references in the party's rhetoric. It would take a little more to combat the sexism and misogyny found in BPP rhetoric.

"Jive Sisters—Don't Read This"

An ad that appeared frequently in the BPP newspaper begins "Jive Sisters—Don't Read This." The ad stated, "The Black Panther Party needs typist! If you can type well and want to work for liberation, call 863-6459 in San Francisco." This ad offers other kinds of contradictions and inconsistencies found in the BPP rhetoric. As stated above, the Panthers professed a desire to work with homosexuals but had a hard time getting rid of the homophobic references in their rhetoric. And while women were said to be just as instrumental to the revolution as men, ads such as the one above still appeared in the BPP newspaper.

A few people writing during the 1960s and 1970s analyzed the rhetoric of the Black Power Movement and the BPP.[4] However, they did not offer any critical look at the women in the movement or the things they did to influence BPP rhetoric. For example, Phillip S. Foner (1995) compiled a collection of BPP speeches and writings in his recently re-released *The Black Panther Speaks,* and he gave space to the works of Huey P. Newton, Bobby Seale, Eldridge Cleaver, David Hilliard and Fred Hampton. He placed the BPP women in one section titled "Black Panther Women Speak," which took up only 20 pages of the 280-page text. In the introduction to this section, Foner writes, "[F]rom the early period, too, Black women were important in the work of the Party. Nor was their activity confined to the typewriter and mimeograph machine. Panther women spoke at rallies and meetings and were interviewed in the underground press" (1995, p. 145). However, the importance of the Black Panther women is not reflected in Foner's collected speeches and writings—which is both unfortunate and remiss, since women such as Kathleen Cleaver, Elaine Brown, and Erica Huggins played key roles in shaping the party.

Elaine Brown (1992) wrote that her first encounter with blatant sexism in the BPP occurred when she visited national headquarters in Oakland for the first time. Brown did not help the sisters prepare the food when she arrived and had the audacity to sit in the room with the men as they talked. She quickly got a firsthand account of what a sister's role in the revolution was thought to be. Bobby Seale, the BPP chairman and co-founder, motioned for the only other sister in the room to join them and told her, "Marsha, tell the sister here what a brother has got to do to get some from you." Fifteen-year-old Marsha stood at attention and began:

> First of all, a brother's got to be righteous. He's got to be a
> Panther. He's got to be able to recite the ten-point platform

and program, and be ready to off the pig and die for the people. . . . Can't no motherfucker get no pussy from me unless he can get down with the Party. . . . A sister has to give up the pussy when the brother is on his job and hold it back when he's not. 'Cause sisters got pussy power. (Brown, 1992, p. 189)

Instead of working to put Brown in her "place" as a woman, the speech, which received "right-ons" and "ooh-wees" from the brothers, only incensed her and caused her to begin to evaluate the chauvinism in the BPP.

Although Brown paints Seale as the chauvinist who had fifteen-year-old girls give speeches about their pussy power, Seale tells a different story in his book *Seize the Time: The Story of the Black Panther Party and Huey P. Newton*. Seale portrays himself and other leaders of the BPP as the true purveyors of women's rights:

When Eldridge and Huey and the Party as a whole move to get rid of male chauvinism, we're moving on that principle of absolute equality between male and female: because male chauvinism is related to the very class nature of this society as it exists today. . . . The party is working hard and fast to break down male chauvinism: at the same time that we are moving on this matter in relation to the community, we are also moving and changing in relation to ourselves. (1991, p. 394)

Seale created a space in which Panthers operated as role models for Black men on the proper way to treat Black women. Seale also provided a striking contradiction and inconsistency. "A lot of the brothers in the Black community who only think of the sisters as secondary—brothers who are pimping sisters and think that this is the way life has to be—have begun to see that the examples that are being set by the Black Panther Party are more progressive. They see us winning on a higher level and treating sisters on an equal level" (Seale, 1991, p. 398). However, only a few pages earlier in his text, he characterizes the sexual conduct of women in the party in much the same way that Elaine Brown describes above. He makes reference to Sister Marsha chastising some brothers in front of a barbershop who made a pass at her. She told them, "[L]ook, brother, you're not getting none of this! . . . The only way you can get close to me is to get hip to some of the real ideology of the Black Panther Party" (p. 395). He also gives credit to Los Angeles Panther leader Bunchy

Carter for coming up with the notion that sisters should not "go to bed" with men who weren't "doing any revolutionary work" (p. 396).[5]

Several dual contradictions can be seen in other actions of the BPP—such as the response to women in leadership positions. Bobby Seale (1991) describes a scene of Panther men and women working in harmony: "[T]hey [women] want to be treated like human beings. And we've found that the sisters work better in the party when they're treated like human beings. If a sister's in charge and taking responsibility to do something, the brothers follow her orders. They don't say, 'I ain't going to listen to no woman" (p. 398). It should also be noted that the BPP was forced, in the later years of the organization, to let women move up in ranks. Huey Newton had to pick Elaine Brown to take over the party when he left the country because she was next in line and most of the BPP leadership was either in jail, in exile, or dead. Also, police repression and infiltration resulted in the advancement of women. As Angela LeBlanc-Ernest writes in her article "'The Most Qualified Person to Handle the Job': Black Panther Party Women, 1966–1982" (1998): "[T]he Party's decision to close ranks further contributed to the increased opportunities for women to fill nontraditional roles" (p. 310). Thus, although women had been a part of the BPP since the beginning, and women such as Kathleen Cleaver and Erica Huggins held leadership positions, it took such outside circumstance as police repression to create a space for other rank-and-file members to move up in the ranks.

It should also be noted that the party did not send a strong message of inclusion, sensitivity to women's issues, and faith in their ability to lead until Newton placed Brown in control of the party while he was in exile. This action disproved the notion that only a jive sister would want to do more than type for the BPP newspaper. Placing Brown as leader of the BPP helped enforce a ban on derogatory words against women and placed more women in leadership positions. As Brown relates:

> There was one result of all this I had failed to think through:
> I had introduced a number of women in the Party's administration. There were too many women in command of the affairs of the Black Panther Party, numerous men were grumbling.
>
> "I hear we can't call them bitches no more," one brother actually stated to me in the middle of an extraordinarily hectic day.
>
> "No, motherfucker," I responded unendearingly, "You may not call them bitches 'no more.'" I turned brusquely to

> Bill, my bodyguard, and told him to make note for Larry to
> deal with "my brother here." (1992, pp. 362–363)

Brown used her executive power and the muscle that went along with it to ensure that no derogatory remarks against women were made. She used her power to "deflect most of the chauvinism of Black Panther men" (p. 363). Besides giving women key positions, she also made an attempt to secure respect for those women, and for herself. On a larger scale, her actions can be viewed as an attempt to ensure that the BPP maintained a respect for all women in their discourse and actions.

Power to the People/Repression of the BPP

Hugh Pearson (1994) offers a scathing critique of the BPP that accuses party members who have recently released autobiographies of overly implicating the FBI and the CIA in the BPP's downfall. He paints the party as a bunch of thugs and criminals. He writes that drugs and Black on Black crime—Panthers offing other Panthers as opposed to the "pigs"—are important factors contributing to the BPP's ultimate demise. However, Earl Anthony suggests a different analysis of why the Panthers failed. Anthony, a confessed FBI and CIA informant, claims that he was forced to either become an informant or go to prison on a trumped-up murder charge. He writes, "And what eulogy is there for the rest of us who picked up the gun. We found that trying to make a revolution in this country is like spitting in the wind, it will blow back into your face" (1990, p. 191). I believe that the truth is a mixture of both of these accounts. The BPP, as can be seen in some of the examples and contradictions discussed here, were by no means perfect. But they were also undeniably the targets of heavy government and police repression because they were trying to create revolutionary change and encourage coalitions. Many lost their lives—or large parts of their lives in the case of the many political prisoners—because of their political beliefs and activism.

The BPP's ideas and work toward a united struggle, which manifested itself in a willingness to work not only with radical whites, but gays and women as well, led to the party's ultimate demise. It is the inclusiveness of their revolutionary vision that I feel frightened the American government the most. To have a Black radical group such as the BPP be so successful at bringing various groups together to in essence stop the oppression of Black people was not to be condoned at that time. Separatism was still encouraged, especially as the nation was just coming out of an era of racial segregation. Also, their alliances with White radical groups made Black people just coming out of segregation a bit skeptical. In spite of repression, the BPP continued to form coalitions across race and worked diligently to remove homophobic and sexist language from their rhetoric. Perhaps there is something we can learn from their struggles as we work toward these same goals today?

In the foreword to Newton's posthumously published doctoral dissertation, *War Against the Panthers: A Study of Repression in America,* his second wife, Fredericka Newton, writes, "The Party was Huey Newton's essence and his life's work, left behind as a personal legacy, a foundation, a work not yet complete, a seed sown to flower today's barren fields" (1996, p. vii). And these words seem fitting to close an essay written during the "uprooted homelessness of now" (Baker, 1995, p. 7)—an essay concerned with finding out where the BPP went wrong in order to continue to build on the legacy of the Party. Tracye Matthews (1998) describes the legacy of the BPP in her article "'No One Ever Asks, What a Man's Place in the Revolution Is': Gender and the Politics of the Black Panther Party 1966–1971."

> Through its ideology, rhetoric, imagery, and praxis, the BPP engaged the dominant culture in a debate about the parameters of Black racial and sexual identity and its impact on politics and policy. . . . They also engaged each other and the larger Black community about what it meant to be a Black woman, man, comrade, revolutionary—not in the abstract—but in the heat of political struggle. (1998, p. 294)

Matthews's words confirm the focus of this essay: The BPP changed the way Black people were viewed in the American public sphere, and in the process it changed the way Black people looked at themselves. The Panthers had contradictions, like any other group in society, but they tried to work through them. They were not a group content to sit in a coffee shop and talk about revolution while discussing Marx, Lenin, Ché, and Mao. They were trying to implement the ideas of these revolutionaries and revolutionary thinkers.

Newton describes the purpose of his doctoral dissertation as an "intent to forge an analysis capable of informing and instructing those who are devoted to and must continue to grapple with these outstanding problems in need of being resolved if ever democratic government in America is to achieve any degree of substance consistent with its theoretical suppositions and ideals" (1996, p. 6). Newton realized that change still has to be made for America to reach its full potential as a democracy.

And in order to start working on change today, I think it would behoove all of us to take a look at the BPP, the things they tried to accomplish, and the rhetoric they used to do so. We need to make present the absent rhetoric, learn from their multiple revisions and innovations. Many of the problems that the Panthers organized to fight against in the late 1960s are still present today. The ways in which they went about fighting are just as relevant. By learning from the contradictions that befell them, we can start to reconstruct their rhetoric into an innovative and revolutionary rhetoric for today. We can then learn from them and perhaps move the people.

Notes

1. I use the term *Black community* in this essay because during the time that the BPP was active the proper term, *Black communities*, was not used in the same ways that it is today—as a way of documenting the vast diversity of Blackness in the United States. The Black Power Movement was meant to be a unifying movement and as such strove for a unified Blackness and a unified Black community.

2. When we look at what is left of the Black Power Movement today, cultural nationalist projects such as Kwanzaa and Afrocentric-based Black studies programs, it's not hard to make the case that cultural nationalism was more successful in drawing in the masses.

3. This skepticism and distrust of Whites is one of the reasons why Stokely Carmichael and H. Rap Brown only joined the BPP briefly. Both noted problems with White students taking over SNCC as their major reasons for leaving that organization and felt that the BPP's coalitions with Whites would lead to the same outcome.

4. Other useful works on this subject not mentioned in this essay are K. Borden (1973), Black Rhetoric in the 1960s: Sociohistorical Perspectives. *Journal of Black Studies, 3,* 423–431; M. S. Cummings (1972), Problems of Researching Black Rhetoric: Review Essay. *Journal of Black Studies,* 503–508; P. C. Kennicott, & W. E. Page (1971), H. Rap Brown: The Cambridge Incident. *Quarterly Journal of Speech, 57,* 325–334; P. C. Kennicott (1970), *Rhetoric of Black Revolution* by Arthur L. Smith: Book Review. *Journal of Black Studies,* 209–211; and H. W. Simons (1970), Requirements, Problems, and Strategies: A Theory of Persuasion for Social Movements. *Quarterly Journal of Speech, 56,* 1–11.

5. There are several different accounts of who actually started "pussy power." Brown attributes it to Seale. Seale attributes it to Bunchy Carter. And there are other accounts that point to Eldridge Cleaver as the mastermind behind the phrase. For the purpose of this essay, it is more important simply to note that the phrase existed.

4

The Literary Foremother: An Embodiment of the Rhetoric of Freedom

Jacqueline K. Bryant

CRITICS NOTE THAT EARLY BLACK WOMEN WRITERS SUBVERT THE familiar stereotypical representations of Black women in various subtle and creative ways. This essay, then, seeks to substantiate the subversion of, particularly, the mammy stereotype as a discursive practice. It seeks to illuminate the existence of communicative power structures in character portrayal and dialogue through the lens of an Afrocentric rhetoric in Harriet Jacobs's *Incidents in the Life of a Slave Girl Written by Herself.* Jacobs's text exemplifies how communicative power structures confirm a hierarchical relationship between a major character, the younger Black woman as mulatta heroine, and a minor character, the older Black woman as literary foremother, in the works of early Black women writers.

Interestingly, early Black woman writer Harriet Jacobs constructs two older Black women characters, Aunt Marthy, the heroine's grandmother, and Aunt Nancy, the heroine's aunt. Both possess language and behavior that reflect elements of an Afrocentric rhetoric. Both also contribute to the subversion of a mainstay in early American literature, the stereotypical mammy figure—the faithful, submissive, hardworking, older Black woman whose language and behavior perpetuate the myth of White superiority.

The expected characteristics of the familiar mammy figure and her roles associated with work and responsibility, in the context of the White woman, undergo a shift when we study the works of early Black women writers. Images now emanate from the perspective of the Black woman.[1] Subservient behavior still surrounds the older Black woman, but in many instances this behavior is a requisite posture for freedom. The older Black woman seemingly emerges as the stereotypical mainstay; however, close reading reveals the more complex figure—the literary foremother—in the works of early Black women writers. Alice Walker (1983) suggests the term *foremother* in her essay "In Search of Our Mothers' Gardens" in which she explains that these older Black women were creative despite the constraints of physical and mental abuse, space, and time. By whatever means, these older Black women, in general, pass on creative genius in the forms of storytelling, language style, and creative arts. Spirituality and morality contribute to her creativity. This gifted, older Black woman, this foremother, is unaware that her voice is laden with cultural wisdom, spiritual insight, and generative power. As the unassuming visionary that possesses a hope so intense that it directs circumstances, this literary foremother guides those who hear her minimal and often inarticulate voice.

In response to Jacobs's construction of two older Black women characters, the clearly vocal Aunt Marthy and the nearly silent Aunt Nancy, Claudia Tate determines that the single chapter entitled "Aunt Nancy" serves as an epilogue to Aunt Marthy's story (1992, p. 31). I disagree with Tate's assessment of the chapter "Aunt Nancy" and, by association, her assessment of the character Aunt Nancy. I argue instead that the limited textual space of this chapter parallels the minimal voice of the character Aunt Nancy. It is, in fact, the minimal voice and repetitive message of freedom that clearly define Aunt Nancy's relationship with her niece, the heroine, and distinguish Aunt Nancy as the older Black woman who more effectively embodies an Afrocentric rhetoric than the more vocal Aunt Marthy. According to Molefi Kete Asante, "A true Afrocentric rhetoric must oppose the negation in Western culture; it is combative, antagonistic, and wholly committed to the propagation of a more humanistic vision of the world" (1987, p. 170). A discursive practice of early Black women writers results in the construction of the foremother figure—a figure that clearly opposes and subverts the mammy image—an image that members of the dominant culture needed to create and perpetuate. One example of the strength of the foremother figure's ability to subvert through the use of powerful language emerges in speech situations that involve the foremother and the mulatta heroine. Black women writers inscribe the foremother in speech situations that result in a direct or an indirect impact on the life of the mulatta heroine or principal character. That is, despite her minor role as the older Black woman, the foremother uses language that invariably influences the principal Black female character. The foremother's language reflects her view of the world—the view of Black cultural wisdom that conflicts with the view of White dominant ideology. Elements of this prevailing ideology are often incorporated in the mulatta's world view; however, following speech situations in which the foremother and the mulatta participate, the mulatta generates specific responses in the forms of language activity, behavior, decisions, and/or actions that can be linked to the generative power of the foremother's words. Whether the foremother is ideal or flawed, whether she is physically free or enslaved, her powerful language frames the foremother-mulatta relationship in the works of early Black women writers.

In Harriet Jacobs's *Incidents in the Life of a Slave Girl Written by Herself* (1861/1987), Aunt Marthy plays the role of grandmother and significant older Black woman, and Aunt Nancy plays the role of the foremother figure in the life of the author and protagonist. Within the construction of this significant work, I will use language content to identify and examine the roles of Aunt Marthy and Aunt Nancy in light of their life experiences, to discuss their influence in Jacobs's life, and to determine Jacobs's responses to their influence. Although Aunt Marthy plays a much larger role in the story of Jacobs's escape and, in many ways, seems to be the vocal and nurturing older Black woman, the peripheral and nearly silent Aunt Nancy more effectively embodies an Afrocentric rhetoric that resists oppression and subverts the stereotype of the older Black woman.

Like other early Black women writers, Jacobs makes language choices in character portrayal. As Jacobs creates her textual beings, she also re-creates the elements of the sentimental novel and the slave narrative in order to tell *her* story—the experiences of the enslaved Black woman. She deconstructs sexual morality through the lens of enslavement and presents its complexity to her reading audience. As she re-creates the elements of the novel and narrative through the telling of her story, Jacobs reconfigures the social and literary stereotypes of Black and White women (Doriani, 1991, p. 207; Carby, 1987, p. 61; Tate, 1992, p. 27; Yellin, 1985, p. 273).

It is clear that the images of Black and White women differ in the works of early Black and White women writers. As early Black women writers portray the older Black woman as a revision of the stereotypical mammy portrayed in early White women's works, they also yield vivid detailed descriptions of White women in their works, including slave narratives such as Jacobs's. Many White women writers, however, depict Black women in stereotypical modes in fictional and nonfictional works. They seem to have known Black women only in terms of their work and responsibilities. While engaged in continuous tasks in the Flint household, Aunt Nancy resembles the portrait of the mammy figure; however, Jacobs repeatedly undermines the stereotype. One example occurs when Jacobs mockingly interjects that "[m]y aunt was taken out of jail at the end of a month, because Mrs. Flint . . . was tired of being her own housekeeper" (1861/1987, p. 101). It is more important for Mrs. Flint to maintain her social status as mistress than to continue to punish Aunt Nancy for her quiet protest—her secrecy regarding Jacobs's escape.

According to Minrose Gwin, the White woman's ambivalence toward the Black woman and her inability to acknowledge the Black woman's humanity illuminates a "pattern of connection and rejection in southern racial experience," and it is an experience that is mirrored in the literature (1985, p. 109). Jacobs clearly inscribes White and Black race relations between women and between men and women. The language of literature clearly mirrors these social concerns of the period, for Jacobs presents evidence of the mixed heritage of each generation of her family by simply telling her story.

Jacobs mixes praise and admiration in the inscription of her grandmother, a significant figure in this work. Aunt Marthy, an entrepreneur, is well loved in the community by both Blacks and Whites (1861/1987, p. 6). She owns a "snug little home" surrounded by the necessities of life. Jacobs sees her grandmother as loving, sympathetic, patient, and hopeful. Aunt Marthy is a balm; she has the power to soothe and to heal. Jacobs is hopeful when she hears Aunt Marthy's voice within the confines of her home—a place that captivates her aural, tactile, and olfactory senses (p. 17). Outside the perimeter of this nurturing environment, however, contentment is elusive. It is the home, the domestic ideal, that makes everything seem so right when Jacobs is in the presence of this wise, older Black woman—a woman whose life experiences reflect that she was freed, re-enslaved, and eventually freed again.

Aunt Marthy not only participated in but also orchestrated the final action that marked her freedom. As Linda (the character representing Jacobs) would do later, Aunt Marthy takes control of her situation. She resists the garb of chattel by posing as chattel. Because of her popularity in the community, Dr. Flint arranges to sell Aunt Marthy under the shadow of privacy; however, Aunt Marthy thrusts the intended transaction into the light of the publicity: "When the day of sale came, she took her place among the chattels, and at the first call she sprang upon the auction-block. Many voices called out, 'Shame! Shame! Who is going to sell you, Aunt Marthy? Don't stand there! That is no place for you'" (p. 11). No one outbids her dead mistress's sister who purchases her for $50.00 and releases her immediately from the bondage of slavery (p. 12). According to Martha Cutter, this passage represents discourse that is both communal and performative (1996, p. 221). Afrocentric rhetoric assumes discourse that resists oppression. Interestingly, Aunt Marthy remains silent, yet her action of voluntarily mounting the auction block generates protest from the community. Aunt Marthy essentially transforms the auction block into the political stump. Her singular, silent act generates the communal, vocal action that ultimately wins her freedom. The community and Miss Fannie, her dead mistress's sister, erect a strategic language front that overrides Dr. Flint's secret maneuvers. Through discourse, Aunt Marthy and the community dismantle the economic, communicative power structures that surround the auction block when they join forces to make a public shame out of what Dr. Flint wished to make a private gain.

This action douses the expected heat of financial fervor surrounding the auction block—the life force of the system of slavery. The auction block is a stark reminder that the enslaved were viewed as objects. It reduces every person of African descent (whether mentally enslaved or mentally free) to the lowest common factors of merchandise, property, and economic profit and loss. The auction block extinguishes the spirit of the enslaved because it disrupts families and creates fear, anxiety, and madness, all for the sake of someone else's economic gain. Aunt Marthy, then, challenges the system, wins her freedom, and maintains her family unit. She is proactive in her counter move to Dr. Flint's plan to sell her.

Aunt Marthy serves as a model for what Jacobs would do later in that she, too, plans and participates in an action that steals the reins of power. Arguably and ironically, Jacobs steals the reins of power from Dr. Flint when she submits to another White man's pressure for sexual relations, bears two children by this man, imprisons herself in a garret for seven years, and eventually escapes the bondage of slavery. It has been said repeatedly that "where there is no slave there can be no master." Aunt Marthy serves as an earlier and Jacobs as a later model for this maxim.

The modeling influence of Aunt Marthy's language is evident when the young Jacobs attempts to comfort her younger brother, William, after their father's mysterious death: "Perhaps we might before long be allowed to hire our time, and then we could earn money to buy our freedom" (p. 10). These words parallel the actions of Aunt Marthy, who uses her midnight baking as a means to save money and purchase the freedom of her children (p. 6). The strengthening influence of Aunt Marthy also emerges when Jacobs's language resonates Aunt Marthy's disdain for Dr. Flint: "My grandmother had already had high words with my master about me. She had told him pretty plainly what she thought of his character" (p. 53). In response to Dr. Flint's accusations following the revelation of Jacobs's pregnancy ("He talked of . . . how I had sinned against my master."), Jacobs replies forcefully, as she utilizes the discourses of resistance, sass and backtalk: "I have sinned against God and myself, but not against you" (p. 58). Although viable rhetorical forms of resistance, the enslaved Black woman's sass and backtalk are not comparable to the well-documented abolitionist oratory of, for example, Charles Lenox Remond and Frederick Douglass (Gilyard, introduction, this volume). Nevertheless, the presence of sass and backtalk is relevant in the identification of the Black woman's voice in the Black literary tradition. Certainly Jacobs's use of such rhetoric clearly links to the strengthening influence of Aunt Marthy's actions, more so than her words.

Aunt Marthy is a model of strength and support, but her perspective, intertwined with a mother's possessive love, is problematic. She is strong and honest and demands respect, but her language reveals that her perspective is impaired by enslavement when she envisions freedom for her children and grandchildren. For example, when the bounty hunters capture her youngest son, Benjamin, after his attempted escape, Aunt Marthy pleads with her son to "trust God" and to "be humble." Benjamin refuses and chooses freedom (p. 22).

One still credits Aunt Marthy for influencing the lives of her son Benjamin, her daughter Aunt Nancy, and her granddaughter Harriet Jacobs, for she places family first and privileges the collective over the individual. Aunt Marthy labors for the freedom of her family, and, in doing so, clings to the belief that freedom can be bought and that one must pay into the system in order to be free of the system. Aunt Marthy's son and daughter, Benjamin and Aunt Nancy, develop a view that opposes their mother's. Both possess a consciousness of liberation. Both know that freedom is their birthright and that the system of slavery is merely a deterrent. Benjamin will leave all for freedom, while Aunt Nancy will persist in her revolutionary stance of "freedom now." Aunt Marthy will remain with her children in virtual enslavement until her death, or until all of her children and her granddaughter, Jacobs, are free.

Even though *Incidents in the Life of a Slave Girl* "mourn[s] the persistent violation of black womanhood, maternity, family, and home"

(Tate, 1992, p. 26), Jacobs continues in her battle against sexual oppression. Thus, Jacobs identifies the White man, Mr. Sands, not Dr. Flint, as the father of her child. Even though Aunt Marthy judges her granddaughter in line with strict Victorian views of the time and the system of slavery, Jacobs loosens the restraints that would keep her mentally and physically bound. She pleads with her audience, her grandmother, and all who judge according to rigid definitions of morality. Jacobs argues that the enslaved Black woman does not live under the same conditions as the White woman, and thus she believes "that the slave woman ought not to be judged by the same standard as others" (p. 56). Jacobs speaks clearly and consistently for all enslaved women. Even though the title of her work, *Incidents in the Life of a Slave Girl Written by Herself,* connotes singularity, Jacobs speaks *for* women and *to* women. Hers is a battle against oppression that is consistently communal and gendered. Jacobs's efforts cannot be interpreted as acts of individualism as Shirley Wilson Logan observes in Frederick Douglass's seeming individual fight for freedom (see chapter 1). Jacobs redefines sexual morality for the sake of all enslaved women. She imparts vitality outside the rigid boundaries of marriage, race, and even outside her respect for Aunt Marthy's inflexible views.

Although Aunt Marthy is highly respected among the town officials, friends, and family members, her strong views concerning efforts to escape to freedom run counter to the views of the Black community. With escape comes the danger of capture and torture. Aunt Marthy longs to protect her children, so she cries in anguish when her grandson William escapes from Mr. Sands and remains in the North. Aunt Marthy is obviously the exception to the rule in the Black community, for even her neighbor Aunt Aggie is puzzled over her sadness, since sadness and freedom are mutually exclusive. She urges Aunt Marthy to rejoice in her grandson's escape to freedom: "Git down on your knees and bress de Lord! . . . [H]e is in free parts; and dat's de right place (p. 135). Aunt Marthy disregards the voice of the community and still communicates deterrence when she speaks directly to Jacobs about her anticipated escape: "Stand by your own children, and suffer with them till death" (p. 91). Aunt Marthy does not realize that Jacobs, like her brother William and her Aunt Nancy, possesses a different worldview and thus a different view of freedom. Oppressed people do not work for freedom or ask for freedom; they take freedom.

Despite all the drawbacks associated with Aunt Marthy's character, she clearly represents a refutation of the stereotypical mammy figure as shown in her defiance of Dr. Flint and the priority she attaches to her own family. Modeling a true Afrocentric rhetoric, Jacobs, the Black woman writer, challenges the stereotypical, the conventional, and the ideological. Jacobs's portrayal, not only of Aunt Marthy but also of other enslaved women, contradicts the image of enslaved women as subservient victims. For example, a neighbor servant, Betty, emerges in a portrait that seemingly casts her as the stereotypical mammy figure in White women's literature. Predictably, Betty's mistress describes her as "so faithful that I would trust my own life with her" (p. 99). Betty's voice, however, emerges not to praise her mistress but to console Jacobs, the fugitive, temporarily sheltered in the home of the sympathetic White benefactress. Betty consoles Linda with tough love by saying, "Lors, chile! what's you crying 'bout? Dem young uns vil kill you dead. Don't be so chick'n hearted! If you does, you vil nebber git thro' dis world" (p. 101). Even though Betty has no children, she possesses the cultural attributes of mothering and mother wit when she diagnoses Jacobs's condition, assesses the situation, and takes action: "You's got de highsterics. I'll sleep wid you to-night. . . . Something has stirred you up mightily. When you done cryin, I'll talk wid you" (p. 108). Ironically, both Betty and Aunt Nancy are childless, yet both exemplify a sense of community in the maintenance of the extended family. Betty and Aunt Nancy communicate freedom, the tie that binds the community of the enslaved. Jacobs, then, associates cultural attitudes and attributes with the older Black women who make up her community, especially with Aunt Nancy. Although both Aunt Marthy and Aunt Nancy possess characteristics of the foremother figure as they play the role of distinguishing the mulatta heroine, it is Aunt Nancy who, though emerging in fewer speech situations, makes the greater impact on Jacobs's life.

It is, indeed, ironic that Aunt Marthy, who is free, is consciously bound, and Aunt Nancy, who is enslaved, is consciously free. Aunt Nancy possesses a consciousness of liberation and speaks liberation even though she is physically and spatially bound. Alice Walker separates this intuitive knowledge from textbook knowledge when she captures in her foremothers the sense of knowing that Aunt Nancy possesses. Walker refers to those foremothers who "knew what we must know without knowing a page of it themselves" (1983, pp. 242–243). Similarly, Aunt Nancy has not experienced freedom, but she embraces freedom and wants in life, for Jacobs and her children, what she will experience only in death—freedom from enslavement. Aunt Nancy desires freedom so much that Jacobs's experiencing it will serve vicariously for her. Aunt

Nancy transforms everything she does to work toward the liberation of Jacobs and her children. She never complains when she participates in Jacobs's movement toward freedom, even taking risks to spy for Jacobs. While "faithfully" serving in the Flint household, Aunt Nancy willingly serves as a reporter when she obtains information and communicates that information to Jacobs during her self-imprisonment in the garret. She realizes fully the significance of this information to Jacobs's safety and plans for her eventual and successful escape.

Although Jacobs shares her own experiences in the Flint household with the reading audience, she does not share the experiences of Aunt Nancy, who lives in the same household for years as a housekeeper and waiting maid. Jacobs also does not tell the reader about Aunt Nancy's physical features, thus Aunt Nancy's younger brother Benjamin must serve as the basis for a sketch of a textual portrait: "He was a bright handsome lad, nearly White; for he inherited the complexion my grand-mother had derived from Anglo-Saxon ancestors" (1861/1987, p. 6). Also, when the slave trader purchases Benjamin following his impris-onment, "He said he would give any price if the handsome lad was a girl" (p. 23). The reader, then, deduces that Aunt Nancy was an attrac-tive Black woman and thus a presumed victim in the hands of the ob-sessive Dr. Flint. Did Jacobs suppress her knowledge of Dr. Flint's sexual abuse of Aunt Nancy to protect the name of her dearly beloved aunt? Jacobs admits in the preface of *Incidents in the Life of a Slave Girl Written by Herself* that "I have not exaggerated the wrongs inflicted by Slavery; on the contrary, my descriptions fall far short of the facts. . . . I had no motive for secrecy on my own account, but I deemed it kind and considerate towards others to pursue this course" (p. 1). The title of Jacobs's work informs the reader, too, that her work is limited to the revelation of the incidents in *her* life, not the incidents in the lives of Aunt Marthy and Aunt Nancy.

As noted earlier, Jacobs reserves chapter twenty-eight for Aunt Nancy, but this chapter still does not render the complexity of her person. Jacobs's personal view of Aunt Nancy is that "she was, in fact, at the beginning and end of every thing" (p. 12). In the Flint household, she is the housekeeper, waiting maid, and nurse, for "nothing went on well without her" (p. 144). Jacobs also says that her Aunt Nancy is "old" during the time that she slept with her while she lived in the Flint house-hold: "At night I slept by the side of my great [*sic*] aunt, where I felt safe. He was too prudent to come into her room. She was an old woman, and had been in the family many years" (pp. 32–33). Aunt Nancy must, however, be roughly the same age as her mistress, Mrs. Flint, because Aunt Marthy was forced to wean her own baby (Aunt Nancy's twin sister and Jacobs's mother) early so as to accommodate the needs of the baby that would mature to be Mrs. Flint (p. 7). At the age of fifteen, Jacobs comments that Dr. Flint is forty years her senior; thus, he is approximately fifty-five years old (p. 27). Mrs. Flint is his second wife and his junior (p. 34); thus, Aunt Nancy, even though Linda describes her as "old," is some years younger than Dr. Flint.

This analysis leads to the likelihood that Dr. Flint attempted to victimize Aunt Nancy over the years as he did Linda. This suspicion arises not only because of the evidence of her younger age and physical beauty, implied in the text, but because of the number of babies she bore prematurely. Jacobs says that Aunt Nancy married a "seafaring man" at the age of twenty (p. 143), so her husband was seldom at home. Even though she was married, Mrs. Flint insisted that Aunt Nancy sleep on the floor outside her chamber: "But on the wedding evening, the bride was ordered to her old post on the entry floor" (p. 143). This ongoing involuntary separation from her husband leads one to question how Aunt Nancy became pregnant six times and lost six babies before she was permitted to sleep in her own quarters. Even after moving into her own quarters to sleep, Aunt Nancy becomes pregnant two more times and both babies die. Jacobs, like others in the community, knew Dr. Flint to be the father of eleven children of slaves (p. 35). Everyone knew that he removed those slaves who publicly acknowledged his paternity because it was a crime for an enslaved Black woman to identify the White father of her child (p. 13).

These textual implications of Aunt Nancy's experiences in the Flint household also strengthen my argument about the close and meaningful relationship between Aunt Nancy and Jacobs. Theirs is familial and experiential in nature, as is evident in the foremother's limited, repetitive, and powerful messages to the mulatta heroine and the mulatta heroine's limited, meaningful, and responsive references to the foremother. The nature of their relationship is also configured on textual implications and omissions. Omission and silence are meaningful in language use.

In contrast to Aunt Marthy, not once do we hear Aunt Nancy condemn Jacobs while she maneuvers through the mire of enslavement and oppression. Aunt Nancy communicates one clear message—freedom now. This enslaved, older Black woman who possesses a consciousness of liberation is referred to only intermittently in the text and does not have the privilege of direct language use at the same level as her mother, Aunt Marthy. Aunt Nancy is, however, permitted voice later in her life when she communicates the message of freedom to Jacobs during her self-imprisonment in the garret: "I am old, and have not long to live . . . and I could die happy if I could only see you and the children free" (p. 144). Aunt Nancy communicates the urgency of freedom, for she sees the systemic perpetuation of enslavement when she gazes upon Jacobs and her children. Whereas Aunt Marthy's language discourages escape, Aunt Nancy's language encourages escape—freedom by any means. Jacobs recalls her aunt's powerful message: "She said if I persevered I might, perhaps, gain the freedom of my children; and *even if I perished* in doing it, that was better than to leave them to groan under the same persecutions that had blighted my own life" (p. 144; emphasis added). The foremother's language in this example, even though reported indirectly, makes a significant impact on the mulatta heroine and reinforces her determination to claim freedom.

Aunt Nancy's language reveals the power of characterization. Her messages are clear, concise, and repetitive—nothing replaces freedom. Through language, this foremother conveys a meaningful attitude, a clear perspective, and a purposeful determination. Even though Aunt Nancy uses her voice minimally, the family relies on her common sense and balanced judgment (p. 144). Clearly, Aunt Nancy guides Jacobs as she recalls, "When my friends tried to discourage me from running away, she always encouraged me. . . . [S]he sent me word never to yield" (p. 144). Of Aunt Marthy, Jacobs recalls, "Most earnestly did she strive to make us feel that it was the will of God; that He had seen fit to place us under such circumstances; and though it seemed hard, we ought to pray for contentment" (p. 17). It is because of Aunt Marthy that Phillip refuses to seize the opportunity for freedom when, on an errand, he meets his brother Benjamin in New York shortly after Benjamin's escape. Aunt Marthy's belief that she will earn freedom through perseverance and hard work influences Phillip to forgo freedom in the North and to return to enslavement in the South (p. 25). Jacobs confesses just prior to her attempted escape that Aunt Marthy influences her thoughts and actions: "My courage failed me, in view of the sorrow I should bring on that faithful, loving old heart" (p. 91). Aunt Marthy's language inhibits her. Aunt Nancy empowers her.

Not only is the foremother–mulatta heroine relationship based on familial ties and suspected abuse but Aunt Nancy and Jacobs share similarly traumatic physical experiences. Jacobs describes the circumstances surrounding her first birth: "When my babe was born, they said it was premature . . . ; but God let it live"(pp. 60–61). Likewise, Aunt Nancy is described as having "given premature birth to six children; and all the while she was employed as night-nurse to Mrs. Flint's children" (p. 143). After a total of eight births and eight deaths, Aunt Nancy resolved, "it is not the will of God that any of my children should live" (p. 144). Further, during her self-imprisonment, Jacobs suffers inadequate physical mobility in the garret and overexposure to the weather: "My limbs were benumbed by inaction and the cold filled them with cramp. . . . even my face and tongue stiffened, and I lost the power of speech" (p. 122). Of Aunt Nancy, who suffered the physical hardship of sleeping on the floor for years, she says: "My aunt had been stricken with paralysis. She lived but two days, and the last day she was speechless" (pp. 144–145). The ties that bind Aunt Nancy and Jacobs are familial, experiential, and reciprocal, for upon overhearing her Uncle Phillip tell someone else, "[s]he [Aunt Nancy] is dead," Jacobs faints and awakens with a fixed gaze (p. 145). Phillip's death pronouncement is generative; in the power of the word, death is life for Jacobs, and death is freedom for both Jacobs and Aunt Nancy. Thus, from an African cultural perspective Phillip enacts Nommo the generative power of the word, for the spirit of Aunt Nancy, now Jacobs's ancestor, truly binds with Jacobs's spirit and quickens her seven-year dormancy. It is only after Jacobs hears of Aunt Nancy's death that she realizes the urgency to escape from her seven-year self-imprisonment, and from enslavement to freedom. Aunt Nancy, "who had been my refuge during the shameful persecutions I suffered from him [Dr. Flint]" (p. 143), symbolically continues to serve as a refuge for Jacobs. Just as the foremother sheltered Jacobs physically within the confines of the Flint household, so she shelters her spiritually in her move toward freedom.

In conclusion, Aunt Marthy, who is prominent in the text, is the mother figure to Jacobs because she protects, sacrifices, advises, and loves within the boundaries prescribed by the institution of slavery. Aunt Marthy longs for freedom for her children and grandchildren, but she is willing to work her way out of an oppressive system according to the rules and laws of the oppressor. Her words and actions create ambivalence. The true foremother, Aunt Nancy, on the other hand, is not prominent in the text in terms of the space permitted for her language and the language of others regarding her. To increase Aunt Nancy's presence in the text would likely have resulted in revelations about her marital relationship and her oppressive experiences in the Flint household. Although Aunt Nancy, in her role as foremother, is permitted little space for language use, her message of freedom for Jacobs and her children is clear: "'I shan't mind being a slave all my life, if I can only see you and the children free'" (p. 129). Aunt Nancy's message is clear, concise, and repetitive, giving her voice a greater force than Aunt Marthy's. Freedom requires no deliberation, negotiation, or transaction; it is to be attained by any means. In response to Aunt Nancy's repeated message, Jacobs releases herself from her seven-year self-imprisonment in the garret of her grandmother's home and escapes to the North. Jacobs struggles to attain freedom and to maintain freedom, for she lives under the shadow of enslavement in the form of the Fugitive Slave Law. Jacobs moves guardedly through nineteenth-century cities such as Philadelphia, New York, and Boston. Ella Forbes (2003) explores the political climate of nineteenth-century Black society in these major northern cities. It was this climate, thick with the rhetoric of resistance, that infuses a boldness in Jacobs and enables her to maneuver successfully in public and private spaces in her continued struggle for freedom. With Aunt Nancy's rhetoric of freedom still resonating in the southern spaces of her mind, coupled with the rhetoric of resistance against the Fugitive Slave Law surrounding her in the North, Jacobs, the protagonist and Black woman writer, engages in a true Afrocentric rhetoric as she chooses to challenge negative representations of enslaved Black women. Jacobs opposes Western cultural assumptions when she joins the chorus of the Black women's voices of resistance and boldly tells her story, *Incidents in the Life of a Slave Girl Written by Herself*.

Note

1. I use the term *Black* because it is inclusive. It encompasses Africans living in America and the Diaspora. Acts of resistance and subversion are not exclusive to women of African descent living in America.

5

Ties that Bind: A Comparative Analysis of Zora Neale Hurston's and Geneva Smitherman's Work

Kimmika L. H. Williams

Introduction

THE GENERAL PURPOSE OF THIS ESSAY IS TO IDENTIFY THE CEN-
trality of the work of two early African American women scholars—Zora
Neale Hurston and Geneva Smitherman—in the developing study of
African American rhetoric (AAR). Widely regarded as pioneers in the
African American Vernacular English (AAVE) discourse, both scholars
incorporated an ethnographic perspective on the forms, styles, functions,
and efficacy of AAR. As cultural and linguistic pioneers, these scholars
actively researched the language of Black America at a time when African American speech was not even considered a *dialect*. The *unenlight-
ened* thought African American speech was simply Black nonsense, and
they made little attempt to acknowledge the effectiveness of its eloquence
or the breadth of its rhetorical style. This essay is written in an attempt
to critically evaluate and extend the canon by analyzing the early work
of these Black women linguistics pioneers.

Locating the Analysis

Hurston's and Smitherman's work provided the foundation for the developing study on AAR. Despite the reality that Hurston's and Smitherman's work initially looked at African American language features nearly
forty years apart, both identified the dynamic nature of language strategies in AAR and their functions as persuasive means of communication.
By focusing on the similarities and differences between what Hurston
called the elements of Negro expression, in the 1920s through 1938, and

the components of Black English made popular in Geneva Smitherman's findings in 1977, it is my intention to critically delineate those nodes of intersection in each of the scholar's work by looking at the morphology, syntax, phonetics, lexicon, and discourse practices of AAVE speakers, identifying Hurston's and Smitherman's foundational contributions to the ongoing study of AAVE and AAR. While Smitherman's first work *Talkin and Testifyin: The Language of Black America* (1977/1986) and Zora Neale Hurston's "Characteristics of Negro Expression," first published in 1934 and subsequently in *The Sanctified Church* (1981), did not include enough detailed information about the methodology each employed, the subsequent publication of Hurston's unfinished texts, *Go Gator and Muddy the Water* (1999) and *Every Tongue Got to Confess: Negro Folk-Tales from the Gulf States* (2001) and Smitherman's *Talkin that Talk: Language, Culture and Education in African America* (2000) go a long way to fill that void.

Contextualizing the Discourse

"Language" is both evidence and the product of *culture*. A "cultural construct," all living languages are dynamic and continually undergoing change (Lippi-Green, 1997, p. 8). If language is to remain functional and an effective tool for persuasion, it must be *fluid*—consistently "reinventing" itself so that it can continually meet the needs of language speakers. Languages that fail to change become static and are thus doomed to die out (Lippi-Green, 1997, p. 10). The flexibility and fluidity of AAVE, (in the areas of style, "grammaticality," morphology, and syntax) speak to the ways in which language "functions" in a society and tends to be two of the more consistent elements of AAR that can be traced through language histories (Lippi-Green, 1997: pp. 10–40). Hurston's and Smitherman's work remains consistent with at least two of the prevailing theories in AAVE: (1) that the language spoken by African Americans can be classified as a language in of itself, (evolving because of the consequences and the history of enslavement, classified as a dialect because of the position of powerlessness of its speakers); (2) that the ancestors of today's AAVE speakers were from diverse multilingual ethnic groups (each with a first *African* language already in tact); (3) that these people were strategically targeted for the exploitation of their labor by culture and region (Holloway, 1991)[1] and were forced into contact language situations necessitating the development of a functional process of communication;[2] (4) and most importantly, that the ways in which some African Americans speak and the nature of that expression is still informed by cultural referents that grew out of African linguistic traditions (Turner, 1949; Dillard, 1973; Baraka, 1963; Asante, 1990a, 1990b).

Characteristics of African American Expression

Living Art—Secular, Sacred, Dramatic

"Its not what you say but how you say it." African American speakers use lexicon and modes of discourse for persuasion and both Smitherman and Hurston identify African lexical retentions in AAVE. Smitherman's earlier work insisted that critics of the discourse must have a clear understanding of the importance of "the oral tradition" in African American culture to fully comprehend the linguistic rules and the cultural importance of the narrative, the poetics, the dozens, the sermonizing, and the storytelling that inform AAR.

Keith Gilyard's introduction in this volume discusses one of the many multiple functions of AAR as a ready way to establish, identify, and maintain group membership. The rhetoric and the oral tradition historically served as a counter hegemonic strategy of resistance. The oral tradition has always functioned as an educational tool and can also signal religious and cultural unity. If persuasive speaking begins from a "shared premise," then the use of AAVE can be said to trigger a collective epic memory. Its use immediately identifies African American speakers' cultural competency—that is, values, beliefs, and definitions (Simons, 1976). In a given communicative event, even though the persuasive "intent" may vary, as demonstrated by Smitherman's and Hurston's work, modes of discourse in AAR are integrally linked to "verbosity" and the theatricality of oral expression, influenced by the African oral tradition.

One of the most notable elements of persuasive speaking is having a unique style of delivery. To accommodate this culturally cherished practice, AAVE speakers incorporate a number of "showy" modes of discourse such as exaggerated speech, signification, call and response, speaking in tongues, circumlocution, and rhythmicality as a way of demonstrating individual verbal acuity. Smitherman (1977/1986) writes:

> In Black America, the oral tradition has served as a fundamental vehicle for gittin ovah. . . . Through song, story, folk sayings and rich verbal interplay among everyday people, lessons and precepts about life and survival are handed down from generation to generation. (p. 73)

What Smitherman calls "verbal interplay," Hurston identified as "drama" in 1934. That drama, according to Hurston, is one of the most important and readily identifiable elements of AAVE. Although, "mimicry" is evidence of something larger, broader, and more inclusive in African American culture, Hurston postulates that the broader "thing" or element at the core of our communications and expressions is this predisposition for drama: "Every phase of Negro life is highly dramatized. No matter how joyful or how sad . . . everything is acted out. . . . There is an impromptu ceremony always ready for every hour of life" (1981, p. 49).

Both Smitherman and Hurston identified African American language speakers' use of an active language style as an element of persuasion. AAVE speakers interpret language as that which is composed or symbolic of imagery and "pictures." In this way, "moments" in the drama of life become hyperextended. Thus, one act or action can be described in relationship to another. Hurston called this strategy, the "poetical flow of language" (1999, p. 144). Her research suggested that African Americans think and, by extension, speak in images and in pictures. "[E]ven with detached words in his vocabulary—not evolved in him but transplanted on his tongue by contact—[the speaker] must add action to it to make it do" (1981, p. 49). The creative use and choice of action words provides the foundation for AAR.

In an excerpt from *Their Eyes Were Watching God,* Hurston illustrated the "hyperextended" nature of the drama of "action" in AAVE. Hurston's novel, first published in 1937, was labeled "dialect." This prime example of African American literature is filled with image-heavy dialogue where descriptive "actions" are compounded and compressed—one atop the other.

> Naw, you gointuh listen tuh me one time befo' you die. Have yo' way all yo' life, trample and mash down and then die ruther than tuh let yo'self heah 'bout it. Listen, Jody, you ain't de Jody ah run off down de road wid. You's whut's left after he died. Ah run off tuh keep house wid you in uh wonderful way. But you wasn't satisfied wid me de way Ah was. Naw! Mah own mind had tuh be squeezed and crowded out tuh make room for yours in me. (1937/1978, p. 133)

Critically evaluating the language as rhetoric, Janie's line in the preceding excerpt "Have yo' way all yo' life" functions as indictment and as an assertion of fact. The use of "have yo' way" as opposed to "had your way" is deliberate. The word choice of *have* specifically blurs the lines of temporality and, linked to the holistic African acceptance of near-past and remote-past, this first statement speaks to the fluidity of time. It is not just Jody's past actions that he is being indicted for; but even now, right up to this final scene, Janie accuses him of still "having his way."

"Trample and mash down" is a particularly interesting use of descriptive verbs as a persuasive technique. To trample someone is a very violent act. It indicates not only power and control over an individual's body but also over the individual's will; otherwise, one would surely "get out of the way." In its totality, "trample and mash down and then die ruther than tuh let yo'self heah" again is very deliberate. The phrasing symbolizes (concretely) Jody's level of power over self, as well as others.

In the passage, when the speaker notes that Jody is no longer "the Jody" that Janie "run off down de road wid. You's whut's left after he died," it signals to the reader that Janie is not accusing Jody of becoming a new person per se (as if that in itself wouldn't be deceitful enough); but much more hurtful, she accuses him of being the mere residue, or shadow, of the man he once was. In the action verb phrase "run off tuh keep house wid you" the speaker refers to not only the work of maintaining a relationship but also to the expectation of the *shared roles* in the physical labor or work of making a "home" that she had once believed they would have. This is clearly evidenced by the use of the phrase "wid you," as opposed to "fer you."

The last line, "Mah own mind had to be squeezed and crowded out tuh make room for yours in me," speaks to the totality of power and control that Jody exercised over Janie. Victimized and emotionally abused, Janie admits to being powerless with this deliberate choice of words because, as she says, ultimately, her mind was "squeezed out."

Hurston demonstrated that the speech of African Americans draws heavily on figurative linguistic strategies meant to identify the speaker as a member of the community and then to invest the listener in the totality of the communication event. AAVE, and by extension AAR, incorporates a lot of metaphor and simile. A *metaphor,* as a strategy in African American verbal expressions, may use the comparison of one thing to another without the use of the terms, *like* or *as.* An example of this rhetorical strategy in African American language can be observed in the following item: "Baby . . . you got me in the grip of your glue."

In comparison, a *simile* explicitly compares two things, considered quite different from one another. Much like its function in metaphor, the simile specifically uses identifiers *like* or *as.* The example "Aunt Ada smells like trash truck juice, don't she?"[3] speaks volumes in exposition. Hurston suggests that one of the most important contributions that African American language speakers have made to the languages of the

Americas has been this abundant use of metaphor and simile as figures of speech in AAVE (Hurston, 1981, pp. 51–52).

Mimetic

Both Smitherman and Hurston discuss the significance of mimicry in AAVE. Smitherman argues that mimicry, mocking, and imitation are often employed as a language strategy in AAR. In speech events, African American language speakers may mimic the animate and/or inanimate sounds around them to enliven their communications and to further invest the listener into the totality of the speech event via alliteration, onomatopoeia, or intonation. As a persuasive technique, AAVE speakers may imitate individual speech patterns, sounds, or utterances of others to authenticate that which is being communicated. Consider the following example collected by Smitherman (1977/1986): "Told you she wasn't none of yo friend; [singing] 'smiling faces.'" (p. 95). With this example, Smitherman demonstrates the use of performance for rhetorical effect and for the establishment of ethos.

Hurston proposes that mimicry is an art unto itself. Before the development of discourses on AAVE and AAR, critics of African American art and culture suggested the Eurocentric viewpoint that African Americans imitate out of inferiority. Discussing the linguistic competence of colonized Blacks in 1774 Virginia, J. F. D. Smyth (1853) concluded that the best Blacks could do was acquire imperfectly the English language. Similarly, Peter Kolchin (1993) notes that early scholarship relative to Black culture prevailed in its emphasis on Black imitation of White behavior. On the other hand, discussing Black culture of the antebellum period, John W. Blassingame (1972) underscored the fact that many enslaved Africans imitated their masters' shouting at camp meetings and at their own segregated religious services as a means of incorporating layers of meaning. This view corresponds to the work of Hurston that argued that "imitations" by Black folk could either be celebratory—or a critique (1981, p. 59).[4] And again, Smitherman (1977/1986) also discussed mimicry as a deliberate means of establishing authenticity or for ridicule or rhetorical effect (p. 94).

African American speech then is inherently creative incorporating other elements of drama and verbal dexterity.[5] How often have we heard spirits, plants, animals, a rock, or a tree given anthropomorphic characteristics? In an interesting encounter in my research, one "brother" described something that had happened to him, relating it with all its dramatic nuances:

> Man, I don't know what was on its mind. That rock jumped
> up and tripped me . . . fell flat on my face, yes I did! I tell ya,
> them rocks be trippin'!

Interconnected

Recognizing, accepting and being able to express one's part in "the drama
of life" is part and parcel of the African worldview that has survived as
a cultural, spiritual, and linguistic "residual" incorporated into African
American expressions. Both Smitherman's and Hurston's work referred
to long-standing sociocultural linguistic traditions and a deep-structured
African worldview that informs "the rules" of AAR. That African
worldview, according to Smitherman, includes the "underlying thought
patterns, belief sets, values, ways of looking at the world and the community of men and women that are shared by all traditional Africans"
(1977/1986, p. 74).

This African worldview dictates interdependence and a holistic approach to humankind's relationship to God and to nature. It is replete
in the AAVE of the *Brer Rabbit* stories, the mythoforms about cultural
heroes like *High John the Conqueror*, right down to conversations about
cultural icons in the "'hood"! This notion of "necessary interdependence" and its strategies to effect or create an amalgamation and consensus of thought and ritual (i.e., culture) was reinterpreted from African village life to the subsequently "imposed-upon" communities of
plantation culture in early American history. As a result, vestiges of those
communal modes of behavior have survived in many Black communities since enslavement. Couple those strategies for mutual interdependence with Hurston's first assertion that for African Americans, "all life
is drama," then logic would dictate that good drama should have an
audience (1981, p. 49).

In African American social interactions, particularly those emblem-
atic of group membership, when these mini-dramas—disagreements,
fights, love-making, or grief—are being done well, there is no negative connotation or pejorative badge of misconduct attached to "the
players" when done in public, or within ear shot of someone else. As
Hurston's work asserts, "[L]ove-making and fighting in all their branches
are high arts" (1981, p. 61). This is not just another way of essentializing
Black folks. Rather, according to Smitherman, the collective ethos that
mediates successful African American rhetoric draws on a shared set of
experiences and thought processes for making sense of the world.

Sharing historical experiences doesn't necessarily mean, however, that all individual people of African descent automatically exploit African American language variables.[6] African Americans are not automatically bound to adhere to an African (American) worldview, but the absence of shared experience on behalf of a small percentage of people does not negate its existence on behalf of the many.[7]

"Nommo," as Gilyard (introduction, this volume) concurs, "is the African belief in the pervasive, mystical, transformative, even life-giving power of the Word." Smitherman (1977/1986) argues that this linguistic orientation reinterpreted by American African Nommo realizes "fundamental unity between the spiritual and material aspects of existence" (p. 75). The ontology of African-influenced spirituality includes (1) God, (2) spirits, (3) men and women, (4) plants and animals, and (5) inanimate objects or "things." In the African worldview, each of these items are regarded as harmonious, mutually inclusive, interacting elements that constitute all life. The African worldview, then, is a tool used to view and articulate the world, and it is consistently drawn upon in nearly all forms of AAR, including African American "mythoforms" and the drama of everyday speech.

Functional

Another construct particular to AAVE that Smitherman addresses is the use of the serial negative in AAR. Coining the phenomenon with regard to AAVE, "serial negators" appear to be connected to the African worldview and the philosophy of "curlinear" time. These predispositions in African American language evolved as a way to further enhance the character context in communication events. Similar rules of tense, with regard to present, past, remote past, and future tense in be/non-be verb constructions in AAVE, likewise apply in serial negators. "Whereas the old double negative goes back to Shakespeare and is in abundant use among [English-speaking Europeans and American] whites today, triple and quadruple negatives are the sole province" of AAVE speakers (Smitherman, 1977/1986, p. 30). Smitherman identified two rules in AAR that can be applied to serial negative constructions.

(1) If a negative statement is composed of only *one* sentence, then *every* negatable item in the statement [will] be negated. (p. 30; italics in original)

(2) If, however, the negative statement involves *two* or more sentences combined together as one . . . all negatives indicate

positives and all negatives, *plus one positive* indicate negatives. (pp. 30–31; italics in original)

In be/non-be verb constructions, a string of negators such as "ain't,
never, not" can be used to express present, past, remote past, and future tense as in the following item: "You know I don't be awake when I
be sleep." In much the same way, a series of negators within the body
of the same sentence can speak to the continuity of the negative value
and the temporal condition. In this way, in accord with the African
worldview, time is fluid, and AAVE speakers have devised ways to speak
to that temporal fluidity, even in their negative constructions.

"Ain't got none," is a recognizable "double negative" that appears
frequently in AAVE. In the present tense, we understand quite succinctly
that the speaker doesn't have any. "Ain't *never* got none," on the other
hand, is a triple negative, or tri-negator, which can apply in both past
or future tense, signifying that the speaker hardly *ever* has any of whatever the desired "thing" is.

The phrase "Ain't never had none neither" is an example of a quad-
negator that could be used in both present tense and remote past.[8] Layered with social meaning, this item simply means that the speaker recognizes that he or she, like so many before, has never had (and quite
probably never will) have any of the desired "thing."[9]

Hurston and Smitherman find an interesting juxtaposition between
AAVE speakers and their predisposition toward angularity or building
of contrasts in their language. At the same time, African American language speakers are innately drawn to creating rhythms. The predisposition toward angularity contrasted with notions of rhythm and finding
balance helps to infuse AAR with its kinetic force. The tonal semantics
in "rhyme," according to Smitherman, becomes a communicative strategy to affect both balance and musicality. "The most effective signifyin
and cappin have rhyme as a prime ingredient" (1977/1986, p. 146). The
juxtaposition between those items that rhyme and the ones that do not
in a given communication exchange creates an angularity in the language
as point/counterpoint. As an example, Smitherman cites this lexical utterance: "I would if I could, but I ain't cause I cain't" (p. 146).

In her creative endeavors as a fiction writer, Zora Neale Hurston allowed more of her personal views about African retentions and culture
to surface through her characters such as Lias, in *Their Eyes Were Watching God* (1937/1978, p. 148); but as an anthropologist, Hurston allowed
her informants and their aesthetic products (prayers, songs, folktales,

and the like) to speak for themselves. In Hurston's scholarly writing, there are only a few instances when she pointedly addressed the notion of "African retentions," specifically with regard to song, dance, and spirituality. Hurston's fieldwork collecting folk tales in the Gulf states in 1927, recently published posthumously by her estate, goes a long way to fill that void.

In the section "Witch and Hant Tales" in *Every Tongue Got to Confess,* Hurston included a piece by a Georgia barber that speaks to both the cultural, morphological, pragmatic, and syntactic retentions in African American discourse:

> There was a witch woman wid a saddle-cat who could git out her skin and go ride people she didn't like. She had a great big looking-glass. When she git ready to go out she'd git befor dat glass naked. She'd say: Gee whiz! Slip 'em and slip 'em agin!" And de old skin would slip off and she'd get out. . . . And she'd go back and spread de old skin out at de fire place and tell de skin, "So remember who you are." (2001, p. 63)

Filled with a multiplicity of layered meaning, "riding people" refers to spirit possession, so much a part of so many African-centered spiritual rituals (Hurston, 1999, p. 96). The "looking-glass" references memory and reflecting back as a way of coming outside of oneself. In this short excerpt, evidence also exists of Nommo and word magic in the incantation or "oral prescription" that activates the "transformation." Chiding the skin to "remember who you are" admonishes listeners to always be mindful of their historical present, as well as their historical past. As John Edgar Wideman writes in the foreword of Hurston's text, "[T]hese narratives from the southern states instruct us that talk functions in African American communities . . . as a means of having fun, getting serious, establishing credibility and consensus, securing identity, negotiating survival, keeping hope alive, suffering and celebrating the power language bestows" (p. xx).

Spiritual

Religious oratory has been central to the African American rhetorical tradition (see Gilyard, introduction). With regard to spirituality and modes of expression relative to sacred communicative strategies in the Black church, "the congregation is restored to its primitive alters under the new name of Christ . . . the expression known as "shouting" . . . is nothing more than a continuation of the African possession by the gods" (Hurston, 1999, p. 96).

Both Smitherman and Hurston recognized that many of the linguistic strategies they were identifying as integral components of AAR were easily recognizable in the formal and informal speech of African Americans. As a deep-structured mode of discourse, African American speakers employ many of the same language strategies, such as serial nouns, image-heavy verb-noun constructions and serial negators, both in their secular *and* their sacred communicative events.

"Whatever the Negro does of his own volition, he embellishes. . . . His religious service is for the greater part excellent prose poetry. Both prayers and sermons are tooled and polished until they are true works of art" (Hurston, 1981, p. 54). Thus, the linguistic rules in religious services and oral rituals are very much a part of African American culture. The Black preacher's sermon, according to Smitherman, represents an important connection in the African American oral tradition. Harkening back to Mbiti's ontology, the traditional Black church is far more than just a religious unit. Instead, it serves an equally important social function as well.

Above and beyond Nommo (as the power of the word) (Jahn, 1989, pp. 121–155) and the rules of call and response, the African American church is replete with Africanisms from the "tongue-speaking" to the "vision-receiving" on to the "spirit-getting" (Smitherman, 1977/1986, pp. 150–155). Spirituality and Nommo are indelibly interrelated as "Nommo refers to "the magic power of the Word, [and] was believed necessary to actualize life and give man mastery over things" (p. 78).

In African American culture, the power of Nommo is represented in all aspects of AAVE. That "power" infuses "use value" and cultural capital with the strategies employed in AAR, and as Bourdieu teaches us, symbolic or cultural capital can often times easily be converted into "real capital" (1991). In the African American oral tradition, then, Nommo creates and is created by "word-warriors," preachers, griots, and rhetoricians who become "technicians of verbosity."

One example of a representation of Nommo in religious oratory can easily be heard, felt, and identified even in the following, short, excerpt from Martin Luther King's famous "I Have a Dream" sermon/oration. In the passage, both the cadence and the word choices all work together to help create Nommo: "With this faith we will be able to work together, to pray together, to struggle together, to go to jail together, to stand up for freedom together, knowing that we will be free . . . one day" (1963/

1996, p. 676). Dr. King's verbalization of his vision, his dream, must be articulated and transmitted to the hearts and minds of his listeners before it could begin to be taken as a possible reality. Neither Hurston nor Smitherman found many distinctions made between the sacred and the secular. Many of the linguistic rules learned in church were and are transposed into daily expressions. "Touch your neighbor" and "show your love" come right out of the traditional Black church and can be heard daily on BET and out of the mouths of many everyday African Americans (and others via pop culture or familiar contact). Further, it should be noted that because of the linguistic boundary shifting prompted by the media and television evangelism, many non–African American preachers are now yielding to the tonal demands of their increasingly diverse congregations and adopting linguistic strategies and linguistic rituals such as the once-marked "speaking in tongues" (Appiah & Gates, 1999, p. 434).

AAVE is participatory. Smitherman identified call and response as an integral mode of discourse. Providing an interesting lexicon of the kinds and types of calls and responses in her research, Smitherman found evidence of this rhetorical strategy in not only the sacred but also in the secular arenas as well (1977/1986, p. 107). Because of Smitherman's work, some of the *functions* of call and response in AAR were identified for the first time. As a linguistic strategy, call and response allows AAVE speakers to reach for balance and harmony, to move their audiences. The call-and-response process, when functional, enables AAVE speakers to tap into one another's deep-structured shared field of experience and is tied to establishing group membership.

Call and response can involve verbal *and/or* nonverbal communications. I remember hours, days, and years spent sitting in a "too-too" warm and crowded Pentecostal church in West Philly. If I "crunched" candy, whispered too loudly, or innocently "wiggled," my parents would turn and look in my direction. They didn't have to say a word. By facial expression, angle of the body, or gesture, both my parents could (and would) communicate a whole *wealth* of information or admonishment!

The nonverbal forms of call and response in the secular arena still include some of the very same features that Smitherman observed in 1977, such as "high fives," handshakes, the snapping of fingers in a demonstrative gesture, and the rolling of one's eyes (that used to get me in particular trouble when I was a youngster!). In the church, the rocking back and forth, the waving of a hand, and the jumping up and down are likewise still considered appropriate forms of call and response in

African American sacred rituals—with the exception, perhaps, of specific Black Catholic and/or Lutheran denominations.

Secular forms of call and response in AAR continue to include "Dig dat," "Preach!" "Sho' you right!" "You know?" "Stop—," and (more recently) the popular addition of "You go girl . . . !" More research needs to be done to further update the kinds and types of "new creations" that continue to make up the more contemporary lexicon in this linguistic strategy.

In the sacred arena, "Preach!" is also an appropriate form of call and response within the dictates of those communicative events. In church settings in some very diverse African American communities, I have found that "Go 'head," "look out," "Teach," "Do Jesus," and "Lord, have mercy, Father" are still as prevalent in use today as appropriate forms of call and response in sacred forms of AAR, as they must have been when Smitherman did her initial research prior to 1977.

Even when the kinds and types of appropriate calls and responses change, the *function* of that particular linguistic strategy, as a mode of discourse, remains the same. From providing the rhythm in repetition through choral "humming," to the participatory "completers function" (when "hearers" or audience members will complete the ending words or phrases of the main speaker's sentence unconsciously "in vesting" listeners in the communication event), there are a number of culturally specific linguistic strategies peculiar to AAVE that are still being deployed.

According to Smitherman's work, call and response strategies function as proof of the efficacy of AAR by instigating and encouraging:

- "co-signing" (with its "Uh-huh," "yes, Go 'head now") as re-affirmation
- encouragement—when the listener entreats the speaker to continue in the current line of reasoning
- repetition—of a singular sound or set of sounds to provide the rhythm, underbeat, or bass so that the speech event incorporates musicality
- completers—when the audience finishes whole trains of thought for the speaker
- and "the On T," (which Smitherman lists as the most powerful, and the most verbal, method of call and response that acknowledges something said that is "on the money" or "dead on time", if you will!) (Smitherman, 1977/1986, p. 107)

Of course, the very nature of AAR demands improvisation and creativity, even in regards to mode of call and response. In this regard, AAVE language speakers are always reinventing new affirming sounds, movements, words, and phrases to add to the growing lexicon of the call and response modality.

Preaching "spirit-filled, dramatic" sermons is a necessary component of the oral tradition. Though spirituality is expected in sacred performances, it is also expected in secular performances by Black orators from politicians to the Johnny Cochrans of the world, even to the raps of street hustlers (Rivers, 1977, pp. 28–37). "Proverbial statement-making" in AAR has a direct correlation to the "sermon-preaching from the pulpit." These communication strategies further contribute to the continuation of African American culture by passing on generational, regional, or otherwise highly specialized proverbs and proverbial expressions. "One monkey don't stop no show." "If it don't fit, you must acquit!"

Smitherman lists "indirection" and "tonal semantics" as two other elements of AAVE that can also be linked to verbal/oral strategies with roots in the traditional Black church. She describes "indirection" as a strategy when the speaker makes a point through the power of suggestion and innuendo (1977/1986, p. 97). This concept that Smitherman identifies is similar to the notion of "asymmetry" that Hurston's text discusses. Each of these very participatory strategies relies on call and response as a mode and method of persuasion.

In these instances, it is solely up to the listener to decipher and explicate the "total" meaning of the AAVE spoken and to accept for face value whatever surface meaning may be applicable. (As this feature in AAVE is often used in signifying and code switching, it is rarely as effective in AAR unless both speaker and listener are good at "circumlocution" or indirection.)

Narrative

What Zora Neale Hurston called the tendency toward "folklore" in 1938, Smitherman referred to as "narrative sequencing" and the "storytelling tradition" in 1977. In analysis of this strategy in AAVE, Smitherman includes a discussion of storytelling, Toasts, lies, braggadocio, signifying, and Playing the Dozens (pp. 157–166). In AAR, the AAVE language speaker, griot, or storyteller uses voice, gestures, body, tone, and sounds as tools to bring a story or image to life—and it makes no difference whatsoever if the story be true, or not!

Hurston's research also speaks of "the absence of the concept of privacy." Some would say that the "absence of the concept of privacy" accounts for the freedom African Americans take with regard to talking about all aspects of life—public ones as well as those, considered by others, to be quite private. Contrary to the public vulnerability historically written into other African American aesthetic cultural products such as blues lyrics, poetry, and contemporary "rap," it has been suggested that "Black folks don't put their business in the street." But, in fact, as Hurston suggests, "Black folks' can't keep nothing secret, and [so] they have [often been accused of having] no reserve" (1981, p. 60).

In Hurston's discussion on "Negro expression," she defends the supposed tendency that "Black folks are always tellin'," by pointing to the traditional African and then, by extension, African American predisposition to "community" or communal living either for survival, subsistence strategies or for strength in numbers. Identified in many cultures, those instances of "public telling" utilize various strategies in the function of gossip and oftentimes can reinforce/reinform social rules of behavior (Barns, 1996; Price, 1993; Bodine 1996).[10]

Just as AAVE speakers create rhythm and musicality in their speech, originality and improvisation are likewise important to narratives in AAR. What Smitherman (1977/1986, pp. 118–119) identified as "signification" implicates Hurston's notion of the "absence of privacy."

In AAVE, signification refers to the verbal "art of insult." Stretching the rules of social behavior and the boundaries of individual space, signification or verbal insults can be used for humor, to make a point, to talk about somebody, or to "tell them off" without really hurting feelings. Still a very current mode of discourse in the African American community, *signifying* is "public Dis-ing" or verbally showing disrespect. Playing the Dozens with its terse "your mama so fat . . ." jokes popularized in film, media, and popular cultural events such as *Def Comedy Jam* is a subcategory of signification.

There are specific rules and rituals to "playing the dozens" that provide the social and linguistic "space" for one speaker to "dis" the kinfolk of another speaker in verbal rounds. Depending on the verbal prowess and acuity of the language combatants, the dozens can either get more humorous or more insulting, the further the players go back through ancestral lines (Smitherman, 1977/1986, p. 131).[11]

Narrative is a fundamental mode of persuasion in AAR. The content of narrative is just as important as the delivery. To resonate with a Black audience, the Black rhetor uses many culturally approved methods of communication.

The Will to Adorn

Both Hurston and Smitherman identified Black stylings in language, which point to eloquence and ways to make the English language over in an Africanized fashion. Hurston identified this phenomenon as "the will to adorn":

> [The African American's] ideas of ornament does not attempt to meet conventional standards, but it satisfies the soul of the creator. In this respect the American Negro has done wonders to the . . . language . . . he has made new force words out of old feeble elements. (1981, p. 51)

This kind of "accessorizing," according to Hurston's analysis, "satisfies the soul" (pp. 51–52). The African-influenced "will to adorn" has a direct link and natural extension to language, as one's culture informs all aspects of one's life. As Asante (1993) argues, "[N]o displaced people ever completely lose the forms of their previous culture" (p. 234). Hurston's work identifies three integral African American linguistic contributions to the language that have a direct connection to "the will to adorn":

1. First, the abundant use of metaphor and simile (as aforementioned)
2. Second, the double descriptive, and
3. Last, the use of verbal nouns or nouns from verbs

It would seem, according to Hurston, that African Americans modify and adapt words to better fit the image-heavy descriptions of person, place, and thing.[12]

Since AAVE is a dynamic language, in AAR particular lexical items and syntactical "creations" may change to fit our constantly evolving language needs.[13] It is interesting to note that even though AAVE language speakers make varied changes to the language, other elements of the language remain consistent. In this way, AAVE is continually reinvested and reimagined by "creating" image-heavy lexical items and expressions, using deep-structured, African-centered language strategies.[14] As Hurston (1981) suggested, the unadulterated English language, without the benefit of acculturation and the African aesthetic, cannot meet the needs for the breadth and depth of African American experience—

hence "the adornment." "It arises out of the same impulse as the wearing of jewelry and the making of sculpture." (p. 53)

Rather than calling the linguistic strategy "the will to adorn" as Hurston did, Smitherman (1977/1986) labeled this strategy "exaggerated language" and discussed its frequent use along with a technique that she labeled "image-making." Smitherman noted that African Americans often incorporated "uncommon words and rarely used expressions" to add weight to their communications. "Sometimes the whole syntax of a sentence may be expressed in an elevated, formal manner" (94). Those images, metaphors, and other kinds of imaginative language allow AAVE speakers to communicate in even more creative ways.[15] These "metaphorical constructs," according to Smitherman, are representative of exactly what gives AAVE its poetic quality. "The figures of speech created in Black linguistic imagery tend to be earthy, gutsy and rooted in plain everyday reality" (Smitherman, 1977/1986, p. 97).

Dialect

The most striking dissimilarities between the work of Zora Neale Hurston and Geneva Smitherman was not in how each of the women identified the features of AAR but, rather, in the explanations that they each offered for the reasons *behind* the development of AAVE in the first place. Hurston believed that much of the variation and adaptation that African Americans imposed on the English language in the precolonial years of second-language acquisition as a result of enslavement had nothing to do with linguistic "laziness" (the prevailing Eurocentric thought of the time) but instead was dictated by rules of physiology and the desire to achieve a better comfort level while producing vocal sounds. We should note, however, that when Hurston was writing, much of the literature on language development at the time (now considered racist) was predicated on Darwinian notions of physiology and eugenics. By 1977, the Black Power Movement and Black studies movement as well as modern sociolinguistic theories of language acquisition and development influenced Smitherman's theorizing.[16]

Hurston's analysis is inherently problematic today precisely because it did attempt to discuss phonetic features in the language that African American's speak by pointing to anthropology and physiology.

Hurston's drawing on Enlightenment and Darwinian paradigms is where her work on AAVE and AAR falls short. To her credit, though, we must acknowledge that Hurston was familiar with the concept of "contact language" development, as can be noted in her explanation for the dramatic nature of Black expression. Hurston wrote, "[E]ven with detached words in his vocabulary—not evolved in him but transplanted on his tongue by contact—[the speaker] must add action to it to make it do" (1981, p. 49). At the time of Hurston's writing, scholars such as Melville Herskovits were just uncovering culturally appropriate data about the linguistic and cultural practices of Black people. Thus, her early explanations could be perceived as giving the academic audience what it expected to hear while at the same time implying correlations between the development of AAVE with "first language" residuals from African languages. Hurston was, however, researching and writing from 1927 to 1938, before *the language* of African Americans was even recognized *as a language;* and there are many who would say that the battle is still being fought.

The most telling criticism of Geneva Smitherman's work in *Talkin and Testifyin: The Language of Black America* is that she does not reveal enough of her qualitative field methods of what was studied, who the informants were, and how the data was collected; however, the strengths of her findings on AAR far outweigh many of those concerns. Both Hurston's and Smitherman's writing styles and findings helped lend credibility to the developing discourse on AAR and AAVE. Both of these women's rhetorical styles exhibited the power of the language.

Smitherman's strength lies in her explanation of contact language fusion; and her work references a dynamic lexicon, citing African lexical items such as *gumbo, okra,* and *yam* that were, no doubt, incorporated into AAVE undetected by tyrannical overseers bent on robbing early African Americans of every remnant of their respective cultures (Smitherman, 1977/1986, pp. 14–15). For many of those speakers, their developing second-language skills needed to be functional enough to readily understand and/or appropriately respond to their oppressors—the Dutch, the Portuguese, the German, the Quaker, the Irish, the English, the Italian, the Spanish, the Mexican, and the French. Thankfully, these transplanted Africans developed a myriad number of linguistic strategies to "retain" as much of their native cultures as they could.

Historians and linguists have suggested that (contrary to the beliefs held by early cultural scholars) probably few of these Africans "relinquished their African languages immediately, [but] they all found themselves in a situation in which they had to learn [and persuasively use] an auxiliary language in a hurry in order to establish communication in the heterogeneous groups into which they were thrown" (Dillard, 1973, p. 74).[17] By tracing African rules of grammar to ethnic groups brought to particular regions (Bendor-Samuel, 1969; Bamgbose, 1970), scholars such as Smitherman have gone a long way in establishing the pan-national continuity of AAVE.

Conclusion

This essay offers evidence that both Hurston and Smitherman identified many of the same salient features, fluidity, and dynamics of AAR nearly forty years apart from one another's research. Using their work, contemporary scholars have gone on to further the discourses of AAVE and AAR. With the body of literature in and around the language that African Americans speak, like the scholarship collected in this volume, we now recognize that AAVE is not only a language consistently and constantly being reinvented by its users but also that modes of discourse in AAR, facilitated by the use of AAVE, have made substantial contributions to American rhetoric as a whole.

The consistency in some of the other modes of discourse that both scholars identified in AAR, including linguistic grammaticality, function, theatricality in form and style of delivery, abundant use of metaphor and simile, double descriptives, and complex noun-verb constructions is remarkable. Images, metaphors, and imaginative language strategies (such as the serial negator, serial verbs, verb/noun constructions, and call and response) found in AAVE language allow speakers to communicate in creative, effective, and persuasive ways.

The sheer volume of research contesting the importance of AAVE in school, in the media, and in the political realm is still quite telling. Those of us in the field know that as a construct language "is used as a way to limit or validate discourse." (Lippi-Green, 1997, p. 77) In their respective research, Hurston's and Smitherman's work laid the groundwork for the discourses we must continue. We won't know where we are going if we don't know where we have been!

Notes

1. According to Holloway's discussion of the slave trade (1991, pp. 1–18), there were strategic reasons why certain cultures were actively hunted and sought after in the African slave trade. Many of those decisions were inextricably tied to a colonial awareness of indigenous bodies of knowledge and modes of production that American and Caribbean planters strategically tried to capitalize on in efforts to maximize slave labor in their growing plantation economies.

2. For more information about sociohistorical factors of plantation economy and the demographics influencing the development of language varieties in the Americas, see John Victor Singler's article "African Influence upon

Afro-American Language Varieties Consideration of Sociohistorical Factors," in Salikoko S. Mufwene (Ed.) (1993), *Africanisms in Afro American Language* (Athens: University of Georgia Press), pp. 235–253.

3. One of the favorite simile constructions that I found in my research was the following item: "Girl, chile . . . he was as sexy as a cool drink of water on a hot summer's day!"

4. Hurston also suggested that for other examples of improvisation, researchers can pay particular attention to the instances of mime, pantomime, and dramatic action in the everyday gestures of Ebonics speakers.

5. "Yeerp?" is a contemporary AAVE expression used by young men trying to get the attention of young women in urban areas in and around one field site in Philadelphia. Recognized as a contrived amalgamation of "What's up?" according to respondents in my research, the sound has been given new meaning as a synonym for "Yo" or "Hey you!"

6. In one African American region, "some suds" becomes a recognizable lexifer and an appropriate beverage for adults after work or on weekends. Miles away, in a northern, much more urban region, "a forty," some "dawg," or "brew" are some of the same terms readily identified by like members of a similar group for that very same desired beverage. Transplanted beyond their respective regional borders, each thirsty speaker understands the others' parched need for libations as "African languages . . . defy genetic boundaries (Mazrui, 1992, p. 76).

7. The media and popularity of African American culture has helped to blur the linguistic boundaries between regions and races so that some of these terms may be familiar outside of traditional geographic or racialized boundaries. Through vehicles of popular culture such as rap, Hip Hop music, poetry, and drama, other language speakers and ethnic groups are being exposed to the cultural terms, lexical items, and (some would argue) knowledge of the African World View and layered meaning inherent in Ebonics.

8. With the assistance of Darrell Witherspoon, to date, I am in the process of cataloging interesting examples of serial negators like some of the following examples: double negative—"I ain't goin' no where"; tri-negator—"He don't know anything *about nothin'*!"; quad-negator—"Ain't no Muslim gonna have nothin' to do with none of that."

9. In my research, the most complex serial negator that I've come across is a penta-negative or quint-negator as in the following statement: "I ain't gonna do nothin' with nothin' I ain't got nothin' to do with!" In that statement, there are fully five words that constitute negative value, and yet the speaker's intention to mind his or her own business is both clear and exact.

10. Sandra Barns offers a discussion of the function of gossip in public space in contemporary Nigeria; Sally Price's text looks at instances of gossip in Saramakan songs; and John J. Bodine looks at the function of gossip in Taos culture as a way to promote conformity in that unique Native American community.

11. In my research, that biting repetition when engaged in "the dozens" affects the weight and value of the insult as perceived by the listener.

12. You should note here how I have used the term *image-heavy,* creating a more powerful adjective by combining adjective and noun.

13. An example of contemporary verbal-nouns or noun-form-verb constructions is in the following scenario: Right after the verdict from the infamous O.
J. Simpson trial was reached, a young, African American gentleman overheard
on a fairly large college campus "created" a very interesting verb from noun.
The "brother" was referring to an apparent physical altercation between himself and a young female. "I had to O.J. her, Man—whop! Right in the mouth!"
[Of course, inserting a feminist/womanist critique, this paper would be much
longer if we spoke to the social implications of that "creation."] However, the
point of the "creation" should, nevertheless, be quite clear.

14. As a performance poet and playwright, I too am often guilty of trying
to institutionalize "first-language" sensibilities from AAR with academic text.
In my creative work, I am particularly fond of the tendency toward using serial nouns and serial verbs that is so much a part of AAVE. In my play *Dog Days:
The Legend of O. V. Catto,* two female characters in nineteenth-century Philadelphia begin a verbal brawl for the title character's affections, when Fanny Mae
Jackson stops her nemesis, Mrs. Chase, dead in her tracks with a string of serial nouns.

> "Now just wait a minute, darling, Honey, Baby, Sweetie Pie, Baby
> cakes, I don't think so! Now we's both big girls, sweet thing; but
> don't be gettin' in over your head! Don't be confusing "friendship"
> with anything else, 'cause O. V. ain't interested. Trust me!" (Will-
> iams, 1998)

With each serialized noun used, the stakes are raised exponentially. In the
text, the words become separated from their individual meanings of endearment.
By stringing the several nouns together (Darling . . . Honey . . . Baby . . .), the
terms become much more insulting and/or intimidating because they become
weighted now with negative value. These kinds of serial nouns and serial verbs
in AAR further point to African retentions in the language that African Americans speak. According to Molefi Asante, the African American tendency toward
serial verb construction as a way to enhance and express *levels* in our communications is quite similar to the kind of serial verblike constructions that appear
in some West African languages to express action, and these occurrences are
further proof of the tendency in AAR towards linguistic "adornment" (1990a,
p. 26).

15. As an example of this feature, Smitherman cites Martin Luther King Jr.
and his use of the phrase "incandescently clear" in one of his many sermons,
or the young brother who asks for a date in a far more elevated manner:
"[W]ould you care to dine with me tonight on some delectable red beans and
rice?" (Smitherman, 1977/1986, p. 94).

16. In my research into the early Ebonics of nineteenth-century African
Americans (using oral histories, personal texts as in letters, journal entries, and
song, along with the so-called African American dialect poetry of Paul Laurence
Dunbar), I (as have many linguists) noted the absence of the *th* fricative in be-
ginning and final sounds in the lexicon of AAVE terms from the 1800s. In some
West African languages, according to Lorenzo Turner (2002), in particular Ibo,
Hausa, and Yoruba, the *th* fricative is seldom present, and African speakers more

often rely on the voiced alveolar stop *d* sound, instead—even when English is the second language of those African speakers.

17. David Dalby (1972), among others, documented a notable predominance of Wolof being used as a lingua franca among early West Africans in the thirteen colonies (Brewer, 1970).

Part Two

Visions for Pedagogy of
African American Rhetoric

6

The Multiple Dimensions of Nubian/ Egyptian Rhetoric and Its Implications for Contemporary Classroom Instructions

Clinton Crawford

IT IS IMPERATIVE TO PROVIDE A CULTURAL AND HISTORICAL CONtext to help in our accurate understanding of the two expressions from the Nile Valley complex under review. By providing this framework, the rhetorical tradition could be fully understood and appreciated. Before that is done a preface is warranted. This volume takes a sharp detour from the so-called classical Western academic pantheon, which elects to advance the foundation of rhetoric with Platonic and Aristotelian affiliation. Given this view, ancient Africa is relegated to the compost pile of historical rhetorical tradition as evidenced in the deliberate attempt to obfuscate its rhetorical tradition from textbooks. This intellectually dishonest and amoral behavior follows a consistent pattern advanced by those who insist on a dominant hegemonic paradigm that continually seeks to obviate, omit, and preclude the African contribution to human culture.

Against the above background, one can see the correlation between European rhetors and philosophers who are impelled by the same argument: that no substantive rhetorical tradition could be ascribed to Africa. Nonetheless, these same rhetoricians are willing to concede that the proverbs, storytelling, and oral traditions of West and Central Africa are the only known category of African utterances that are not documented. To further repress the African contribution to the science of argumentative, speculative, and contemplative behaviors of speech, Kemet (ancient Egypt) is conveniently removed from the continent of Africa, and its early inhabitants are misrepresented in terms of their cultural and racial identity. For example, when the inquisitive student asks about the Kemetic (ancient Egyptian) tradition, such a student might still be instructed that Kemet is in the Middle East, thus persuading one to reject the physical geographic truth that Egypt is indeed on the northeastern quadroon of the continent of Africa (Crawford, 1996). Kemet was not oriented toward the Mediterranean as is implied in the term *Mediterranean world* but, rather, it was culturally, economically, and racially directed toward the inner most southerly direction of Africa. The attempt at continually deploying inaccurate information about Kemet's past with respect to its cultural connection to the rest of Africa, in all its deliberations and dimensions, is very distressing. This act of intellectual destabilization constitutes part of the miseducation for all people. Cheikh Anta Diop's *Cultural Unity of Black Africa* (1978), a germinal work of our time, which reconnects many ancient and modern African cultures through biogenetics, linguistics, social organization, cosmology, rites of passage, and so on, is most noteworthy and instructive for the reader.

This essay and the book in general attempt to recover the deliberately discarded files and replace them on the hard drive of the African and African American rhetorical tradition. Without question, Africa has the longest recorded history of written documentation dating back forty thousand years (Crawford, 1996, p. 101).

Given the dominant Eurocentric academic agency of misinformation and miseducation about ancient and contemporary Africa, one should not be surprised that in most contemporary discourse about Ta-Seti (ancient Nubia), an unmistakable manifestation of ancient African Nile Valley culture preceding Egypt, is that its relationship to Kemet is a subsidiary one. Ta-Seti is primarily presented as the place where the Kemetic people (ancient Egyptians) satisfied their thirst for the precious metal, gold, and the coveted frankincense and myrrh. Indeed, the South was the source for ancient Egyptian wealth—the immense stone quarries, the source of the Nile, the papyrus plant used for paper and ship building—but it was also the source for Egyptian culture. During the fifth millennium B.C. in Upper Nubia, the technologically advanced Khartoum neolithic culture already had in place a burial tradition that included objects such as pottery, personal adornment, and tools, which were the possessions of the deceased. This practice was later seen in ancient Egypt. Today, very few scholars are willing to contest that the development of Nile Valley culture came from the southeast: Ethiopia and Nubia.

Notably, Yosef ben-Jochannan (1970) recounts that Nubia is merely chronicled in the context of ancient Egyptian pharoanic dynastic history of the New Kingdom. ben-Jochannan and Bruce Williams (1989b), two of the leading scholars on Nubia, provide us with a time line for a civilization already established approximately 4000 B.C.E., about a millennium before ancient Kemet. As stated above, numerous attempts are made to continually misrepresent the history and relationship between Egypt and Nubia. In some other bewildering moments of the discourse, the Nubians and the Egyptians are depicted as unrelated neighbors and enemies, thus the justification for Nubia's repression in favor of the beloved culture, Egypt, the darling of art historians, archaeologists, historians, philologists, and anthropologists.

It must be made clear that the people of Kemet consistently acknowledged the people from Ta-Seti/Nubia, those from south and central Africa, as models of pharaonic rule, builders of pyramids, skilled in the art of mummification, and creators of the characters of Medew Netcher and Medew Nefer. According to Gerald Massey (1881), the general region of Ethiopia and Nubia was called "Land of the Gods." Cheikh Anta Diop's *Cultural Unity of Black Africa* (1978) and Theophile Obenga's *Ancient Egypt and Black Africa* (1992) provide compelling evidence that Kemet and Ta-Seti belonged to the same cultural complex. Essentially, there were no cultural and linguistic differences, except for some regional variations. This should not be alarming to us, since one can find the same features of regional variations in modern-day cultures. The United States of America is one modern example of a culture with a myriad of regional variations. Furthermore, throughout the history of Kemet, the Ta-Setians/Nubians always came to the aid of their kin when they fell victims to invading forces. Ronuko Rashidi (1989b) tells us that in the Middle Kingdom, Amenemhet I (1991–1971 B.C.), whose name when translated means "the triumphant son of a woman from the land of Nubia" was instrumental in keeping the Asiatic invaders out of the lower Kemetic Delta area. Again, during the New Kingdom period (750–656 B.C.), Nubian pharaohs Piankhi, Shabaka, and Taharqa reclaimed, reunified, and restored ancient Kemet for its final walk of glory in history before Kemet's demise (Rashidi, 1989a, pp. 184–185).

Since the enormity of the historical and cultural expressions that connect ancient Egypt and the rest of the Nile Valley civilizations are voluminous, one cannot chronicle them in this short essay. This overview sets the stage for a contextual examination of some of the dimensions of the rhetoric of Nile Valley peoples, particularly Egypt and Nubia. It is therefore appropriate and urgent to posit the following explication here in our discourse. Nile Valley cultural rhetoric is based on the fundamental concept of Ma'at: truth, justice, virtue, reciprocity, balance, and righteousness, among other tenets. This fundamental approach to life is demonstrated in the pedagogy of the educational system, learner/hearer, art, speech, written communication, deep thought, sciences, and in every aspect of daily life of Nile Valley peoples (Crawford, 1996; Carruthers, 1995; Hilliard, 1995). The world has the benefit of the radical thinking of Nile Valley cultural expressions through the Medew Netjer (Mdw Ntr). *Medew Netjer* is defined as sacred speech that is measured, principled, and ordered. In this light, one can advance a well-reasoned position for inquiry, observation, and possible implementation in contemporary classroom instructions and the culture at large. However, the Nile Valley cultural complex under review reflected the awareness of the complementary force *Isfet*. *Isfet* is the counterbalance of Ma'at. Isfet does not represent the goals and standards for a righteous person in society. It is the embodiment of injustice, an amoral ecology of disunion, falsehood, and disorder. Ma'at and Isfet are two banks of the same river, as it were. In Asa Hilliard's, Larry Williams's, and Nia Damali's (1987) translation of *The Teachings of Ptahhotep*, the oldest surviving book in the world, the fifth instruction, is most fitting to make the point about Ma'at and its oppositional force, Isfet:

> If you are a man who leads, a man who controls the affairs of many, then seek the most perfect way of performing your responsibility so that your conduct will be blameless. Great is Ma'at (truth, justice and righteousness). It is everlasting. Ma'at has being unchanged since the time of Asar. To create obstacles to the following of the laws is to open a way to a condition of violence. The transgressor of laws is punished, although the greedy person overlooks this. Baseness may obtain riches, yet crime never lands its wares on the shore. In the end only Ma'at lasts. Man says, "Ma'at is my father's ground." (pp. 18–19)

A more in-depth discourse on the following important concepts, Ma'at, Mdw Ntr, and Medew Nefer, which have affected every aspect of life within Ta-Setian and Kemetic culture is therefore appropriate.

The discussion about Ma'at, Mdw Ntr, and Medew Nefer not only defines the arena out of which Nile Valley rhetoric emerged but essentially helps us to understand the singular focus of the world's oldest civilizing force. Thus, the singular objective of Nile Valley rhetoric was creating a just society, one in which men and women were treated equally. Hence, it is both urgent and appropriate for a more in-depth definition of the above-identified concepts, which have affected every aspect of life within the Nile Valley complex that included Ta-Seti and Kemet.

Definition of Medew Netjer and Medew Nefer

Jacob Carruthers's work *Divine Speech* (1995), offers the most accessible explanations of Mdw Ntr/Mdw Nfr. *Medew Netjer*[1] (God Speech) and *Medew Nefer*[2] (Good Speech) are terms that approximated in the Greek provisos "theology" (divine speech) and "logos" (reasoned speech). Again, one experiences the duality of all things manifested in speech. In the Nile Valley complex, the practice of good speech (Mdw Nfr) prepared one for divine speech (Mdw Ntr); hence, they were inextricably linked together. It is important to note here from the outset in this very contentious academic climate that while there was no specific term such as *philosophy* used in ancient Kemet/Egypt, the concept existed in the doctrines and theories that were established prototypes, models, and archetypes long before their appearance in later Greek doctrines and theories of Platonic and Aristotelian schools (Crawford, 1996; Onyewuenyi, 1993). For example, divine speech and particularly reasoned speech, advanced by Aristotle and Plato, respectively, were models explicated in the popular contemporary Greek philosophy. These concepts, as we have seen above and will be detailed later, were already entrenched in ancient Kemet/Egypt. Also noteworthy, the primacy of the origin of Kemetic "philosophy" and its influence on other cultures, particularly Greece, can be attributed to close geographical proximity of ancient Kemet/Egypt, northeast corridor of Africa, to the Greek peninsula in the Mediterranean Sea. Albeit St. Augustine proclaimed that the term *philosophy* (love of wisdom) was credited to Pythagoras, both Herodotus and Diogenes Laetius recall that Samos native Pythagoras had secured the appropriate consent from African high priests to study at the Egyptian Mysteries school (Onyewuenyi, 1993, p. 47). This Greek sage, Pythagoras, acknowledged his debt to his Egyptian teachers by calling himself a follower of wisdom. On the other hand, Plato, the father of what is now called Western philosophy, gave his version of philosophy by using the legendary Socrates. Socratic teachings, as we must all know by now, were not documented by Socrates. Interestingly though, a student of Socrates, Plato, used *Doctrines of Rebirth, Transmigration of the Soul; Being and Becoming; Idea and Form;* and *Creation of the Universe,* which were all prototypes of Pythagoras, who was, as I mentioned above, a student of ancient Egyptian Mysteries school (Onyewuenyi, 1993, pp. 227–229). (Also see Plato's *Republic* for a detailed explanation on the rudimentary tenets of Greek philosophy.)

While neither time nor space allows for a protracted explanation on the ancient Egyptian origin of Western philosophy, one must not neglect to reflect on the doctrine of the soul and the immortality of the soul attributed to Aristotle and other Greek philosophers. The Greek eyewitness and historian Herodotus categorically stated that the ancient Egyptians were the progenitors of this doctrine and that they were the first to have maintained that the soul of man was immortal. (For further discussion, see Herodotus's *Histories,* 1956, p. 124.) One can also refer to Hegel's *History of Philosophy* (1832/1964) and *Lectures on the History of Philosophy* (1833/1983), in which he candidly discusses the influence of ancient Egyptian teaching on Pythagoras and others. Equally concrete is citing the *Doctrine of the Opposites,* espoused by Pythagoras, in the theory of "completeness and harmony" based on the number ten: odd/even, limited/unlimited, hot/cold, good/evil, male/female, light/darkness, rest/motion, square/oblong, left/right, and one/plurality, for which the "unification of any set of these opposites achieves harmony in the universe and in one's personal life" (Onyewuenyi, p. 172). Clearly, the *Doctrine of the Opposites* belongs to the Ma'atian forerunner, which is discussed below (James, 1954; Van Sertima, 1989; Chandler, 1999).

As we shall learn later, in the Grecian cultural context, the pursuit of wisdom was substantially different to the practice of the Kemetic people (ancient Egyptians). The word *Medew Netjer,* in the Nile Valley cultural complex, denotes the formal written language, particularly the dramas on the walls of the pyramids, temples, and tombs. Consequently, when the Greeks called the Egyptian written language hieroglyphs (sacred inscription), these foreigners were not only describing what they saw but were also translating the Kemetic term narrowly (Carruthers, 1995). It might be instructive to immediately cut through the anticipation and cite the major difference between the Greek worldview and the Egyptian worldview. The single fundamental difference in these two seemingly contesting pantheons is the concept of Ma'at. On the one hand, in the Greek cultural philosophical context, the material and exterior expression of forms and ideas were of paramount importance with the incipient separation of body and mind; whereas in the Egyptian context, the embodiment of the metaphysical and physical expression of the cycle of life was embraced. Hence, the concept of Ma'at dominated every facet of Egyptian life.

Definition of Ma'at

For many people who might not be familiar with the Kemetic literature and culture, the word *Ma'at* would be a relative new one, if not entirely unknown. Granted the complexity and multidimensionality of Ma'at, it would be misleading for me to attempt to describe this concept in a few simple explanations. One is hard-pressed to offer an attempted outline for understanding Ma'at, which is a very complex philosophical concept. Nonetheless, Oba T'Shaka (1995) reports that in ancient Kemet the principle of unicity or twin-ness was manifested through Ma'at, and that "Ma'at was both a cosmic and earthly law" (p. 114). The person in society and the cosmos at large were inextricably linked by the order of Ma'at. To understand Ma'at, one must contemplate its duality of simplicity and complexity and its implications for cosmic, social, and personal understanding.

Theophile Obenga (1989), the distinguished African linguist and philosopher, gives the best approximation of Ma'at. He writes:

> Ma'at is the primordial principle which gives order to all values. Ma'at is the substantive ingredient in the cosmic order, part of Truth and Justice that allowed the pharaoh (for all that he was and symbolized) to protect the country from disorder, from chaos, from famine, from misery, and that all men living in society must conform to Justice and Truth, to Ma'at, the Supreme Virtue, guide and measure of all human activity. (p. 317)

Summarily then, Ma'at is the preestablished harmony in the cosmos, felicity supreme, an invitation to all men and women in society to do and speak, think and act, to live according to what is true, normal, harmonious, according to virtue, with all the hieratic, traditional, transcendental, imperative, and absolute implications that the word *virtue* takes on in the mentality of the African people from the Nile Valley (Obenga, 1989, p. 318).

Any attempt at defining the above-identified precepts of Ma'at, Mdw Ntr, and Medew Nefer in Nile Valley cultural expressions is incomplete without reference to Tehuti. Nile Valley civilization had such great regard for god speech and good speech that the inhabitants designated a deity for thought, speech, and writing called Tehuti. The model of Tehuti gave rise to the scribal tradition, a position revered in ancient Kemet. Wayne Chandler (1999) described Tehuti as the personification of "universal wisdom and truth . . . the scribe of the Gods" (p. 24). More than three millennia later, the Greeks renamed him *Hermes Mercurius Trismegistus,* "the thrice-great, the great-great, the greatest great and master of masters" (p. 24). Subsequently, the teachings of Tehuti became known under the disguise of the Hermetic philosophy instead of Kemetic philosophy (see Massey, 1881; Chandler, 1999). One must exercise caution, though, for in the transposition of cultural knowledge the context changes, much of the original Kemetic meanings are lost in translation. In the case of the Hermetic doctrine, as Chandler points out, the Greeks were (and the present-day Western academic culture is) more concerned with the superficial nature of "empty speeches . . . an insane foolosophy of speeches" (1999, p. 25). By contrast, the Kemetic people were not given to empty speeches but were persuaded by sounds that engendered action (Chandler, 1999, p. 25).

The best examples of Kemetic action as it relates to rhetoric can be seen in the summary of the seven principles or laws of Tehuti cited by Chandler from the *Divine Pymander.*

- The Principle of Mentalism: *All is Mind; The Universe is Mental;*
- The Principle of Correspondence: *As above, so below; as below, so above;*
- The Principle of Vibration: *Nothing rests; everything moves; everything vibrates;*
- The Principle of Polarity: *Everything is dual, everything has* poles, everything has pairs of opposites;
- The Principle of Gender: Gender is in everything; everything has Masculine and Feminine Principles; Gender on all planes;
- *The Principle of Rhythm: Everything flows out and in; everything has its tides; all things rise and fall . . . and;*
- *The Principle of Cause and Effect: Everything has its Effect; everything has its cause.* (Chandler, 1999, pp. 35–38; italics added)

Given the definition of Ma'at posited above, one can observe that Tehuti's precepts are fundamentally based on Ma'atian principles of balance and reciprocity, which are in effect universal laws, devoid of humans' conjectures of chance and coincidence.

Some Dimensions of Nubian/Egyptian Rhetoric

Much of Nile Valley rhetoric, particularly Tehuti's teachings, has been sublimated in Greco-Roman, in modern-day European philosophy, and in the indigenous teachings of India and China. Therefore, to understand the importance of Nubian/Egyptian rhetoric, it is instructive for one to return to the creations, a variety of narratives from the Nile Valley.

First, Nile Valley cultures viewed creation as a continuous process contiguous with the rising of the sun and events in human history such as the constant effort to establish and reestablish order and righteousness in the midst of chaos and evil. Thus, one finds *creations* rather than a *creation narrative*.

To understand why there are creation stories rather than a creation story, one must be cognizant that the African way of narration, and as a matter of fact African life in general, is concentric. Historically, African people have emulated and lived in harmony with nature. Nature, they observe, is constantly changing and re-creating itself. Oba T'Shaka (1995) helps us to understand the African observation of nature by using the example of the spiral rotational path of the planets, each with its own timely cycle and course of motion. This macro example shows how the cosmos is continuously moving and changing. Similarly, the microcosmic example of the rising and the setting of the sun provides a daily reminder of change, motion, and transformation. The Africans from the Nile Valley complex and their predecessors framed their thought to include intellect and intuition, masculine and feminine, heavenly and earthly, all of which are firmly synthesized in paramount order of Ma'at. Linear movement is therefore unnatural to the African psyche (T'Shaka, 1995).

Wallis Budge's (1960) *The Egyptian Book of the Dead* (in reality the book of Ma'at), and Maulana Karenga's (1984) translation of *Selections from the Husia*, which is a compilation of many sacred books of wisdom, provide a comprehensive view of Nile Valley rhetoric, hence, their importance as instructive sources for our conversation. Among the compilation of books translated in the *Husia* text, *The Book of Knowing the Creations*, is one of the foci. Note the title of the book defines itself as *Creations* rather than *Creation*, since the people of inner Africa and the Nile Valley complex (Kemet, Ethiopia, Ta-Seti) viewed creation as a continuous process. The central argument put forth in this view persuades us that the first creation and the first event of time are synonymous. The rationale for this view is steeped in the Nile Valley complex's observation of nature and human history; for example, the sun resurrects itself each day, and human beings are constantly in pursuit of maintaining order over chaos, an act similar to that of Ra, which is explained below (Karenga, 1984, p. 3).

Wallis Budge's translation helps in reflecting on the radical thinking of people of the Nile Valley complex. Hence, the following is posited:

> Before time existed . . . He existed before nothing else existed
> and what existed He created after He had come into being.
> He produceth, but was not produced; He begat Himself but
> never begotten. . . . God is mother and father, the father of
> fathers and the mother of mothers. God hatheth make the
> universe with all its forms. (1960, p. 107)

In the Nile Valley cultural complex, the coming out of the darkness of the primeval waters of Nun, and the uncreated being calling forth himself in the form of the rising sun are central. Ra, the source of light, provided energy for all that was dormant. Simultaneously, Ra, the creative intelligence, manifested as Kheper, *the one who comes in being and brings into being* through the utterance of the sacred word, called forth all forms and living things. The new genesis included Shu (the power and principle of light and air) and Tefnut (the power and principle of water—heaven and earth). Shu was the male principle of the sky and the transformative medium for people to change from mortal to immortal, and Tefnut was his female twin companion, representing the sun and water as well as the defender against alien forces. These two forces were also regarded as the feminine and masculine systems of harmonious existence, Ausar and Auset. Upon this foundation of twin-ness, the creation of Ausar and Auset (Osiris and Isis), which is the synthesis of male and female, followed. Horus, Seth, and Nephthys were brought into being one after the other and subsequently gave rise to the many coming afterwards. In the Osirian drama emerging from the *Creations,* Seth, the personification of fear, slew his brother Osiris (good) and scattered his dismembered body over the land. Isis, the devoted one, never rested until she recovered the parts of her husband's dismembered body, which was mummified and resurrected. Horus, the son of Isis and Osiris, attempted to avenge his father's death but met a formidable opponent in his uncle Seth (Karenga, 1984; T'Skaka, 1995; Crawford, 1996).

George G. M. James (1954) gleans from this drama that Osiris, Isis, and Horus constituted the Divine Trinity, which was revered throughout antiquity in the likeness of father, mother, and son. A more recent interpretation arising out of the aforementioned triadic relationship, Chandler (cited in Van Sertima) writes: "Osiris was the greatest God of Egypt, Sun of Saturn, celestial fire and reincarnation." Chandler identifies Isis as the "virgin mother and personified nature . . . woman clothed in the sun of the Land of Khemi." Horus was referred to as "loved of heaven" and "beloved of the Sun . . . born from the womb of the world" (1989, p. 131).

What we can also glean from the narrative of the *Creations* are some of the members of the Christian holy family that remain a part of the doctrine of Christianity—father, son, and Holy Spirit, minus the female presence. If time and space were afforded here, one would see many of the same aspects of transformation, death, and resurrection that existed long before Greek culture and Christianity. Another important and instructive point that needs to be made here is that the major European and so-called Middle Eastern religions—Judaism, Christianity, and Islam—have their genesis, like human culture and the human species, in the southern cradle of civilization, Africa (ben-Jochannan, 1970; Diop, 1974). Many of the fundamental precepts of these religions were already institutionalized and codified in the Nile Valley cultural text commonly called the *Egyptian Book of the Dead, Pyramid Text, the Coffin Text, the Memphite Theology, the Amarna Letters,* and other texts relevant to this particular discussion. The spiritual genius insights and observations of the Africans out of the Nile Valley complex profoundly influence Judaism, Christianity, and Islam. For example, the virgin birth concept first illustrated in Ausar, Auset, and Heru (Isis, Osiris, and Horus) in the creations narrative cited above bear witness to this argument that all three of the world's major religions also have virgin birth. Edward Bynum (1999) contends that we should not be surprised that in an agrarian culture that astutely observed nature's cycles of growth, maturation, harvesting, and planting reinforced the natural perception of seen and unseen cycles in the natural world. He further points out that making the correlation between planting of the human seed in the body of women, growth and pregnancy, birth, maturity, and then death and the symbolism of rebirth are obvious conclusions for any group of people (p. 113). Further, the concept of monotheism, the worship of one God, practiced by all major world religions today, was firmly entrenched in Nile Valley cultures, even before the reformer Akhenaton revived it during his reign (New Kingdom, eighteenth dynasty).

Theophile Obenga extrapolates another salient point from the *Creations* matrix. He identifies a philosophical text in which Nile Valley inhabitants posited their radical thinking of the beginning of beginnings when there existed the abysmal water with all the elements for the genesis of life. This text was chiefly concerned with speculations in "question of origins . . . Life and Death . . . Truth and Justice . . . primordial waters of Nun . . . social order and chaos . . . the emergence of matter . . . Nun and Ma'at . . . created and uncreated beings . . . existence and

existing . . . before time and space . . . cosmogenesis . . . the cosmic All"
(Obenga, 1989, pp. 292–294).

The text above helps with the possibility for further contemplation
deriving from the description given about the complex rhetoric of the
early civilizations from the Nile Valley. For example, the duality of all
things in the cosmos and nature are illuminated in the paradoxical idea
that there was nonexistence and existence at the same time, that the
uncreated created himself or herself and called forth all that was, all that
is, and all that will be. From him or her all things in the universe came
into being. One can therefore arrive at a plausible conclusion that all
things are an extension of the creative intelligence. Hence, it makes perfect sense to appreciate the insistence on the consciousness of being and
becoming, good and evil, earth and heaven, water and fire, air and wind,
space and time, male and female, above and below, and the unity of all
things as opposed to the individuality among things.

Again, it is important to note that underpinning all the deliberations
and contemplations in the Nile Valley complex is Ma'at. It was the sta-
bilizing force in many areas of Egyptian life (i.e., the cosmology of the
beginning of beginnings, the building of pyramids and temples, the system of governance, and the balanced principle of life in ancient Egypt).
The voluminous corpus of the rhetorical tradition of petitions, instructions, confessions, complex plots in literary texts, wisdom teaching,
progressive arguments, fine speech, eloquence, examples of delight, and
Ma'at influenced all light-hearted poetics.

What happened to the Ma'atian ethic? This seems like an obvious
question at this juncture of our discourse. One view postulated is that
the literature and the texts were never really understood, hence, the
academic and intellectual mistreatment of Ma'at. Maulana Karenga
(1989) emphasizes that the last centuries of Ma'at, which were toward
the end of the longest surviving civilization known to humankind of
approximately 4,500 years, coincided with the first centuries of Christianity. This newly configured doctrine, Christianity, not only supplanted
Ma'at but also systematically attacked it. The symbolic use of animals,
sculpture, and architecture were not understood by invading foreign
forces; thus, they scourged and supplanted Ma'at. Under the order of
Theodosius fourth-century and Justinian sixth-century dictum, Ma'at
was outlawed (Karenga, 1989, p. 352). Therefore, only by carefully
studying the Egyptian Ma'atian ethics can one reconstruct and eradicate
many of the misunderstandings held today about Africa's past, its pres-

ent, its potential for the future, and the one-dimensional education system that is on the brink of disrepair.

The Education System: An Overview

It is meaningful to underscore that the people of Kemet did not separate "religion" and everyday life. Hence, people lived "religious" lives, and their instructions were based in theology, quite similar to traditional African societies of today. George G. M. James (1954), Asa Hilliard (1986, 1995, 1986), Jacob Carruthers (1986, 1995), and others recount that the pedagogical approach used in the instructions of the neophyte commenced with the *"observation of nature."* Along the path of education, accounted for by Hilliard, the student was allowed to develop the direction natural to his or her interest with the final choice at the advance stage in either political leadership or knowledge and wisdom. One had to be cognizant of the consequence of his or her choice, for the choice of ambitiousness inevitably led to limitedness. Ambition is said to be the cataract of one's intuition, one's creativity, and ones' worldview. Conversely, if one elected to sacrifice personal ambition, then he or she consciously became a guardian against the path fraught with the illusion of satisfaction. His or her path led directly to the limitless reservoir of wisdom (Hilliard, 1986, p. 144).

Quite specifically, the student's instructions were given in formal organized institutions known as the Mystery Lodges, with three distinct grades of students. George G. M. James (1954) provides the following categorizations:

(a) The Morals—probationary students who received instructions but were peripheral with respect to the experience of inner vision;

(b) The intelligentsia—those who had attained the inner vision and by implication had received mind or *nous;* and

(c) The Creators or Sons of Light (the enlightened)—who had become identified with or unified with light, which is a signifier of true spiritual consciousness. (p. 27)

These three grades are equivalent to Initiation, Illumination, and Perfection, respectively.

During each stage of intellectual development in the agency of the Mystery School System, students were put through rigorous disciplinary, intellectual, and physical exercises overseen by high priests who tested them to ensure the development of body and mind. Our present-day university system may echo some of the concepts of the Mystery System of ancient Egypt. For the student, education not only prepared him or her for eternal happiness but also demanded knowledge of the ten virtues and Seven Liberal Arts aimed at liberating his or her soul. As a consequence, James points out that the neophyte was expected to manifest the following virtues:

> Control of thought, control of actions, steadfastness of sur-prise, identity with spiritual life or higher ideals, evidence of having a higher vision in life, evidence of a call to spiritual orders, freedom resentment, confidence in the power of the Master/Teacher, confidence in ones own ability to learn, and primary is readiness for initiation (1954, p. 30).

Of course, it is the final virtue, *readiness for initiation* that fully em-bodies what the Mystery System represents. One of its axioms reads: "[W]hen the pupil is ready, then the master will appear" (James, 1954, p. 31). Also complementing the ten virtues, the student curriculum con-sisted of the Seven Liberal Arts: Grammar, Arithmetic, Rhetoric and Dialectic, Geometry, Astronomy, and Music. Beyond this training, suc-cessful students were admitted to the Holy Orders, which allowed for specialization in the *secret system of language and mathematical sym-bolism.* In the case of the more advanced students, the phenomenon of magic was emphasized. James (1954) incorporates Herodotus' writings when he describes the Egyptian priest's capacity, "controlling the minds of men (hypnosis) . . . the power to predicate the future, and the power over nature by giving commands in the name of the Divinity and accom-plishing great deeds" (p. 27), to make the point about the advanced nature of education in Kemet. (See also Herodotus, 1928, *History of Herodotus,* G. Rawlinson, trans., for further information.)

Rhetoric of Instruction/Pedagogy

The *Rhetoric of Instruction* brings us into the realm of the methods and strategies that were used as the vehicle for the transmission of knowl-edge. At its base, initiation was the major aim of this comprehensive system. In ancient Egypt, and as a matter of fact in all ancient African educational systems, the narrow vocational goals were subordinated to

- unity of person, unity of group, and unity with nature;
- the development of social responsibility;

- the development of character; and
- the development of spiritual power.

Asa Hilliard (1986, 1995) and James (1954) convey that these higher aims were the vehicles that propelled the education process. Vocational-skill training was merely a small part of the whole process of education. In this system, little thought was given to the inept intellectual capacity of the student. Conversely, most of the attention was placed on the character as an impediment or as a facilitator to educational development. While one can point to the fact that the individual undertook learning, it was the collective body of students rather than the individual that was paramount in the worldview of this system. The magnificence of Egyptian educational system is manifested in the enormous feats of engineering, voluminous documentation, and stability of an antecedent culture that lasted for thousands of years. The process was designed in such a way that one experienced a true rebirth over the course of a successive series of personal and social transformations. Hilliard (1995) emphasizes that students were engaged in a deeply interactive and comprehensive process. This process included interaction among students and students and teachers, socialization being a major objective of the educational enterprise (p. 78). Content was conveyed through a variety of media—stories, parables, examination of signs, symbolism, use of proverbs, songs, dances—all to convey a special view of the world in which the people lived (Hilliard, 1986, p. 144). The master/teacher modeled the type of behavior the initiates were expected to learn. They (master/teachers) were always alert in a position to respond and to nurture the students' direct educational experience in order for them to move to higher levels of understanding. Even though some scholars in the field may argue that the educational process was broadly "religious," I must depart from this generalization and argue for the specific scientific nature of the Kemetic system of thought. An in-depth study of Egyptian art, architecture, and language in my own work *Recasting Ancient Egypt in the African Context* sheds light on this detour (Crawford, 1996, pp. 85–89). Since I don't have the luxury of time to engage in a protracted discourse around what some deem religious rhetoric, let me share some cogent insights. The commonly held misconception is that the ancient Egyptian rhetoric of "religion" is based on the pantheon of many anthropomorphic gods, and as such, religion can be relegated to myths and superstitions without consistency or significance.

To address this misconception, one must note that the Kemetic belief system derived from a fundamental system of coherent and intricate ordering of thought, observed in the explication of the beginnings of beginnings. "Religion" fiercely interfaced with science, art, and philosophy. For example, the temple built on a rectangular floor plan was so constructed to acknowledge the four elements, the four directions, and the law of opposites, as it were. In fact, nowhere else can one identify a better synthetic of science and art or reason and emotions than in Egyptian art, language, and culture. African deep thought (and by extension African science) does not merely concern itself with naturalism or materialism but also recognizes the existence of psychic forces or phenomena. The acknowledgement of the spiritual and the physical is one of the cornerstones of the Kemetic rhetoric of symbolic logic. For example, pyramid building, the anthropomorphic representation of deities, and the elevated social and spiritual role women played in ancient Egyptian culture are three noteworthy points of reference to bear out the aforementioned observation.[3] The pyramids were not merely elaborate burial edifices for the pharaohs. The dualism inherent in this structure, with its subterranean dimensions and the imposing upper massive vertical structure, was indeed necessary to create engineering balance against the forces of gravity. The symbol logic behind the pyramid also reinforces the coexistence of the spiritual world/netherworld (symbolized by the substructure) and the world of physical existence by the exterior vertical structure. Similarly, the woman's role in society gained prominence since the narrative of the beginnings laid the foundation for her importance as essential to life. The goddess Isis (Auset), representative of the female principle, was a divine deity who provided an equal and balanced relationship for the god Osiris (Ausar), representative of the male principle. Africans from the Nile Valley complex and from inner Africa had no obtrusive question about the equality and importance of women. This argument was resolved, if it ever became an issue, with the elevation of the woman to goddess. In Nile Valley cosmology, the first goddess, Ma'at, was the daughter of Ra and wife of Tehuti, both of whom assisted in the creation of all things. She was both symbolically and physically the source and continuation of life. Isis was also the goddess of medicine, and as such, she was imbued with many powers of healing, which many modern Egyptologists wrongly identified as magical. In her honor, many temples of life, which we call hospitals today, were erected. Symbolism was the corner stone of Nile Valley complex rhetoric. The feather was the symbol of Ma'at present at the Hall of Judgment when one died. The person's heart was evaluated by weighing it on a scale against the feather of Ma'at. Ma'at is word, action, and deed in the physical realm, and the divine in the metaphysical dimension.

Education and Rhetoric for Governance

No area of Nile Valley culture was left unattended with respect to the protocol and general conduct. In this regard, education was no exception. As a matter of fact, education was accorded high priority. Both Carruthers (1995) and Hilliard (1995) cite the master pedagogy, Ptahhotep's remarks before he presented the treatise of pedagogy for the "learner/listener/hearer" (Hilliard, 1995). Ptahhotep petitions the Pharaoh, the representation of Ra and Ma'at: "May I instruct him with the speech of those who heard" (Carruthers, 1995). Ptahhotep was asking permission to pass on the knowledge of those who procured wisdom and listened to the Gods before they left for the ancestral world. Hence, education in Kemet begins with the transmission of knowledge from elders to juniors through the divinely sanctioned word. Teaching was therefore a sacred and spiritual task, as one mantled himself or herself with the responsibility to prepare the next generation for posterity beyond the narrow confines of what contemporary societies call the curriculum. As was pointed out earlier, the word was of a sacred and divine order: Mdw Ntr (God Speech) and Mdw Nfr (Good Speech). Let it also be reemphasized that one's education could take two paths: public servant or priesthood. In the context of public service, the primary focus was on wisdom for governance or what most might call political philosophy, while others prefer to call it *African Deep Thought* (Hilliard, 1995; Carruthers, 1995). From the Kemetic worldview, those who elected governance had to be individuals who were well educated and self-disciplined with the propensity to ensure national order and maintain conformity with Ma'at. Since Mdw Nfr (Good Speech), Mdw Ntr (God Speech), and Ma'at are inextricably linked in this culture, this union became the major vehicle of governance. Given the fact that Mdw Nfr included both the process and the product of intergenerational conversation, instruction became a social obligation. Hence, education for governance became an important part of one's training.

A window into education for governance in the Nile Valley complex (Kemet and Nubia) would be appropriate to open here. Pharaohs, prime ministers, viziers, other dignitaries, and commoners followed written instructions by their elders, who were expected to follow in the footsteps of their forebears. Carruthers conveys that the written instructions comprised part of the corpus of the larger curriculum text used for the education of future scribes. Schoolboys studied and copied their lessons not only for penmanship and literary form but also for decorum, ethics, and social values. If one can recall, Aristotle called these instructions the master science, which is referred to as political science today. Instructions in the realm of scribal schools highlighted conduct and orientation of officials to their duties and functions. Scribal schools prepared the core of governmental officials and others who made up parts of the bureaucracy from clerks to prime ministers (Carruthers, 1995, p. 116). One can speculate that children of royal families were also educated at these scribal schools. Conclusively, what we know is the following: children from all walks of life were exposed to the wisdom teaching from the scribal school. *The Satire of the Trade*, or the Dua Khety (Lichtheim, 1975; Crawford 1996), is testimony to this fact. This text illuminates the importance of formal scribal education as a prerequisite to governance and clarifies that a career in government was opened to ordinary families as well as to nobility and the elite. Judging from the proliferation of the many written texts, for example, from recipes for beers to highly complex letters describing the beginnings of beginnings, one cannot ignore the high degree of literacy, contemplation, and wit in ancient Kemet.

Several texts survived the destructive invasions of Egypt, which can give us a firsthand insight into some of the instructions. Three of these well-known texts include *The Instructions of Ptahhotep* from the Old Kingdom, fifth dynasty; *The Instructions of Amenomope* from the eighteenth Dynasty (considered the master teacher of his day); and the *Shabaka Text* from the New Kingdom, twenty-fifth dynasty. This particular text is sometimes referred to as the Memphite Theology, and it constitutes the corpus of a version of some of the most ancient wisdom teaching. Let us focus on the *Instructions of Ptahhotep* for a moment, because it reinforces the substance of the traditional rhetorical concept of governance. Maulana Karenga and Jacob Carruthers (1986), Carruthers (1995), Hilliard (1986, 1995), and others identify *Instructions of Ptahhotep* as the oldest complete text surviving from the Old Kingdom. Because of its timeless value, this text is considered the epitome of content and form for scribal education in Egypt, and certainly appropriate for contemporary education. The text focuses on manners and the attitudes of officials as well as ordinary people in various typical situations. Among Ptahhotep's thirty-seven teachings, Hilliard identified fourteen as antiviolence commentaries, that is, "the root cause of all violence is greed," as greed begets violence at the individual and collective level. Ptahhotep's teachings reflected the major tenets of Kemetic culture, which espoused "to know, to study, to become wise" (Hilliard, 1995, p. 79).

One can also add that Budge's (1960) translation of *The Book of the Dead* (correctly called the *The Book of Coming Forth by Day and Night* by some African-centered scholars such as ben-Jochannan, Asa Hilliard, Molefi Asante, Carruthers, Karenga, and others) contains many books of antiviolence rhetoric. For instance, in the Papyrus Ani, at the Great Judgment in the Hall Ma'at, the forty-two admonitions repeated by the person before the god Un-Nefer on this occasion reflected the antiviolence nature of the Nile Valley complex. Here are some examples:

> I have not committed sins against men;
> I have not opposed my family;
> I have not acted fraudulently (or deceitfully) in the Seat of
>   Truth;
> I have not wrought evil;
> I have not defrauded the humble man of his property;
> I have not plundered the offerings in the temples;
> I have not defrauded the gods of their cake offerings. (Budge,
>   1960, pp. 573–574)

Every statement in the Hall of Ma'at required one to denounce violence at all levels: person, community, and divine.

Further, to illuminate the enduring relevance of Ptahhotep's teachings, an extension of the Ma'atian ethic, for our present day with respect to governance, the following is highlighted: "if good men and women hold office then government will be good." Equally important, too, "the quality of the education determines the quality of the office holder." This is a perfect synthesis of governance and education in which the students—listeners, hearers—are the embodiment of harmony, antiviolence, and order. These are qualities not commonly found in contemporary education and society.

Ptahhotep's treatise was also pertinent to the general populace. For example, in Karenga's retranslation, one finds, "Be not arrogant because of your knowledge. Take counsel with the ignorant as well as with the unwise. For the limits of knowledge in any field have never been set and no one has ever reached them. Wisdom is rarer than emeralds, and yet it is found among the women who gather at the grindstones" (1984, p. 41). The profundity of this statement lies in the belief of the Nile Valley complex that wisdom does not only lie in the parlor of one person's experiences.

In every instance of education for governance, the virtue of good speech and wisdom was primal. Ptahhotep proclaims: "[W]ords are more powerful than fighting." Carruthers notes that the people of Kemet were well aware that actual disunity occurs when wisdom itself is disunited. Further, they recognized the fact that since Ma'at is closely tied to governance, this accentuated the vigilance that wisdom and governance must be balanced at all times against the challenge of deception.

Instructions of Ptahhotep teaches that government must be benevolent, thus ruling more by reward and promotion rather than punishment. Do right is the cornerstone of governance. A student credo read as follows: A self-disciplined person is one who speaks wisely, because he only speaks when he has something substantive to say.

All of the instructions from *The Book of Amenomope* retranslated by Maulana Karenga (1984) are also instructive for us in contemporary times as they were for the ancients, for example, Instruction III: "Do not argue with the contentious, nor provoke them with words. Pause before those who interrupt and give way to those who verbally attack you. For the unrestrained person is like a storm which bursts like a flame in a pile of straw" (p. 59).

Another important instruction from Amenomope reads: "Keep your tongue away from words of detraction, and you will be one loved by the people. You will find your seat in the Temple of God and your gifts shall be among the offerings to your Lord. You will be greatly honored in old age, duly concealed in your coffin, and safe from the wrath of God" (Karenga, 1984, p. 60). Implicit in the examples cited from Ptahhotep and Amenomope are the same dialectic of dualism used by philosophers many centuries later (Karl Marx's dialectical materialism is an example).

Also within the Memphite Theology text, we see the use of the doctrine of the four elements (AIR, WATER, FIRE, EARTH) and four qualities (Hot, Cold, Wet and Dry) sometimes referred to as the principles of the opposites. In the perspective of the ancient Egyptians, for example, among their pantheon of Gods each had both a male and a female principle, already discussed earlier in this chapter. This pantheon has nine gods with Atum as the one Great Neter (God); Shu (Air) and Tefnut (moisture); Geb (earth) and Nut (sky); Osiris and Isis (husband and wife), Seth (brother and evil one), and Nephthys (sister of Isis). These pairs are the many manifestations of the supreme god, Atum.

Reference was already made to the curriculum of the Seven Liberal Arts (James, 1954), but these must be seen in the light as adjuncts to the initiate's highest goal—self-knowledge. Hence, "Know thyself" was inscribed in temples of learning to remind students of their primary purpose. The essence of education was nature itself or the person. The study of nature helps one to reflect on his or her human nature, which is in effect one aspect of nature.

Let us now briefly examine a case of relations with the general public: First, let me set forth how arguments were made. (1) The prologue which gives the context and significance of the matter under review; (2) Maxims provide the precedence already set forth (i.e., the rules for good speech, Ma'atian ethics, and the treatment for those who are in violation of these tenets.) Maxims give directions for relationship with higher authorities, relations with peers, and relations with the general public. (3) The epilogue emphasizes through many examples the wisdom of the educational process, showing the importance of listening, obedience, self-control and silence, measured speech, Ma'at, and one's divinity and its connection between the earthly role and God (Carruthers, 1995, p. 126).

Relations with the General Public

Of course, there are many maxims set forth for government officials, but only one will be addressed here. The Kemetic people recognized that the power government officials had was ingrained with the potential for problems; hence, those entering public service must be committed to "right doing." In this instance, instructions for leadership were very deliberately focused on Ma'at. For example, in Carruthers's translation, Maxim 4 contains a scenario that involves a high official and a troublemaker who is a poor person. The instructions admonish the official not to be oppressive against the troublemaker because he is weak, but his punishment comes through the reprisal of the judges. In other words, the heavy-handedness of the one in power is not necessary against the weak and ordinary offender, since the law of enforcement will punish the transgressor. This maxim sets the example for other relationships between government officials and ordinary people. The troublemaker or the petitioner absolutely had the course for appeal as well (Carruthers, 1995, p. 127).

Essentially, in ancient Kemet, order, justice, balance, and virtue were at all times foremost in the instructions of the student and the people of the general populace. The student can be a pharaoh, any dignitary, and common folk. It was Ma'at, the balance of all things, that permeated every aspect of this culture.

Implications for Present-Day Classroom Instructions

It is no secret that the educational system is an abysmal failure for our young people across gender and race. Evidence of a failed educational system is manifested in the poor reading scores nationwide and the correlation between low reading scores and the incarcerated Black male, who is disproportionately placed into the prison industrial complex. A high incarceration rate in any society is a direct reflection of poverty, hopelessness, self-hatred, and miseducation. That students from the U.S. school system find themselves at the bottom of the list of advanced countries in sciences, for example, is another reflection of a failed educational system. Thus, we are faced with a generation of people who have no moral and intellectual compass as well as a lack of substantive intellectual stature. A pedagogue should be concerned about the (mis)education and plight of all students. Given the sad academic state of the African-descended child, I am most perplexed and must therefore move to rectify this condition. The student is in the midst of the *Maafa* (Ani, 1994), which is a process that continuously strips the person of African descent of his or her spiritual, educational, and socialization process—cultural genocide. This process has completely denuded him or her of Ma'at. It is therefore relevant and urgent to return the African to the standard of behavior where speaking and doing right, Ma'at, become the vehicle for living in a just society. Too often, scholars and teachers assemble at conferences to discuss the crisis of our academic institutions, but after the "feel good" sessions, they return to their respective institutions to continue down the path that has no light to uplift the human spirit. The ancient architects have set the blueprint forth for us in the complex of Nile Valley culture. The doors of the twenty-first century are open; its time to take a deliberate look at the code of value and virtues unmatched by any ancient and modern culture anywhere. Most people in the profession of teaching and learning represent some of the best minds in this nation today. It is therefore our responsibility to mantle ourselves with the information for substantive change. Pedagogues can no longer nominally engage their students in schooling. They must cultivate learners/listeners and engage them in an educational process that synthesizes an education for governance and human harmony with nature and cosmos. This approach means going beyond the conventional limited boundaries of Western thought of selfish, materialistic, and punitive behaviors.

Some immediate mechanisms must be implemented to change a course of further disintegration of our education system. Here is a short proposal on this matter:

1. *Real democratic education.* The curriculum must reflect and address the specific concerns of all students, including African-descended students, especially as it relates to their political, cultural, and historical background.

2. *Pedagogical relevance.* The method used to teach students must be appropriate to their learning styles. For example, much of the research shows that students of African ancestry learn best through the "talk time approach," "hands-on, creative use of their home language, and the teachers' approximation and understanding of their students' culture."

3. *Academic excellence.* All disciplines must maintain the integrity of high academic standards.

4. *A return to a mastery of the Seven Liberal Arts*: Grammar, Arithmetic, Rhetoric and Dialect, Geometry, Astronomy, and Music.

5. *The moral character of the student must not be neglected; hence, cosmology, cosmogeny, a strong moral ethical foundation of doing good, speaking truth to power, and an all around spiritual development should be included in the curriculum. Self-development and skills development must complement each other.*

In this abbreviated probe, I have attempted to show that the people of the Nile Valley complex sought Ma'at as the moral compass to chart their way through long-lived and exemplary civilizations. The ancient African endeavored to be one and the same with Ma'at, the cosmic order. The challenge for the twenty-first-century person and the teacher, more specifically for our purpose, is to transform himself or herself by uniting with the Ma'atian order that advocates balance between human and cosmos, human and divine world, human and the state, human and society, and human to himself or herself. The role of the teacher is directly related to educating the new generation for governance. We are witnesses to a culture of disunity and a lack of wisdom in our classrooms. This observation can also be extended to all agencies in the culture at large. The central question that confronts us is: What must the concerned person do? Some of the outlines are illuminated in this short essay, which we can build upon in subsequent conversations. One immediate consideration for practitioners and scholars is to recast conventional rhetoric into its accurate historical continuum to reflect the Nile Valley complex and other indigenous African cultures.

Summary and Conclusion

This essay has particular relevance to the restoration of the African worldview for all those who have an interest in reshaping their fractured African consciousness. The Nile Valley cultural complex laid the foundations for all the major cultural institutions that followed in western Asia and early Greco-Roman cultures. The principle rhetoric of Ma'at, which permeated the fabric of all forms of education, for example, education for governance, was paramount in crystallizing the Nile Valley cultural complex that lasted for several millennia. Once we begin to rethink the old engagement of African unity with an inward and outward African focus, it is Ma'at that will replace the disorder and ignorance that have penetrated our cultural unity and continuity. Today, in this new century and millennium, our very survival depends on an educational system infused with a global African cultural content and an awareness of our Pan-African needs. Such an educational system must seriously take into consideration the physical and metaphysical aspects of the global African culture while viewing itself as a major part of world culture and not as an appendage. Undoubtedly, an educational system with a framework that engages the Ma'atian ethics can reform the African personality and that of all human beings. An educational system that allows for the expression of the creative genius and rhetoric of Tehuti, Ptahhotep, Amenomope, Frederick Douglass, David Walker, Marcus Garvey, W. E. B. Du Bois, Kwame Nkrumah, George Padmore, Edward Wilmont Blyden, Malcolm X, Martin Luther King Jr., Yaa Asantewaa, Fannie Lou Hamer, Sojourner Truth, Ida B. Wells, and the many others who articulated truth and righteousness of the human condition in the face of injustice and barbarity must be a critical consideration. However, the architects of this renewed system must not make the same mistakes of our present form of education that has many major failings. The most glaring failures are the compartmentalization of knowledge, Eurocentrism, colonization of information, and an education that is restricted to the recipient class of the intelligentsia. Those who do not belong to the privileged stratification lie outside the grace of the academy. In the reconstruction of rhetorics for a just society, education, social justice, equality, and an elevation of the human condition (the "know thyself" axiom), the learning process must include the entire cycle of life in all its dimensions. If a system built on truth, equality, balance, justice, reciprocity, and righteousness characterizes the culture to which we subscribe, people would not have to haplessly look for a sociopolitical leadership. Speaking truth, acting in a just way, listening, learning, hearing, and observing nature constitute the vehicles by which wisdom and truth are transmitted. Cultural communion has always been important for African people in which knowledge is transmitted through the medium of intergenerational communication. Let me grasp the final initiative here to recontextualize the core of the African axiology; it takes the entire community with its entire general cultural ambience (formal and informal) to help mold the stable and well-adjusted human being. The aforementioned formulation must continue to be the hallmark of a civilized humanity.

An added sage piece of wisdom from the African axiology coming out of the Nile Valley cultural complex of Kush, Kemet, Axum, Dinka, and inner Africa is appropriate: "I am because we are and because we are therefore I am" (John Mbiti, 1969). This statement constitutes one of the reasons why the Nile Valley complex and other African cultures lived in relative peace in advanced stages of society. It takes all of us to prepare the next generation for posterity, governance, and peace. Shemhotep!

Notes

1. Medew Netjar (God Speech) is the utterance of the gods in Kemetic thought that is pure and uncontaminated.

2. Medew Nefer (Good Speech) is the utterance of human beings; though powerful and creative, it can be misleading.

3. They exemplify balance, one of the principles of Ma'at.

7

Modeling Orality: African American Rhetorical Practices and the Teaching of Writing

Lena Ampadu

ENGLISH TEACHERS HAVE LONG BEEN ENGAGED IN THE SEARCH to find effective ways to improve their students' writing ability. From examining method to curriculum to the students themselves, they have grappled with this lingering pedagogical challenge (Bartholomae, 1987; Smit, 1994; Winterowd, 1994). My study responded anew to this effort to address this longstanding problem by focusing on improving students' writing using imitation of African American texts as linguistic models. What students imitated, however, were oral practices in writing, which many believe hinder the development of effective prose style or prevent students from being in control of their writing (Cook-Gumperz, 1993; Kolln, 1991). However, others highly value oral practices used in writing and maintain that it is natural for inexperienced writers to rely on the discourse rules with which they are familiar (those that have a basis in speech) to produce a piece of written discourse (Robinson, 1983; Welch, 1990). One language researcher, in fact, believes that the use of speech in writing may be "a positive and even rich contribution to the writing and social development of a writer" (Horowitz, 1995). Another popular composition researcher, Peter Elbow (1985), maintains that the best writing has voice or the life and rhythms of speech, and unless students are actively trained to translate speech into writing, they will write prose that is "dead, limp, and nominalized" (p. 291). Like Elbow, linguist Akua Duku Anokye (1997), strongly endorses the belief that oral language has qualities that can enhance writing (pp. 229–231). She argues that African Americans come from a lineage that values the oral tradition, evidence of which can be found among the values and linguistic practices of West African peoples (230). My study takes its inspiration from the kind of attitude that both Elbow and Anokye have professed.

This chapter examines the effects of using African American oral texts in teaching inexperienced writers to improve their persuasive writing style. This goal is in keeping with the objective of this volume in that it promotes texts, often overlooked as exemplars of literacy, as models for student writing. The view that I expound upon is that incorporating repetition schemes that are speechlike strategies into the persuasive writing assignments of college students facilitates their efforts at developing a clear, elegant writing style. Students, therefore, participated in an instructional unit in which they imitated repetition (anaphora, antithesis, parallelism, and chiasmus) to determine the effects of this imitation on their persuasive writing style. The primary question that formed the backdrop of this research follows: How does college students' participation in an instructional unit emphasizing the imitation of repetition (anaphora, antithesis, chiasmus, and parallelism) in selected African American texts shape the students' choices of repetition schemes in persuasive writing style in an introductory African American literature class?

Few studies exist that focus on the oral dimensions of language as they affect the teaching of writing to college students. Additionally, African American rhetorical practices have not been highlighted to teach literacy and writing skills to college students who are of varied racial/ethnic backgrounds. Most studies have focused mainly on the effect of such texts on only African American students (Balester, 1993; Fox, 1994; Lee, 1993; Redd, 1995). This study adds to the existing research investigating the role of the interrelationship between orally based and written language practices in writing (Chafe, 1993; Horowitz, 1995). Thus, it will explore the dynamic relationship between orality and literacy (Ong, 1982). Finally, it will add to the body of research and scholarship melding Western classical rhetoric and African American rhetoric to teach writing (Logan, 1996; Moss, 1994; Redd, 1995).

Why Use African American Texts as Models?

Many style textbooks often quote examples from American speeches to illustrate effective repetition, with some of the most frequent examples being famous lines from speeches by John F. Kennedy and Abraham Lincoln (Corbett & Connors, 1998). What is not always noted is that African American texts are exemplars of audience-involving texts, which include highly orally based forms, such as letters and speeches. Moreover, many prominent African American writers and orators have been influenced by the oral tradition, an important dimension of African American rhetoric, rooted in the culture of African Americans (Abrahams, 1976; Asante, 1987; Smitherman, 1977/1986). Beginning with Maria Stewart's groundbreaking "Lecture Delivered at the Franklin Hall" (1832/1995) and including Dr. Martin Luther King's classic "Letter from Birmingham Jail," (1963/1997) one can find evidence of this rich rhetorical tradition. These texts provide fertile ground for the study of repetition and provide rich examples of a lively, elegant style created in part by sentences that create complexity of thought and ideas through vivid language and balanced, rhythmical sentences filled with anaphora, antithesis, parallelism, and chiasmus. This style has features of Black preacher rhetoric with its many Biblical allusions and call-response created by a series of rhetorical questions, anaphoric phrases, and parallel listings. These devices help to make arguments more powerful by using such devices as the Black jeremiad, which heightens the pathetic appeal of one's writing, and the series of rhetorical questions, which effect a call-response style that highly engages the audience, as well as parallel listings, which dramatize the writing and liken the discourse to that of the Black preacher.

In fact, one scholar has argued that the speeches of nineteenth-century African American women orators, especially those of Frances E. W. Harper, should be employed as a means of teaching writing to college students because they exemplify excellent rhetorical and stylistic features (Logan, 1996; also see chapter 1). African American texts should no longer be associated mainly with a history and tradition of illiteracy but should move to the fore of the writing classroom and exercise some influence on the writing and literacy skills of college students, regardless of their racial and ethnic backgrounds.

Why Should We Imitate Schemes of Repetition?

Before answering the question posed in the aforementioned subhead, I will define *repetition*. As used in this study, it refers to an involvement strategy in which a word, phrase, or larger unit is used more than once to create meaning through strategies based on sound (Tannen, 1994). It functions to communicate ideas and move audiences. For the purposes of this study, repetition is created solely by the schemes of repetition identified in classical Greek rhetoric as anaphora, antithesis, chiasmus, and parallelism. However, repetition has a long-standing tradition in

African American rhetorical practices, since its use is far more prevalent in societies in which prime importance is attached to the spoken word (Tomlin, 1999). Carol Tomlin, a rhetorical scholar who has studied mostly Black British rhetorical practices by comparing them with similar African American practices, has identified different forms of repetition in a variety of domains, including political speeches, songs, sermons, and informal conversations (1999, p. 148). Noted intellectual Henry Louis Gates Jr. named repetition as one of the master verbal tropes in Black rhetoric (1988, p. xxiv).

Texts that include repetition allow the audience to participate because repetition evokes a certain sense of sound; its musical, flavorful rhythms deeply involve the audience by triggering emotions (Tannen, 1994), effecting the same kind of rhythmic impact that poetry has on its listeners, the same kind of impact that excites a cultural or ethnic group to anger or ecstasy at the sound of a beating drum (Miles, Bertonasco, & Karns, 1991), or the same kind of influence that arouses emotions among Black religious audiences (Pipes, 1951/1992). Since effective writing considers audience, repetition is a logical strategy to use to help writers create engaging discourse.

In Afrocentric terms, Stewart used *Nommo* (Smith, 1972), the potency of the word; consequently, like the Black preacher of old, she was able to move and fascinate audiences through her abundant use of one type of repetition, known as anaphora. This device successfully assists in involving the audience in discourse through its repetition of initial words in successive phrases or clauses. Common in speeches, it can heighten the dramatic appeal of the oral text. It can heighten the dramatic appeal of the written text, as well.

Similarly, *chiasmus,* repetition in which word order is reversed in consecutive clauses, can, as one sociolinguist observes, significantly involve the audience in oral discourse (Tannen, 1994). (Chiasmus is sometimes referred to as antimetabole, when repetition of words occurs [Corbett & Connors, 1998]). Not only does repetition create engaging discourse but it also facilitates an eloquent style of writing. In Western rhetorical theory, the practice of cultivating such a style can be traced to Gorgias, who placed special emphasis on antithesis, the repetition of contrasting words, phrases, or clauses (Corbett & Connors, 1998), and parallelism, the repetition of similar grammatical structures (Strunk & White, 1979; Corbett & Connors, 1998). Continuing the practice of Gorgias and other early rhetoricians, many contemporary prose stylists take the following stance on the role of repetition in developing writing style: parallelism, when used effectively, is one of the principal means by which writers can achieve eloquence, largely because of its powerful repetition and because of its symmetry and balance (Miles et al., 1991).

Repetition is also one of the ways that writers produce clear, coherent writing (Miles et al., 1991; J. M. Williams, 1997). Parallelism, for example, displays logical, orderly sentences. When Frederick Douglass (1852/1997b) uses this string of parallel words and phrases in his "What to the Slave Is the Fourth of July?" he shows that he gave careful thought to producing his writing:

> To him, your celebration is a sham; your boasted liberty, an unholy license; your national greatness, swelling vanity; your sounds of rejoicing are empty and heartless; your denunciations of tyrants, brass fronted impudence; your shouts of liberty and equality, hollow mockery; your prayers and hymns, your sermons and thanksgivings, with all your religious parade, and solemnity, are, to him, mere bombast, fraud, deception, impiety, and hypocrisy. (p. 388)

Writers who create these kinds of sentences with parallel elements demonstrate that they have taken the time to create balanced, orderly sentences achieved through the repetition of words and phrases. These types of sentences contribute to a style of writing that elicits reader attention by using a certain amount of balance and order that, as Mary P. Hiatt (1975) suggests, provides examples of discourse that are not left to chance—they do not "just happen" (p. 63). An elegant, clear writing style has sentences that are symmetrical because they have been well planned.

Finally, writers who create an elegant, clear style help to build their ethos or character. Such credibility was especially important to orators who had to overcome constraints of race, gender, or both, as some of the speakers in this study had to do. If their style could build their ethos and morality, then they were more successful with their audiences. Writers who exercise their options by creating balanced, rhythmical sentences help to establish themselves as mature, sophisticated, and credible writers.

Why Should We Use Imitation to Teach Writing?

Should writers be taught to deliberately imitate the style of other writers? Ancient Western rhetoricians from Cicero to St. Augustine have argued for integrating this training into the teaching of writing. A firm believer in imitating models, Cicero (1990 version) insisted that the most effective method for using models was to allow students to copy only those models with exemplary features.

Even today, the prose models approach to the teaching of writing has much support. Evidence is found in the many literary and rhetorical works that have included favorable testimony by established writers on the imitation of style. For example, *Classical Rhetoric for the Modern Student* (Corbett & Connors, 1998) included testimony from diverse writers, including Malcolm X, Benjamin Franklin, and Somerset Maugham, attesting to the advantages of copying a writer's style to improve their writing. In his *Narrative,* Frederick Douglass (1845/1997a) maintained that he was able to learn the techniques of writing by studying and modeling the rhetorical strategies found in *The Columbian Orator.*

Instructional models advocating the teaching of style as worthy of imitation abound in rhetorical and composition pedagogy textbooks and in textbooks focusing exclusively on the teaching of style. However, these methods and models are limited because they rely on either the personal opinions of the writers or pedagogical techniques that have not been tested through empirical means.

Yet other educational practitioners oppose using imitation as a means to teach writing. Donald Murray (1985) believed that since imitation distances the students from their own writing problems, it is largely inadequate as a pedagogical method for today's society. Echoing this idea that models are inadequate tools for teaching writing was noted composition scholar James Moffett (1983), who had observed the relationship of models to the student's own writing. Moffett pointed out, "Models don't help writing and merely intimidate some students by implying a kind of competition in which they are bound to lose" (p. 108). Mina Shaughnessy (1977) maintained in her now classic text *Errors and Expectations* that models distract writers from a consciousness of their own writing process.

Many opponents thought that it was neither reasonable nor desirable to have students imitate the styles of older, established writers because their works were not models of good contemporary prose and were, therefore, inappropriate for today's students (Farmer, 1991). In addition to the theoretical critics, empirical researchers like George Hillocks (1986) seem to agree that modeling or imitation has little effect on writing improvement.

After examining the arguments both for and against using imitation to teach writing, I conclude that there are enough convincing reasons to continue to use it to teach writing: not only does it provide inexperienced writers with much needed models for "good writing" but it has been successfully used by writers through the ages. Also, since there exists only a paucity of empirical data on the use of models to teach writing, no decisive argument for rejecting the use of models can be made. This study, then, makes an important contribution to the literature of research studies examining imitation to teach writing. By focusing on the oral dimensions of language, it does something that few other studies on imitation have done.

The Theoretical Basis for Teaching Writing Using Imitation

Does theory support using imitation to teach writing? Almost every pedagogy is informed by theory; therefore, this study is no exception. The warrants for consideration of imitation in writing pedagogy are found in Vygotskian thought. Lev Vygotsky (1986) advocates "intelligent, conscious imitation" as distinct from "automatic copying" in the teaching of writing (p. 95). Furthermore, Vygotsky (1986) considers imitation to be a social activity in which one learns in the presence of another, such as a more experienced teacher or peer, who guides the pupil to a higher level of development by giving him or her the opportunity to solve problems through imitation. One should therefore use imitation to teach writing because the theoretical concepts maintain that imitation grounded in social conception of imitation is essential to teaching language.

Although Eurocentric thought and study provide insights into the teaching of writing, much can be gleaned from an Afrocentric paradigm, based in the oral culture of African Americans, to assist students in producing written discourse that is stylistically rich and persuasive. In other words, African ideals, values, culture, history, traditions, and worldview must inform any literary, artistic creations, and analyses (Asante, 1987, p. 5). With such a framework in mind, Keith Gilyard (introduction), a key African American rhetorical scholar, has noted that the study of Black pulpit oratory represents an essential component of rhetorical study. The Black church, the primary vehicle for the delivery of such rhetoric, is identified in most published studies as one of the main settings for speech interactions in the Black community (Smitherman, 1977/1986; Tomlin, 1999; Gilyard, this volume). The Afrocentric paradigm in this study, therefore, encouraged the imitation of texts emphasizing the use of Nommo (A. Smith, 1972), with its emphasis on the importance of the word and religious discourse, especially that emulating the Black sermonic tradition. As a way of distinguishing Black rhetoric from persuasive discourse identified in Eurocentric terms, Ronald Jackson (1995) has proposed an Afrocentric model in which Nommo underscores the dynamism of Black rhetoric (p. 154).

Other distinguishing characteristics of this type of Afrocentric framework, especially in religious rhetoric, consists of the Black jeremiad, a rhetorical device, used by Blacks to warn Whites of the impending doom and wrath of God that they would suffer for having participated in American slavery (Moses, 1982). The relationship between speaker and audience signifies another type of distinctive dimension of Black rhetoric. One such example is call-response, in which the audience constantly participates by responding to the speaker, and in most cases the audience members act as coproducers of the text or discourse (Mitchell, 1970; Smitherman, 1977/1986). Indeed, in the African world, an understanding of both the religious and the spiritual is an integral part of the noetic process. Finally, since this study emphasizes repetition, a sound-based practice, it employs a category identified by Smitherman (1977/1986) as tonal semantics, the use of voice rhythm and vocal inflection to convey meaning. This emphasis on sound, which bears a direct relationship to African-based knowledge, can be found in many forms of Black creative discourse (Richardson, chapter 8, this volume).

With this culturally based outlook in mind, several researchers have concluded that students from an African American Vernacular English (AAVE) background write discourse that is influenced by the Black religious tradition (Noonan-Wagner, 1981; Visor, 1987). This theoretical framework laid the groundwork for the participants in this study to enhance their abilities as word artisans who preserve the importance of orality and, like the orators of ancient Greece and Africa, command respect and authority by exploiting the oral to express themselves in writing by emulating these orators of old.

Methods and Procedures

The sample population consisted of thirty-four college students in one section of the class Survey of African American Literature offered during a sixteen-week semester at a mid-Atlantic university, where the student population is predominantly White. Approximately 86 percent of the students enrolled in the course were European American, while 14 percent were African American. Papers were collected from everyone in the class; however, six participants were chosen, using purposeful sampling methods, to provide cases that would likely yield "information-rich" data (Gall, Borg, & Gall, 1996, p. 218). The participants' papers were randomly chosen from among the best twenty papers, that is, those that clearly and lucidly made their points, were coherent, and well organized and from among those writers that indicated, based on the initial questionnaire (Ampadu, 1999), that they had not significantly used stylistic imitation before enrolling in the class.

To answer the primary research question, I compared the writing samples collected before instruction with those collected after instruction to determine not only the quality and quantity of repetition schemes present in each writing sample but also the way the repetition schemes helped to influence human thought and actions. For both writing samples, two raters counted the frequency of and reported the quality of the repetition schemes as *very effective, effective,* or *not effective* based on a quality rating scale (see appendix C, Ampadu, 1999). Then, I, along with two observers, analyzed their home assignments to determine if they were able to locate examples of the types of repetition schemes in their readings, analyze them, and write an imitation of the scheme. Next, two other instructors and I observed their group presentations to determine if they were able to locate and analyze examples of the types of repetition schemes in Douglass's (1852/1997) "Fourth of July" speech. We recorded our observations using the guidelines on the observation form (see appendix J, Ampadu, 1999).

During this instructional unit, students produced three writing samples in class. They were allowed one hour to produce each sample. Writing Sample A was written before the actual instruction began. Writing Sample B was given at the end of the third week of instruction, and Writing Sample C was given at the end of the fourth week of instruction.

Details of each writing sample follow. For Writing Sample A, students wrote a short speech, two to three pages (blue book length), by imitating the language/stylistic choices of an excerpt of Henry Highland Garnet's (1848/1997) speech "An Address to the Slaves in the United States of America." The students' speeches addressed an audience in which a large number of people were unfriendly and hostile to many of the ideas being proposed. Frequently, these audiences were composed of hecklers whom the clergy and the press often incited to anger (Lipscomb, 1995). Therefore, the speeches had to be very persuasive and convincing. In writing their speeches, students were directed to pay careful attention to grammar and style.

For Writing Sample B, students produced a speech arguing against the enslavement of women, after studying model speeches and speechlike texts that liberally used repetition strategies. These speeches included

Frederick Douglass's (1852/1997) "What to the Slave Is the Fourth of July?"; Maria Stewart's (1832/1995) "An Address Delivered Before the Afric-American Female Intelligence Society of Boston"; and Sojourner Truth's (1878/1997) "Ain't I a Woman?" In addition, they closely studied the repetition strategies of Frederick Douglass's (1845/1997) *Narrative of the Life of Frederick Douglass* and David Walker's (1829/1997) *Appeal,* a tract. Though the enslavement of any human being is unacceptable, students were asked to argue against the enslavement of women because launching such an argument would allow them to focus intensely on one aspect of slavery they had studied in some of the model texts. "Arn't I a Woman?" by Truth (1878/1997) elevated the status of woman by pointing to her as the mother of Christ and argued for the equality of women. By having students write about topics similar to those in the model texts in the instructional unit, I had hoped that students would have more confidence in their ability to imitate these texts since they (the students) would be familiar with the kinds of arguments made for and against the enslavement of women.

For Writing Sample C, students wrote an editorial letter responding to Barbara Jordan's (1976), "Who Then Will Speak for the Common Good?" This writing was done at the end of the fourth week and was the final assessment of their writing. Unlike those of previous writings, the topics for this writing were more contemporary, because students were directed to write using a contemporary perspective when addressing the social problems Jordan mentioned in her speech. Students wrote to a real audience because they wrote to the editors of the *Sun,* intending to have their letters published for the readers of this newspaper.

To incorporate multiple perspectives into the reporting of the research, the researcher collected the data using triangulation; therefore, data was collected through observation, content analysis forms, and writing samples.

Observation was used to determine whether students could identify the various repetition schemes in their reading and could write their own imitations of the various repetition schemes based on the models. Three people acted as observers—the researcher and two other veteran English instructors. All observers recorded their impressions in a journal, as well as on an observation form that the researcher designed (see appendix J, Ampadu, 1999). All observers took careful notes since the use of multiple observers allowed for them to "cross-check each other's finding and eliminate inaccurate interpretations" (Gall et al., 1996, p. 345).

The researcher and two other observers were present during the class sessions, when the concept of repetition was first introduced; when the students participated in group discussions and reported on their analysis of the selected African American texts used in this study as models for repetition; when students discussed their homework; and when students orally presented their group reports. The third observer listened to audiocassette recordings of the class session, because she was unable to attend the class session. To increase the validity of the study, all observers had been trained as to what kinds of information to observe by listening to audiotaped class sessions recorded during the pilot study.

Analysis of Writing Samples. Students' writing samples were analyzed by two raters using content analysis to locate the four examples of repetition identified by Joseph Williams (1997) as characteristic of an elegant style: antithesis, anaphora, chiasmus, and parallelism. Raters first identified the frequency of the repetition schemes in the writing samples and then evaluated the quality of each of the schemes. Reliabilities for the raters' scores, determined by the Pearson product moment raw score method for writing samples, was highly significant. They reached .98 for the first set of samples, .90 for the second set, and .91 for the third set.

In order to increase the reliability and validity of the writing samples, the researcher carefully designed the exercises in the three writing samples so that they paralleled each other in terms of oral and written directions, time allotted for completion, writing tasks, and reading materials needed to complete each writing task. The directions and tasks used in the writing sample were tested for clarity in a pilot study. Also, principles of writing from current research were incorporated into the design of the writing samples. For example, in one of the writing samples, students were asked to write an editorial letter to a major newspaper. Writing such a sample addresses contemporary composition theory that maintains students who write for assigned audiences, whether they be real or imaginary, produced better quality papers, increased students' motivation, and improved the persuasiveness of some student writing (Flower & Hayes, 1980; Redd-Boyd & Slater, 1989).

Six participants wrote speeches, but a sampling of the types of repetition schemes that one participant produced appears below:

> Participant E—For Writing Sample A, Participant E has written a speech entitled, "In Due Time," whose premise is that Africans will be vindicated for having been treated unjustly as a result of being enslaved when the time is ripe. (See speech below.)

In Due Time

What a deplorable state of being have Africans, brought to American, been placed in! We have been infiltrated in our homeland by outsiders and captured. However, perhaps the worst part of the whole thing is that our own people are the ones who have sold us into this condition. Jealously, envy, greed, power, and material goods have been the driving forces behind our enslavement. Would you sell your brother, sister, or even your own mother for some guns and dried fish? Conversely, would you offer me items of value for the lives of my family or even my own life?

Surely, evil is the driving force behind slavery, the enslavers, and the slave masters. However, to make this whole conspiracy believable and to make it sound like a good thing, those involved mix in some goodness by introducing us to Christianity. Now there is a twist to the whole situation! They will take a line from the Bible that may say something like slaves are to be humble servants to their masters, and they will use this line to keep slaves in check. What they won't tell them is a line like, "the first shall be last and the last shall be first." As such we remain blind to the fact that salvation shall be upon us in due time.

Henry Highland Garnet speaks of what God requires of us in his "Address to the Slaves of the United States of America." He speaks of how we are to love God and our neighbors as ourselves as well as to follow the commandments. I believe he is addressing this to slaves in that despite the condition they are in, they can still live their lives according to god's will. However, this can also be addressed to slave masters in that they are contradicting their words with their actions.

To the slaves of the United States of America—"The first shall be last, and the last shall be first." In due time!

The speech begins by calling attention to the slaves' plight that occurred as a result of the avarice of Africans themselves. This participant has written examples of each type of repetition scheme: one example of anaphora, one of antithesis, one of chiasmus, and three of parallelism. In addition, the student clearly participates in the African American rhetorical tradition with his use of rhetoric that incites and calls for audience participation. Just as Denmark Vessey and Nat Turner had been known to incite their followers with quotations from the Bible (Moses, 1990, p. 113), this writer forges a link to this tradition "whereby God always sided with oppressed peoples" (Moses, 1990, p. 113) by arguing that God will punish the enslavers for having been a part of the evil system called slavery.

The first instance of parallelism is used in the introductory section of the speech, "Jealousy, envy, greed, power, and material goods have been the driving forces behind our enslavement." This listing paints the selfish motives of the enslavers, as well as the Africans who sold their fellow men and women into slavery. This series is followed by a rhetorical question which makes an emotional appeal to the audience by including a series of relatives, "Would you sell your brother, sister, or even your own mother for some guns and dried fish?" This listing parallels Garnet's parallel list of relatives. Again, the device of parallelism highlights the consequences of the role of Africans as participants in the slave trade by listing each relative affected by this heinous behavior.

In the next sentence, the author once again uses parallelism to illustrate his point: "Surely, evil is the force behind slavery, the enslavers, and the slave masters." In this list, he carefully informs his audience of the evil nature of the institution of slavery by using parallel words that equate the roles of each person involved with slavery. The author then uses anaphora to explain how the slave masters used biblical scripture to justify enslaving Africans, "They will take a line from the Bible that may say something like slaves are to be humble servants to their masters, and they will use this line to keep slaves in check." The device of anaphora serves to emphasize the actions used by these evildoers to justify slavery.

The writer then uses antithesis to contrast "what they won't tell" with what "they will tell." Finally, the writer uses chiasmus to conclude his paper, though not an original one: "The first shall be last, and the last shall be first." In using this biblical quote, he builds his ethos and nicely establishes a crescendo for his conclusion by reiterating the theme of the speech: that no longer shall Africans continue to be last, but their lowly circumstances will be reversed in due time. By establishing this crescendo, the writer uses Nommo, where he gains attention, inspires, and excites his audience. Again, the strong use of biblical allusion clearly signals participation in the Black sermonic tradition. Overall, the author's use of rhetorical schemes and language skillfully assists in creating a persuasive message and tone.

After instruction, this participant in Writing Sample B produced a speech entitled, ". . . But What of the Woman? Freedom for Woman, as

Told by a Man," which begins its argument by stating the privileges that the writer has enjoyed as a free Black man and arguing that woman should partake of the same privileges because she has played a prominent role in helping to develop man socially, intellectually, and physically (See speech below.) The title places the speech squarely in the African American oral tradition with its use of the words "As told by," reminiscent of the "As told to" tradition associated with the slave narratives.

> ### . . . But What of the Woman? Freedom for Woman, as Told by a Man
>
> I have fought for my freedom with words, with violence, and with spirit. Many of my fellow men have died fighting to gain for me what should already have been mine to claim . . . freedom. I know what it is to have life taken from me and to feel the joy of having life renewed; you know what it is to take life and to witness its return while seeing the error of your ways.
>
> I stand before you this day a free man, but what of the woman? For two score and two years I have been in this so-called land of the free, and women have remained at the backbone of my existence here. They have nurtured me, scolded me, and placed me in royal regard. I would not have the intellect nor the ability to write this essay to you today had it not been for women.
>
> Surely, you enslavers have made a grave mistake by granting freedom to myself and my brethren. For if my mother, my wife, my sisters, and my daughters do not receive the same freedom I have received, the same joy I have felt, the same breath of life I have breathed, then vengeance shall open her bloody red eyes and extend her wings of darkness upon you. For the only thing worse than a man's revenge is a woman's scorn.

The first sentence states bluntly, using parallel phrases, "I have fought for my freedom with words, with violence, and with spirit." By repeating *with* before each word in the series of parallel phrases, the author convinces the audience of the intensity of his struggle. It is followed by antithetical clauses that contrast the experiences of a former male slave who has not always enjoyed the benefit of liberty with those of White males who have stripped others of their liberties: "I know what it is to have life taken from me and to feel the joy of having life renewed; you know what it is to take life and to witness its return while seeing the error of your ways." The writer points to the positive contributions of women to others by listing them in the following statement, "They have nurtured me, scolded me, and placed me in royal regard." This parallel listing gives equal weight to the actions in which women have engaged to assist men in their development as human beings.

He then follows this statement with a series of parallel words and phrases that constitute a Black jeremiad, a warning to Whites that they will pay for the sins of slavery: "For if my mother, my wife, my sisters, and my daughters do not receive the same freedom I have received, the same joy I have felt, the same breath of life I have breathed, then vengeance shall open her bloody red eyes and extend her wings of darkness upon you." His repeated use of *same* in each preceding phrase heightens the drama of the passage, enhanced by listing each person equally affected by the evil institution. The writer concludes forcefully by rendering the Black woman as one whom the audience should fear more than the Black man with the antithetical statement, "For the only thing worse than a man's revenge is a woman's scorn." His use of oratory is unmistakably in the Black preaching tradition, in which rhythm heightens the emotional appeal (Pipes, 1951/1992). The speaker enlivens the presentation by using techniques based in sound culture. The rhythmic use of *same* creates a dramatic effect much like that described as tonal semantics (Smitherman, 1977/1986). In Writing Sample B, the writer uses five instances of parallelism and two instances of antithesis, two of which were judged effective. Taken together, the participants have produced several examples of anaphora, antithesis, and parallelism in both Writing samples A and B, as shown in table 7.1.

The total number of repetition schemes in each model text was then used to calculate the percentage of repetition schemes that each student

Table 7.1. Total Number of Repetition Schemes for All Participants

	Writing Sample A Frequency	Writing Sample B Frequency
Anaphora	8	9
Antithesis	8	3
Chiasmus	1	0
Parallelism	9	15
Total	26	27

$n = 6$

produced in Writing Sample A in comparison to the total number of schemes found in each model text. As shown in table 7.2, the three-hundred-word sample taken from Garnet's speech, which was the model text for Writing Sample A, included one example of anaphora, one example of antithesis, one example of parallelism, and no examples of chiasmus. In comparison to the total number of repetition schemes in the model text, the repetition schemes in participants' Writing Sample A had fairly low percentages of each scheme, as indicated in table 7.2. Further results showed that the highest percentages students produced were for anaphora and antithesis. The lowest percentage was for parallelism.

Table 7.2. Percentage of Repetition Schemes Participants Produced in Writing Sample A

	Total in Model	Percentage Produced
Anaphora	1	12.5
Antithesis	1	12.5
Chiasmus	0	0
Parallelism	1	11.1

Conclusions and Discussion

In this section, I summarize the results in relation to the two research questions proffered. To answer these questions, I reported the number of times the students used the schemes of repetition in three writing assignments, the percentage of schemes they produced, and the quality of the schemes as determined by the raters.

I compared the two writing samples, Writing Sample A and B, and found that overall, students produced a higher percentage of repetition schemes based on the total number of repetition schemes in the model texts for each category. Students produced the same percentage of examples of chiasmus as that produced in Writing Sample A. Most of the schemes produced were effectively written.

When comparing the results of Writing Sample C with those of Writing Sample A, I found that the number of repetition schemes produced for Writing Sample C was fewer. The percentage of anaphora produced in Writing Sample C was seventy-two times that produced in Writing Sample A. The percentage of antithesis produced was three times that produced in Writing Sample A. There was no change in the percentage of chiasmus. Most of the schemes of repetition were effectively written, some exhibiting freshness and originality. These findings seem to suggest results contrary to what critics of using models purport. Lindemann (1995) maintained that the style of models was too sophisticated for students to copy and that length interfered with the students' ability to imitate the models. Instead, the results appear to lend some support to the notion espoused by advocates of imitation from Cicero (1990 version) to Tate (1993), who believed that using models helps writers learn what good writing is and that it promotes eloquence.

Students were able to benefit from instruction emphasizing three of the schemes of repetition: anaphora, antithesis, and parallelism. Thus, it appears that though students became knowledgeable of chiasmus through instruction, the instruction had little effect on the students' ability to incorporate this scheme of repetition in their persuasive writing style.

The one example of chiasmus, "and the first shall be last, and the last shall be first," was an example of a commonplace from biblical literature. The student in this study, like the students in Redd's study (1995), wrote this chiasmus, relying not on models but on commonplaces. Redd's students, who were enrolled in an historically Black university wrote commonplaces peculiar to African American culture, whereas the student in this study conducted at a predominantly White university wrote one from a more widely shared culture. Writing this commonplace exhibits students' participation in the sharing of group values passed down through religious discourse in the oral tradition of African Americans. Its use also helps to effect call-response by effecting a total identification of the audience with this passage. One could imagine hearing the audience respond with a "Yes" or "Amen." Since the one scheme of chiasmus was produced in the pretest before instruction, it appears to suggest that students' choices of repetition schemes can sometimes be influenced by factors outside of the instructional unit.

One finding was that parallelism in the postinstructional writing sample (Sample B) increased by five times the number in the preinstructional writing sample (Sample A), where $n = 6$. Another finding illustrated that 86.6 percent of the schemes of parallelism the students produced were effective. This effectiveness suggests that students were able to successfully produce sentences that illustrate clear, elegant writing by using balanced, rhythmical sentences using the criteria for effective style that they studied in the instructional unit.

Most students were able to imitate effectively by either closely imitating a passage of the texts being studied or by imitating the scheme. Some were able to recall stylistic techniques from the model texts without the aid of the text when writing their speeches. When producing Writing Sample A, participants most commonly imitated the parallel list that focused on family members. Given that this kind of list was first presented in Garnet's speech, the model for Writing Sample A that was given before instruction, it appears that students remembered this listing and were able to produce it in writing Sample B after the instructional unit. Thus, five out of six of the students in the sample of six (83 percent) used parallel listing in Writing Sample A, whereas only three of the students (50 percent) used it in Writing Sample B. This finding is consistent with Hiatt's (1975) research and seems to lend support to the idea that if parallelism is written artfully it can be an indicator of style. Also, the fact that students appear to remember the parallel listing from a model given before instruction shows that students' choices of schemes of repetition can sometimes be directly influenced by those presented as part of the research study, but not as part of the instructional unit. Thus, the effectiveness of an instructional unit can be enhanced by factors that are outside of the actual instruction in the instructional unit, such as a pretest.

An additional measure of quality used was that of rhetorical and stylistic analysis. As noted in the previous analysis of participants' writing samples, many of the schemes were rhetorically effective when evaluated within the context of the writing assignment. A close analysis of Writing Samples A, B, and C revealed that the writers were able to use the schemes effectively to convey appropriate meanings. For example, parallelism was used to express thoughts in a balanced, orderly manner. Antithesis was used effectively to convey contraries. Anaphora was used effectively to emphasize ideas. Since there were no instances of chiasmus after instruction, its use could not be evaluated.

Many of the schemes of repetition produced in the writing samples exhibited freshness and originality. This finding is consistent with the one in a study by Phelps and Mano (1986), in which the student was able to create fresh forms after studying original models. It also seems to lend support to Vygotsky's version (1986) of imitation, which maintains that imitation should be done intelligently and not mindlessly and automatically. Students in this instructional plan were encouraged to imitate in a careful, intelligent fashion.

Students produced more schemes of repetition after using models when writing speeches as opposed to writing editorial letters, even though the letters had some of the qualities of speech. Therefore, it appears that when the goal of a writing assignment is the creation of a more direct oral text, such as a speech, as opposed to an editorial letter, writers produced more qualities associated with clarity and elegance. This study then appears to offer some support for pedagogy emphasizing those models from the African American tradition, primarily the speeches used in the instructional unit in this study. Overall, it appears that instruction in the imitation of repetition may in fact encourage participants to choose to use more elements of repetition in the persuasive writing style when they use speeches as model texts to write a speech.

One thing that writers must bear in mind is that merely including schemes of repetition in one's writing does not ensure a persuasive writing style, but using them increases the likelihood of such. Although schemes of repetition can improve the rhetorical import and effectiveness of writing, they should be used with skill and variety to effect a style that is appropriate to the writing situation and context. Since this study was concerned with composing antislavery speeches and editorial letters, the mastery of schemes of repetition as a way of improving one's writing style should not be confined to these specific genres. Certainly, using these schemes should help enliven the prose style of varied prose essays and narratives. Imitation, as advocated in this study, is only one of the many ways through which a writer may acquire an effective prose style (Corbett & Connors, 1998).

When crafting these speeches, writers participate in a rhetorical tradition of African Americans grounded in a dynamic oral culture with strategies that help the rhetor to create messages spontaneously, to captivate audiences and allow the audience to participate in creating effective discourse, and to use this type of rhetoric to critique society and argue for effecting social change.

8

Coming from the Heart: African American Students, Literacy Stories, and Rhetorical Education

Elaine B. Richardson

WHILE ONE OF THE GOALS OF THE STUDY PRESENTED HERE WAS to make visible vernacular discourse/rhetorical patterns and strategies in students' texts, the scope of identified strategies and policies is broader. Extending the research tradition interested in exploring vernacular discourses and literacies in relation to school discourses and literacies, this essay focuses attention on the academic personas acquired by two African American students. Exploring issues surrounding Black students' acquisition of school and rhetorical personas may help us to understand how to help them acquire critical stances that will help them participate more meaningfully in official sites providing rhetorical education. Although it is a fact that many people of African ancestry do not identify with African American culture, hardly any of us can escape the aura of race and class issues since they are interwoven into the cultural fabric of our society.

Background

Freedom through literacy has been an important trope in stories about literacy acquisition for African Americans. These complex stories revolve around issues of dominance, suppression, economics, culture, racism, freedom, equality, and justice. As Valerie Smith (1987) notes, this narrative runs throughout the experience of many African Americans. Literacy, in and of itself, helped to develop and organize the thoughts of Frederick Douglass, Richard Wright, Maya Angelou, Malcolm X, and others; however, it was the application of literacy in its expanded uses and senses that helped these great Americans to create new stories about their lives, by inventing lives for themselves and making life better for others.

In fact, literacy stories permeate the history of Black people in the twentieth century. In the enslavement era, those stories concerned laws against Africans learning to read and write, and they were transmitted by word of mouth and through enslavement narratives. During Reconstruction and Jim Crow eras, stories reflected how literacy was used as a gatekeeping function, for example, how literacy tests operated to deny African Americans the right to vote. The lives of Booker T. Washington and W. E. B. Du Bois have come to symbolize two dominant stories about African American literacy during the twentieth century: Washington's narrative focused on helping Black folks develop literacy skills necessary for them to function within the roles established for them by White society, whereas Du Bois's story proposed that a "talented tenth" be academically educated to lead Black people to political, cultural, economic, and social freedom. This education would not limit the possibilities of what Blacks could do or become and would rival the education received by the most privileged White Americans. Another important theme circulating in various stories about literacy in American culture is reflected in a well-known childhood Black folk rhyme that sums up a truth that critical race theorists and others are paid great sums to stretch out into lengthy texts and speeches:

> If you black, get back
> if you brown, stick around
> if you yellow, you mellow
> if you white, you right

This rhyme illustrates the mostly unwritten rule: the closer you and your ideology are to White supremacist ideals, the better your chances of assimilating into mainstream White middle-class society. Most Black people living in any era know that story. The ideologies of White supremacy clearly resonate through these earlier literacy narratives and are still a major motif in stories about literacy education in our classrooms today. In contemporary times, though, the visibility of White supremacist ideologies is, ironically, at once the backbone and the distant background in literacy education. Let us explore some of these insidiously visible, yet obscured, stories.

This one comes from many scholars who identify African American culture as a subculture of American culture. They believe that most African Americans are non–second language learners and that the shift from African American Vernacular English (AAVE) to "Standard English" or the language of wider communication (LWC) is one that should be "natural" for them. African American language is reduced to a dialect rather than seen as a discourse involving a system of living in the world with others (Gee, 1996). These scholars are unable to identify a dominant ethos underlying African American lifestyle that transcends geographic boundaries. As the story goes, (middle-class) African Americans assimilate to middle-class school culture and acquire literacy much the same as European Americans, since the two are so closely related. Yet the question arises: Black Americans have been in this country since 1619. Why, as a group, have they been lagging behind their White counterparts?

Read that story against this one by John Ogbu, which is largely absent from discussions of the literacy education of Black students. Ogbu (1986) looks at the Black literacy experience from a historical perspective and finds that Black education was never geared toward qualifying Blacks for "desirable" positions in society, but menial ones. He recites the Black struggle for education and the conflict, mistrust of institutions, job ceilings, and disregard for academic efforts as reasons why African Americans often choose survival strategies that do not require them to reject their culture or their language and that puts them at odds with school culture. Ogbu rejects theories that explain Black literacy lag in terms of cultural differences per se. He believes, rather, that the historical conflict between African and European Americans causes many Blacks to develop oppositional survival strategies because they see mainstream institutions as oppressive vehicles used to advance cultural supremacy. Development of counterlanguage is one of these survival strategies (Morgan, 1993). When we look deeper into African American ways of knowing, interpreting, and being in the world with others, we will see other survival mechanisms. Alternative or cultural literacies exist for various groups, not just African Americans. Academicians call these alternative literacies (Cook-Gumperz & Keller-Cohen, 1993; Camitta, 1993; Street, 1993; Gee, 1996; Gundaker, 1998). Everyday Black people call it, "makin a way out of no way." However, researchers have not completely worked out how to exploit these alternative literacies into an effort targeted toward stemming the trend of literacy underachievement in educational institutions by African American students.

Further still, there is another story that distinguishes African American orientations to knowledge making. The experiences of slavery and oppression and retention and reinterpretation of African cultural forms in the American context influence these orientations. One example of a distinct African orientation to knowledge can be found in sound culture. Ideas conveyed through sound span the entire spectrum of African American experience. Specific examples can be found in Black discourse practices such as tonal semantics. Music, such as the blues, jazz, and Hip Hop, represents forms of creativity within free yet definite patterns that transmit meaning through sound. It is important to make visible the stories of the development of oppositional cultural strategies and African retentions, not to make excuses for why Black students are not achieving standard literacies at the rate of White students. But these stories offer insight into vernacular literacies operating within American culture that, if seriously explored, could help us to accelerate the literacy education of African American students.

Janis Epps (1985) explains,

> It is Freire's definition of literacy, "a conscious intervention in one's context," which has eluded [African] Americans and kept us from becoming truly literate. We have not been allowed to acquire true literacy. That acquisition would necessitate an analysis of who we are and would point a critical finger at the continued racist and classist nature of America. Such an analysis would not focus simply on the horrors of slavery, but rather on the horrors of the legacy of slavery in American classrooms today. (p. 155)

On the page, we have mostly rewritten the American story of slavery. But the underlying ideologies that dominate literacy practices in our classrooms are still oppressive. Even after Emancipation, Reconstruction, the Civil Rights era, *Brown vs. Board of Education,* busing, multiculturalism, the problem still remains: How do we move African American students into an increasingly highly technological future without replicating the traditional paradigm of cultural oppression and structural racism? To date, the major invisible legacy of slavery in our classrooms is the transmission of White supremacist–based literacy practices, which function to erase Black vernacular survival literacies. I do not mean here to suggest that White teachers who practice bashing Black cultural learning styles damage Black students. I mean that *all* teachers who have not had training in linguistic diversity and literacy education lack the skills necessary to support culturally relevant learning. From the beginning of the African American experience, education was not designed to empower African Americans but to socialize them into "productive citizens" who become consumers of dominant cultural literacy.

Stuckey (1991) makes a critical point when she asks if the possibility exists that the same tool (literacy) that has been used to oppress can be used to empower? To heal the scars of slavery, the silencing, the othering, the devoicing, the unnecessary cultural erasure of African American students, we must begin writing new stories of African American literacy and rhetorical education.

Balester's (1993) exploration of African American college student writers attests to the fact that some African American students, of their design, devise ways to use AAVE rhetorical patterns successfully in their writing. Redd's (1993) work goes a step further by having students experiment with "styling" or use of Black language patterns in their writing. However, there are not a wealth of studies that explore African American college students' language and literacy practices as they have affected their lives and learning.

The present study elucidates social practices that influence students' academic literacy identities. It seeks to give a broader perspective of African American discourse community students in its analysis of two differently gendered and economically classed students in its presentation of two African American students. One of the students takes more pains to disguise her words behind the words of others (a closet speaker), and another leans toward using the AAVE discourse style.

Method

The two students discussed here are a male and a female, Mickey and Rhonda (pseudonyms). They were selected from demographic surveys distributed to a beginning writing class that had as its focus the literatures of many ethnic groups, including European ethnics, Latino Americans, Native Americans, Asian Americans, and African Americans. I interviewed Mickey and Rhonda for ninety minutes using Seidman's three interview procedure (thirty minutes per session). I interviewed the students twice individually and once together. All sessions were tape-recorded. I asked both participants the same set of questions but left them free to change topics even as I always brought them back at natural points during the conversations to questions that I had posed. I met them as they were enrolled in a beginning writing course at a major midwestern university. I observed their classes over the semester and analyzed pieces of their writing.

Rhonda appears to conceal her speech and cultural identity so as to appear in conformance with dominant cultural expectations more so than does Mickey. Thus, I refer to Rhonda as a closet speaker/writer.

What I am referring to here as "closet speaking/writing" is equivalent to "fronting" (Canagarajah, 1997, pp. 188–189). A related if not similar strategy is "racelessness." Fordham (1996, p. 358) defines this strategy as one that high-achieving students use as a survival strategy in environments that are based in dominant monocultural ideologies. On the other hand, Mickey's speech and writing appears to bear the Black mark. What follows then is a condensed report of an ethnomethodological study that included the interviews of these two students. Attending to the literacy stories of African American students may help us to help students see how they are positioning themselves rhetorically, in academia, in the Black literacy tradition, and in the world.

Theoretical Framework

My analysis and interpretation of the students' texts and contexts is informed by African American–centered language, rhetoric, and composition theory. African American–centered language, rhetoric, and composition theory focuses on the language and literacy practices that people of African ancestry have used to make life better for themselves, to change worlds, and to achieve goals. A major assumption of African American–centered rhetoric is that the Black language tradition is inextricably linked to the Black literacy tradition. Further, use of Black language is an ideological as well as rhetorical stance. "The Afrocentric scholar finds the source of a people's truth close to the language. . . . United States Ebonics serves as the archetype of African American language" (Asante, 1990c, p. 10). The African American–centered approach seeks to explicate the production of African American knowledge or epistemology in order that we may develop appropriate language and literacy pedagogies to accelerate the literacy education of Black (and all) students. Woodson's classic analysis of miseducation, published in the early 1930s, contributes to the African American–centered language project. He demonstrated that the traditional teaching of language, along with politics, mathematics, literature, religion, history, and other major areas of study, creates sometimes harmful imitation and conformity on the part of African Americans. In other words, African Americans sometimes uncritically acquire the standard dialect along with uncritical acceptance of the dominant narrative, helping to continue traditions of White privilege and Black oppression. With respect to language education, Woodson held that omitting the linguistic history of "the broken-down African tongue" (i.e., AAVE) from the curriculum teaches the African American to despise her mother tongue. Furthermore, Black students were directly taught to hate Black speech, which indirectly taught them to hate themselves. Thus, the African American–centered approach to literacy research and education seeks to advise and revise the story of miseducation in Black students' literacy education.

African American–centered language theory grows out of the Black studies movement of the 1960s, which advanced the idea that Black studies was practical in the education of African American students (and all students) in a multicultural world. Since the 1960s, some educators have embraced multicultural and African American–centered educational philosophies, because it became apparent that the "equal education" in mainstream classrooms that civil rights workers demanded for African Americans was still not equal. Multicultural education is built on the premise that there are culturally informed ways of constructing knowledge, that there is culturally empowering information, and that students can be made conscious of this knowledge and exploit it to their advantage—academically; politically; economically; socially; spiritually; and, of course, culturally. In this way, then, African American–centered education seeks to accelerate the learning of students of African descent by conscientizing them to their language, learning, and literacy traditions that are relevant to them, exploiting this knowledge in their acquisition of other discourses.

Related Literature

It is this line of thinking that led scholars to look into the literacies of African American rhetorics and AAVE-oriented students (Ampadu, this volume; Smitherman, 1994; Ball, 1992; Redd, 1995; Canagarajah, 1990; Noonan-Wagner, 1981; Visor, 1987) among others. A fundamental aspect of this research has been to identify and define Black discourse styles or Black rhetorical patterns as these manifest themselves in AAVE speaking students' texts. Most of this research has sought to explore and expand the literacies of AAVE-oriented students by having a deeper understanding of what informs the students' approaches to literacy. Noonan-Wagner (1981) is influenced by Smitherman's (1977/1986) suggestion that much of the Black discourse style is maintained and transmitted by the linguistic and cultural traditions of the Black church. Noonan-Wagner hypothesized that writing of students from the Black vernacular culture would reflect features of the Black preacher's rhetoric. Using teachers who were trained to identify features of Black rhetoric, the following were found to be those most closely associated with the writing of AAVE speaking students: "references to the Bible, redundancy, sermonizing and/or moralizing, use of quotations, and word choice" (1981, p. 18). In exploring the relation between the AAVE speaking students' texts and the oral tradition, Visor (1987) finds that such students' writing evinces "cultural contextualization features (CCF)." She points out that such features are identified in the literature pejoratively as unsupported assumptions, disconnected ideas, unexplicated examples and truncated logic. In terms of the AAVE oral tradition, the students used repetition, indirection, shared knowledge, and fraternity of perspective.

Ball (1992) identified AAVE oral tradition features in students' informal written and oral expository texts. She found that AAVE-speaking students insert narrative into written expository text and sometimes use it to carry the main point, which is not a standard rhetorical device. Ball further identifies the circumlocutory pattern. She describes circumlocution as a series of topics that are implicitly linked to a main theme but that seem illogical and pointless to speakers of the language of wider communication or so-called Standard English. Ball also found that AAVE students prefer orally based patterns in their writing. After students were trained to recognize two mainstream patterns of text organization and two vernacular-based organization patterns, students preferred vernacular-based organization patterns (narrative interspersion and circumlocution) in both academic and conversational tasks.

Smitherman conducted a study that focused on the identification of a distinctly Black discourse style in the writing of seventeen-year-old AAVE-speaking students. Smitherman's (1994) work with the National Association of Educational Progress (NAEP) included around 2,800 essays. She found many discernibly Black features in the writing of such students. Further, an important finding of her research was that the Black student writers who used more Black discourse in their essays scored higher than those students who did not.

In this research tradition, I have been looking into Black students' writing and their understanding of their literacy experiences. My work extends previous work on AAVE discourse patterns because it analyzes students' "ways with words," as a means of figuring out how to use Black discourses more forcefully and powerfully, to help students to acquire critical vernacular discourses of the Black literacy tradition that helped to change this nation, and to develop Blackademic writing. Blackademic literacy is another way of referring to African American language and literacy traditions; these include language usage beyond (surface-level) syntax, phonology, vocabulary, and so on into (deep level) speech acts, nonverbal behavior, and cultural production. In this conceptualization, the role of language as a major influence in reality construction and symbolic action is emphasized. The multiethnicity of symbols is more apparent in this view (Asante, 1974). This perspective places emphasis on rhetorical context and the language users—their history; values; and social-cultural, political, and economic position. Furthermore, in this approach to the understanding of African American narrative and literacy, Black creativity is a response to absence and desire and can often be traced (in part) to an "economics of slavery." (Baker, 1984) In this frame of reference, Black language usage is explored through the lens of a Black language tradition, in which language is employed for the purposes of various sorts of freedom.

Literacy Stories and Discussion

Both students pointed to situations in their educational experiences that could be attributed to the way they think of themselves and the ways that they presented themselves in writing. Mickey told me a story about what seemed to be a formative experience for him. He wrote a paper in twelfth grade on the topic of what it meant to be African American. He said that he learned a lot from writing it but that his teacher told him his writing style would not be accepted by White America. When Mickey was asked, "why not?" He explained that "I write from my heart, not from my mind." He said that his teacher encouraged him to continue to write the way that he did. Perhaps that teacher was on to something. My guess is that Mickey's teacher valued his style but had no training in helping him to exploit it to his advantage. Though many would probably take issue with her strategy, I think she probably guessed that he would naturally develop his style as he wrote more and more during his academic sojourn. My work in this area has led me to believe that the path of the vernacular is a good one for such vernacular-oriented students. Once students realize that writing their words is not acceptable, stereotype threat sets in and they get caught between two worlds, writing something that is neither AAVE nor academic English but something else, referred to by some as interlanguage.[1] Stereotype threat refers to a phenomenon in which designated social or cultural groups can become adversely affected academically or otherwise by stereotypes of high magnitude (Steele & Aronson, 1995). Many of such students get funneled into basic writing because of this, a trend that I hope African American–centered rhetoric and composition practice can reverse. Nevertheless, I think we can get a clearer idea of what Mickey meant when he spoke of writing from the heart if we examine a literacy event that occurred the semester in which I met him. He said,

> I wrote this one paper about Proposal A, and it was like, I was tellin that it would do nothin for school funding. . . . And it was like a white student wrote about how his school was so beautiful. . . . And I was like what is this? He got a 4.0, and I got a 2.0. . . . I wrote that paper from my heart!

In the Proposal A paper, referred to above, Mickey wrote,

> In another political style robbery, Governor John Engler attempts to steal more money from the taxpayers of Michigan. . . . From my data I found that areas with very low property are funded very low. Southgate, a predominately white district where academic achievement and property values are low reminds me much of Metro Detroit.

Using written Standard English criteria, the draft of the Proposal A paper has punctuation errors, some nonstandard verb forms and the like, and some unclear sentences; Mickey asks thirteen questions in a six-page paper. He has no reservations about using "I," personal reflection, or experience to validate his points. Mickey's style combined with personal reflection and testimony give his writing a distinct voice and conversational tone, which are attributes of the African American English discourse style. Here is an extended example of Mickey's writing:

> The next question should be how will this new $10.2 billion in funds be dispersed from district to district? School funding in Michigan, obviously can't be equal because if it was then the Detroit school district wouldn't be 18 million dollars in debt. What can Engler's proposal do for the equality of school funding? If you read through what he says you know his Proposal A or his Statutory Plan will do nothing for the equality of school funding. Does the economic class of a district determine it's funding? I think so. If the area a students lives in is considered to be a "better" district than another. Then the student in the "better" district will receive a better education. America is suppose to be based on equality. But you know it is not because, there obvious differences in the funding of public schools. Politicians often use the excuse of drugs and crime to justify the unequal funding of

schools. Are politicians saying, if a district is high in crime and drugs then it should be denied the same education that a district that is not high in crime and drugs is receiving? I think so. They are high in crime and drugs because they don't have money or education. This shows how America uses the educational system to maintain the rich and the poor. Proposal A is another political heist that will rob the tax payers and deny poor districts the same education as wealthier districts.

Mickey tries to validate his ideas and perspective by incorporating language from the register of research in his use of the terms *data* and *found,* terms associated with objectivity and credibility. He mixes the Black style with the research register in this way because use of the Black style is usually evaluated as "emotionality" rather than "rationality." In the sanctioned standard paradigm, emotionality is subordinated to rationality. The Black voice is traditionally drilled out of the college composition classroom, though many of us think that the Black voice has the ability to break a complex idea down into four lines or less as illustrated by the Black childhood rhyme that invoked this muse. June Jordan (1985) agrees that

> [o]ne main benefit following from the person-centered values of [AAVE] is that of clarity. If your idea, your sentence assumes the presence of at least two living and active people, you will make it understandable because the motivation behind every sentence is the wish to say something real to somebody real. (p. 129)

Jordan says that "if you speak or write [AAVE], your ideas will necessarily possess that otherwise elusive attribute, voice."

Mickey's multivocal discourse is not deemed academic enough and the way in which the instructor interpreted academic standards obligated her to assign the grade of 2.0, or a low C, which Mickey protested, as it did not reflect the level of commitment and deep thought that he felt that he put into the writing. In reflecting on the work he put into his paper and the 2.0 grade he got, Mickey says, "She said [the instructor] it wasn't clear. But I mean how could it be when it was deep? That's something I don't understand." Mickey's words point to the complexity of living in a society struggling to balance the scales. The scales contain life, liberty, the pursuit of happiness (or the distribution of wealth and resources) on one side, and race/culture, gender, and class on the other. How can it be clear when it's so deep? Mickey did not return to school the following year. He is just the kind of student who could benefit from African American–centered literacy education, a writer from the heart and soul. But most academic environments do not engage the hearts of students like Mickey. Such students are largely unrewarded for demonstrating competence in their home language, and by and large such students' cultural orientation is not tapped as a source of acceleration or education. Mickey's writing displays something closer to emotional spirituality, which can be attributed to his socialization in Black culture, influenced by the African worldview. In the African worldview, the spiritual dimension represents another way of knowing. This spirituality-cum-epistemology is powerfully enabling and could be used to help Mickey develop his own sustaining ideologies.

The female consultant in this study, Rhonda, told me a story about a literacy event that happened in fifth grade. I believe this event influences the way she represents herself in academic speech and writing. A Korean American who "hung out with whites" accidentally hit her with a hockey puck in the shin while playing field hockey at her predominantly White school. She screamed, "Ouch that hurted!" The Korean American schoolmate "corrected" her speech while everyone laughed and she cried. She said her White friends used to correct her all the time, too, and this helped her learn to codeswitch early on in certain situations.

In the initial questionnaire that Rhonda filled out for me, she identified the following as characteristics of good writing:

> if you use words correctly, use proper grammar
> if your sentences are complete and understandable
> if you organize information effectively

During our interview, Rhonda explained how free she felt to write what she wants in her papers:

> She (the instructor of the course) let's us write about what we want to write about. You know we read the material and when we get to the part where it's time to write papers, your whole topic comes from you. . . . I like when I can write about who I want to write about and say what I wanna say.

I noticed that in the beginning of our interviewing, Rhonda appeared to be a strict Standard English speaker. But as our conversations progressed, she occasionally integrated more AAVE features in her speech. However, her writing does not reveal a hint of her AAVE voice. Below is a very interesting excerpt from her writing. In it, Rhonda's voice is hardly discernible. In her response to Toni Morrison's *The Bluest Eye,* she writes:

> Claudia describes Maureen as a disrupter of seasons, a high yellow dream child with long brown hair braided into two lynch ropes that hung down her back. . . .
>
> There was a hint of spring in her sloe green eyes, something summery in her complexion, and a rich autumn ripeness in her walk [*sic*]. (Rhonda)

Although Rhonda says she feels free to say what she wants to say in her writing, it is hard to distinguish her words from Morrison's. It is clear that many of the words in the first sentence are Morrison's. The second sentence reads like plagiarism, although it could be a case of improper citation. The point is that the student's voice is not discernible. Note, too, Rhonda received a 3.5 on this paper. There's a lot to be said about an academic system that encourages instructors to reward structure over originality. In the Black rhetorical tradition, students are challenged to do they own thang with the form. But because Rhonda was in an academic classroom where study of the Black voice or Blackademic discourse is not seen as central to the acquisition of academic discourse, her attempts to pattern herself off of Morrison are not guided, perhaps not noticed. I think, too, that Rhonda's absence of voice is related to her not wanting to be "hurted" again, so she rides in on the bridge called Morrison's back, perhaps a little too heavily, to really get her ovah.

Rhetorical stances are informed by and express certain ideological stances. Bakhtin (1981) is one scholar who has argued convincingly that the historical, ideological, and sociological context that one associates with literacy and language use influences meaning. One's language orientation influences the ways in which one describes the world. Mickey's rhetorical/ideological stance appears to be "I am an AAVE speaker. It is not acceptable in the classroom, but I gotta come from the heart." Rhonda's rhetorical/ideological stance is a bit different: "I am an AAVE speaker. It is not acceptable in the classroom, so I'll get behind somebody else's big heart." She constructs an academic persona for herself that gets her "ovah." She plays the game within the structure of the system. As discussed by Woodson, Rhonda is engaged in imitation, though there is nothing inherently wrong with imitation. Imitation should be used as a means to an end not the end itself. In short, this, too, is a legacy of slavery in the classroom. Rhonda is not really given room to aspire to the level of creativity of Morrison or other Blackademic writers, who excelled in spite of the system. Morrison is renowned for her ability to critique racism and depict the humanity, culture, and resilience of Black people in her writing. Morrison's use of Black language is sanctioned by the powers that be because it is deemed art or creative and not "academic" or standard. I might add, too, the course's instructor was pro–Black language. However, as a representative of the profession, she is held accountable for teaching "academic discourse." Within the confines of what she has to teach in a particular semester, the instructor is not free to teach a language-based course but a course that is a traditional university writing course that belongs to her department and not her. I don't have the space here to go into the ways that institutional structure prevents educators from facilitating liberatory literacy. That's another essay. In any case, Rhonda should have the opportunity to be exposed to African American–centered literacy education. She could possibly benefit from the stories told by Harriet Jacobs, Toni Morrison, Zora Neale Hurston, Frederick Douglass, Malcolm X, and others whose literacy stories reflect the African American experience of negotiating discourses and identities. What these great Black writers did was to repeat and revise themes of the Black experience, using their own writing to expand what was written before. They turned tropes upside down and inside out.

Language has always been a site of negotiation and resistance for African Americans in White middle-class society. Being an African American male complicates the situation further for students like Mickey. He was very conscious of his position in society as a Black male. He was an avid reader of African American history and very astute in politics. How do we help him to construct an academic persona that he can live with, one that will help him to develop his voice and not discredit his attempts to make knowledge in a way that feels right to him? Is it necessary to symbolically make students say Toby, whipping their voices into accepted forms?

Creating New Stories

As the old folks say, "Ain't nothin new under the sun. Everything you did has already been done." What I am calling African American–centered literacy practice is really nothing more than bringing to the center that which has been common knowledge in traditional African American ways of knowing but not in mainstream classrooms. Many African Americans exploit the tradition of Nommo, power of the word, the connection among language use, rhetorical posture, and ideological stance. Of course, everyday folk don't call it by all these academic names. But they knew the power of the Black voice. It has a place in our society. The Black story of literacy is one about achieving in the face of a no-win situation. All educators should have a knowledge of the basics of language and literacy acquisition and how and why students' home language patterns and ways of knowing may or may not surface in their writing. I believe we must allow students to explore, experiment, and exploit these features. We must develop ways of nurturing students' cultural literacy experience, showing them how their literacies can be used to intervene in their contexts and to succeed in a society in which only one kind of literacy is valued. Perhaps we can change that story, too. African American–centered approaches to composition may help us to revise those old stories of dominant and oppressive literacy practices. African American–centered rhetoric and composition emphasizes the political essence of the Black voice in American history, the very sociopolitical history of what it means to be Black and to write, and the contrasts between the AAVE discourse style and the discourse conventions of academia. There are values embedded in these language varieties. Reflecting more deeply on these may move us in new directions, may help us to create new multivoiced rhymes that ring true with literacy and justice for all:

> If you (are) white, that's alright
> if you('re) yellow, you('re) still my fellow
> if you brown, keep gettin down
> And if you black, you on the right track

Note

1. For a discussion of interlanguage, see, for example, Eleanor Kutz's chapter in V. Zamel & R. Spack (Eds.) (1998), *Negotiating Academic Literacies: Teaching and Learning Across Languages and Cultures.* (Mahwah, N.J.: Lawrence Erlbaum Associates); or see Jerrie Cobb Scott's chapter in W. Glowka & D. M. Lance (Eds.). (1993), *Language Variation in North American English: Research and Teaching* (New York: Modern Language Association).

9

The Rhetoric of Democracy: Contracts, Declarations, and Bills of Sales

Victoria Cliett

> Town maps registered the street as Mains Avenue, but the only
> colored doctor in the city had lived and died on that street, and
> when he moved there in 1896 his patients took to calling the
> street, which none of them lived near, Doctor Street. . . . Some of
> the city legislators, whose concern for appropriate names and the
> maintenance of the city's landmarks was the principal part of
> their political life, saw to it that "Doctor Street" was never used
> in any official capacity. And since they knew that Southside
> residents kept it up, they had notices posted in the stores,
> barbershops, and restaurants in that part of the city saying that
> the avenue . . . had always been and would always be known as
> Mains Avenue and not Doctor Street. . . . It was a genuinely
> clarifying public notice because it gave Southside residents a way
> to keep their memories alive and please the city legislators as
> well. They called it Not Doctor Street.
> —Toni Morrison, *Song of Solomon*

IN *SONG OF SOLOMON*, THE RELATIONSHIP OF AFRICAN AMERICAN
discourse in society is exemplified in the evolution of "Not Doctor Street."
The naming of "Not Doctor Street" does not only exhibit a unique facet
of African American discourse but how African American discourse, in
political confrontations, changes but remains the same in a continual re-
constitution of language. "Not Doctor Street" becomes part of political resistance and historical referent(s), engaging the act of "signifying."
The cultural skirmish of "Not Doctor Street" between African American citizens and city legislators is a microcosm of larger and older traditional political discourse in which African American discourse even
within the language of Standard English, can have cultural dissonance.
This chapter will explain how nineteenth-century African American

discourse as used by Frederick Douglass and David Walker engage sophisticated acts of "signifying" within and against Standard English.

Enslaved people of African descent manipulated their situations the best they could to survive their hostile situations. They adapted language, art, thought, religion, work, everything that they were made to endure, to their own means and purposes. This is the making of African American culture, a culture developed out of struggle for freedoms and resistance to oppressions. The critique of social injustice and hypocrisy in American democracy is a significant theme in African American culture. In the nineteenth century, especially, African American activists exploited the available means of the time to problematize notions of text and subjectivity. Through their use of analogies, irony, and metonymic language, semantic inversion, to name a few, African American rhetors signified their alternative visions of democracy even within the genre of American literature. Smitherman (1977/1986, p. 82) defined *signifyin* as negative critique, witty put-downs and indirect references. *Signifyin(g)* has also been defined by Gates (1988) as a theory for understanding African American literature and discourse. Gates uses the *(g)* to indicate that there are always at least two layers of meaning that could be implicated in this mode of language use, vernacular and standard. Because of their powerless rhetorical situation, people of African descent needed to code their language. This semantic system indicates Black experiences. Following Gates (1988), I define *African American discourse* as texts that reference themes of Black experiences with a signal difference. Through examination of nineteenth-century Black rhetors' campaign against standard or traditional versions of democracy and citizenship, I will illumine their use of signifyin and other Black discursive practices. By so doing, I hope to broaden our conceptions of African American discourse and discursive practices and correct restricting perceptions of African American discourse as merely "dialect."

The conventions of signifying in nineteenth-century political rhetoric centered on dismantling notions of natural law, the language of citizenship, and the symbols of the American Revolution and the republic. The idea of democracy assumes a natural relationship between a subject/citizen and a community in which the subject/citizen is represented within the community and is also a representative of the community. "We" as used in political/legal documents invoked a code of social relations that appeared to be universal and natural, but relative to White, male upper-class property owners. A tenet of the performative "we" is that African American writers must perform within the formalized frame of Standard

English and its ideologies. "We" was used to invoke a democracy in which everyone was "self-evident." Self-evidence implies a relationship in which everyone understands a universal truth. "Self-evident" as used by Thomas Jefferson suggested a rhetoric in which "I's" speak for the "we" and vice versa. "Self-evident" as referred to in the Declaration of Independence promoted unity between language and thought and between subject and nation. African American persons have historically been disenfranchised from this relationship, not able to represent a "we." Signifyin(g) "played on" the role of the addressor and the addressee.

"We" is the first person plural. "We" references a subject that speaks. The "we" speaks not only for himself or herself but for other persons— "I's"—subjects who have given the "I" permission to speak for them. This subject who is representing can speak for the community. The singular "I" has the consent of the other "I's" to speak for them to participate rhetorically and historically. But the political "we" as expressed by Jefferson does not represent all individuals; a rhetorical gap that African American political discourse plays on and engages.

When Thomas Jefferson drafted the Declaration of Independence, he wrote: "We hold these truths to be self-evident, that all men are created equal." The "we" was not just an assembly of individuals. It was the assembly of a nation with representative values and beliefs for that discourse community. Jefferson authored a document that presumably spoke for all individuals. There is the presumption that "self-evident" invokes individual authority based on a transparent ideology. (Wills, 1978, p. 182) This belief has more in common with Scottish philosopher Thomas Reid, who believed a self-evident truth was accessible by everyone at any time, regardless of how much money you had or your station in life; reasoning is not needed. Jefferson believed that in order for truth to be self-evident everyone must recognize it wherever they are; it is universal (Payne, 1982, p. 112).

If we look at *self-evident,* as some scholars believe Jefferson meant it, an individual possesses truth independently of the outside world; nothing can be added or taken away from him. Furthermore, Jefferson believed that people can only know about themselves and their God-given rights through these self-evident truths, rights being defined as the "law in the nature of man" (Payne, 1982, p. 116). In nineteenth-century political rhetoric, the American Constitution was a document that listed the "unalienable rights" that the Declaration said mankind had. After the Civil War, the Thirteenth, Fourteenth, and Fifteenth Amendments were added to the Constitution to ensure that ex-slaves could be recognized as participating members of the "we." But if equality was self-evident, why did it have to be amended? The opposition of these mutually exclusive rhetorical operations generates the act of signifying in nineteenth-century African American political discourse: contesting hegemonic ideology and reaffirming African American subjectivity simultaneously within the "homogenizing" language of Standard English.

African American writers, ex-slaves, and activists, such as Frederick Douglass, used the warrants of the Declaration of Independence to secure an audience. Within slave narratives, the act of signifyin(g) could be practiced simply by using a different pronoun or omitting certain information. Slavery and racism placed Africans and African Americans as passive objects within texts; the "performance" was written for them and disenfranchised them as active writers. The freedom of an enslaved person was not necessarily determined by physical restraint although violence certainly underwrote it. The physical body and voice of the slave were translated through the text of the White master, the enslaved person becoming invisible. The deprivation of liberty and the yoke of colonial exploitation were paired with literal ignorance, as the southern states forbade persons of African descent to learn to read or write (see Gates, 1988; Anderson, 1995). Thus, the formerly enslaved person initiated the rhetorical act to establish independence. The slave narratives are not just literary pieces; they are sites of negotiation seeking to establish the truth of the ex-slave's experience and to provide self-evidence of earned citizenship. The writing and the written document became the media through which the enslaved or marked person resisted oppressive colonization acts. Williams Andrews (1988) in To Tell a Free Story outlines this literary struggle:

> In a number of important black autobiographies of this year, however, a quest more psycho literary than spiritual can be discerned. It is spurred by many motives, perhaps the most important of which is the need of an other to *declare* (Andrew's emphasis) himself through various linguistic acts, thereby reifying his abstract unreality, his invisibility, in the eyes of his reader, so that he can be recognized as someone to be reckoned with. Such declarative acts, as we shall see, include the reconstructing of one's past in a meaningful and instructive form, the appropriating of empowering myths and models of the self from any available resource, and redefining the language used to locate one in that scheme. (p. 3)

Through the writing act, persons of African descent resisted the oppression of colonization, and through declaration, formerly enslaved writers could signify on the assumptions of authorship. As the American forefathers could establish a new country through rhetorical and legal texts, the enslaved person used the English language to revise and resist a harsh reality. The slave existed not as a whole or complete individual in colonial rhetoric but as a document being manipulated through the linguistic acts of the text. If a will dictated that a slave be given to a certain relative, that act was carried out. A pass issued by the master of the plantation ensured that the slave could travel off the plantation safely. For that reason, the experiences of reading and writing had much significance, for example, in slave narratives of people such as Frederick Douglass and in the writings of people such as David Walker, in particular. The texts of Frederick Douglass are sites of numerous conflicts between the ex-slave, colonial rhetoric, and issues of self-evidence. Douglass is an example of how the formerly enslaved, although nominally free, was enfranchised through the political agenda of the abolitionists in order to have some rhetorical visibility. The textual relationship between Frederick Douglass and William Lloyd Garrison is an example of how the formerly enslaved still had to appease the political agenda of abolitionists. In later years, when Douglass ideologically broke away from the Garrisonian abolitionists, he was only replaced at the forefront of the movement with other formerly enslaved Africans to represent the Garrisonian abolitionist ideologies (Andrews, 1988).

Frederick Douglass's ideas of freedom were not prescribed by those sympathetic with him, although that might certainly appear so as he gained his literacy from interacting with his oppressors. In describing his relationship with Sophia Auld, Douglass writes of her kind nature, which encouraged him to ask her if she would teach him to read (1855/1969, p. 145). When Sophia Auld stopped her lessons under the influence of her husband, she subsequently began to treat him poorly. Douglass's desire for literacy became more intense as he learned that it was not what Hugh Auld, his master, wanted for him. At the time that Douglass was forbidden to read and write, he also understood what it represented. Reading and writing would become the "pathway from slavery to freedom" (1845/1997a, p. 49). Most important, Frederick Douglass learned signifyin(g) not only as an oral and writing act but as a reading act as well:

> Very soon after I went to live with Mr. and Mrs. Auld, she
> very kindly commenced to teach me the A, B, C. After I had

learned this, she assisted me in learning to spell words of three
or four letters. Just at this point of my progress, Mr. Auld
found out what was going on and at once forbade Mrs. Auld
to instruct me further, telling her, among other things, that
it was unlawful, as well as unsafe, to teach a slave to read.
. . . Whilst I was saddened by the thought of losing the aid
of my kind mistress, I was gladdened by the invaluable instruction which, by the merest accident, I had gained from
my master. . . . The very decided manner with which he spoke,
an strove to impress his wife with the evil consequences of
giving me instruction, served to convince me that he was
deeply sensible of the truths he was uttering. . . . What he
most dreaded, that I most desired. What he most loved, that
I most hated. That which to him was a great evil, to be carefully shunned, was to me a great good, to be diligently sought.
(1845/1997a, pp. 49–50)

Frederick Douglass engaged doubly conscious readings of the dominant culture, enacting the practice of signifyin(g). Douglass's lesson in
cultural values highlights an important point: that signifyin(g) is a practice that goes beyond language and dialect, pen and paper. Those who
learn to discern and negotiate cultural signifiers and systemic social practices learn a more sophisticated literacy practice that is the art of sig-
nifyin(g). Critically literate students learn that what is taught always
serves the interests of the state. Those who are oppressed must actually
take what is being taught and decode in order to resist oppressive state
practices. This knowledge of literacy that Douglass acquired would be
burdensome for many reasons; he would be aware that those in power
determined his identity. When Douglass grieves at the thought of "being a slave for life," in the 1845 narrative, it may not be that he thought
physical freedom was elusive but that his identity, which he knew to be
that of a man, was represented as subhuman "slave" in the self-evident
world of elite White male discourse and the near impossibility of transforming that representation. We may note that even to this day, the Black
male and female image is controlled and policed by the state and its
media. After comprehending the words *abolition* and *abolitionist,*
Douglass felt satisfaction because he knew this was something that his
master would not want him to know (1845/1997a, p. 56). Learning for
Douglass no longer necessitated a teacher. Literacy no longer represented
reading and writing. He saw these as tools to gain access to power.

Signifyin(g), then, is a means by which the power of the dominant culture's ideology can be taken apart.

These observations and interpretations relate to the textual argument at hand, as they give insight on how literacy, freedom, and self were a means of force to resolve the instability of double consciousness. The movement toward emancipatory literacy that took place beyond Douglass's writings were just as important, since many slaves, especially Douglass, were pressured only to write or speak regarding certain incidents. From Douglass's reconstruction of his life, we can gain insight as to how the oppressed-oppressor relationship influenced his writing.

The years after the 1845 narrative, Douglass laconically reflected on how abolitionists themselves marginalized him. William McFeely documents a statement in which Garrison, after hearing Douglass's speech, proclaimed that by a "miracle" "a chattel becomes a man," although it is clear that in the years preceding, Douglass never once considered himself anything less (McFeely, 1991, 9. 95). Douglass recounts that after he gave his speech, Garrison followed him, "taking me as his text," seeing Douglass as an object instead of a subject (1855/1969, p. 358). Even after listening to Douglass speak, Garrison does not attribute Douglass's eloquence to Douglass the visible being; instead, Garrison uses his own representation and compares the speech of Douglass to Patrick Henry's, referring to Douglass the person as that "hunted fugitive" (1855/1969, p. vii). In subsequent speeches, Douglass was introduced by John A. Collins as a "graduate from the peculiar institution," with his "diploma written on his back" (p. 359). Generally, Douglass was introduced as "chattel," "thing," "property," the chairman assuring everyone that "it" could speak (p. 360). Douglass recounts:

> Fugitive slaves, at that time, were not so plentiful as now; and as a fugitive slave lecturer, I had the advantage of being a "*brand new fact,*" [Douglass's emphasis]—the first one out. . . . During the first three or four months, my speeches were almost exclusively made up of narratives of my own personal experience as a slave. "Let us have the facts," said people. So also said Friend George Foster, who always wished to pin me down to my simple narrative. "Give us the facts," said Collins, "we will take care of the philosophy." (p. 361)

Here, Douglass breaks down the signifiers critiquing the values of the abolitionists. Now in the company of those who professed emancipation, Douglass was all too painfully aware that oppressive ideologies were ever present, the "I's" and the "we's" were not one in the same.

From the writings of Frederick Douglass, parallels to the contemporary composition classroom can be drawn. Like the antislavery movement, the notion of the democratic writing classroom works with an idea of emancipation. The crux of the practice of signifyin(g) in the nineteenth and twentieth centuries emerges from incompatible and oppressive language systems. Oppressed individuals use signifyin(g) practices as a form of emancipatory literacy that dismantles the hegemonic systems of language and makes new meanings that surpass those of the original language by reconstituting reality and recoding meaning, recontextualizing history, and deconstructing the values of the dominant culture. Frederick Douglass in a speech entitled "The Anti-Slavery Movement" employed these signifyin(g) conventions to put the antislavery movement out of the hands of the abolitionists and put focus on the purpose of antislavery itself. In the introduction of his speech, Douglass does not introduce antislavery within the movement itself; instead, he introduces opponents of the antislavery movement John C. Calhoun and Daniel Webster, who have taken the antislavery movement seriously:

> The late John C. Calhoun . . . probably studied it as deeply, though not as honestly, as Gerrit Smith, or William Lloyd Garrison. He evinced the greatest familiarity with the subject; and the greatest efforts of his last years in the senate had direct reference to this movement. . . . He never allowed himself to make light of it; but always spoke of it and treated it as a matter of grave import: and in this he showed himself a master of the mental, moral, and religious constitution of human society. (1855/1969, p. 457)

Douglass forthrightly addresses the worthiness of the abolitionist cause but puts the abolitionists and the antiabolitionists on the same level, consequently putting ownership of the antislavery movement outside that of the abolitionists and making it one in consideration of what is right. In Douglass's discourse, antislavery is not a movement owned by the abolitionists but a truth about human freedom that any citizen believing in the value of a human life would embrace. Douglass's signifiyin(g) on the abolitionists is a reminder to them to not forget what the real purpose of antislavery was.

In another signifyin(g) practice, Douglass seemingly uses two contradicting ideas: facts and evidence. He states: "[O]f the existence and power of the anti-slavery movement, as a fact, you need no evidence" (1855/ 1969, p. 458). Logically, facts are supported by evidence, but here, Douglass dismantles the traditional modes of thinking supported by the dominant culture and oppressive modes of language. The reader and listener are forced to reconsider the meaning of "evidence" and truth as it relates to the justification of enslavement. Also, Douglass once again takes the antislavery argument out of the abolitionist discourse and puts it in a domain of its own merit.

As demonstrated by Ampadu (chapter 7) African American speeches and rhetoric developed in the nineteenth and the twentieth centuries provide excellent material for literacy and rhetorical education. There is a rich tradition of rhetoric in African American culture that is generally underused, if used at all, in the classroom. Unfortunately, traditional rhetoric and writing vis-à-vis the White forefathers is taught more often than a diversity of cultural discourses.

David Walker's *Appeal to the Coloured Citizens of the World* (1830/ 1995) is a straightforward political pamphlet addressing the status of African Americans in nineteenth-century America. Much of Walker's treatise "signified on" Thomas Jefferson's theories of citizenship and the natural abilities of Africans. Jefferson's writings provided Walker with his primary arguments against the assumed inferiority of Africans. Walker had a significant amount of respect and admiration for Jefferson, as Jefferson played a central role in creating the philosophical fabric of the American republic (Wilentz, 1995, p. xvi). Walker's *Appeal* targeted the ideas of Jefferson because the tide of proslavery and racism was becoming more entrenched in the ideological and political arena of America and was picking up momentum (Hinks, 1997, p. 205–206). Jefferson's *Notes on the State of Virginia* influenced much of the racial thought in the 1820s (Hinks, 1997, p. 206).

The Declaration of Independence and *Notes on the State of Virginia* were documents that addressed equality and moral aptitude that commanded Walker's attention and response. Walker takes a text from Jefferson and signifies on Jefferson's theories and assumptions about people of African descent and the attitudes of Whites in general:

> And those enemies who have for hundreds of years stolen our
> *rights* [Walker's emphasis], and kept us ignorant of Him and
> His divine worship, he will remove. Millions of whom, are
> this day, so ignorant and avaricious, that they cannot con-

ceive how God can have an attribute of justice, and who
mercy to us because it pleased Him to make us black—which
colour, Mr. Jefferson calls unfortunate!!!!!! As though we are
not as thankful to our God, for having made us as it pleased
himself, as they (the Whites,) are for having made them
White. They think because they hold us in their infernal
chains of slavery, that we wish to be White, or of their color—
but they are dreadfully deceived—we wish to be just as it
pleased our Creator to have made us. . . . But is Mr. Jefferson's
assertion true? Viz. "that it is unfortunate for us that our
Creator has been pleased to make us *black*." We will not take
his say so, for the fact. (Walker, 1830/1995, p. 12)

Walker strategically dissected Jefferson as the preeminent architect
and author of American ideology, specifically calling into question how
Jefferson, the foremost speaker on American liberty and equality, could
also be a slave owner and a proponent of African inferiority. Along with
Walker, James McCune Smith and William Hamilton were other persons
of African descent who strongly challenged Jefferson's views on the inferiority of persons of African descent (Hinks, 1997, p. 178–179). Walker
recognized that as an authorized and respected author, Jefferson's beliefs would be entrenched in America's consciousness. Walker encouraged people of African descent to refute Jefferson's ideas (Hinks, 1997,
pp. 207–208).

It was important to meet Jefferson on his own ground regarding ideological beliefs of inferiority, scientific nationalism, and objectivity. Walker
establishes reasoned and logical arguments to Jefferson's in his *Appeal*
(1830/1995). Walker's task was to take on science's claim as objective
and observable reality as promoted by Jefferson and uncover the racist
foundation. Walker did this by discussing the moral abomination inflicted on Blacks. Walker believed that if Blacks were inferior, it was a
result of the constant and brutal degradation by Whites (Walker, 1830/
1995, pp. 15–16; Hinks, 1997, p. 210). Walker asserts that Whites were
not objective; rather, they were only detached from their own moral
obligations and racial uplift. They refused to acknowledge their own
degradation; the issue was not about scientific fact (Walker, 1830/1995,
p. 17; Hinks, 1997, p. 210).

Walker strategically used pathos to point up the shortcomings in
Jefferson's theories of nationality. One might think that Walker might
undercut his own argument by moving away from objectivity, but Walker's

purpose was to assert the humanity of Blacks within the assumed detached animal nature of slavery (Hinks, 1997, p. 211). Walker used emotionalism to connect with the Black audience and bring about "internal coherency and self-respect" (Hinks, 1997, p. 211). Clearly, this is an effort on Walker's part to resolve the double consciousness of Black experiences, through the advocacy of an "internal revolution" (Hinks, 1997, p. 226). This idea of internal revolution demonstrates the effects of double consciousness and the intertextuality of African American identity. It is not a physical revolution but the psychological war that must be won.

The internal war that Walker addressed concerned the "perversion of natural instinct." Slavery's greatest crime was the manner in which it transformed Blacks (Hinks, 1997, p. 217). Walker unequivocally abhorred slavery, but he believed that Blacks played a complicit role in their enslavement, and he spoke out against the passive role that reinforced their servitude (Walker, 1830/1995, p. 25; Wilentz, 1995, xv–xvi). The aid of a Black woman in foiling an escape was a sore point with Walker. The incident demonstrated the "natural" tendencies that were structurally established. It was not natural for the slave to assist the oppressors (Walker, 1830/1995, p. 25; Hinks, 1997, pp. 218–219).

But it may be too premature to chalk up the emotionalism in the *Appeal* to mere rhetorical strategy, as Hinks suggests. The structure of double consciousness elicits dual readings in American society that necessitate the African American subject to see himself or herself simultaneously in the detached gaze of White America and the frustration of Black. It is the "objectivity" that creates the tension within Walker's emotionalism and is the strong undercurrent in the signifyin(g) practices he undertakes. The journey of self-knowledge on part of African Americans is a journey into the systematic process of reading history and structure. The self-knowledge of African Americans was self-knowledge of an "operation" of slavery and its ideological foundations.

Walker's great fear was that in the absence of clearly upheld alternative definitions of self and of the African past, the individual's tendency to organize personality around a single dominant understanding of self would be unavoidably shaped by representations of Black character and worth made by slaveholders. Walker addressed the way identity was related to perception and the reading of the "sign." He recognized that this perception of self was part of an organized system (Hinks, 1997, 216–222).

The understanding of the self revolved around signs and significations established within contracts. Walker's assertion that Whites were "natural enemies" was a critique on the assumptions of natural inferiority that were prevalent in the early nineteenth century. Walker asserts that there is no "natural" bond between the slave and the master. There was no "mutually derived contract"; hence, this is one informed reading of "natural enemies" (Hinks, 1997, p. 220). To make this point, Walker recounts an uprising of slaves in which two White men were killed and another injured. The injured White man was assisted by a Black woman. Walker uses this incident to address the "natural" justification of the woman's action:

> Here my brethren, I want you to notice particularly in the above article, the *ignorant* and *deceitful* actions of this coloured woman. I beg you to view it candidly, as for *eternity!!!!* Here a *notorious wretch,* with two other confederates had sixty of them in a gang, driving them like *brutes*— the men all in chains and handcuffs thrown off, and caught two of the wretches and put them to death, and beat the other until they thought he was dead, and left him for dead; however he deceived them, and rising from the ground, this *servile woman* helped him upon his horse, and he made his escape. Brethren, what do you think of this? Was it the natural *fine feelings* of this woman, to save such a wretch alive? (1830/1995 p. 24; Walker's emphasis)

The discourse of "natural enemies" in Walker's *Appeal* takes seemingly natural beliefs of human rights, liberty, and happiness and places them over the beliefs of the proslavery movement. By "naturalizing" the idea of slaveholding Whites and enslaved Blacks being antagonistic to each other, Walker also opens the door to make observations about White slave owners and the colored woman much in the way that assumptions were made about the natural capabilities of Blacks. Also, by recasting Whites as "natural enemies," Walker is legitimizing the emotional response to the brutalization of slavery. If it is natural to enslave Blacks and treat them worse than animals, then, as consequence, it is natural to hate Whites; acceptance and happiness in an oppressive institution cannot be natural.

It is a major act of signifyin(g) when Walker says that the dominant culture's conceptualization of freedom is predicated on how Whiteness is embedded in freedom, not for the sake of freedom alone. It is a brilliant move on Walker's part that he attacks the presumptuousness of Western theories of inferiority. One of the artificial notions of the "contract" is that Blacks wished to be White. Not true: they merely wanted to be free.

Signifyin(g) strategies in nineteenth-century democratic rhetoric focus on a textual contract that asserts "natural" relationships between the individual and the social world. The operation of signifyin(g) then requires a metonymic strategy and reversal of traditional rhetorical strategies. The rhetorical strategies and foundation of African American subjectivity engage the stripping away of assumed legitimacy of structural, read, rhetorical "contracts" based on their one-sidedness or lack of mutual agreement.

As consequence to the idea of the democratic writing classroom, there are cultural mores that students are expected to practice in the writing classroom. The dominant culture has subtle and not so subtle ways of rupturing agreement between "minority" students and knowledge. The culture of Black struggle is not in agreement with the ideologies of Standard English, which many teachers try to divorce from historical and contemporary reality. Standard English is based in White supremacist ideologies, whether we like it or not. Black skin has been inscribed by the dominant culture as a representation of a subject that is not knowledgeable, not an authority in the classroom, and disruptive to traditional academia. Minorities are considered incompatible signs of knowledge and literacy. The idea that certain cultures are not agreeable with the predicate of knowledge seems to be an unspoken clause in the contract of democracy. Self-evident equality doesn't seem to be so self-evident after all, and recognizing the equality of all linguistic and cultural systems of knowledge does not figure into the sentence. Rather than correct the text of the dominant culture, "minorities" pay the price for the inconsistencies.

Learning a superficial conception of Standard English should not be the goal of the writing classroom; the goal should be to learn to communicate ideas effectively and to revise unjust texts of the world.

Although the founding fathers were slave owners, they conceived universal equality in "all men" as a means of establishing the republic on irreducible principles of truth. Benjamin N. Cardozo states that the inconsistencies of "all men" is an example of a principle expanding itself "to the limit of its logic" (Higginbotham, 1978). Black activists and White sympathizers would expand the principle of "all men" until it was a self-evident truth universally.

The aftermath of the "Renaissance of Rhetoric" has left a strong commitment in composition scholars to create a "democratic classroom," in the sense that currently not all voices are heard, that the pedagogy of Standard English has brought with it much cultural oppression. Paulo Freire (1994), considered one of the "founding fathers" of liberatory pedagogy, stated in *Pedagogy of the Oppressed:*

> It is as transforming and creative beings that humans, in their permanent relations with reality, produce not only material goods—tangible objects—but also social institutions, ideas, and concepts. Through their continuing praxis, men and women simultaneously create history and become historical-social beings. (p. 82)

It is this social-historical being that has been identified by composition theorists as the potentially liberated subject:

> We enter the process of theorizing the relation between popular culture and critical pedagogy by arguing for educational practice as both a site and form of cultural politics. Our project is the construction of an educational practice that expands human capacities in order to enable people to intervene in the formation of their own subjectivities and to be able to exercise in the interest of transforming the ideological and material conditions of domination into social practices that promote social empowerment and demonstrate possibilities. (Giroux, 1993, p. 189)

James Berlin (1993) states:

> Composition Studies is undertaking projects in both pedagogy and research that parallel those in cultural studies. Some of these efforts signal the emergence of a social epistemic rhetoric, a rhetoric that considers signifying practices in relation to the ideological formation of the self with a context of economics, politics, and power . . . social epistemic rhetoric argues that the writing subject is a discursive construction, the subject serving as a point of conjecture for a plethora of discourses—a rich variety of texts inscribed in the persona of the individual. (p. 108)

Freire (1994), Giroux (1993), and J. A. Berlin (1993) refer to the "transformation" of the subject, a subject that is formed by social and historical forces. Obviously, rhetoric is defined more by what it does, rather than what it is. In fact, opposition to (multi)cultural ideas in writing classrooms is rooted in the belief that rhetoric cannot "do" anything; it can only be taught. But if we turn to the construction of democracy, we can see that rhetoric is very much involved in the political process and his-torical-social subjects in the United States.

Democracy, in the broadest sense, means government by the people, individual voices with collective and equal participation in choosing a form of government. Individual "I's" are working for the good of a "we." "We hold these truths," and "We the people," from the Declaration of Independence and the Constitution establish that the foundation of the American government was wholeheartedly republican in which "each inhabitant placed his consent . . . approving its sovereignty and bend-ing its allegiance to it" (Sollors, 1996). Composition studies, as a disci-pline, is not ignorant of the Platonic allegiances of the founding fathers:

> In rhetoric, there is history and culture and language with political and personal implications. Plato saw a plurality of the senses as somehow base, good only insofar as the senses could lead to the supersensible, to the one unifying principle of another plane of existence, the ideal, the Idea of the Good. He argues against democracy, as a kind of government that would have everyone running after sensual self-interest, a kind of anarchy. . . . Plato was an influence on Cicero; Cicero was an influence on the Founding Fathers. (Villanueva, 1993, p. 77)

Ultimately, the "I" can be expressed only as it contributes to the so-cial formation of the "we." Unity can never be sacrificed for individual interests. The "I/we," then, becomes a relevant dialectic for composi-tion studies. Contrary to what more conservative educators might think, the introduction of culture and the disciplinary ideologies it has brought with it does serve as a useful platform for interrogating history and rheto-ric, although of late, there are some who may not be clear on how to use it (Bahri, 1998).

James Berlin outlines in his essay, "Contemporary Composition: The Major Pedagogical Theories" (1997), four elements of the composing process: writer, reality, audience, and language. The differences between major pedagogical theories lie in different perceptions of the relationship between these four elements. Hence, neo-Aristotelians, or the Classicists, believe that "the material world exists independently of the observer and is knowable through sense impressions" (p. 235). The Positivists, or Current Traditionalists, believe that "truth is discovered through induc-tion alone." This methodology has its roots in the logic of John Locke and Francis Bacon. The speaker adapts the language to correspond to the objects in the material world; senses are irrelevant. The neo-Platonists or Expressivists believe that the material world is unreliable; hence, senses are of no use. "[T]ruth is discovered through internal apprehension, a private vision of a world that transcends the physical. . . . [T]ruth can be learned but not taught" (Berlin, 1997, p. 235). Berlin argues that this theory is best envisioned by two speakers breaking free from different beliefs and biases to arrive at knowledge through a painful process. Language may not be able to communicate truth, but it can reveal the realities of the material world. Current composition theorists, the Expressivists, believe consequently that "all good writing is personal." Finally, the New Rhetoricians, with whom Berlin identified himself, believe that "truth is dynamic and dialectical, the result of a process involving the interaction of opposing elements. It is a relation that is created, not pre-existent or waiting to be discovered." All four elements are involved in the dialectic (Berlin, 1997, p. 242).

And so, when we look at the phrase "We hold these truths to be self-evident, that all men are created equal," there is a relation between writer/reader, audience, reality and language that is implied for the citizen. A text such as the Declaration of Independence offers a new view on how the rhetoric of the founding fathers created citizenship. Even more important, when we look at the responses of Black intellectuals and writers to slavery and the agenda of Reconstruction, we can see how rhetoric can be oppressive and/or liberatory. Ideas on social constructivism or expressivism can be uncovered not only for contemporary composition studies but also cultural studies, and studies of African American literary criticism.

In legal studies, scholars have pointed out how race and civil rights have not been compatible with the ideals of natural language and law; Blackness in the public sphere is not a sign of enfranchisement. Patricia Williams stated (1991), "When I get up in the morning, I stare in the mirror and stick on my roles. . . . I dab stringent on my pores that I might be a role model upon whom all may gaze with pride. . . . I hunt for this set of expectations that will go best with that obligation" (p. 196). Karla Holloway (1995) recalls the charge from her social world to represent the image of a respectable Black woman in public life. Holloway also observes that Washington, D.C., is not a state because of its very public Black majority. Self-evidence is intertwined within the relationship of culture and conduct. Within the "we," Holloway sees herself as a Black woman who is not in control of how she is read as a self-evident text.

Within the larger issues of civil rights, "self-evident" is problematic because the language put forth by the government has never reflected the rights of African Americans. Manning Marable (1991) in *Race, Reform, and Rebellion* recognized Reconstruction and the Civil Rights eras as social movements that "expressed a powerful vision of multicultural democracy and human equality" (p. 3). Democratic ideals were only social movements; they still have not become self-evident in law. Derrick Bell (1987) recognizes that the conversations of racial justice have been repeated and redundant. The unfinished business of civil rights demonstrated how race as a text of self-evidence has become a barrier. Racial justice and civil rights become an agenda to unveil the truth of freedom by finding the right language. The debates on affirmative action are an example of how the racial casting of equality has eclipsed freedom.

The texts of Frederick Douglass and David Walker challenge the injustices of slavery in more refined rhetorical approaches when one examines how the signifiers and signs are rearranged. The signifyin(g) practices of African American discourse do not solely reside in dialect or culture but can cross boundaries of genre, ideology, and language, resulting in not just another snappy comeback but a useful metacritique on the shaping of discourses and cultures and the twenty-first-century writing classroom.

Part Three

Visions for Research in African
American Rhetoric(s)

10

Looking Forward to Look Back: Technology Access and Transformation in African American Rhetoric

Adam J. Banks

The folks promoting this nonsense—I call them "tricknologists"—
are the high tech equivalent of the three card monty dealers you
see on street corners. You know the game: they get you to follow
one card, and all the while the real action is somewhere else. Well,
that's exactly what the New Age tricknologists are doing with the
Digital Divide debate. The trick is simple: the first step is to narrow the definition of the Divide, by saying that computer ownership and Internet usage are how we measure minority participation in the new, high-tech economy. In fact, all these statistics
prove is that minorities are closing the gap in becoming consumers of technology, not in being producers or equal partners. . . .
Saying that the Digital Divide is closing because minorities have
greater access to computers is like saying minorities have a stake
in the automobile industry because they drive cars, or that they
are Bill Gates because they own Microsoft Office 2000.
                    —T. Taborn, "The Art of Tricknology"

What is usually missing in our celebrations of African American
history is a focus on how technological change contributes to the
structural basis of African American history. The entire sweep of
African American history needs to be examined on the basis that
technological change creates the main structural context for the
grand historical narrative of enslavement and the subsequent
freedom struggle.
                    —A. Alkalimat, "Technological Revolution and
                Prospects for Black Liberation in the 21st Century"

YOU WON'T FIND TOO MANY ENGINEERS IN AFRICAN AMERICAN
rhetoric anthologies, but Tyrone Taborn, as publisher of *US Black Engi-*

neer: Information Technology is obviously grounded in the tradition. His magazine is billed as "the African American community's technology magazine," continuing in the history of periodicals committed to advocacy for African American people. As is clear in the quote above, taken from the February 2001 "Community Awareness" issue, Taborn and his staff understand technology as one of the major battlegrounds for African American struggle in this era of post–Civil Rights retrenchment. More than just an intriguing rhetorical performance in its own right, Taborn's article shines a spotlight on the connections that have always existed between communication technologies, questions of access, and the African American rhetorical tradition in ways that allow a new look at that tradition and how scholars might engage it in a new century. The history of African American rhetoric is, in many ways, one of individual writers, speakers, visual artists, and designers mastering, manipulating, and working around available technologies, even when access to them had been denied the masses of Black people. By concentrating on this connection between communication technologies and rhetorical production, by looking forward to look back, African American rhetorical scholars can not only offer far richer analysis of those speeches and writings that have always been considered to be within the tradition but can also open it up beyond just the word and show that it has always been multimedia, always using *all* the available means in resisting racism and pursuing justice and equal access on behalf of African American people. Finally, the Digital Divide itself is a rhetorical problem at least as much as it is a technical one. As a field that has always had to address issues of access either directly or indirectly, African American rhetoric is poised to make substantial contributions to minimizing that divide, if technological issues make it onto scholars' and students' maps of the field.

It might seem odd to attempt to argue that the entire African American rhetorical tradition can be read with a focus on the importance of technologies and African Americans' access to them. After all, the story of African American rhetoric to this point has been primarily understood as being about the mastery of "the word"—both oral and written—throughout our history. Examples of this focus—mostly on speeches and essays—abound, from foundational texts defining the scope of African American rhetorical study to articles analyzing specific rhetorical performances, regardless of the disciplinary homes of African American rhetorical scholars. Those who define African American rhetoric strictly as persuasion and concentrate their work on African American public discourse (A. Smith, 1969; Smith & Robb, 1972; Golden & Rieke, 1971;

R. J. Walker, 1992), as well as those who work in linguistics, interpersonal and group communications (Asante & Gudykunst, 1989; Cummings & Daniel, 1995) have been very consistent in this focus in their coverage of the history of African American rhetoric. This is not to say that individual scholars in Black rhetoric have not discussed technology issues: Richardson (2003) in particular has been very clear about the ways discourses function as technologies, for example, and it is difficult to engage the Hip Hop tradition at all without some attention to these connections. However, the mastery of spoken and written language remains the frame that organizes the field.

Using such a frame works, obviously, for many reasons—not only because of its congruence with the events of that history but because it allows a relatively coherent view of it. Because African American history has been so much about antiracist struggle; and because that struggle has been so consistently about demonstrating or making the argument for African American equality; and because our greatest victories often emerge from the linguistic and argumentative brilliance of poets, teachers, grassroots organizers, preachers, politicians, essayists, and musicians—all people who work with words—it makes sense to organize that study around the spoken and written word.

A focus on "the word" allows for a somewhat stable narrative. We can link the power and commitment of Stevie Wonder's music (Atwater, 1995) to the development of Malcolm X's political voice and his ability to not only take the best of the African American homiletic tradition but also turn that tradition on its head, to Carol Moseley Braun's signifyin' on Jesse Helms in formal legislative debate (Crenshaw, 1997),[1] to innumerable unnamed people across historical eras and social, political, and economic circumstances based on their use of argument to pursue a collective agenda on behalf of Black people, whether that agenda be one of resistance and revolution (Smith, 1969) or access to some notion of "the good life" (Golden & Rieke, 1971). More importantly, "the word" as the organizing trope of African American rhetorical study provides scholars and students with a foundation on which to offer that narrative unshaken by the rapid changes that occur in communication media. It doesn't matter whether we talk about poetry that was assumed to be imitative because it could not be conceived that it was written by an African American person, as in the case of Phillis Wheatley, or whether we talk of the multimedia connectivity of Tom Joyner's attempts to get Black folks to "party with a purpose,"[2] the same analytical tools allow us to talk about all African American rhetorical production.

This is not an easy argument to make, though—especially in the current context of the Digital Divide in which the common assumption is that Black people don't exist. At least not on-line we don't—or so we might be led to believe. Caught between cyberspace theory that argues race is irrelevant (and that it should be) on-line, a history of African American social and political struggle that seems to privilege cultural production over scientific and technological production, and conversations about access that attempt to argue that one only need to own a particular tool to have that access, African Americans occupy a Discursive Divide far broader than the digital one that we've all heard about during the last few years. We have all witnessed conversations, either in scholarly or broadcast media, about what African American people supposedly don't do (own computers, embrace technology, enter science and technology careers), and why we supposedly don't do these things. Add to the pervasiveness of that discourse the fact that African Americans do often have a healthy dose of technological skepticism, fostered by a long history of witnessing the ways technologies have been used to create ways to subjugate or exterminate people (the two words *Tuskegee Experiment,* uttered in the presence of Black folk, are enough to remind any doubter about the depth of that awareness), and it would be easy to understand why African American rhetorical scholarship has followed the path that it has.

Another reason why the Digital Divide and other technological divides are so pervasive and why it might be difficult to make the connections that I'm pressing for is a lack of a solid understanding of what actually constitutes meaningful access among many of those who are legitimately concerned with technology issues. The rigidity of these technological divides should help make it clear why there is so much at stake in the connections between technologies and people's lived experiences, and the ways those experiences inform social, cultural, political, and economic struggle. Even the Clinton administration's efforts to address the Digital Divide seemed based on a definition that amounts to the same access African American children have to public education or African American Floridians to the franchise: a vaguely articulated right to be in the same space, *if* one navigates all the other barriers that prevent that presence (U.S. Department of Commerce/National Telecommunications and Information Administration [hereafter Department of Commerce], 1995, 1998, 2000).

In the academy, for the few scholars who do take up the Digital Divide or technology access as important issues, access is either defined as the mere ownership of or proximity to a computer or Internet connection, which Taborn critiques in his response to a Pew Foundation study of African American computer use, or access is solely the responsibility of those groups trying to get it. They must own computers, they must learn how to use them, they must come to know and appreciate the conventions set up in this new space, and they must unconditionally accept the ways technology will "transform" their lives. But the Digital Divide is about far more than just computer ownership. Science and technology issues shape the power relationships that have historically provided the exigence for African American rhetors, and they have influenced—tangibly and intangibly—the rhetorical situation through the dynamics of control that determine who gets to speak to whom, in what circumstances, and to what degree those messages are mediated, as I will discuss later.

Even with all of the difficulties that might prevent one from connecting African American rhetoric and technology issues, these connections have been and are being made in African American studies. Over twenty-five years ago, Herman and Barbara Young in "Science and Black Studies," urged African American studies programs to make study of the sciences a more central part of their curricula: "[M]ost Black Studies courses have been concentrated in the fields of humanities, history, and social sciences. They have neglected one area of special significance in achieving their objectives, which is the contributions of Black men [and women] to the fields of science" (Young & Young, 1977, p. 386). For Herman and Barbara Young, more focus on these achievements would help meet all of African American studies' major disciplinary goals, including "provid[ing] alternative ideologies for social change" (p. 386).

A quarter of a century later, few African American studies programs have answered the call. Abdul Alkalimat, African American studies director at the University of Toledo, is one of those who has, however, by explicitly linking technology to inquiry in African American studies. In addition to creating eBlack, the on-line presence of Toledo's Africana studies program, and in Alkalimat's words, the "virtualization of the Black experience," he uses the current moment's conversations about technology to keep discussions about what African Americans can and should do with technolog(ies) grounded in past struggle.

Alkalimat argues in an article published on cy.Rev (www.cyRev.com), "Technological Revolution and Prospects for Black Liberation in the 21st Century" (2001a), that the relationship between technological change and the economic, social, cultural, and political struggle of African

American people is the missing link in the "history of African American history." Technological advances that improved the mechanization of the cotton and auto industries bring this relationship into relief for Alkalimat: "Cotton and auto, as the leading sectors of the US economy— 19th century agricultural and 20th century industrial production— helped to structure more than 150 years of African American labor. It has been this economic structure of how agriculture and industry have utilized African American labor that has set the stage for all of African American history" (2001a). The perfection of the cotton gin provides the quintessential example of this relationship between technology innovation and African American struggle in Alkalimat's analysis, as it is the creation of the cotton gin that made cotton king and slavery even more profitable than it had been by the 1800s (2001a).

What makes this relationship important for the study of African American rhetoric is the fact that not only did these technological changes structure the conditions in which African American people lived but they influenced the environments in which they organized to resist those conditions. Just as the cotton gin mechanized the cleaning of cotton and created incredible demands for slave labor, Alkalimat notes, the mechanical cotton picker made sharecroppers obsolete and was thus another important factor in what is commonly known as the "second great migration" of African Americans to the North (those migrating from the South after 1940) and led to conditions becoming favorable for the Civil Rights Movement to emerge. He shows a similar pattern of high demand for African American labor being created and then obliterated by technological change in the automobile industry, and he points to the staggering unemployment statistics for African American men in the 1980s and 1990s in northern cities as evidence.

One need not agree with the breadth of Alkalimat's claim that "the most profound historical changes are linked to changes in technology" to take from his analysis an understanding that important connections exist between technological history in the United States and African American struggle. An important part of this connection is the relationship between communication technologies and rhetorical production, which is just as strong as that which Alkalimat sketches in African American history. It is this relationship that I want to point to, as a way of extending Alkalimat's argument and making it relevant for African American rhetorical study. Advances in communication technologies do not simply amount to insignificant changes in the medium. All technologies come packaged with a set of politics: if those technologies are not inherently political, the conditions in which they are created and in which they circulate into a society are political and influence their uses in that society (Winner, 1986), and those politics can profoundly change the spaces in which messages are created, received, and used. The potential of the changes in these spaces can be staggering when considered in light of the communicative possibilities they can either open up or shut down. One's ability to understand and operate within those changed spaces determines whether her or his linguistic dexterity is even relevant—as any faculty member who has been flamed (translation: dissed) on an E-mail listserv will be happy to explain.

African Americans' ability to make the move from "ideology to information," and to take African American experience into new technological spaces, to digitize African American history, struggle, and celebration, is not only important to survival for Alkalimat but a move that offers possibilities that did not exist before: "While ideological struggle has persisted the information revolution has undercut the material conditions for ideological ignorance. The information revolution has increased our capacity to produce, store, distribute, and consume all texts—written, oral, and visual" (Alkalimat, 2001b). The Web site eBlack, as a model of what is possible when African American studies, traditions, and struggle, are digitized, is currently comprised of five programs or parts: a listserv, a distance education component, a community service initiative helping local churches to create and maintain Web sites, a Web site for the Black Radical Congress, and a research Web site on Malcolm X. Alkalimat notes that while many of the community members and activists involved were skeptical about whether cyberspace could be an important site of struggle, organizing in this way not only allowed participants to document their work in spaces they could control but also prevented "factionalism and a hardening of ideological lines" (2001b).

What is important about Alkalimat's work with eBlack is not just that the histories and work of African American leaders, activists, and organizations can be put on-line but that cyberspace can transform that work because it is a space that, for all of the barriers to access that exist now, can allow more direct control of one's message than other media. As the Internet is currently constructed, a person who has a connection can view any site he or she wishes (that is not password protected, of course), and those with messages to share can target them directly to those they want to reach, unhindered by a television network's assumptions about African American people or the limited range of AM radio or cable television public access channels. And it is far easier to own the means of production than it is a television station, radio station, newspaper, or magazine. So the possibilities for individual activists and rhetors are impressive, but they are just as bright for students and scholars of African American rhetoric. Imagine, for example, if as a result of eBlack's work with churches in the Toledo area, or of any effort in any town, that twenty years from now, two or five or ten churches in that area have Web sites that have archived all of their pastors' sermons (either in print, audio, video, or some combination of forms) over that twenty-year period, with examples of church bulletins, directories, activities, and newsletters as well. One of the most studied forms in African American rhetoric, the sermon, becomes much easier to study thoroughly, because many of the five challenges to offering rhetorical criticism of sermons that Lyndrey Niles (1995) identifies can be greatly minimized:

> 1. Most African American sermons were not and are not prepared in manuscript form
> 2. Most African American sermons through the centuries were not and are not tape recorded during delivery
> 3. Some preachers are reluctant to release copies for criticism
> 4. Since most African American sermons are in dialogue form, manuscripts may not satisfactorily represent what actually took place in the church
> 5. Sermons in the African American tradition were not written to be read. Much of the real impact, therefore, is lost unless the critic knows how the words would have sounded, and can picture the delivery in his or her mind as he or she reads the manuscript. (p. 81)

As I noted earlier and as Niles's list shows, African American rhetoric has always been multimedia, has always been about body and voice and image, even when they only set the stage for language. And again, even with a definition of African American rhetoric as being about the word, careful considerations of how current technologies can extend our study will provide a much richer body of work for rhetorical criticism and analysis.

This is not just about the politics of a particular writing, speaking, or designing space, nor is it just about the benefits that can exist for students and scholars of rhetoric. Technologies shape all five of the classical canons and greatly affect the rhetorical situation, however one might

define the concept. Whether the technology involved is a soapbox, mega-
phone, printing press, typewriter, telegraph, microphone, television,
radio, or Web site, the tools available affect the means available because
of how they configure relationships between rhetors and their potential
audiences. What gave Hip Hop such powerful potential in African
American (and later worldwide) culture was not the lyrics, the break-
dances, or the content or quality of individual "bombs" or grafitti paint-
ings. The magic that could have produced a movement was in the ways
young African American men and women used every technology available to seize public space for themselves long before official organs like
major record companies or Billboard magazine would sanction their
efforts and then forced their way into access to more mainstream technologies to even further write, rhyme, and tag their bodies and their
stories into public discourses and imaginations. From two turntables, a
mixer, and the biggest speakers imaginable (or in some cases, just a
microphone or a pen and a notebook full of rhymes or even just the
human voice in the battle rhyme tradition) to flyers and posters used to
promote parties, to late-night radio shows and networks of callers being organized to create buzz for records and artists, to independent—
well, once-independent—record labels, to Chuck D's defense of Napster,
to Russell Simmons's bum rush of U.S. Senate hearings on music content, Hip Hop—at its best—has always been about taking, jacking, access to the means of production, however inequitably those means had
been distributed.

Lest one assume that the relatively obvious case of Hip Hop is the
only moment in the African American rhetorical tradition to be shaped
in important ways by the relationships between specific communication
technologies and rhetorical performances, let me briefly offer two other
examples. Thousands of books and articles have been written for scholars, students, and the general public that speak to the rhetorical brilliance
of Malcolm X and Martin Luther King, Jr. One might even go so far as
to say that their combined persuasive brilliance accounted, in part at
least, for the rise of African American rhetoric as a distinct field of study.
Their speeches and writings have been collected, anthologized, and analyzed from a seemingly endless range of perspectives.

And that discursive brilliance deserves every bit of the attention it has
received and more. But as Keith Gilyard (1991, 1996) points out regularly, there are and were many in African American communities all over
space and time who had King's or Malcolm's oratorical gifts.[3] Little, if
any, of those books and articles accounts for either their most impor-

tant or most successful rhetorical performances. In a personal interview (August 15, 2001), Gilyard noted how little attention communication technologies are given in the study of African American rhetoric:

> There *are* some random mentions of television or radio in conversations about African American rhetoric, but little sustained inquiry about what those relationships were. Taylor Branch makes mention of how King used television, and Mike Dyson talks about the influence that watching King on TV as a nine-year-old boy had on his life, but no one is pushing those questions. If you really want to talk about it, I'd say that the success of Malcolm's rhetoric was deeply connected to the albums that were out there. Not everybody was gathered around that soapbox on 125th Street, but everybody did have those speeches at home on wax.

An extension of Gilyard's comments would suggest that as valuable as the innumerable speeches, sermons, letters, editorial pieces, essays, and books that they wrote were, one could argue that the single most important rhetorical achievements in both King's and Malcolm's careers occurred on television. What transformed a Civil Rights Movement from a set of disturbances led by a "rabble rouser" to a coherent national movement led by one who would become a Nobel Prize winner and national hero depended greatly on King's grasp of how television worked as a rhetorical tool.

King knew that because of national television news, he had a vehicle for demonstrating, almost instantly—as contrasted with the weekly publication cycle in national newspapers and magazines, or even the dailies—the extreme nature of White racism and the moral justice of civil rights protesters and their cause. And even beyond the relative speed with which these messages could be carried was the fact of video footage: instead of mere still photographs, or the verbal or written descriptions of writers and television anchors, Americans could see the action happening. For all of King's eloquence with the written and spoken word, it was a visual rhetoric of innocent protesters being beaten and hosed, of masses of Black people being willing to sacrifice all they had, of callous politicians that he could count on to put extreme words with those hoses and beatings that made the appeals successful. In spite of all of the work that has been done on the intellectual and philosophical underpinnings of King's tactics during the Civil Rights Movement, however, studies exploring the rhetorical underpinnings of his radical, aggressive nonviolence—especially as it relates to what was still an emerging technology at the time—are nonexistent.

The same argument could be made for Malcolm X: again, not in any way opposed to the focus that has been given to his oral and written ability but alongside it. While Malcolm X was verbally brilliant, the Nation of Islam has always had verbally gifted mosque leaders and spokesmen. But the Nation had been dismissed as either an irrelevant cult or as extremist, even early in Malcolm's own career. One moment, carried on television, is important to how we view him as a rhetor, and it possibly changed Malcolm's role in the movement. On July 13–17, 1959, the television special "The Hate that Hate Produced" aired nationwide, bringing Malcolm X and the Nation of Islam to the public's attention. While this is not the space to offer a detailed analysis of that television moment, let me suggest how rhetorical analysis can also take into account questions of how the technology of the medium and issues of access to it can shape the rhetorical situation in ways that a communicator must reckon with in order to be effective.

While a person who is interviewed on a television show does get a chance to speak directly to many different audiences, that person in some ways has very little control over what gets spoken. In the case of Mike Wallace's special on the Black Muslims (as the Nation of Islam was called then) and Malcolm X, Malcolm was presented on a television show that writers, directors, producers, and television executives planned and approved. Contemporary relevance is obviously a factor in why networks pursue news specials, and this relevance is calculated by the number of potential viewers such a special might attract.

So once a concept is approved, the special is planned, footage is collected, research is performed, the episodes of the series are planned, the reporter's narrative written, and interviews performed, all before the public sees the individual invited to appear on it, even when the special is live. So decisions have been made about what to include and exclude, even from individual interviews; how those segments will be arranged; and how the reporter will comment on them, both before and after. The interviewer knows much sooner than the subject what questions will be asked, and in what order, and how much time the subject will be given to answer-even when guests receive some briefing on those questions in advance. And even after all of that, the interviews, the speeches, or whatever else might be presented about an individual or organization is edited with consideration for time constraints, commercial slots, the interviewer himself or herself (after all, any news show is far more about the anchor or the talent than any individual guest), and the biases of those involved in the process.

With all that in mind, consider the television landscape for African Americans in 1959, if in 2001 organizations such as the NAACP still have to threaten boycotts of networks over hiring practices and issues of representation. Television, 1959: What role did African Americans play in the overall business of this communication space? What writers, engineers, videographers, reporters, anchors, directors, or producers worked on television? Where could an African American leader go to present a message on television where African Americans played at least some part in deciding how that message would be shaped and received?

To consider this specific news special, since it was the only game in town for Malcolm at the time, how does one answer questions when the interviewer controls the questions and the conventions of turn taking; when an entire staff overtly shaped the context before the interview happened and had the power to edit as it saw fit without even consulting the person interviewed before the special aired, or even on live television; and when the staff can pace the show in such a way that the interviewer got the first, last, and arbiting words? In such a situation, how did Malcolm manage the interviews despite this tremendous difference in access and power? How did he respond to what he knew was a stacked rhetorical deck on a four-day special whose title took for granted the widespread assumption that he and his group were hatemongers? How can these considerations help us to appreciate even more Malcolm's cool under pressure on the program, his incredible quick-wittedness and argumentative focus in his answers to the questions asked him?

This is not an attempt at a definitive reading of either Malcolm X or Martin Luther King Jr. Rather, I'm trying to suggest how a change in the analytic tools we bring to bear on the study of African American rhetoric can allow us to do what we have always done better; take us to texts and performances that we haven't given as much consideration to; *and* by taking access however we can get it, by committing to work with new technologies, acquire far more control over messages than we have had at other times in our history.

As powerful as this potential is, however, it is anything but a given. The slightest look at how African Americans and other people of color are used in technology marketing remind us of just how slippery the notion of controlling one's message really is. Lisa Nakamura, in her chapter in the edited collection *Race in Cyberspace* (2000) demonstrates the ways many television advertising campaigns for computers and

Internet services contribute to the construction of cyberspace as White by default, even as those campaigns seem to offer a vision of inclusion in the new economy. James Stewart, in his 2001 Martin Luther King Jr. Memorial Lecture at Pennsylvania State University, examines the disturbing ways King's oratorical gifts and the critiques of globalism that he embraced late in his career have been summarily co-opted by global capitalist forces in an advertising campaign for the telecommunication networks company Alcaltel. There is already a narrative in place about African Americans, technology, and technology access that must be disrupted. Tyrone Taborn's words in the beginning of this chapter and his work with the journal *US Black Engineer: Information Technology* offers ways that it might be.

Just as access to an education depends on far more than the mere right to attend the same school as someone who already has that access, meaningful access to technology requires much more than a computer or Internet connection, or television, or radio, or any other individual tool. Taborn articulates many of the important differences between common assumptions about technology access and what it really demands: "Measuring the *real* Digital Divide means looking at many factors, including: quality of Internet content and its relevance to us, computer literacy rate and level of computer skills among African Americans, employability and employment rate of African Americans in technical jobs, representation of African Americans as owners of high-tech enterprises" (2001, p. 8). Those who use such narrow definitions of technology access as mere proximity to a computer connected to the Internet (Department of Commerce, *Falling Through The Net,* 1995, 1998, 2000) or rate of diffusion (Rogers, 1985, Pew Foundation, 2001), Taborn continues, "would love to have us focus all of our energy on putting computers into every school, to guarantee themselves another generation of technology consumers. But the real issue for the African American community is how to use technology to become technology innovators and producers" (p. 8).

In his list of characteristics of the "real" Digital Divide, Taborn is critical of the differences in material conditions that make up gaps in access between people of color and Whites, but he also examines content and literacy, issues that are entirely about writing with, for, and about technology. While Taborn includes those concerns, I want to foreground them and push his definition a little further, to suggest that the Digital Divide, and technology access more broadly, is primarily a rhetorical problem, or at least as much as it is a material one. Access to computers and Internet technologies is about the writing of content, but it is also about how documentation and training materials are created, about how policy is written to either ensure inclusion or foster marginalization, about how technologies are marketed, and even about how interfaces—the spaces where users who are new to a given technology learn how to use it—are written and designed. It's about the communication networks that exist in real communities that persuade one that he or she must develop new sets of literacies and that let people know where they can go to work on them if they do.

The rhetorical part of the problem of access begins with the definitional problems that I've outlined and includes the fact that so few in the academy, the corporate sector, and government see it as a problem worth addressing in a serious, sustained way. It includes the fact that race, gender, and many other factors are often ignored in deciding how computers and other products are tested to minimize problems users might have. It involves the ways that interfaces, the environments either onscreen or in a physical place where users interact with a computer, show little understanding of how to genuinely consider those who use them, even when their creators are genuinely concerned about providing more equal access. These rhetorical problems—print, oral, visual, and design problems—are so important because they construct the experiences that users have with computers, software, and other tools, just as the assumptions of a teacher, the environment of a school and its classrooms, the content of the curriculum, and that particular teacher's and school's grading and disciplinary policies make all the difference in the quality of a student's access to education.

A serious consideration of the relationships between technologies and rhetorical production throughout African American history can dramatically reshape African American rhetorical study, opening up new spaces for inquiry even while giving us new ways to help our students and the public appreciate how African American language and cultural productions have been used as technologies. The opportunity that such an approach opens up is, as I see it, connected by four vital tasks: (1) to reexamine those works and communicators who have been a part of African American rhetorical study—the poems, the plays, the sermons, the essays, the pamphlets, the newspapers, the journals and others—and to ask how a strong reading of those texts as technological, as well as linguistic and argumentative performances, can help us appreciate the language and persuasion in them even better; (2) to look for ways to open up what we think of as the African American rhetorical tradition, to pay just as much attention to image, body, and design as we do to language in attempts at persuasion; (3) to pay careful attention to the relationships that exist between race and emerging technologies so that we can teach students how to operate with those changed, and changing, spaces; and (4) to integrate the work we do as thoroughly as possible with the technologies that are available to us now, borrowing, stealing, jacking access to them however we must.

Notes

1. In her article "Resisting Whiteness' Rhetorical Silence," Carrie Crenshaw examines debate within the U.S. Senate Judiciary Committee between Moseley-Braun and Jesse Helms over the insignia of the United Daughters of the Confederacy. Crenshaw reports that Moseley Braun responded to Helms's silence about the relationship between the Confederate flag and slavery with a patterned silence of her own: by repeating "we all know" over and over again, she signifies on his silence with her own silence that uncovers what Helms would rather avoid.

2. The *Tom Joyner Morning Show* is a syndicated radio show, rated number one in the nation in urban markets. Joyner frequently invokes this phrase to describe his show's aims. The show itself combines a mock soap opera, comedians as hosts, and weekly live performances in cities that carry it with political commentary and foundation work on behalf of historically Black colleges and universities.

3. In fact, Gilyard's work in *Voices of the Self* (1991) and *Let's Flip the Script* (1996) is built on the premise that rhetors like King and Malcolm emerge from deeply rooted rhetorical and discursive traditions in African American communities, and that for all of the work in composition that has branded Black students as remedial writers, these students come out of these same traditions, and that these traditions can be foregrounded in writing instruction.

11

We Is Who We Was: The African/ American Rhetoric of *Amistad*

Kermit E. Campbell

Dry your tears, Africa!
Your children come back to you
their hands full of playthings
and their hearts full of love.
They return to clothe you
in their dreams and their hopes.
—Bernard Dadié, "Dry Your Tears, Afrika!"

Since the beginning of the nation, white Americans have suffered
from a deep inner uncertainty as to who they really are. One of
the ways that has been used to simplify the answer has been to
seize upon the presence of black Americans and use them as a
marker, a symbol of limits, a metaphor for the "outsider." Many
whites could look at the social position of blacks and feel that
color formed an easy and reliable gauge for determining to what
extent one was or was not American. Perhaps that is why one of
the first epithets that many European immigrants learned when
they got off the boat was the term "nigger"—it made them feel
instantly American. But this is tricky magic. Despite his racial
difference and social status, something indisputably American
about Negroes not only raised doubts about the white man's
value system but aroused the troubling suspicion that whatever
else the true American is, he is also somehow black.
—Ralph Ellison, "What America
Would Be Like Without Blacks"

IN SPITE OF ALL THE HYPE, OR MOST LIKELY BECAUSE OF IT, I HAD
resolved that I wouldn't see it. Oh, I didn't doubt that it was just as
everyone (including my wife) had described it: monumentally tragic,
romantic, historic. Yes, it was all of these, I discovered many months later

when I finally gave in and saw it at home on video. Indeed, it was deeply tragic, and yet, I soon realized, its tragedy bore little relation to me. It was intensely romantic, but its romance moved me only superficially. And, yes, it was historic, yet its fatal history somehow seemed to negate or overshadow my own. But then one rather uneventful day while writing at my computer I happened to remember an intimate connection: Shine. "Oh yeah," I loudly pronounced to myself, "my man Shine." He took part in that historic-tragic-romantic event that everybody's so stirred up about, didn't he? In fact, wasn't he the real hero? Let's see, how does the story go? Ah yes, . . .

> The eighth of May was a hell of a day.
> I don't know, but that's what my folks say.
> The news reached the little seaport town
> That the old Titanic was finally goin' down.
> There was a fella on board they called Shine,
> Was so black he changed the world's mind.
> Now Shine was downstairs eating his peas—his black-eyed
>   peas—
> When the water come up to his knees.
> Shine said, "Captain, Captain, I was downstairs eating my
>   peas
> When the water come up to my knees."
> Captain said, "Shine, Shine set your black ass down
> I got ninety-nine pumps to pump the water down."
> Shine went back downstairs looking through space.
> That's when the water came up to his waist.
> Shine said, "Captain, Captain, I was downstairs looking
>   through space
> When the water came up to my waist."
> Captain said, "Shine, Shine set your black ass down,
> I got ninety-nine pumps to pump the water down."
> Shine went downstairs, and he ate a piece of bread.
> That's when the water came above his head.
> Shine said, "Captain, Captain, I was downstairs eatin' my
>   bread
> And that damn water came above my head."
> Captain said, "Shine, Shine set your black ass down,
> I got ninety-nine pumps to pump the water down."
> Shine say, "Look here, Captain I'm a scared man.

I'd rather be out there on that iceberg goin' around and 'round
Than to be on this big mother—— when it's goin' down."
So Shine hit the water and he begin to swim,
With ninety-nine millionaires lookin' at him.
Big man from Wall Street came on the second deck.
In his hand he held a book a checks.
He said, "Shine, Shine save poor me,
I'll make you as rich as any black man can be."
Shine said, "You don't like my color and you down on my race,
You better get yo ass overboard and give these sharks a chase."
Now the Captain's daughter came out on the second deck
With her drawers in her hand and brassiere around her neck.
She said, "Shine, Shine, save poor me,
I'll give you all this white ass your eyes can see."
Shine say, "there's some of that on land, there's some of that
    on the sea,
But the some of that on land is the one for me."
And Shine swum on.
Now when the news got to port, the great Titanic had sunk,
There was old Shine on Main Street damn near drunk.
A whore said, "Shine, daddy, why didn't you drown?"
Shine said, "I had a cork in my ass, baby, and I couldn't go
    down!"
                    (adapted from versions recorded in Roger Abraham's
                        Deep Down in the Jungle and Bruce Jackson's
                        Get Your Ass in the Water and Swim Like Me)

Now that's a historic-tragic-romantic tale I can relate to—though, I
must admit, its bawdiness makes for more comedy than tragedy. But of
course the toast is myth, grand hyperbole, if you will. Shine (a shine?)
plays no part in the "real" *Titanic* story, at least that is what we have
been led to believe based on historical accounts and cinematic portray-
als such as director James Cameron's critically acclaimed *Titanic*. There
are no Black heroes in Cameron's *Titanic*—no Black Leonardo Dicaprio
for Black teenage girls to swoon over, no Black Kate Winslet for young
Black boys to imagine bangin' in the back of a Model T, no Black captain or ship designer for Black men and women to take pride in for
bravely going down with the maiden vessel. *Politically Incorrect* talk
show host Bill Maher would, I am reminded, rail at this compulsion to
insist on including, say, racial minorities in everything, in a historical

event in which they clearly did not take part. But what does Maher, or any of us, really know about the accuracy of recorded history? Case in point: a June 2000 report by *Ebony* magazine that a Black family was, in fact, aboard the *Titanic*. Apparently, a Haitian man, his French wife, and their children were among the passengers on the ship, but not until recently was this Black element in the *Titanic* story brought to light through an exhibit of the Chicago Museum of Science and Industry.

In any case, I'm intrigued by the fact that some ten or twenty years after the sinking of the voyager *Titanic* in April 1912, some African Americans somewhere devised their own account of the event—one that over time has become a classic toast in the African American oral tradition. This appropriation of the *Titanic* story in the African American oral tradition suggests the felt need among some African Americans to rewrite history in their own image, even where no authentic record (or acknowledged one) of such history exists. But make no mistake, there are those not-so-rare occasions when a long forgotten or neglected historical moment is recovered. This seems to me to be the case with the Steven Spielberg movie *Amistad*, which was also based on historical fact. Eclipsed by *Titanic* at the box office in 1997, however, *Amistad* did not prevail upon the nation's consciousness nearly as much as *Titanic* did. Perhaps many people, even some African Americans, assumed that *Amistad* was *Roots* revisited—another radical revisionist film designed to sear already guilt-ridden White consciences and rekindle the waning Black rage of the Afrocentric movement. Whatever the reasons for its lackluster appeal at theaters, *Amistad* recounts a prodigious historic event little known to most Americans. And yet, it is one that, unlike *Titanic,* has everything to do with being an American, everything to do with Shine, everything to do with me—a descendant of Africans and African American slaves, mixed with unspecified amounts of Native American and Caucasian blood. In a rather indirect way, the account of the *Amistad* Africans also has everything to do with rhetorical history, with nineteenth-century American oratory and civil protest, the subject of this essay.

Specifically, in this essay, I argue that the *Amistad* Africans—as brave defendants in their moral and legal fight for freedom from captivity and slavery—left an indelible imprint on American oratorical culture. They, of course, were not the first or the last Africans or African descendants to do so; however, like no other slave or African captive before or after them, the *Amistad* Africans' story was heard before the highest court in the land, the United States Supreme Court, and their cause was championed by a man who represented, at various times, the highest executive and legislative offices in the U.S. government, the former president and then congressman John Quincy Adams. Represented as such by Adams, the capture of the *Amistad* Africans and their trial before the Supreme Court, I believe, stand as a defining moment not only in American judicial history but in the history of American rhetoric and racial politics. Yet it is an unwritten or forgotten chapter in the history of racism and rhetoric in America—for we have assumed that American rhetoric is, as Toni Morrison states about American literature, "free of, uninformed, and unshaped by the four-hundred-year-old presence of, first, Africans and then African Americans" (1992a, pp. 4–5). Historians of rhetoric and rhetorical theorists, I maintain, must account for this undeniable presence, that in our attempts to construct histories of rhetoric or conceptualize rhetorical practices we must look for the many lacunae in the dominant rhetorical texts (and contexts). That should be our first task. Our second task should be to determine the lasting impact of this dark presence on what we do, on what we have long perceived to be *The Tradition* of American or Western rhetoric. If we wish American rhetoric to reflect our national history and character accurately, then we must begin to engage critically in what Paul Gilroy calls the "theorisation of creolisation" or "hybridity" (1993, p. 2).

I propose to discuss these matters by focusing on three stages in what I call a hybrid African/American rhetorical history: (1) *Who we was* for a synchronic account of our rhetorical past, the *Amistad* rebellion and the trial before the U.S. Supreme Court; (2) *Who we are* for a brief diachronic look at the omissions in current constructions of our rhetorical history; and (3) *Who we gonna be* for prospects for our rhetorical future, that is, my hope for rhetorical studies that reflect the hybrid racial/ethnic identities that have long constituted our national culture and discursive practices.

Who We Was as Africa's Victims, America's Victors

For readers unfamiliar with it, let me begin by recounting the *Amistad* saga as we know it. The time was April 1839; the place was a slave factory at Lomboko,[1] a harbor on the coast of Sierra Leone, West Africa. From about five hundred men, women, and children originally taken by the Portuguese slave ship *Tecora* to Havana, Cuba, fifty-three Africans were purchased by Spaniards José Ruiz and Pedro Montes and were placed aboard the schooner *La Amistad* for a short journey to Puerto Principe, east of Havana. During this part of their journey, Sengbe (or

Joseph Cinque as he was renamed by his Spanish enslavers) somehow managed to seize upon a nail, with which he was able to pry open the lock to his shackles. A revolt then ensued, as one by one the newly freed Africans took up arms against their captors. Within a fairly short time, the Africans subdued the seven-man crew and prevailed. At last, they were headed home—east to Africa, or so they thought. To safely navigate the ship to the African coast, two (three according to some reports) members of the crew were spared, Ruiz and Montes. The two of them feign compliance with the plan to sail back to Africa, for at night when the Africans were asleep they steered the schooner west toward Cuba or the slave-holding states of the American South. Adrift for several days as a result of this clever plot, the ship was spotted and seized by the U.S. brig *Washington* in Long Island Sound in August 1839. The African rebels were at once arrested and taken to New London and later New Haven, Connecticut, for imprisonment and subsequent trial. In the course of an eighteen-month period, up to March 1841, the Africans were tried in three courts, including the Supreme Court, before they were finally set free and allowed to return to their West African homeland.

Thus far, I have referred to the *Amistad* collective as "Africans," as if they saw themselves as a singular, unified, and homogeneous group. These fifty-three (actually some forty-four or less by the time they appear before the Supreme Court) captives were a mixture of different African tribes, including the Temne, Fula, Kissi, Sherbro, Lokko, Ibo, Mandinka, and Mende (or Mendi in some documents), the predominant group. Unfortunately, we aren't told very much about each of these tribes in the film or in the various historical narratives (e.g., Mary Cable's *Black Odyssey: The Case of the Slave Ship "Amistad,"* 1977; Howard Jones's *Mutiny on the "Amistad,"* 1987), but from novelist Alex Pate's rendition of the David Franzoni and Steven Zaillian screenplay, we do get a brief introduction to the Mende, the tribe to which Sengbe belonged. The Mende—according to Pate whose notes on this are quite consistent with reputed historian John Blassingame in *Slave Testimony: Two Centuries of Letters, Speeches, Interviews, and Autobiographies*—were farmers, hunters, garment makers, teachers, and doctors (1977, p. 182). Sengbe, in fact, was a rice planter and son of a village leader in Mende. Had he not been taken captive and sold to repay a debt he owed to a Vai tribesman, he would have assumed his father's position as a leader in the Mani village of Mende. Although the details on this are sketchy, the Mende apparently had a village judicial system and, according to Blassingame, a written language (1977, p. 30). The Mende were not as formidable in war as the Temne (their neighbors); however, they were competent warriors, well prepared to defend themselves when the occasional battle erupted (p. 183).

One of the more interesting characteristics of the Mende, I have found, is the importance they place on ritual practices in daily life. Pate explains that "[f]rom birth to death, the Mende would call upon the generosity and wisdom of the ancestors to guide them. Much of their culture was governed by secret tribal organizations, like the Poro for men, and the Sande for women, that regulated and celebrated nearly every significant event in a person's life" (pp. 182–183). Sengbe himself, a young man of about twenty-five years at the time of his capture in February or March 1839, appeared to be an avid adherent of these ritual practices.

Two particular scenes in the film version *Amistad* provide very telling glimpses of African or Mende cultural practices that bear on rhetoric. The first of these is a burial ceremony that takes place while the *Amistad* Africans await trial in New Haven. After contracting a disease, Fala, the sole Kissi among them, dies and is put to rest. As is the custom in burial rituals (or so it would seem based on the screenplay), Sengbe (played by Djimon Hounsou), in this case, first washes the body with a warm cloth and then takes a sharp instrument to make a cut across the back of one of Fala's hands. After he does this, he says (in Mende, of course), "There. You'll be recognized when you return" (Pate, 1997, pp. 174–175). Representing what appears to be multiple religious faiths (e.g., Muslim for the Temne and a kind of creationism for the Mende), each tribe offers its own distinct chant or prayer on behalf of Fala.

First, the Mende:

> Fala, Fala, be accepted in the paradise of the creator.
> *Yes, Fala, be accepted in a blanket of heaven.*

Then the Temne:

> One God, One God, God
> Prophet Muhammed
> Peace and blessing be upon him until the day we die.

The Ibo voice added:

> Bear it, bear it, bear it,
> Bearing it is best.
> Whosoever the burdens come upon,
> *Bearing it is best.* (p. 175; italics in original)

Resolved to pay proper tribute to Fala, Sengbe proclaims above their chants: "The unexpected always happens. We did what we could, but our efforts were in vain. The proud warrior, Fala, is dead" (p. 176). Maseray, one of the three young girls among the captives, then adds "a long plaintive song" (p. 176). The enactment of this ritual and the participation of each individual and group among them prompt Pate to liken the event to a staged play. Indeed, quite unlike traditional Christian burial rites in this country, the ceremony bears witness to one among many cultural practices the Africans may have remembered and sought to preserve while detained in the United States.

It's difficult to say how closely this rendition of a burial ceremony approximates the ritual practice among inhabitants of Sierra Leone or West Africa in the nineteenth century. Nevertheless, it effectively captures what Western scholars (see Arthur Smith) have come to understand about African cultural practices generally, that is, that they often depend on some form of communal engagement and performance, what's commonly referred to as *call and response*. One could, on the other hand, attribute this practice to the influence of African American Christian churches, for the Africans or "Mendians" were once said to have responded animatedly "in the manner of the congregation of the Colored Baptist Church" upon hearing a brief "sermon" given by Sengbe at one of their farewell meetings (Owens, 1953/1968, p. 296). But it is more likely that the influence came from the opposite direction, if not from the *Amistad* Africans themselves, certainly from enslaved Africans at an earlier time. In any case, as a ceremonial event, one requiring a specialized discourse, the ritual might be considered an example of what in ancient Greek rhetoric is called epideictic—only in this case the rhetoric consists of multiple speakers, a mix of speech genres, and various performative acts.

If Pate or Franzoni and Zaillian were for some unimaginable reason trying to score rhetorical points for the Africans with this rendition of a West African burial, they didn't stop with the epideictic. They ventured further even to the point of intimating that the Africans were up on their deliberative rhetoric as well. For Sengbe didn't head up the burial ritual by default; he was elected for that honor by the majority of the Africans who favored him over Yamba, his chief rival for leadership of the *Amistad* captives. The import of this election was, apparently, not lost on Theodore Joadson, a free Black American of New Haven who volunteered his time to assist in the *Amistad* case. Pate tells us that "Joadson had watched the scene with pride. He'd never imagined that Africans, his own forefathers, had ever been able to deliberate, to vote" (1997, p. 174). Apparently, neither had George Kennedy imagined it, for his *Comparative Rhetoric: An Historical and Cross-cultural Introduction* states unequivocally that voting traditionally has not existed in any non-Western society (1998, p. 65). But then Kennedy probably knows nothing about the story of Sengbe and the Africans captured aboard *La Amistad*.

The other scene in Spielberg's *Amistad* that reveals Mende or African cultural and discursive practice occurs in a private meeting John Quincy Adams (played by Anthony Hopkins) held with Sengbe just before the U.S. Supreme Court trial and in the trial itself when Adams presents his closing argument. The meeting between Adams and Sengbe came about because Sengbe, by way of his translator as messenger, continually prevailed upon Adams and Roger Baldwin (the attorney who successfully defended the Africans in the lower courts) questions about the case. Conscious of the odds against them, Adams says advisedly to the inquisitive African brought to his study in chains, "I'm being honest with you. Anything less would be disrespectful. I'm telling you, preparing you, I suppose, explaining to you that the task ahead of us is an exceptionally difficult one" (Pate, 1997, p. 289). To this, Sengbe responds, referring to his ancestors "We won't be going in there alone. I will call into the past, far back to the beginning of time and beg them to come help me at the judgment. I will reach back and draw them into me. And they must come, for at this moment, I am the whole reason they have existed at all" (pp. 289–290).

From Sengbe's statement, we see that Adams may have learned from Sengbe the value the Mende place on their ancestral past and the role it plays in determining an individual's present course of action. When Adams spoke before the Supreme Court following this encounter, he related Sengbe's story and incorporated it into his argument in the case.

> "Tradition. The Mende believe that if one can summon the spirit of one's ancestors, then they have never left and that wisdom and strength they fathered will come to his aid." He then walked to a wall lined with portraits of famous Americans. "Thomas Jefferson. Benjamin Franklin. James Madison. Alexander Hamilton. George Washington. John Adams." He stopped there and stared at the picture of his father. Adams regarded the picture and seemed to be talking to it when he continued. "We have long resisted asking you for guidance.

Perhaps we've feared in doing so, we might acknowledge that our individuality, which we so revere, is not entirely our own. Perhaps we've feared that an appeal to you might be taken for weakness. But we have to understand finally, that this is not so. We understand now." He looked at Cinque again. "We have been made to understand and to embrace the understanding that who we are is who we were." (Pate, 1997, pp. 298–299)

John Quincy Adams's dramatic appeal to the Court gave the Africans their freedom. But were it not for Sengbe, were it not for the *Amistad* Africans, neither Adams nor the Court would have so greatly appreciated the scope of the founding principles of the young nation: liberty and justice for all. Sengbe gave Adams and the nine justices of the U.S. Supreme Court their raison d'etre gave them the moral and ideological link to America's heritage as a free and independent nation. But is this what really happened? Did Sengbe and the others really introduce an African consciousness to American judicial rhetoric?

Who We Are as a People Followed by History like Shadows

Admittedly, the Spielberg version of Adams's speech before the Supreme Court inadequately represents the 135-page document Adams actually wrote and presented at the trial in February and March 1841 (see the Basic Afro-American Reprint Library, 1968). In this latter version, there appears to be little or no influence from Sengbe's stories. Rather, there we see references to early Western civilization (e.g., the Romans) and to traditional American precepts: natural rights, justice, and liberty. For instance, Adams remarks in his opening that

> I derive consolation from the thought that this Court is a Court of JUSTICE. And in saying so very trivial a thing, I should not on any other occasion, perhaps, be warranted in asking the Court to consider what justice is. Justice, as defined in the Institutes of Justinian, nearly 2000 years ago, and as it is felt and understood by all who understand human relations and human rights, is—
> "Constans et perpetua voluntas, jus suum cuique tribuendi."
> The constant and perpetual will to secure to every one HIS OWN right."

And in a Court of Justice, where there are two parties present, justice demands that the rights of each party should be allowed to himself, as well as that each party has a right, to be secured and protected by the Court. This observation is important, because I appear here on the behalf of thirty-six individuals, the life and liberty of every one of whom depend on the decision of this Court. (Basic Afro-American Reprint Library, 1968, pp. 3–4)

One cannot dismiss the discrepancy between the two versions. Perhaps for the sake of entertaining as well as enlightening viewers of the film, Spielberg took some liberties with the degree of influence he imbues Sengbe as having on the former president. It certainly made for an enormously dramatic scene toward the close of the movie when Adams connects our most sacred documents—the Declaration of Independence and U.S. Constitution—to a simple story told him by an unlearned African rice planter. Still, I am inclined to think that Sengbe and the *Amistad* Africans did have some effect on Adams's way of thinking about his argument on their behalf before the Court. In fact, portions of Adams's lengthy defense do suggest, at the very least, a conscious awareness of similarities between the African struggle for freedom and the fight for democracy in ancient Athens, which of course was the political pretext for Greek rhetoric.

Cinque and Grabeau are uncouth and barbarous names. Call them Harmodius and Aristogiton, and go back for moral principle three thousand years to the fierce and glorious democracy of Athens. They too resorted to lawless violence, and slew the tyrant to redeem the freedom of their country. For this heroic action they paid the forfeit of their lives; but within three years the Athenians expelled their tyrants themselves, and in gratitude to their self-devoted deliverers decreed, that henceforth no slave ever bear either of their names. Cinque and Grabeau are not slaves. Let them bear in future history the names of Harmodius and Aristogiton. (pp. 86–87)

As further evidence, one might also look to the letters Sengbe and the others wrote to Adams once they had acquired enough English to inscribe their thoughts in the new language. Among the collection of letters printed in *Slave Testimony,* only two are actually addressed to Adams, one dated January 4, 1841, a month or so before the Supreme

Court trial, and the other dated November 6, 1841, shortly before the Africans were to return home. The January letter would have reached Adams before the trial and might have had some effect on his thinking. Yet, the letter wasn't authored by Sengbe, and so it doesn't speak to any of the matters Sengbe discusses with Adams in the private meeting portrayed in the film. The letter was written by an eleven-year-old boy named Ka-le, one of the first of the Africans to learn to write English. Before Adams "talk[ed] to the grand court," Ka-le wanted to tell him the truth about the Mende, about the true thinking of the Mende (Blassingame, 1977, p. 33). In much of the letter, Ka-le strongly refutes what Americans have been saying about them, but more importantly, he writes that they have souls and would feel sorry not so much for themselves but those (i.e., Americans) who lied to them about their freedom. The excerpt below picks up on the concluding paragraph of Ka-le's letter.

> Dear friend Mr. Adams, you have children, you have friends, you love them, you feel very sorry if Mendi people come and carry them all to Africa. We feel bad for our friends, and our friends all feel bad for us. Americans no take us in ship. We on shore and Americans tell us slave ship catch us. The say we make you free. If they make us free, they tell truth, if they no make us free they tell lie. If America people give us free we glad, if they no give us free we sorry-we sorry for Mendi people little, we sorry for America people great deal, because God punish liars. We want you to tell court that Mendi people no want to go back to Havana, we no want to be killed. Dear friend, we want you to know how we feel. Mendi people *think, think, think.* Nobody know what he think. (p. 34)

In reality, perhaps Adams didn't learn the secret of Sengbe's strength, that is, the importance of a strong, even intrinsic link to the wisdom of one's ancestors. But if nothing else, Adams must have learned from Ka-le, Sengbe, and the whole *Amistad* affair what truth and freedom meant to the Africans, even more than what these meant to the Americans (those who were citizens) of his day. In this sense, Adams may have come to see rhetoric and oratory as African American rhetorician William Allen had a decade later: "Orations worthy the name must have for their subject personal or political liberty; and orators worthy of the name must necessarily originate in the nation that is on the eve of passing from a state of slavery into freedom" (1852/1998, p. 232). But if we look beyond the immediate issue of the *Amistad* case, perhaps we'll find that Adams did, in fact, see rhetoric in this way. Long before *Amistad*, in an entry in his journal of 1820, Adams states, "Never since human sentiments and human conduct were influenced by human speech was there a theme for eloquence like the free side of this question now before Congress of this Union. By what fatality does it happen that all the most eloquent orators of the body are on its slavish side?" (qtd. in W. L. Miller, 1995/1998, p. 185).

And eloquent oratory was something that Adams knew well. As a Massachusetts congressman, he had engaged often enough in the free side of this theme for eloquence. Toward the end of the twenty-fourth Congress in February 1837, for instance, he waxed eloquent on the constitutional right of any human being, slave or free, to petition Congress.

> [I]f the Creator of the Universe did not deny to the lowest, the humblest and the meanest the right of petition and supplication, were they to say they would not hear the prayer of these petitioners because they were slaves?
>
> If this House decides that it will not receive petitions from slaves, under any circumstances, it will cause the name of this country to be enrolled among the first of the barbarous nations. (qtd. in W. L. Miller, 1998, 268)

Not only as a rhetor but more importantly as a rhetorician Adams knew eloquent oratory. For this same John Quincy Adams who argued for the Africans before the Supreme Court and who served petitions against slavery for nine years in Congress had, in point of fact, held the Nicholas Boylston Chair of Rhetoric and Oratory at Harvard University, the very first endowed professorship of its kind in North America. In this capacity, Adams gave several lectures on classical rhetoric and oratory, which his students subsequently published as *Lectures on Rhetoric and Oratory* (1810/1962). However, had it not been for a chance reading of an article in the *Journal of Blacks in Higher Education* (Hill, 1997/1998, pp. 18, 102), the link between Adams the eloquent orator against slavery and Adams the Harvard lecturer and author of a treatise on rhetoric would have otherwise escaped me. No historical accounts of nineteenth-century rhetoric that I'm aware of relate Adams's Harvard lectures to his speech in the *Amistad* case or to his many arguments against slavery in Congress (see W. L. Miller, 1995). Nan Johnson's *Nineteenth-Century Rhetoric in North America* (1991) doesn't mention Adams's *Lectures* or his oratory in the *Amistad* trial. And although

Gregory Clark and S. Michael Halloran's *Oratorical Culture in Nine-teenth-Century America: Transformations in the Theory and Practice of Rhetoric* (1993) does mention Adams as a professor and practitioner of rhetoric, the book says nothing about his *Amistad* speech or his efforts to abolish slavery in Congress (or for that matter, slave oratory and abolitionism—see Royster's review in *College English*, 1996a).

Of course, I would be remiss if I neglected to admit that there was a substantial lapse of time between Adams's tenure at Harvard (1806–9) and his appearance before the Supreme Court in the *Amistad* trial (1841). In fact, the slavery issue doesn't come up in his *Lectures*—in which case, it would seem, Adams's later involvement with the slavery issue has no bearing on his prior contribution to rhetorical history. Yet, the concept of an "oratorical culture" that Clark and Halloran offer as a character-ization of the rhetorical climate of the early nineteenth century seems to me to have everything to do with slavery—if not because of the ora-tory of an accomplished political figure and rhetorician such as Adams, then certainly because of the rhetoric of distinguished abolitionists such as Lewis Tappan, William Lloyd Garrison, Frederick Douglass, and even unlearned fugitive slaves. Indeed, according to Blassingame (1977), the oratory of fugitive slaves was immensely popular around the time of the *Amistad* trial:

> JOHN A. COLLINS, AN AGENT of the American Anti-Sla-very Society, asserted in 1842 that "the public have itching ears to hear a colored man speak, and particularly a slave." Before and after that date many former slaves appeared before northern audiences and recounted their tales of bondage and freedom. Dramatic, filled with pathos and humor, these speeches by men and women fresh from slavery elicited sym-pathy, tears, and increased interest in abolition. Drawing on the black oral tradition, the fugitives delighted their audi-ences. During one speech the audience reportedly "cheered, clapped, stamped, laughed and wept, by turns." (p. 123)

Given the popular appeal of fugitive slave oratory, why then wouldn't it constitute part of nineteenth-century oratorical culture? Why wouldn't the oratory of African American free persons share in this oratorical culture? And why wouldn't the works of Black rhetoricians (not just orators) such as William Allen, Hallie Quinn Brown, and Newell Hous-ton Ensley (see Foner & Branham, 1998) be listed among the rhetorics of that time? Perhaps for the same reason that the Haitian Joseph

Phillippe Lemercier Larouche was omitted from the records of the *Titanic*'s victims. Larouche, Ensley, Brown, the fugitive slave or her freed brethren are not the story being constructed here. The story or history rendered here is, as Morrison so deftly states, "the self-conscious but highly problematic construction of the American as a new white man" (1992a, p. 39). Even Adams (albeit the film's version of him) recognized the truth of this proposition when he asserted hypothetically before the Supreme Court that "[i]f he [Sengbe] were white and his enslavers British, he wouldn't be able to stand, so heavy the weight of the medals we would bestow upon him. Songs would be written about him. The great authors of our time would fill books about him. His story would be told and retold in our classrooms" (Pate, 1997, p. 297).

Who We're Gonna Be as Killers of the Rhetorical Lion

Some time after the death and burial of Fala, Baldwin and Joadson visited Sengbe to seek his help with the court case. Baldwin had succeeded in winning the case with the judge, but the political establishment was able to have that judge removed and thus nullify the favorable judgment. Baldwin therefore needed Sengbe to speak in court, to tell the story of his perilous journey from Africa to America. Sengbe didn't feel that he could speak for all the Africans aboard the *Amistad,* but as Baldwin so astutely observed, he was unique among them. After all, he had killed two lions, one the wild beast he slew back in Mani and the other the civilized beast he conquered aboard the *Amistad*. Now, by speaking before the court, Sengbe was called upon to battle another lion, one that John Quincy Adams later told him "is threatening to rip our country in two" (Pate, 1997, p. 288). In the end, Sengbe had his day in court; and what a momentous day it was, for on this very day he struck a blow against the greatest lion of them all—legalized discrimination based on race—the beast that stood between him and life and liberty.

By taking a close look at the *Amistad* case in this essay, I have tried to suggest that the African soul, or as Morrison puts it, American Africanism is deeply rooted in all that is America, even America's rhetorical tradition. Whether the representations of Adams, Sengbe, or the *Amistad* trial are completely accurate misses the point, well, actually ignores the point because revision and rediscovery have repeatedly proven accepted knowledge or fact inconclusive, even partial. The beloved Thomas Jefferson we knew before we had heard about Sally Hemmings was a mythic or at least incomplete figure of our national consciousness. Thus, in the spirit of Sengbe and in the tradition of the

Mende—America's African forebears—I propose that we slay the lion that haunts America's conceptualization of her rhetorical history. I propose that we become killers of the construction of the new White man still ensconced in our stories or accounts about rhetorical moments, practices, and texts. For if this new White man ever existed in reality, it was a reality shaped by the non-White, by so many other persons, moments, practices, and texts. British sociologist and cultural critic Paul Gilroy hints at this in *The Black Atlantic: Modernity and Double Consciousness:*

> If this appears to be little more than a roundabout way of saying that the reflexive cultures and consciousness of the European settlers and those of the Africans they enslaved, the "Indians" they slaughtered, and the Asians they indentured were not, even in situations of the most extreme brutality, sealed off hermetically from each other, then so be it. This seems as though it ought to be an obvious and self-evident observation, but its stark character has been systematically obscured by commentators from all sides of political opinion. Regardless of their affiliation to the right, left, or centre, groups have fallen back on the idea of cultural nationalism, on the overintegrated conceptions of culture which present immutable, ethnic differences as an absolute break in the histories and experiences of "black" and "white" people. Against this choice stands another, more difficult option: the theorisation of creolisation, metissage, mestizaje, and hybridity. (1993, p. 2)

If what Gilroy claims here is true (and I believe that much of it is), then what we need is altogether different histories of rhetoric, what I like to call mestizo or hybrid rhetorical histories. This means not just histories that include a sampling of, say, African American oratory or great Native American orators (though we do need substantive accounts of these as well) but historical studies that take into account rhetorical influences across racial and cultural lines. Such mestizo/mestiza rhetorical histories would also take into account these concerns: racist and antiracist discourses; linguistic and cultural displacement and reassertion; essentialist representations of rhetoric and nation; hybrid racial/ethnic identities and discursive practices; the absence of the Other in treatises or theories that purport universal application; the assumption of colorblind or race-neutral theories and theorists; and the inexplicable silences about struggles for literacy, humanity, sovereignty, civil rights, and the right to speak. Fortunately, some of this work is already underway among rhetoric scholars. Jacqueline Jones Royster's paper on Maseray or Sarah (1998) has revealed some interesting implications for rhetorical scholarship. And Raka Shome's use of postcolonial theory and criticism in "Postcolonial Interventions in the Rhetorical Canon: An 'Other' View" (1999) addresses the kind of creolized rhetoric I've briefly touched on here. With such work as a starting point, hopefully, we can further limn out hybrid rhetorical traditions and practices in our studies of rhetorical history and theory. Perhaps then we can, like the heroic figure of John Quincy Adams, be made to understand that "who we are is who we were" (Pate, 1997, p. 299). Or better still, if we truly embraced our creoleness as Americans, we can be made to understand brothas and sistas that "we is who we was."

Note

1. Here, I omit the part of the story that involves their initial capture from their native villages and their rather long transport to Lomboko. For instance, Sengbe's village was reportedly some ten days journey from Lomboko.

12

From the Harbor to Da Academic Hood: Hush Harbors and an African American Rhetorical Tradition

Vorris L. Nunley

AS A JURY WEIGHS THE EVIDENCE AGAINST HIM IN A DIVORCE, John Pearson, the itinerate preacher in Zora Neale Hurston's *Jonah's Gourd Vine* (1934/1990), refuses to call witnesses and refuses to speak in his own behalf. When Hambo inquires about his silence, Jonah's response illustrates what I will argue is a primary strand of an African American rhetorical tradition: "'Ah didn't want de White folks tuh hear 'bout nothin' lak that. Dey knows too much 'bout us as it is, but dey some things they ain't tuh know. Dey's some strings on our harp fuh us to play on an sing all tuh ourselves'" (p. 169).

Pearson's "tactic" of a purposeful, critical silence in front of a racially mixed or White audience reflects a historically significant African American commonplace and rhetorical tactic. The old slave bromide "I'se got one mind for my master, and one for myself" intersects with Pearson's take on when, where, and in front of whom Black folks do what Geneva Smitherman calls "talking that talk" that Black folks don't tend to talk in front of non-African Americans. Though still useful, Habermas's public sphere has been kicked to the conceptual curb. Productively critiqued by Michael C. Dawson (2001), Evelyn Brooks Higginbotham (1993), Nancy Fraser (1990), and others, Habermas's public sphere has not been "safe space" for African American rhetorics and subjectivities. As Doreen Massey (1994), Patricia Hill Collins (2000), Diane Reay and Heidi Safia Mirza (2001), and Carter G. Woodson (1925) have demonstrated, diasporic Africans, women, and others have histories of developing raced and gendered distinctive interpretive communities to offset their exclusion from the public sphere. Though this study is about the African American versions of these counterpublics, it is my position that it has implications for the rhetorical analysis of the cultural artifacts of these interpretive communities.

In this essay, I identify, historically locate, and theorize about a primary strand of African American rhetoric I call *hush harbor* rhetoric. This study is concerned with hush harbor sites and hush harbor rhetoric. African American hush harbor rhetoric is a rhetorical tradition constructed through Black public spheres with a distinctive relationship to spatiality (material and discursive), audience, African American *nomoi* (social conventions and beliefs that constitute a worldview or knowledge), and epistemology. Rhetorical scholarship has undertheorized how spatiality, the politics and poetics of space, mediate rhetorical performances. Through hush harbor rhetoric, I argue for spatiality as a distinctive fourth term of the rhetorical situation. African American hush harbor rhetoric offers both analytical tool and theoretical lens for the study of rhetoric in general, and for scholars interested in African American rhetoric in particular. After establishing linkages to what I consider to be contemporary versions of hush harbors, this essay will provide examples to illustrate the implications of hush harbor rhetorics for public/civic and classroom pedagogy.

> What does architecture have to do with Blackness?
> —D. W. Fields, *Architecture in Black*

> Race matters, but it is clear that space does too.
> —M. Forman, *The Hood Comes First:*
> *Race, Space, and Place in Rap and Hip-Hop.*

Cultural critic Mark Anthony Neal in the superb *What the Music Said: Black Popular Music and Black Public Culture* (1999), convincingly argues that "the initial development and maintenance of covert social or 'safe' spaces of the antebellum South are at the core of the black critical tradition in America" (p. 14). Covert and quasi-public spaces such as beauty shops and barbershops provide safe spaces where Black folks affirm, share, and negotiate African American epistemologies and resist and subvert hegemonic Whiteness. All of the above suggests that scholars interested in rhetoric and in African American rhetoric as practice, tradition, or epistemology must expand the domain of sites and objects appropriate for rhetorical analysis and critique.

From the Enslavement era through the Clarence Thomas–Anita Hill spectacle, African Americans have utilized camouflaged locations, hidden sites, and enclosed places as emancipatory cells where they can come in from the wilderness, untie their tongues, speak the unspoken, and sing their own songs to their own selves in their own communities. Woods, plantation borders, churches, burial societies, beauty shops, slave frolics, barbershops, and kitchens loosed their words and their rhetorics. African American sororities and fraternities, porches, taverns, and other sacred and secular Black spaces and places served as geographies of resistance where countless known and unknown Black bards temporarily escaped the hegemonic gaze of Whiteness to make themselves a world. Enslaved African Americans referred to these spaces as cane breaks, bush arbors, or *hush harbors.*

As part of a larger project, this essay posits African American hush harbors as historic and contemporary safe spaces and spatial palimpsests through which to begin to map African American hush harbor rhetoric.[1] I will offer a dense definitional formulation of hush harbors and of African American hush harbor rhetoric, which I will unpack throughout. Next, I ground hush harbors historically and situate them within the context of African American rhetorical tradition(s). I will provide historical evidence for my claim about the centrality of hush harbors to African American cultures and subjectivities. Disrupting conventional notions of space will be a central gesture, which illustrates the ideological nature of space, how it is gendered and raced, and how space mediates rhetorical practice. It is in this section where I offer space as an explicit fourth element of the rhetorical situation. African American audience and African American commonplaces are pivotal terms in my hush harbor rhetoric theorizing. In the section aptly titled "Black Audience and Black Commonplaces," I attempt to de-suture the terms *African American* and *audience* from the muscle of phenotype and connect them to the ligaments of rhetoric, epistemology, and identity by grounding the commonplace in a sophistic-influenced definition of nomos. In the following section, I then link historic hush harbor spaces and places to what I argue are their contemporary functional equivalents in locations and places such as certain beauty shops, barbershops, churches, and other African American public spheres. Finally, I provide two examples of how hush harbor rhetoric resources can be utilized in classroom pedagogy.

Hush Harbors, Spaces of Emancipation, Sites of Dread
We is gathated hyeah, my brothahs
In dis howlin' wildaness,

Fu'to speak some words of comfo't
To each othah in distress
         Paul Laurence Dunbar, "An Ante-bellum Sermon"

Hush harbor rhetoric is composed of the rhetorics and the common-places emerging from those rhetorics, articulating distinctive social epistemologies and subjectivities of African Americans and directed toward predominantly Black audiences in formal and informal Black publics or African American–centered cultural geographies. Hush harbors as genres of Black public spheres are not Black cultural locations solely because they are situated where Black folks live and gather. Rather, hush harbor places become Black spaces because African American *nomos* (social convention, worldview knowledge), rhetoric, phronesis (practical wisdom and intelligence) tropes, and commonplaces are normative in the encounters that occur in these locations. African American subjectivities are negotiated, affirmed, circulated in these Black spaces and Black cultural sites. Although a segment of this examination will provide an example of how African American rhetorical performance differs in Black hush harbor audiences from those in public spheres of White audiences, it is purposely not the primary focus of this study. Instead, this examination will unpack hush harbor theory and illustrate how African American hush harbor spaces and rhetoric are most functional to its occupants.

Hush harbors are functional because they are Black spaces, offering what Reay and Mirza (2001) describe as a "disruptive discursive space," "spaces of radical Blackness" where hegemonic discourse is not unproblematically reinscribed. These spaces allow African American subjects and subjectivities to be "familiar," "hegemonic," and normative (p. 95). Such spaces of radical Blackness are spaces where Blackness is hegemonic, but not static, and where Black subjects challenge and negotiate their various articulations. An illustrative history of African American hush harbor and hush harbor rhetorics will make the cultural and racialized content of hush harbor spaces, and the function of the rhetorics emerging from those spaces, more apparent.

Architectural theorist Brandford C. Grant (1996) in "Accommodation and Resistance: The Built Environment and the African American Experience" describes race as being "architecturally constructed" and "architecture, building and planning" as "inherently racially constituted activities" (p. 202). Spatial organization of the built environment racialized the plantation house and the slave cabin. Racialization of space in the United States arguably began with plantation residential segregation because as Donald R. Deskins Jr. and Christopher Bettinger (2002) note about the intersection between race and space: "Race is based on exclusion. . . . Space therefore, is an ideal means of creating and asserting racial identities" (p. 57). Even as globalization compresses space thereby increasing mobility and fraying the threads connecting place and identity, Deskins and Bettinger's insight in relation to race, class, ethnicity, and gender is still valid in many parts of the world. Grant (1996) locates the racialization of space as Black within the Enslavement era then links spatial racialization to the habitation of collective Black "neighborhoods" camouflaged from the surveillance of the master and White hegemony in indoor and outdoor communal spaces (p. 206). According to Grant, the enslaved peoples reinterpreted the "communal living in West African villages," to cotton, sugar cane, and rice fields and in the woods and other secret outdoor hiding places (p. 206).

Previously listed locations are described in numerous books, novels, and histories as bush arbors, cane breaks, or hush harbors. Lawrence Levine's germinal text on African American cultural history and practice, *Black Culture and Black Consciousness: Afro-American Folk Thought from Slavery to Freedom* (1997) situates hush harbors historically, verifies their physical existence, and bears witness to their use as geographies of camouflage and resistance. Levine points out that hush harbors were sites where "[s]laves broke the prescription against unsupervised or unauthorized meetings by holding their services in secret, well hidden areas" (p. 41). To be caught was to risk severe punishment because of the hidden transcripts circulating in the spaces. Meetings had to be held in secret. Thus, African American hush harbor rhetoric emerges from the distinctive social epistemologies and subjectivities of subaltern and counterdiscourses. Minister and ex-slave W. B. Allen alludes to the hidden transcripts and the danger associated with them when slaves dared to attend clandestine hush harbor meetings:

> The slaves had turned a large pot down in the center of the floor to hold the sounds of their voices within. But, despite their precaution, the patrollers found them and broke in. Of course, every Nigger present was in for a severe whipping." (qtd. in I. Berlin, 1998, p. 56)

James Scott defines *hidden transcripts* as "non-hegemonic, subversive discourse generated by subordinate groups and concealed from certain dominant others" (1980, p. 14). Slaves of African descent in America constructed a sense of their own subjectivity through these hidden transcripts. At times, slaves feigned ignorance of certain skills to decrease plantation production. Other times, certain objects were left on the grave of the deceased so that they might return and utilize them. All of the above tactics reflect hidden transcripts deployed to retain African retentions in the culture of enslaved Africans.

In hush harbors, slaves did not only address sacred or esoteric issues. Hush harbor spaces enabled enslaved Africans in America to address secular as well as sacred concerns. Eric Sundquist (1993) describes both the sacred and secular functions of Frederick Douglass's version of a hush harbor space where Douglass secretly taught slaves to read and provided them with instruction in politics. Sundquist is worth reading for two reasons. First, he directly utilizes the term *hush harbor* not only as a physical space but as a conceptual metaphor for various sites of "subtle strategies of masquerade" often hidden in plain sight (p. 83). Second, Sundquist alludes to the alternative knowledges, values, and commonplaces making hush harbors productive, generative, and resistant Black public spheres. Nat Turner and Denmark Vesey are believed to have hatched their rebellions in such spaces. While the above examples refer to informal sites, hush harbor sites sometimes transformed into more formal formations as did that once "invisible institution," the traditional Black church, makes evident.

Ira Berlin in *Many Thousands Gone: The First Two Centuries of Slavery in North America* (1999) describes how new institutions, which addressed the problems of formerly enslaved people, rose from "informal, clandestine, associations of Black people created in slavery" (p. 251). White Northerners excluded Blacks from White burial grounds, so "their burial grounds, the graveyard, became the first truly African American institution in the Northern colonies, and perhaps in mainland North America" (p. 62). Roberta H. Wright's and Wilbur B. Hughes III's *Lay Down Body: Living History in African American Cemeteries* (1996) outlines a specific burial practice alluded to by Berlin that reflects alternative worldviews occurring underneath the gaze of White hegemony. Wright and Hughes describe how plots in Braddock Point Cemetery where African Americans were buried in the 1800s faced toward the ocean, "with a view over the sound, since it was believed that their spirits would return to Africa if buried near the water" (p. 65).

Berlin, Wright and Hughes, and others suggest a history, a tradition, an epistemic ground of African and African American discourse and rhetoric, from which a distinctively African American hush harbor rhetorical tradition might be mapped. Formal institutions such as the National Colored Woman's Association, the Black Panthers, and the Southern Christian Leadership Conference all emerged from sequestered or hidden Black public spheres of African American hush harbors. Keith Gilyard's contribution to this volume posits Carter G. Woodson's *Negro Orators and Their Orations* (1925) and *The Mind of the Negro as Reflected in Letters Written During the Crisis 1800–1860* (1926) as "[t]he first standard reference work[s] on African American oratory." Gilyard's contribution is of vital import to hush harbor concerns, as Woodson refers to sequestered spaces in which Black folks speak to each other. Given the apparent importance of spatiality to rhetoric in general and African American hush harbor rhetoric in particular, a discussion about space, ideology, and rhetoric might prove useful.

Space, Place, and Camouflaged Rhetoric

> A whole history remains to be written of spaces.
> —Michel Foucault, *Eye of Power*

Quintilian long ago recognized how spatiality informs the distinctiveness of rhetorics and arguments emerging from particular localities, habitats (places), and haunts.[2] Calling for an examination of rhetoric in relation to space creates a disciplinary location to discuss the spatial (geographical) in the rhetorical and the rhetorical in the geographical. In human and critical geography, it is axiomatic that the spatial is socially constructed and that the social is spatially constructed. Soja (1998), McDowell (1995), and others have written scholarship that does not ignore the materiality of space and the built environment. However, it does recognize how atavistic is the positivistic-Kantian notion of space as abstract, fixed, and outside of social relations. So although Kenneth Burke's (1945) pentad certainly takes space seriously, he does not explicitly theorize space as ideological and discursive and how spatial subjectivity might mediate his pentad.

Architecture theorists Beatriz Columbia (1992) and J. Yolande Daniels (2000), and others writing about architecture have theorized about the ideological nature of the built environment, the physical environment, and the meanings produced by both discursive and physical space. Space is important. Literary theorists such as Raymond Williams and Edward Said (1993) have commented on the importance of space to contemporary theorizing. There is a spatial turn that rhetorical scholarship inadequately addresses. Hush harbor theorizing proceeds by explicitly addressing spatiality.

As a term, *spatiality* disrupts the aforementioned sedimented conceptions of space. Pia Christensen, Allison James, and Chris Jenks's (2000) understanding of spatiality in "Home and Movement: Children Constructing 'Family Time'" intersects with hush harbor theorizing in that it is concerned with explicitly theorizing society and spatiality: "Spatiality is used to capture the ways in which the social and spatial are inextricably realized one in the other: to conjure up the circumstances in which society and space are simultaneously realized by thinking, feeling, doing, individuals" (p. 142).

If the spatial is ideological, then both space and, of course, ideology possess a rhetorical component. In a thoughtful, provocative article, "On Gender and Rhetorical Space," Roxanne Mountford complicates the separation of material and discursive spatialities directly linking the spatial to the rhetorical. For Mountford, rhetorical space is "the geography of a communicative event and like all landscapes, may include both the cultural and material arrangements, whether, intended or fortuitous of space" (p. 42). Renditions of hush harbors in novels are a type of communicative event that justify Mountford's (and my own) use of novels and other texts to illuminate the importance of spatiality and hush harbors. Informed by Henri Levebre and work in cultural and feminist geography, Mountford (2001) argues that the material configuration or spatial location of a site mediates rhetorical performances which enable certain kinds of discourses and rhetorics while constraining others. This is a line of inquiry in understanding African American hush harbors and hush harbor rhetoric. Space, in Mountford's view, both "produces" and "embodies" meaning (p. 42).

However, Mountford overlooks how performances in some African American rhetorical spaces are expressions of a textual and rhetorical tradition. Hush harbor rhetoric and the theorizing I am performing around it explicitly foregrounds radicalized geography, asymmetrical power relations, hidden transcripts, and the traces of historic oppression. For example, one of the works in which Mountford anchors her examination of spatiality, gender, and rhetoric is Toni Morrison's *Beloved* (1987), in which a character, Baby Suggs, delivers a sermon in the woods/wilderness. Mountford understands Baby Suggs's sermon and the trope of the woods as embodying an undomesticated, unofficial, counternarrative outside the bounds of institutionalized, traditional, and patriarchal religious dogma.

My project extends Mountford's specific reading and is concerned with understanding the woods/wilderness trope as spatial and rhetorical palimpsests historically situated within a matrix of African American rhetoric, audience, and commonplaces. Melvin Dixon (1987) in *Ride Out the Wilderness* identifies the wilderness, the mountaintop, and the underground as central tropes in the, African American "search for self and home" (p. 3). Wilderness tropes permeate the African American social-expressive imagination in literature, music, religion, and art. Often viewed as uncultivated, undomesticated, and uncivilized and grafted to dark, othered bodies, the wilderness was constructed as a geography of physical, discursive, and spiritual possibility in the minds of many enslaved African Americans. For example, "Negro" spirituals consistently invoke the wilderness as an emancipatory Promised Land.

> Jesus call you. Go in de wilderness
> Go in the wilderness, go in the wilderness
> Jesus call you. Go in de wilderness
> To wait upon the Lord.
>
> (Dixon, 1987, p. 53)

Hush harbors are temporary homes of emancipatory politics suffused with particular forms of agency and identity. Baby Suggs testifies to the importance of place and identity in Black folks creating themselves a world anchored in the wilderness of their own experience and history. Suggs walks to "a wide open place cut deep in the woods," an outpost where, "She told them that the only grace they could have was the grace they could imagine. That if they could not see it, they would not have it" (Morrison, 1987, pp. 88–89). African American hush harbors are spatialites where Black folks go to affirm, negotiate, and reproduce culture, epistemology, and resistance and to find sacred and secular grace.

African Americans are able to find grace in these spatialities in part because they often circulate outside the gaze of hegemonic relations. I do not claim that these epistemologies are never heard by non–African Americans. Indeed, globalization and technology increase the commodification and the surveillance of rhetoric and the knowledges intertwined within it as the global-local binary collapses. Such a collapse makes a claim for complete cultural and spatial suture problematic. Nevertheless, hush harbor spaces are sites where certain African American counternarratives and narratives are acknowledged, privileged, and spoken and performed differently. My primary concern is to posit hush harbors as offering a resource or location for rhetorical theory, epistemology, and history, and to resist having hush harbors trivialized into little more than sites of social pathology and difference. One specific example of a hush harbor tactic and rhetoric is the speech "The Ballot or the Bullet."

Malcolm X Speaks: Selected Speeches and Statements (Malcolm X & Breitman, 1965/1990) describes the speech "The Ballot or the Bullet" as one of Malcolm X's most memorable. "The Ballot or the Bullet" was delivered at the Cory Methodist Church in Cleveland, Ohio, April 3, 1964, before a predominantly Black hush harbor audience at a Black church during the era's Civil Rights Movement. Declaring his independence from Elijah Muhammad, Malcolm X established the Muslin Mosque, Inc. As part of his independence, Malcolm X began accepting speaking engagements outside of New York, developing and formulating new ideologies while continuing to perform at several rallies in Harlem. Malcolm often spoke about and developed the same themes in front of African American and non–African American audiences.

Five days after establishing the Muslim Mosque, Inc., Malcolm X delivered a speech, "The Black Revolution," sponsored by the Militant Labor Forum (a socialist organization) before a 75 percent White audience at Palm Gardens, New York. Although differently titled, both speeches were concerned with many of the same themes. Malcolm X begins both speeches before both audiences with the phrase "friends and enemies" (pp. 24, 45). This gesture immediately disrupts any notion of a narrow Black Nationalism or Black essentialism often attributed to Malcolm X and other Black rhetors who struggled not just over civil rights but over language, power, and definition.

"The Ballot or the Bullet" and "The Black Revolution" both address Black nationalism, self-defense, White liberal complicity in African American oppression, and the internationalization of African American struggle; but Malcolm X establishes his ethos quite differently with the predominantly African American audience than he does with the White audience. With the White audience, immediately after the friends and enemies reference, he addresses White liberal fears: "Tonight I hope to have a little fireside chat with as few sparks as possible being tossed around" (p. 45). Of course, there is some signifyin' going on because no matter the audience, Malcolm X is the fire in the flint of normalized discourse. Sparks are de rigueur with a Malcolm speech. Nevertheless, Malcolm X does try to become consubstantial with the predominantly White audience, since for the next few minutes of his oratory he invokes the names of Everett Dirksen, George Washington, Patrick Henry, and Abraham Lincoln. It is an appeal to what David Howard-Pitney describes as America's civil religion. In "The Ballot or the Bullet," Adam Clayton Powell, Martin Luther King Jr., and Reverend Galamison are immediately deployed to the predominantly African American audience. His concern is not White fear; it is Black oppression and self-defense against that oppression. In addition, references to enslavement/segregation occur more often in "The Ballot or the Bullet" oratory than in "The Black Revolution." Finally, Malcolm provides a definition of, then an explanation of, the goals of Black nationalism to the Black audience; no such explanation is provided the White audience. Malcolm's pedagogical goal differs for the hush harbor audience.

Too often, African American and other "subaltern" rhetors gain legitimacy in the public sphere through domesticating their rhetoric into the bounds of acceptable debate by appealing to notions of civility and tolerance. Of course, civility and tolerance are needed, but that often camouflages the politics. Civility tends to privilege the politics and the values of those already benefiting from the dominant discourse. Bold, brazen, assertive, insolent, edgy, wild, rhetorically nappy rhetors such as Maria W. Stewart, Fannie Lou Hamer, Ida B. Wells, Martin Delaney, Minister Louis Farrakhan, Malcolm X, and countless others are often supported by significant numbers of Black folks not because they necessarily agreed with their claims or politics but because these speakers are willing to "tell it like they think it is" in front of a White audience. This element of African American rhetoric and epistemology is often misunderstood by the general public as angry, hostile, uppity, arrogant, and uncivil rhetoric.

Malcolm X affirms African American culture and experience in the hush harbor spheres in a different way than he does in non–hush harbor spaces. Hush harbors are Black public spheres because as Michael Warner (2002) illustrates, in public spheres there is a "relation among strangers," "self-organized," "public and personal," a "social space created by the reflexive circulation of discourse" (p. 65). In "Message to the Grass Roots" (1965), Malcolm X argues that Black folks should disagree at home in the closet of the private sphere but present a united front in the public sphere (assumed to be hegemonically White). Malcolm X, Frederick Douglass, and bell hooks all have theorized how racial composition of an audience mediates the performance and reception of African American rhetoric and epistemology. If Aristotle is correct that rhetoric is not persuasion but about finding available means to persuade, then how may scholars find what persuades African American hush harbor audiences?

Black Audience and Black Commonplaces

What do we mean when we say Black audience? Certainly, phenotype is a consideration. But this can hardly suffice. For a speaker or rhetor to become what Kenneth Burke terms "consubstantial" with an African American hush harbor audience, the skin one is in is no guarantee. Phenotype may get you a passport, but African American commonplaces, tonal semantics, mascons, and the tropes and epistemologies connected to them are what get your rhetorical documents stamped and approved. Consequently, my conceptualization of an "African American audience" in relation to African American hush harbor rhetoric includes, but extends beyond, phenotype. Arthur L. Smith's (1972) (Molefi Asante's) concept of hearership is a rhetorically oriented concept that seems to navigate the tension between the Charybdis of the audience as coherent and homogeneous and the Scylla of the audience as idiosyncratic and fragmented.

Smith defines *hearership* in *Language, Communication, and Rhetoric in Black America* (1972) as "[c]ollections or gatherings of persons who maintain, if only for the duration of the speech occasion, a special relationship with each other, if only in the hearing of a speaker" (p. 286). While useful, Smith's definition is not a snug fit with my notion of a hush harbor occasion because as an artifact of a Black public sphere, the rhetor's text alone is not enough to create a public. Hush harbor rhetorics are more socially dense than the hearership definition suggests. Michael Warner contends that texts themselves do not "create publics" and that only when a previously existing discourse can be supposed, and when a responding discourse can be postulated, can a text address a public" (2002, p. 90). Warner's definition suggests a historical resonance not reflected in the Smith explanation. Nevertheless, Smith's concept of hearership is very useful in relation to rhetor, audience, and identity (p. 286).

African American hush harbor audiences then are constructed as Black through experience and the tactics, commonplaces, and *nomoi* reflecting that experience. Certain commonplaces, tropes, and figures circulate with such volume in African American communities that they become entangled with African Americans' subjective experience of themselves. Call and response, signifying, the African American sermonic form, homelitics, the bad man/bad woman trope, are commonplaces that produce and construct Black subjectivities. The commonplace as marker of identity is an important element of hush harbor rhetoric.

The Commonplace and Identity

Sharon Crowley in *Ancient Rhetorics for Contemporary Students* (1994) tweaks the current-traditional description of rhetoric. Crowley provides a conceptualization of the commonplace which seems to implicitly take into account modern insights into language and social epistemology. For Crowley, a commonplace is "Any statement or bit of knowledge that is commonly shared among a given audience or community" (p. 335). Crowley's notion of commonplaces posits them in a generative relation to social practice, doxa (belief), and knowledge. Commonplaces and phronesis de-center the positivistic science notion of knowledge as abstract, theoretical and objective; Crowley's sophistic take on the commonplace re-inserts the social into an epistemological frame.

Commonplaces are more than just sources of argument. Commonplaces connect to experience in such a specific, distinctive manner that the same commonplace may be understood differently in response to various *nomoi*. Susan Jarratt defines *nomos* (pl. *nomoi*) as "[a] self conscious arrangement of discourse to create politically and socially significant knowledge . . . thus it is always a social construct with ethical dimensions" (1991, p. 42). Jarratt links this term to the sophistic tradition and its understanding of the social situatedness of knowledge. African American commonplaces resonate with African American experiences and knowledges and are therefore understood differently and are more likely to be persuasive within African American hush harbors. For instance, sermons derived from the commonplace of the homiletic tradition of borrowing are understood and valued differently in African American culture. Different culturally mediated evaluations and receptions of the sermons of Dr. Martin Luther King Jr. offer a compelling example.

Dr. King has been accused of plagiarizing particular speeches, essays, and so on, by David Garrow and others because he utilized material from other preachers without acknowledgement. Keith Miller's (1998) *Voice of Deliverance: The Language of Martin Luther King, Jr., and Its Sources* recognizes African American homiletics as distinctive oratorical commonplaces within American and African American rhetorical practice. In homiletics, truth is understood as "repeatable" as "shared," and as "truth as best communicated orally, and truth as expressed in story" (p. 115). Truth as shared and repeatable is the important characteristic in the context of my hush harbor exploration. Both Black and White preachers borrowed from other preachers because in this American/African American hush harbor form distinctiveness of articulation, use, and function of rhetoric and its performance are valued by these audiences, not source of origin.

As Miller recognizes, King affirmed much of the traditional Christian message through borrowing: Borrowing "granted his (King's) sermons a ritualistic quality that resonated with those who had heard or read similar or identical themes" (p. 117). African American ministers in the homiletic tradition often utilize material from other ministers. Although African American audiences often expect and celebrate this commonplace of creative borrowing, wholesale lifting (sampling) for its own sake is not condoned. Ministers are required to insert the material into a unique rhetorical performance. Improvisation on preexisting material is rewarded in the African American oral and musical traditions. Thievery is not. Like borrowing, improvisation is well known to be highly valued as a commonplace and as a rhetorical tactic in African American communities. Borrowing enables improvisation. Black hush harbor audiences are persuaded by rhetorical performances that effectively deploy Black commonplaces linking the performed identity of the rhetor to the subjectivity of the audience through culturally derived African American commonplaces.

While the discussions of Baby Suggs, Malcolm X, and Martin Luther King Jr. were anchored in the past, contemporary versions of hush harbors do exist.

Hush Harbors as Contemporary Safe and Unsafe Spaces

Sociologist Zygmunt Bauman (1998) understands that as we enter the new millennium, globalization and technology, for all their obvious benefits, can polarize as well as democratize society: "It emancipates certain humans from territorial constraints and renders certain communication generating meanings extra-territorial while denuding the territory, to which other people go on being confined, of its meaning and its identity-endowing capacity" (p. 18). Hush harbor theorizing allows rhetoricians to take into account the identity-endowing capacity of these spatialities through the everyday rhetorics and practices of people who occupy these sites.

Contemporary versions of hush harbors where African Americans temporarily escape the disciplining gaze of the guardians of dominant culture are barbershops, fraternity and sorority houses, beauty shops, book clubs (mostly women), Hip Hop free-style throw downs, churches, pool halls, front porches, liquor stores, and jook joints. In *Black Feminist Thought: Knowledge, Consciousness, and the Politics of Empowerment* (2000), Patricia Hill Collins theorizes what I posit are contemporary versions of the hush harbor. Collins examines hush harbor spaces as locations where "domination may be inevitable as a social fact, but it is unlikely to be hegemonic as an ideology within that social space where Black women speak freely" (p. 100). Collins's account of hush harbors rightly disidentifies them as separatist. While some may be, most hush harbor spatialities, elements of what Collins describes as "Black civil society," are places of cultural and political reinvigoration, enabling hush harbor occupants to re-enter society with a sense of themselves as subjects not as objects. Collins is well aware of the importance of spatiality to African American women. African American women have a long history of utilizing informal sites such as beauty shops and formal organizations such as the National Association of Colored Women to challenge Black male and White domination. Hush harbors reconfigure and flatten out asymmetrical power relations to provide a measure of safety and solace through authorizing and legitimizing voices that typically lack jurisdiction in non-hush harbor spaces. "This space is not only safe—it forms a prime location for resisting objectification as the other," notes Collins (p. 99). Hush harbors authorize the unofficial, the underground, and under the radar rhetoric and epistemology.

Nevertheless, hush harbor spaces are not utopian respites free from internecine conflicts and contradictions. Space and culture are sites of the entanglements of power around class, race, and gender. Dunbar's "An Ante-bellum Sermon" illustrates how that even during slavery, hush harbor spaces were not entirely safe. Hush harbor spatialities offer possibilities and containment. Since racialized subjects are constitutive of and by the discourses of the dominant culture, traces of hegemonic thinking may take up residence in hush harbor spaces.

As Dunbar complicated antebellum hush harbors, Florence Griffin's (1995) *"Who Set You Flowing?": The African American Migration Narrative* complicates contemporary hush harbors. Recognizing their progressive potential, Griffin believes that "at their most reactionary" these safe havens are " potentially provincial spaces which do not encourage resistance but instead help to create complacent subjects whose only aim is to exist within the confines of power that oppress them" (p. 9). Griffin understands that "hegemonic ideology can exist even in spaces of resistance" (p. 9). She does not trivialize the distinctiveness of African American culture in these Black geographies, but Griffin's interrogation does destabilize romantic, monolithic, and culturally and politically innocent conceptions of hush harbors. Hush harbors are not uniform in rhetorical or political content nor in their capacity to resist hegemonic practices.

The Classroom as Contact and Combat Zone

Most rhetoricians in the academy are required to teach composition. Therefore, it seems necessary to discuss what implications, if any, hush harbor rhetoric and African American hush harbor rhetoric have for the classroom. Language, rhetoric, and composition classrooms provide fertile ground for hush harbor theory and rhetoric. Composing theory takes up the spatial turn and most explicitly engages the politics and poetics of spatiality in relation to the composition classroom. Mary Louise Pratt's (1992) notion of the "contact zone" is illustrative. In *Imperial Eyes,* Pratt defines contact zones as "an attempt to invoke the spatial and temporal co-presence of subjects previously separated by geographic and historical disjunctures, and whose trajectories now intersect" (p. 6). Classroom contact zones are often more like combat zones whose discursive territory and boundaries of karotic appropriatenesses are mediated too often by combatants who under the guise of broader concerns with class, gender, or French theory trivialize or jettison discussions about race.

There are, of course, ruptures and lines of flight for creating new emancipatory possibilities within any classroom and curricula because while power may be everywhere so is resistance. What gets constructed as acceptable debate, constructed as the sound of reasonableness and not as the noise of special pleading, tends to be overdetermined by what is institutionally normative or theoretically sexy. Therefore, discourse in agonistic contact zones tends to reproduce hegemonic constructions due to asymmetrical power relations particularly around the subject positions of some participants based on gender, race, class, or language. Patricia Hill Collins tells how her training as a social scientist inadequately prepared her to examine the subjugated knowledge of African American women because "subordinated groups have long had to use alternative ways to create independent self-definitions and self-evaluations and to re-articulate them through our own specialists" (2000, p. 252).

Collins's insight illustrates how pervasive and insidious are the institutional reproductions of hegemonic relations. Yet even when the discourse in a composition classroom is temporarily tilted toward the interest of the "other," those who benefit from or support dominant epistemologies too often continually try to restore hegemonic relations to the classroom. A personal anecdote will illustrate how well-intentioned individuals can discipline resistant voices into compliance.

As writing instructors at Penn State University, all graduate students in the rhetoric program are required to enroll in a yearlong course in which they address pedagogy, curricula, student management, and other classroom concerns. The year I matriculated through the course, each member of the class was assigned the task of reviewing a rhetoric reader and determining its appropriateness for the teaching of a rhetoric-based writing course. Two of my classmates chose to review a multicultural reader. Although thinking the text was useful and supporting its argument for diversity, the two students critiqued the text for being too race based. They made their argument, with the silent complicity of nodding heads in the class, without interrogating Whiteness as unmarked and normative, without defining their use of the term *race,* and without offering criteria for what makes a text race based or raceless. My colleagues, while offering a perfunctory nod to the nobility of the desire to increase textual diversity, reduced, trivialized, and dismissed the text to the theoretical hinterlands. Of course, one could argue that the students were critically unreflexive and therefore unaware of my aforementioned critique. This is exactly my point. They can be unaware of such a basic critique in ways that one could not be unaware of continental philosophical critiques of Enlightenment concepts of history, truth, and language, and still be taken seriously as scholars. And when I did offer my critique, in an attempt to complicate their McDonalds brand of diversity— diversity as consumption decoupled from power and concerns about who determines what gets consumed as diverse—they countered with examples of Eastern Europeans left out of the diversity loop.

Later, I discussed what happened in class with two African American professors and another colleague. After closing the door and dropping the level of their voices, the professors and my colleagues went on to relate their own stories of how White, male, and class privilege is too often argued for and supported under the guise of complicating race, identity, and diversity in the contact zone of the classroom. Subaltern folks must often construct our own hush harbors within the university (stopping conversation in midsentence, looking down the hall, then closing the office door to ensure the lack of surveillance) in order to assert African American subjectivity without hegemonic intervention from well-intentioned folks. Bearing witness to the unsaid and underrecognized in academic hush harbors is necessary because too often the slightest assertion of a distinctive African American identity and knowledge is met with a "vogue statement"[3] that elides as much about the discourse of race and gender as it reveals: you are essentializing. Hush harbor epistemologies are not inherently essentializing gestures. However, they typically do not privilege the conventional knowledge validation process located outside the thoughts, experience, strategies, and tactics of African Americans and others who occupy hush harbor sites. If pedagogy is more effective when it takes into account the cultural terra firma students bring to class, then hush harbors may offer useful pedagogical and rhetorical possibilities that allow instructors to avoid pedagogical hallucinations, in relation to race, gender, class, and ethnicity.

Hush harbor rhetorics and epistemologies may create a transgressive classroom space because a pedagogy informed by such epistemologies might disrupt notions of civility, consensus, tolerance, and the comfort zone of both teachers and students in contact zones. Nevertheless, instructors willing to expend the extra effort may find useful pedagogic treasure, as did linguist John Baugh and magnet program coordinator Beverly Silverstein with their students.

Shuffling Lyrics, Ellison, Morrison, Thinking Critically

In "Reading, Writing, and Rap: Lyric Shuffle and Other Motivational Strategies to Introduce and Reinforce Literacy" from his book *Out of the Mouths of Slaves: African American Language and Educational Malpractice*, linguist J. Baugh (1999) utilizes a game he developed from years of fieldwork called the "Lyric Shuffle" to assist children in acquiring literacy in reading and writing. Baugh developed the game in response to parents he interviewed who "adopted communal strategies to combat illiteracy" and for children who wanted to improve their reading and writing skills but did not want to have to leave their identities at the hegemonic gate (p. 32).

Lyric Shuffle encourages students to choose songs from popular culture as a starting point. Students from different discourse communities choose different songs, which are transcribed into texts for student use. The game requires the students to rearrange the words into new sentences, new lyrics, or new poems. The game can also be used for basic phonic lessons or sentence formation, vocabulary, and a myriad of other language exercises. Lyric Shuffle can be altered for a variety of student competencies and instructor goals. Baugh shares variations on Lyric Shuffle (sentence shuffle, poet shuffle, grammar roulette, story shuffle) to demonstrate the flexibility of the game's basic concept. As students choose the songs utilized for the game, so they tend to be more invested and motivated in the game.

While first constructed with the concerns of African American parents and students in mind, Lyric Shuffle has obvious applicability in a number of contexts. In the case of African American students, the game is effective in part because it is apparent to the students that the singers/ rappers effectively utilize so-called standardized English without erasing African American cultural referents (jargon, commonplaces, tropes, cadence, etc.). Standardized English and success are decoupled from cultural erasure and linked to student agency. As a result, Baugh believes "these materials can be used to introduce Standard[ized] English without the corresponding stigma of texts that many African Americans directly associate with the dominant culture" (p. 34). The classroom is transformed into a hush harbor site, a safe site, because the rhetoric, pedagogy, and knowledge circulating in and through the site reflect an attempt to inhabit the ground of the students before taking them on a journey to a new territory. Teacher authority is not relinquished; rather, it is used to enable the students to assume agency. Black culture in Baugh's class becomes a generative, productive site. While Baugh linked the students to familiar hush harbor cultural formations that have migrated into mainstream culture (Rap, R & B, and other popular music) to enhance student acquisition of literacy, Beverly Silverstein's version of a service learning program utilizes African American literary texts to enhance critical thinking and reading skills while broadening student knowledge of African American culture.

In Los Angeles, at Crenshaw High School in conjunction with California State University at Los Angeles, Beverly Silverstein developed a service learning program to introduce critical thinking, reading, and writing skills to students.

Using literature and critical theory to traverse the landscape of folklore, music, and the cultural traditions of African Americans, students and adults are constructed as both hush harbor dwellers and hush harbor tourists. Silverstein disrupts the boundary between school knowledge and community knowledge to accomplish her goal. Once a week, a two-hour block of class time is held off campus at a residential home for local residents aged sixty-five or older. Program participants listen to music, read articles, and critically discuss African American literary texts such as Toni Morrison's *Song of Solomon* or Ralph Ellison's *Invisible Man*. Instructors develop knowledge about the participants through school records, meetings with parents, and discussions with the participants. Instructors assist the students and adult residents to excavate the continuities, extensions, and evolutions of African American rhetoric, culture, and social knowledges. Such knowledge often hides in plain sight within rap, jazz, the blues, sermons, and other sites of Black cultural production. Snoop Doggy Dogg's lyrics become a modern variation of the bad man as hero in early African American poetry and folktales; Erika Badu is found to have antecedents in Billie Holiday; and discussions about Ebonics are found to have corollaries in the reception or lack of reception of the "dialect" poems of Paul Laurence Dunbar. African American culture is pried open to critical reflection. Reading becomes explicitly hermeneutical, and meaning becomes contested terrain. Students and adults are able to immerse themselves in critical debate. They struggle over alternative interpretations of Black texts and the cultural contexts from which they emerge. Experience is taken into account but is no longer deemed the authoritative trump card of legitimacy. Hush harbor knowledge centered on African American commonplaces and *nomoi* make critical discussions relevant to the lives of the participants, student motivation increases. As a result, so does student engagement with learning. Over 90 percent of the program's students graduate and attend postsecondary institutions in a public school where college attendance rates are subpar.

Hush Harbors, Possibility, and Democracy

As the old slave bromide "I'se got one mind for my master, and one for myself" indicates, Africans in America have had to flip the script of the prevailing paradigm of the dominant culture to affirm African American epistemology and to ensure psychological, spiritual, and cultural survival. Hush harbors in both their secular and sacred versions provide locations from which a contingent but stable African American rhetorical tradition can be theorized. From the plantation to da 'hood, barbershops, beauty shops, local stores, and churches have provided safe spaces for African Americans to authorize their voices.

Hush harbor spatialities are constructed and maintained in a variety of race, ethnic, gender, class, and theological configurations. Democracy depends on such spatialities. In *Bowling Alone: The Collapse and Survival of American Community,* Robert Putnam (2000) describes the political, social, and psychological vibrancy of such "ethnic enclaves." Hush harbors may serve as a key to replenishing a hollowed-out public sphere where fewer working class and poor folks participate in national elections, where the most popular game shows thrive on a Darwinian survival of the fittest ethos while the social safety net becomes more porous, and where prohibiting African American youths from speaking Ebonics elicits more concern than keeping them out of jail (p. 22).

Ethnic enclaves that continue to exist in the forgotten purgatories of globalization, which render the local both less important to a privileged few who may choose fluidity at their convenience and more important to disempowered nomads and vagabonds who occupy the local because circumstances dictate that they must. Hush harbor theorizing makes the ideology and poetics of these spaces as central to rhetorical analysis as audience, speaker, and message. Scholars and instructors interested in rhetorical theory and history may find methodological and pedagogical possibility within hush harbors. A useful genealogy of African American rhetoric exists in these Black public spheres, flourishing outside the domain of conventional rhetorical study. If classical Western experiential rhetoric and African American rhetorical theory are to have a home in the rock of theoretical significance, then they must go where Black folks go for what they know, and to where they keep the minds they keep for themselves.

Notes

1. See B. Ashcroft, G. Griffiths, and H. Tifflin (1998), *Key Concepts in Post-Colonial Studies* (New York: Routledge). "Originally the term for a parchment on which several inscriptions had been made after earlier ones had been erased" (p. 174), *palimpsest* refers to the traces of writing and history that remain in a text. Hush harbors function as metaphoric spatial palimpsests in which the histories of hush harbor often remain in contemporary hush harbors through the memories of significant numbers of African Americans who circulate through them.

2. See S. Crowley (1994), *Ancient Rhetorics for Contemporary Student.* Quintilian's quote reflects the spatial and social locatedness of argument and knowledge: "For just as all kinds of produce are not provided by every country, and as you will not succeed in finding a particular bird or beast if you are ignorant of the localities where it has its usual haunts or birthplace . . . so not every kind of argument can be derived from every circumstance, and consequently our search requires discrimination" (p. 49). Roxanne Mountford (2001) makes a similar point when she argues in "Gender and Rhetorical Space" (p. 42) that "[t]he material is a dimension too little theorized by rhetoricians, often has unforeseen influence over a communicative event and cannot always be explained by cultural or creative intent."

3. Vogue words (such as *political correctness, globalization, border crossing*) tend to conceal as much about social relationships as they reveal. "All vogue words share a similar fate: the more experiences they pretend to make transparent, the more they themselves become opaque. The more numerous are the orthodox truths they elbow out and supplant, the faster they turn into no-question asked canons" (Bauman, 1998, p. 8).

13

"Both Print and Oral" and "Talking about Race": Transforming Toni Morrison's Language Issues into Teaching Issues

Joyce Irene Middleton

> There were two kinds of education going on: one was the education in the schools which was print-oriented; and right side by side with it was this other way of looking at the world that was not only different than what we learned about in school, it was coming through another sense. People told stories. Also there was the radio; I was a radio child. You get in the habit of gathering information that way, and imagining the rest.
> —Toni Morrison, Interview with Kathy Neustadt

> In this country, . . . American means white, and Africanist people struggle to make the term applicable to themselves with ethnicity and hyphen after hyphen after hyphen.
> —Toni Morrison, *Playing in the Dark: Whiteness and the Literary Imagination*

WHEN TONI MORRISON WON THE NOBEL PRIZE FOR LITERATURE, she told a *Washington Post* reporter that one of her interests as a teacher of literature at Princeton University was to enable her students to "talk about race." While teaching is not an explicit subject matter that Morrison interrogates through her writing, her critique of conflicts in cultural language use mirrors many of the teaching issues in our classrooms. Her work encourages teachers and scholars in rhetoric and composition to explore the implications of her interests in writing to current academic research on race, literacy, and teaching. Morrison's writings ask her readers to think about language issues that modern Western traditions of schooling do not, but should, address. This essay shows how Morrison's language issues may be articulated as teaching issues to help students think critically about issues of race, gender, culture, and writing in the academy. Using Morrison's nonfiction (including her Nobel lecture), I analyze her language issues as teaching issues, I explore the usefulness of theories of orality to student discussions about personal and cultural language use, and I explore the pedagogical implications of Morrison's claims about writing in a racialized society.

Orality and Literacy in Morrison's Nonfiction

Although Morrison's ethos and influence is probably viewed more as a fiction writer than as a nonfiction writer, she has produced a substantial body of interviews and essays that focus on her strong interest in contemporary language use and pedagogy. Her topics, familiar to those of us who teach rhetoric, writing, and literacy, include discussions of memory (see McConkey, 1996), audience, revision, pathos, listening, aurality/orality, and essential relationships between race, gender, and writing. A close analysis of the subliminal language features that she self-consciously structures in her writing shows how orality and literacy work together, in a language that is "both print and oral" (Morrison, 1984b, p. 341).

For example, in an early essay, "Memory, Creation, and Writing," Morrison writes about her literary imagination as a Black woman writer. As she expresses her broad interests in language, she implicitly rereads Western canonical literary values and discusses a range of rhetoric and literacy issues—oral and written memory, listening and reading, construction of audience, and a writer's ethos. Her particular interest in memory as a subject matter focuses on the relationship between memory and rhetorical invention—a "form of willed creation" (Morrison, 1984a, p. 385) that "ignites some process of invention" (p. 386). Morrison speaks here as a writer of fiction, but her concern with how to move her audience is clearly rhetorical. Her audience analysis critiques familiar, traditional conceptions of readers and creates new ones. She writes:

> I want my fiction to urge the reader into active participation in the non-narrative, nonliterary experience of the text, which makes it difficult for the reader to confine himself to a cool and distant acceptance of data. . . . I want him to respond on the same plane as an illiterate or preliterate reader would. I want to subvert his traditional comfort so that he may experience an unorthodox one: that of being in the company of his own solitary imagination. (Morrison, 1984a, p. 387)

Morrison's explicit focus on the "nonliterary experience" and on an imagined "illiterate" or "preliterate" response to her work signifies her search for shifting the habits of readers trained in modern Western patriarchal traditions of reading and literacy (especially students). Further, with her interest in subjectivity and intimacy rather than the familiar "cool distance" in the academy, Morrison positions her reader, a co-creator of the text, as an active participant who not only interprets the text but also, responsibly, creates an empowering language of one's own.

In the same article, Morrison elaborates on her literary interest in the contemporary reader's co-creation of the text. But here Morrison's audience analysis also includes an important cultural perspective on early Western uses of literacy:

> I sometimes think how glorious it must have been to have written drama in sixteenth-century England, or poetry in ancient Greece, or religious narrative in the Middle Ages, when literature was need and did not have a critical history to constrain or diminish the writer's imagination. How magnificent not to have to depend on the reader's literary associations—his literary experience—which can be as much an impoverishment of the reader's imagination as it is of a writer's. It is important that what I write not be merely literary. (Morrison, 1984a, 387)

Morrison's historical focus is not only on the literary genres—drama, religious narrative, or poetry—that she describes but it is also on the psychodynamics of orality (or residual orality) associated with literacy in the early Western cultures that she names. Shakespeare's audience went "to hear" a play, not to see one (Donawerth, 1984). Thus, in this passage, Morrison implicitly questions modern Western literate values and the academic inheritance that informs her contemporary reader's reception of literary texts.

In a more recent lecture, in *The Dancing Mind,* Morrison is much more explicit about the politics of "participatory" reading. She tells the story of a highly cultivated, young, White male doctoral student, now in a prestigious graduate school. At this pinnacle moment of his academic training, he discovers what Morrison describes as "his disability":

> [I]n all those years he had never learned to sit in a room by himself and read for four hours and have those four hours followed by another four without any companionship but his

own mind. He said it was the hardest thing he ever had to
do, but he taught himself, forced himself to be alone with a
book he was not assigned to read, a book on which there was
no test. He forced himself to be alone without the comfort
or disturbance of telephone, radio, television. To his credit,
he learned this habit, this skill that once was part of any literate young person's life. (1996, p. 10)

One can only speculate on the state of the"impoverished" readerly imagination that this graduate student confronted, but one can certainly applaud his actions to "subvert [his] traditional comfort" and to unlearn
habits that have effectively and instinctively constrained his literate and
literary experiences.

Morrison's reader/learner is an active participant, not a passive "received knower." Positioning her reader in this way, Morrison privileges
subjectivity, intimacy, orality, and memory in her writing. If writing as
practiced in the Western tradition "separates the knower from the
known" (Havelock, 1986, 1978; Ong, 1982), constructing its reader as
detached and objective, as Morrison observes, then Morrison creates new
uses of literacy, effectively reclaiming its essential relationship to orality (and oral storytelling). In fact, early Western uses of literacy often
reveal the ways in which orality and literacy work together ("both print
and oral"). In "Unspeakable Things Unspoken: The Afro-American
Presence in American Literature," Morrison discusses the connection
between her own composing process and the participatory text that she
creates. Discussing her interpretative strategies, she states:

These spaces, which I am filling in, and can fill in because they
were planned, can conceivably be filled in with other sig-
nificances. That is planned as well. The point is that into these
spaces should fall the ruminations of the reader and his or
her invented or recollected or misunderstood knowingness.
(1989, p. 29)

Rather than constrain or limit the reader's imagination with familiar
literate conventions, Morrison empowers the literacy of the reader by
making him or her a co-creator of her text. But the reader, like Morrison's
student in *The Dancing Mind,* must be open and willing to actively
participate in her text.

It is important to remember that orality is not simply a synonym for
speech. A more accurate view defines orality as a coherent system of

cultural values for language use—a symbol system that relies on the spoken voice and face to face discourse, but that also includes bodily gestures, strong appeal to the senses, oral memory, and acoustic elements, especially music (see Havelock, 1978). Paul Zumthor, constructing a theory of oral poetry, corrects the view of orality that is limited to speech, and he stresses the significance of bodily presence in any discussion of orality. He states:

> Orality cannot be reduced to vocal action. As an expansion of the body, vocality does not exhaust orality. Indeed, it implies everything in us that is addressed to the other, be it a mute gesture, a look. . . . Body movements are thus integrated into a poetics. Empirically, one notes the astonishing permanence that associates gesture and utterance. (1990, p. 153)

The historically shifting values of the relationship between orality and literacy that Morrison observes in "Memory, Creation, and Writing" may also be usefully illustrated by focusing on Frederick Douglass's development of literacy skills in the early American oratorical culture. In a previous article, I argued that Douglass's own orality and oral memory strengthened his access to the American literacy, public discourse, and schooling of his time. The implicit orality of nineteenth-century American school texts, for example, *The Columbian Orator* that Douglass cites in his *Narrative,* reveals its residual orality in much of its content: rhetorical dialogues that imitate face-to-face argumentation (e.g., arguments against slavery), speeches, poetry, and other models for speech making (Middleton, 1994, 1993).

In her numerous interviews and essays, Morrison talks about elements of Black oral art forms that inform her work. But what gives her art its complex language use and texture is not a simple, static representation of these elements in writing. Instead, Morrison explores the dynamic and often conflicting relationships between these Black oral cultural forms and the dominant Western cultural paradigms for language use. Rather than representing a hierarchical or subordinate relationship between the literate and the oral, as the modern Western tradition of writing generally represents these and as many African American writers have chosen to do, Morrison privileges orality and its values both in characterization and in narration. Thus, readers gain significant meaning from her stories through the spoken/heard quality of the text (listening) as well as from the written/visual quality (reading). As we read Morrison's stories, our imaginations are frequently directed to focus on sounds—the aural world of her stories—and the values of communication that are associated with speaking—body gestures, sensual engagement, phonetic spellings of sounds and words, manipulated silences, music, listening, dialogues, face-to-face discourse, and speaking pictures. If Morrison's writerly efforts are successful, then these elements should stimulate for the reader the intimacy of a spoken word culture and its preservation through oral memory.

An Epideictic Nobel Address Praising Human Speech

The element of a dialogic, participatory discourse—reader/writer involvement—is eloquently structured in Morrison's most powerful essay on language and storytelling, her Nobel lecture, which may be viewed rhetorically as an epideictic address on the virtues of human speech. Using a "once upon a time" opening and narrative frame, Morrison draws together commonplace images from early bardic traditions of oral storytelling. She delivers her text as a parable—an oral speech genre— with a mythic, prophetic tone and a sustained use of metaphors and similes. The first part of her ancient story—a lengthy response to a question raised by several children—is told by an old Black woman, a griotte, who has been blessed with blindness (a metaphor for her highly esteemed wisdom). Telling her tale, the blind woman offers a wide-ranging prophetic view on the state and uses of language, enumerating its many misguided modern attributes: "statist," "sexist," "oppressive," "theistic," "racist," "the faux language of mindless media," "the calcified language of the academy," (she names over twenty-five of these [Morrison, 1995, pp. 319–320]). "The vitality of language," the old woman emphasizes," "lies in its ability to limn the actual, imagined, and possible lives of its speakers, readers, writers" (p. 321). Ending her speech with a memorable, ceremonial tone, the old woman utters an old proverbial statement about language: "Word-work is sublime . . . because it is generative; it makes meaning that secures our difference, our human difference—*the way in which we are like no other life*" (p. 321; emphasis added).

In this frequently cited passage, Morrison signifies the great esteem for the gift of human speech in an oral culture. Praise of human speech is commonplace in the roots of Western culture among the ancient Greeks, especially during their democracy or still later in the age of Erasmus, an early historical print culture that reveals a strong influence of orality (Ong, 1982, p. 16). Today, many contemporary writers of color and postmodern writers blur the lines between the oral and the written, treating all language as a continuum. They play with language and merge the interests of Western prose with the voices and values of their own cultural orality, for example, in works by Morrison, John Edgar Wideman, Gloria Anzaldua, Leslie Marmon Silko, or Gabriel Garcia Marquez. They remind us that the rhetorical power and ability to speak, to tell one's story, to defend oneself, is a highly prized human attribute that continues to characterize our cultural and political histories, experiences and relationships (Middleton, 1995).

As the old, Black blind woman finishes her speech, Morrison's audience must be deeply persuaded by the old woman's ethos and wisdom. Morrison addresses her international audience about the imminent death of language that we face in our age, and the nobility of word—work that is trapped in a race for power and dominance. If Morrison's rhetoric works, she has effectively persuaded her own listeners to accept the lessons of the old blind woman's tale, and we, too, want to "do" language.

But the discourse does not end here. The telling of the tale continues, and after hearing the powerful "call" of the old woman, we hear the "response" of the children throughout the second half of Morrison's Nobel lecture. Through the children's response, the text becomes recursive and rewrites itself. The voice previously constructed as venerable and wise becomes questionable and unstable, and the text begins a crucial intellectual and psychological phase of deconstructing its earlier premises. Through the children's responses, we hear that the blind woman's ethos did not persuade them: "Your answer is artful, but its artfulness embarrasses us and ought to embarrass you. Your answer is indecent in its self-congratulation. A made-for-television script" (p. 322). The children see someone who maintains a critical, objective distance. But they want intimacy, subjectivity—they represent the voice of the future attempting to create a dialogue with the voice of the past.

The extensive response of the children is loaded with potent questions, and in contrast to the stately, monologic character of the old woman's text, the children stress the urgent need for dialogue. With honest passion, they demand answers to their questions:

> Why didn't you reach out, touch us with your soft fingers, delay the sound bite, the lesson, until you knew who we were? Is there no speech, . . . no words you can give us that help us break through your dossier of failures? Don't you remember being young, when language was magic without meaning? We have heard all our short lives that we have to be respon-

sible. What could that possibly mean in the catastrophe this world has become? (Morrison, 1995, p. 322)

The dialogic—call and response—structure of this Nobel lecture creates a strong dynamic tension as Morrison's story explores the implications for thinking about language, rhetoric, and the literary imagination. In another essay, Morrison elaborates on the element of personal involvement and commitment that is implicit in her conception of a participatory reading process. She says: "Writing and reading are not all that distinct for a writer. . . . Writing and reading mean being aware of the writer's notions of risk and safety, the serene achievement of, or sweaty fight for, meaning and *response-ability*" (1992a, p. xi, emphasis added). Thus, as Morrison strategically motivates her reader's involvement in her texts, Morrison's reader/writer finds that her language reflects a site of struggle, marked by questions and answers, ease and dis-ease, speech and silences, telling and being heard. The achievement of co-creating language and meaning together for both writer and reader is praiseworthy and honorable, and Morrison celebrates this successful act in the final lines of her Nobel lecture, when, following a long moment of silence and listening, the old, Black blind woman exclaims, "Look. How lovely it is, this thing we have done together" (p. 323).

Exploring Connections Between Language and Teaching

These conceptual issues about oral and written language use as Morrison represents them help students to reexamine those elements of Western literate traditions that inhibit their ability to understand the relationships between schooling and personal language use (see Middleton, 1994).

Implied in Morrison's interest in participation is a collaboration between writer and reader, or teacher and student, that not only leads to creating new language but also reflects the reader's responsibility for that language-making process (recall the doctoral student's experience in Morrison's *The Dancing Mind*). Morrison's use of orality stimulates a significant shift from the familiar, text-based pedagogy in which the text is valued as the authority in the knowledge-making process. Thus, the students' struggle lies in finding a voice of legitimacy to express knowledge that is not usually associated with *real* learning. Traditionally, students censor their ideas as "only their opinions," subordinating their ideas to the objectivity of book knowledge and teacher authority. The students' problems are emphatic in settings that encourage lively, sustained class discussions and that encourage critical discussions about race, gender, and difference. "At times I do not feel the urge to speak in class," one Black woman wrote in her journal, "because of opinion related topics which may force me to use examples of my individual experience in contrast to someone else's. I realize that my opinions are not based on fact, therefore I just keep them to myself." Student comments such as this one illustrate the new questions that emerge in response to shifting the academic paradigm that not only includes orality in the teaching of literacy but also recognizes the power of ordinary language in this kind of instruction. Kathleen Welch frames these conflicts as cultural and media issues and offers new ways of thinking about the essential relationships between orality and literacy and between ordinary and extraordinary language use:

> In order for people to become persuaded of the empowerment that is possible for them through encoding, they must see the relationship between their own ordinary language—including interior discourse—and that of artistic discourse. This issue provides a powerful means of persuasion for writing instructors. Connecting a student's interior discourse—something that is lived and felt—to a class essay or to a play by Shakespeare acts as an effective means of empowering students. This connection treats conceptualizations, or "how" questions, not "content" or "what" questions. In addition, this connection enables students to comprehend the interconnections of all language use and its existence as a communal activity rather than as the merely private, hermetic possession that many people assume it to be. (1990, p. 162)

Asking new pedagogical questions, teachers and researchers need to talk about these kinds of language conflicts explicitly in class discussions with students. Without creating a means for an intellectual shift away from traditional concepts of teaching and language issues, students are not only skeptical about the legitimacy of the conflicts—who's right? who's wrong?—but they also resist them. This reaction (the resistance of the passive receiver, clinging to the comfort and familiarity that role provides) reflects the vulnerability of students thinking through uncharted territory in the academy. In *Rhetoric and Irony,* C. Jan Swearingen articulates the significance of these traditional academic values in the Western intellectual tradition in general and in the rhetoric and composition community in particular:

> Detachment, objectivity, a certain amount of skepticism, a willingness to question received opinion, command over abstractions, generalizations, and logic, and analytical probity—all these hallmarks of Western thought are so highly valued that they are now conceived of as universals or at least as inevitabilities of human thought. (1991, p. 7)

Within the academy, then, our students are highly trained to listen for information that positions them as "passive receivers of knowledge," "objective," "detached," and "rational." These student behaviors are rooted in a tradition of schooling that is hierarchical and agonistic, an us versus them, a Punch and Judy show that focuses on defeating an opponent. In contrast, empathetic, participatory listening and subjectivity—defining students as co-creators of language and meaning—are no longer required, taught, or valued in the traditional academic curriculum. While Swearingen's observations begin to articulate the kinds of academic problems to be solved, William Reid, in "Literacy, Orality, and the Functions of Curriculum," challenges the basic premises of the hierarchy and conflict between orality, literacy, and Western curriculum theorizing.

> We should consider that it may not, after all, be necessary for oral and literate traditions to be thought of as conflicting. Certainly, the perception of conflict has been almost universal, but I suspect that this is due less to the intrinsic nature of oral and literate world views, and more to the ways in which the resources of literacy have been allowed to become an engine of modernization, using that word in what, I suggest, may be its historic sense. (1993, p. 24–25)

In "Writing on the Bias" in her *Writing Permitted in Designated Areas Only*, Linda Brodkey also effectively critiques the ways in which these dichotomous, conflicting, traditional academic values influence our teaching and our construction of a literacy curriculum. Questioning the subordinate relationship between objectivity and subjectivity, Brodkey observes the contradictions implicit in traditional writing instruction:

> [S]tudents are taught that third-person statements are unbiased (objective) and those in the first person are biased (subjective). Little wonder then that by the time they reach college, most students have concluded that to avoid bias they have only to recast their first person claims into the third

person. Delete "I believe" from "racism is on the rise in this country" or "racism has virtually disappeared in this country," and the assertion assumes a reality independent of the writer, who is no longer the author but merely the messenger of the news or fact. Students learn what they have been taught, and they have been taught that grammatical person governs the objectivity and subjectivity of actual persons. (1996, p. 49–50)

Brodkey's concrete example makes visible the invisibility of this long-standing dichotomous pedagogical stance in the teaching of writing. But further, it moves her readers to interrogate the tradition and raise new pedagogical questions for ways to incorporate more elements of orality and issues of subjectivity into the traditional literacy classroom.

"Black Matters" and Writing in a Racialized Society

Current research on race and cultural studies breaks the precedent of traditional arguments on race (see Crichlow & McCarthy, 1993, p. xix). With an interest in "theorizing" race, scholars have opened debates on race as an intellectual proposition in the academy. Given the paradoxical nature of any discussion about race, that it is both an empty social construction and one of the most violent, powerful, and destructive ways of social organization, these debates are complex, interdisciplinary, and progressive. Based on the distinctions between "race" (the empty category) and "racism" (the use of ideology to establish systems of hierarchy and domination), the current body of scholarship addresses issues surrounding definitions of race, who can talk about it, and antiracism. With a focus on Toni Morrison's nonfiction work on racialized writing, this final section of my essay addresses ways to talk about race and Whiteness as intellectual issues both in theory and in practice.

When Toni Morrison delivered her highly provocative theory (at the time) on literary Whiteness, race, and history during a three-day lecture series at Harvard in 1992, she delivered the first two lectures (that is, the first two days) without allowing for any questions from the audience. As the story goes, she said that she would not address questions until the third day, the last day of that lecture series. While we all acknowledge the intellectual power of those more than ten-year-old lectures in our teaching, research, and publications, I would like to revisit the rhetorical circumstances of that historical moment in which Morrison effectively articulated elements for shaping a new rhetoric of racism. This rhetoric offered new strategies to encourage "talking about race" as an intellectual proposition in the academy.

For example, what do those two days of forced silence say about the rhetorical situation that Morrison faced? From one perspective, Morrison's strategy strikes me as a particularly womanist pose, a reversal of a privileged, familiar, masculine paradigm ("crossfire") that would have allowed for unplanned debate, interruptions, and listening for flaws to attack. Instead, by suspending the moment for response and discussion, Morrison encouraged a different kind of listening—one that would suspend immediate judgment—and critical engagement that she knew her provocative text would demand. Structuring her new rhetoric, Morrison required a new way of listening and thinking about her texts, and she had to. Like many of us, she had to discover ways to dismantle the hostility of race studies in the academy. She had to ensure that her intellectual enterprise would not be misinterpreted as a simple interest in a reversal of power and racial domination but would be engaged with new interest in knowledge transformation.

In *Playing in the Dark*, Morrison critiques and affirms a set of premises that have historically served to inhibit rather than to promote any serious discussion about race in the academy. Effectively, she shifts the critical gaze on race from object (Black bodies) to subject (Whiteness) and from noun to verb. As she reframes the analysis of racialized discourse, she reveals its inadequacies and throws into relief the subjectivity of the reader. It is important to recognize that Morrison's arguments about race are both historical and textual. It is also important to recognize that Morrison is not interested in a simple power reversal of racial hierarchies: "Morrison makes clear that her revision of Africanism diametrically opposes conventional Afrocentricity, which often replicates the imperialistic tendencies of Eurocentric scholarship" (Maselila, 1998, p. 23).

While Morrison's research is literary, her arguments should promote ways to frame a rhetoric for talking about race in the classroom and in our scholarly practices. At least three major claims or premises from her lectures help to demonstrate how Morrison's rhetoric of racism works: her statement that "American means white," her "black matters" arguments that immediately translated into "race matters," arguments, and her argument that "metaphorical race" is more threatening to the body politic than "biological race" ever was.

The rhetoric of her chapter entitled "Black Matters" argues forcefully to counter the claims of the liberal ideas of color-blind rhetoric. In fact, "race matters" has become the signature phrasing to address the ideological confusion implicit in the dominant American cultural descriptions that "race doesn't matter," or that "color makes no difference."—or, as George F. Will recently coined in his new color-blind phrase (in response to the results of the 2000 U.S. Census), that we are simply "ethnic accidents." Perhaps this is the racial progress that Black comedian Chris Tucker desires, "to be America's first black postracial movie star" (qtd. in Hirschberg, 2000, p. 37). Using a "race matters" rhetorical strategy, Patricia Williams describes the detrimental effects of color-blind rhetoric as a "false luxury of a prematurely imagined community, . . . a purity achieved through ignorance," which must be countered with a language that structures a "world in which we know each other better" (1997, p. 5; also see Middleton, 2000). The verbal silence encouraged by color-blind rhetoric is extremely problematic, for there is only one race that this rhetoric serves.

Perhaps the strongest, most recent evidence of the detrimental effects of color-blind rhetoric was in Florida in December 2000 when the media response to the "stolen election" and to Black voters in Florida was to render the various "accidents" as invisible. In a published conversation, "The Invisible People," with poet activist June Jordan, Toni Morrison equated this media event to *Pravda*: "It's like Pravda," Morrison told Jordan, "Or worse! Because there's no news! For example, you wouldn't know there were truly massive protests in D.C. Or who knows about the speeches in Tallahassee? It's a capitalist consolidation of the press— with consequences the same as Pravda: Horrifying distortion and sabotage!" (Jordan, 2001, p. 25). Adding to Morrison's response, June Jordan describes what happened as a "Whites Only" [event] in the public consciousness and on the public forums (p. 25). "Where," Jordan asks, "is there record of any major national newspaper or TV channel attempting . . . to find out what black people were thinking, and why?" (p. 25). With these responses in mind, we may recall Morrison's claim that "American means white" and question what many black voters (and Black nonvoters) really hear when politicians speak repeatedly through all forms of media about "what the American people want."

In the preface to *Playing in the Dark,* Morrison talks about her only short story, "Recitatif" (1983), in which she experiments with her theory of racialized writing. She attempts to remove all racial codes in her writing while at the same time making race essential to the identities of the two main female characters. We know that one woman is Black and that one is White, but we don't know which is which (thus, class issues gain more relevance). If Morrison's experiment works, "to sign race while designing racelessness" (1997, p. 8), she effectively positions us as readers to recognize our conscious and self-conscious act of "racing" her characters (note the shift from noun to verb). Thus, our questions as readers reveal both a strong curiosity about the racial identity of each woman and a horrifying response to acknowledging our need for the correct answers, which obviously do not exist. What does exist, as one student observes, is the reality of racially inflected language and our participation in that language. Responding to these issues in Morrison's story, the student writes: "The absence of racial labels combined with the important roles that race and racism play in the characters' lives shows us that it is not possible for one to live in the United States without being a part of the 'cultural hegemony' of race stratification." Another student writes about how Morrison's text resists any conclusive racing of the characters:

> What exactly are the words and phrases in the story that seem stereotypes of one or the other race and which race and why?
> . . . Twyla's mother danced all night (black?). Roberta's mother was sick (white?). Twyla was taken to the shelter in the early morning (black?).
>
> Twyla's mother said "they never washed their hair and they smelled funny" (white?). Twyla's name (black?). "My mother won't like you putting me in here" (white?). In the first two paragraphs alone, the stereotypes shift the question of race several times.

Scholarly inquiries have also addressed these issues, searching for "the correct" responses to unanswerable questions. In fact, Elizabeth Abel's well-known article on "Recitatif" (1993) involved a direct call to Morrison for help in explaining why White women and Black women construct opposite racial identities for the female characters in the story even though they were using the exact same set of "racial" stereotypes. This early experiment with racialized writing becomes a central feature later in Morrison's novel *Paradise,* which ends without ever disclosing the identity of the only White female character in the story. Instead, readers must formulate their own responses to Morrison's implicit questions: "Why, when, and in what ways does race matter (or not matter)?" While debates about racialized writing can often create a volatile space in our classrooms, the discussions are crucial and essential to our professional growth in rhetoric and composition. New books on racialized writing and literary Whiteness continue to appear and demonstrate a strong intellectual response to Morrison's work among teachers and research-

ers. But open debates among students in the classroom are very difficult to facilitate—and the degree of difficulty increases if the teacher is
already "raced" by students and colleagues (see S. Logan, 1998; Johnson,
1994; du Cille, 1994; E. B. Brown, 1989).

Student responses to these new classroom issues reveal how they face
the implicit contradictions between the study of race as an academic
subject matter, on the one hand, and the academic traditions that de-
value race as an intellectual proposition, on the other. Even when discussions about race are fairly familiar, the unfamiliar discussion about
the politics of Whiteness meets with much resistance, anger, and discomfort (see Giroux, 1997; Ratcliffe, 2000; A. Randall, 2001). Journal and
essay writing helps to illustrate how students think through this new
academic territory and formulate their own arguments of support or
resistance to discussions of race and Whiteness. In one class scenario, a
White female student developed a research project on the social construction of whiteness in Morrison's *The Bluest Eye*. But when she tried to
share her work with other students in the class, she was disappointed
by the dichotomous responses from other White students in her class:

> I think I've seen two common responses from white people
> on the issue of whiteness. Either they are dumbfounded,
> turned off, or resist accepting any such possible argument.
> Or, as shown in this class, they say "yeah yeah" and look too
> eager or too accepting of such a radical, self-questioning
> analysis. I don't know, from the latter response, how much
> white people actually understand what I'm asking of them.
> . . . I think sometimes people look at these theories like clouds
> in the sky. They (the theories) are somehow unearthly, intan-
> gible, too distant. I want to put them in your face. I want you
> to understand what you might have to give up in order to
> create this color-valued society we profess so much about.
> Sometimes, without this deeper understanding, people are all
> too willing to agree with a theory without reflecting on the
> personal implications.

Despite the tensions and conflicts, however, most students agree with
the need for pedagogy on race and Whiteness, noting that if these kinds
of discussions do not take place in the academy, then where should they
(would they) take place? Writing about her critical responses to our class
discussions, another White female student articulates the essential need

for "talking about race" in racially diverse class settings in the academy. On the significance of race, writing, and pedagogy, she observes that:

> [e]ven in my efforts to be anti-racist I still live in a world where the air I breathe is so full of stereotypes, prejudice and racism that it is impossible not to digest some of it. Toni Morrison's *Beloved* makes this point in the encounter between Sethe and Amy. She shows how even through all of Amy's human compassion towards Sethe, the fact that she is white and Sethe is black has forced them to use the oppressive language of racism. . . . This class and my own research enabled me to understand that I am racist, prejudiced, stereotypical, or whatever you want to label me. I have to work everyday, like each of us, to counter what is so ingrained in all of our minds. A diverse class like ours is so important because it allows us the opportunity for change. If we only interact with those of our own race we will keep all those stereotypes locked inside of us with not even the chance to fight them. The strength of our class is that we talk, we listen, and we walk away able to conquer some of those stereotypes and be more aware of ourselves.

These student writings move us to recall some urgent questions in Jacqueline Royster's 1995 Conference of College Composition and Communication Chair's address. With an interest in dismantling the hierarchical relationship between mainstream and marginalized voices, Royster asks the rhetoric and composition community: "How can we teach, engage in research, write about, and talk across boundaries *with* others, instead of for, about and around them? . . . *How do we listen?* . . . How do we translate listening into language and action?" (1996b, p. 38; emphasis added).

Toni Morrison's theory of racially inflected language has provoked many new scholarly publications on the social construction of race and Whiteness in American literary studies; on issues of language, culture, and ownership; and on the politics of pedagogy. Her wordwork to create writing that is "both print and oral" is equally provocative, revealing both her strong value for uses of Western prose traditions and her engagement with culturally distinct oral storytelling traditions. The pedagogical implications for thinking about Morrison's language issues with students are enormous, linking historical and contemporary discourses,

Western and non-Western language uses, and the mutual interests of written and spoken word traditions. In a recent film, *10 Things I Hate about You* (a film loosely based on Shakespeare's *Taming of the Shrew*), a Black male high school English teacher introduces Shakespeare to his class as a "Def Poet" by rapping the opening lines of Sonnet 141 (the moment certainly signifies Langston Hughes's and Claude McKay's experimentation with the Shakespearean sonnet form). The performance could have been better (and, like most Hollywood films, relies too much on clichés and simplistic racial and gender representations). But for talking about race, Whiteness, language and writing, this moment in the film links many of Toni Morrison's language issues together in a single text. Effectively, the film clip stimulates self-reflective thinking among students about their own language use and the texts of their popular culture. More broadly, the clip promotes rhetorical engagement about language and difference. Toni Morrison's language issues move us to think not only about how we use language—a huge conversation in our discipline—but also, perhaps much more significantly, about how language uses us.

14

Found Not Founded

William W. Cook

THE HISTORY OF AFRICAN AMERICAN RHETORIC IN THE AMERICAS
is a history of specific African retentions in both syntax and affective
form, of transformations resulting in syncretistic language rituals and
structures and of "New World" creations. It stands in both a resistant
and symbiotic relationship to the dominant discourses with which it is
engaged. This rhetoric is marked by masking as is evidenced by the frequency with which masks are evoked in literature.

> We wear the mask that grins and lies,
> It hides our cheeks and shades our eyes—
> This debt we pay to human guile:
> With torn and bleeding hearts we smile,
> And mouth with myriad subtleties.
>
> (Dunbar, 1980, p. 71)

African American rhetoric becomes frequently both a rhetoric of deception and a kind of cultural "shibboleth." This masking function is synonymous with what Ralph Ellison calls the representative American
"darky" act:

> The "darky" act makes brothers of us all. America is a land
> of masking jokers. We wear the mask for purposes of aggres-
> sion as well as defense; when we are protecting the future and
> preserving the past. In short, the motives hidden behind the
> mask are as numerous as the ambiguities the mask conceals.
> (1958, p. 1547)

The mask and all of its cultural manifestations may also be read as cultural shibboleth. The term *shibboleth* as used here refers to an incident

reported in Judges 12:6. The Gileadites having defeated the Ephraimites and desiring to prevent their escape across the fords on the River Jordan, devised a language test to distinguish Ephraimites from Gileadites: they asked them to pronounce "shibboleth" which the hapless Ephraimites pronounced, according to their own dialect as "sibboleth." Many Ephraimites were slain for the small difference in language. The term as presently used has enjoyed an expansion. *Webster's Third International Dictionary* defines *shibboleth* as "a use of language regarded as distinctive of a particular class, profession, or group." A further expansion to this 1976 definition has been the tendency to use the term not only in reference to language but to apply it to other aspects of culture. The creativity that has marked language, music, dance, and religion in African American culture may well be the result of an attempt to mask the self from the other and a shibboleth to distinguish members from outsiders. It may be, as Richard Wright observes in *Black Boy*, a weapon to be used against those who delegate the Black self to a subaltern state, both an aggressive and a defensive weapon.

The appearance in 2001 after lengthy litigation with the Margaret Mitchell estate of Alice Randall's *The Wind Done Gone* offers an excellent example of what Ellison calls a "darky" act. This text plays the dozens and otherwise signifies not only with Mitchell's title but with her characters, plot, theme, and novelistic structure. The icon is destroyed by the "change the joke and slip the yoke" maneuver.

Citing Ellison early in this discussion is no accident. His *Invisible Man* (1952/1995) when fully understood, should stand next to works by Smitherman (1977/1986), Baugh (1983), Kochman (1972), and Abrahams (1963/1970) as a thoroughly worked-out study not only of African American rhetoric but of the liberating power of that rhetoric and the cultural forces that it embodies. We trace the progress of his invisible protagonist, invisible because he refuses to assert his identity against the cultural forces that are determined to define him according to the needs of others, invisible because he has lost the very memory of his own language. When we first meet him, his language is marked by slavish imitation of the infamous "Atlanta Exposition Address." We travel with him on a journey that is actually an immersion in blackness, in Black language. This immersion is carefully patterned to include all those sites where language use serves to construct an identity in opposition to external determinants such as the speeches he is given, the Optic White of the paint factory, the white line of the college, or the papers he receives during his travels among cultural worlds. All of these reject the language of his nature because they recognize the danger of its resistant power. He must be made over into that which is needful and supportive of the cultural agenda on which their power is based. His bravura performance of the dozens when confronted by Brother Twobit (see the exchange, pp. 469–471) is nothing like the bafflement he feels when he hears the language play in *The Golden Day.* "Sometimes it appeared as though they played some vast and complicated game with me and the rest of the school folk, a game whose goal was laughter and whose rules and subtleties I could never grasp" (Ellison, 1952/1995, p. 74).

He finds it impossible to participate in the verbal exchanges of the man with the blueprints. His comment on the experience is a measure of how bereft he is of linguistic skill. "I liked his words though I didn't know the answer. I'd known the stuff from childhood, but had forgotten it; had learned it back of school" (p. 176).

The movement of Ellison's protagonist, as the above page numbers indicate, is progressive, since he learns how to avoid imitation and to assume the power of creativity, and regressive as he learns the necessity of grounding himself in the rhetoric of his rearing, hence, Ellison's repeated images of circles and the boomerang of history. The movement of Ellison's protagonist from purpose to passion to perception is marked by sermons, signifying, scathing satire and ridicule, the call-response of Black discourse, improvised speeches, jazzy riffs on language, and the full arsenal of verbal weapons available to an emic speaker.

In 2001, another work was published to coincide with the centenary celebration of a figure almost lost to studies of Black discourse. C. L. R. James's revisionist and "post-colonial" reading of Melville's *Moby Dick,* although written in 1953 with editions in 1978 and 1985, was published in its entirety almost fifty years later. The range of languages available to James is apparent in the unique sound of three of his works: "The Black Jacobins," "Beyond a Boundary," and "Mariners, Renegades & Castaways." That James was seen by progressive writers as a model revolutionary in the war against cultural erasure is certified in Ishmael Reed's (1972) magisterial novel *Mumbo Jumbo.* Having failed to convince young Thor Wintergreen to abandon his cooperative with revolutionary people of color by any other means, Biff Musclewhite uses the sacred icon of White language, literature, and privilege. Black hands must not touch such holy objects. The villain is C. L. R. James, possessed of so many voices and masks that he could not be categorized.

> Son, these niggers writing. Profaning our sacred words, Tak-
> ing them from us and beating them on the anvil of Boogie
> Woogie, putting their black hands on them . . . so that they
> shine like burnished amulets. Taking our words, son. . . . Why
> . . . why 1 of them dared to interpret, critically mind you, the
> great Herman Melville's *Moby-Dick*. (Reed, 1972, p. 114)

This unthinkable offense results in the recovery of the White deserter.
Black control and manipulation of the word is too much for even the
most radical White man to bear. James has committed the sin of sins.
He has dared to declare himself a master of language and, through that
mastery, an independent fashioner of his soul and that of his people.

Careful attention to rhetorical study of our central texts will demonstrate the ways in which Black rhetoric has served as guidon and weapon
in the struggle of Black people "from chattel to esquire." It will demonstrate that there are clear continuities in the rhetorical arsenal as well
as creative leaps over the years. In order to offer yet another instance of
this, we can take our discussion back to the first book of poetry published by an African American.

Let us consider a most unlikely source of information about those
rhetorical strategies used by an artist and a work not usually included
in our discussions: Phillis Wheatley and her 1773 *Poems on Various
Subjects*. In particular, we should examine carefully the opening poem
in that collection. This is the signature poem "To Maecenas." Such a
poem was given the prime position in a collection by artists of her day
in order to certify the author, to acquaint readers of the volume with the
nature of the creator of that work. Wheatley's book was prefaced by the
testimony of a host of prominent White men of her day that she was
indeed the author of the poems included in the volume and that she was
a fairly recent mistress of language and literature. "To Maecenas" skillfully bypasses the authority of such certifiers to effect a radical revision
of literary history. This revision both appropriates and deconstructs the
discourses of her day through its all-out assault on neoclassical norms
of poetic discourse.

The first part of the poem may well be considered the "darky" masking act frequently commented on by students of African American rhetoric. Wheatley surveys the great writers of the Western tradition—Homer,
Virgil, Horace, and (by imitation) Pope. She finds herself dwarfed by such
greatness and silenced by such superior artistry but at the same time she
demonstrates her own ability to create poetry in the tradition she seems

to surrender to all the white masculine models she evokes. She laments her lack:

> But here I sit, and mourn a grov'ling mind
> That fain would mount, and ride upon the wind
>
> (Wheatley, 2001, p. 10)

She acknowledges her inferiority in the closing lines of the first part of the poem.

> But I less happy, cannot raise the song
> The faultr'ing music dies upon my tongue.
>
> (p. 10)

Stanzas five, six, and seven of this seven-stanza poem reveal her real intent. She evokes the name of Terence, a poet who was a slave, who came from North Africa and whose name, according to Wheatley, was accorded "the first glory in the rolls of fame" (2001, p. 10). To compound this audacious act of revisionary literary history, Wheatley uses the only footnote in the entire book. She informs us that Terentius Afer "was African by birth." Here is a tradition into which she can fit with ease. If she is sincere in her praise for the poets of the first part of the poem, poets she cannot hope to emulate, poets who represent a tradition in which her voice cannot be heard, here is the true tradition—one descended from an African slave like herself. Wheatley in this signature poem of her first book transforms the tradition creating thus a legitimating line of descent based on excellence and anchored by another African slave. She determines in the penultimate stanza to "snatch" the laurel of poet and claim it for herself. The poem, which begins as a traditional neoclassical evocation replete with the requisite classical references and tidy heroic couplets, is revealed to be a brilliant act of artistic subversion, one worthy of later Black poets who also signify on the tradition.

Just as African American writers were intent on following the literal as opposed to the intended meaning of the epideictic rhetoric of American foundational documents like the Declaration of Independence, so too they created, after the example of Wheatley, modes of disclosure in those texts that afforded spaces for their own particular inscriptions of self. Frederick Douglass, in his *Narratives,* calls such inscription "writing in the spaces left."

Having commented elsewhere on Douglass's rhetorical assault on the dominant discourse of his day (Cook, 1993), I will refrain from rehearsing that argument here. I will note, however, that in his letter to Mr. Auld, in his Fourth of July oration, in his only work of fiction *(The Heroic Slave)*, as well as in the better-known *Narrative of the Life of Frederick Douglass*, Douglass demonstrates how well he has turned the lessons he had learned from Caleb Bingham's progymnasmata, *The Columbian Orator*, to uses never anticipated by Bingham or those like Abraham Lincoln and others who found this work a source of their own libratory and forensic discourse. Those classical oratorical figures such as membrum, epanalepsis, synonymia, and anaphora so carefully presented by Bingham for emulation found a new use in Douglass's texts and in his oratory. By presenting in *The Heroic Slave* Madison Washington, who was both slave and master of sublime expression, Douglass disproved the claim that Blacks were incapable of such expression. Mr. Listwell, Douglass's surrogate for White America, heard Washington and was converted by him before he saw him. Not knowing that he was listening to a Black man, his admiration was not blinded by notions of racial inferiority:

> Long after Madison had left the ground, Mr. Listwell (our traveler) remained in motionless silence, meditating on the extraordinary revelations to which he had listened. The speech of Madison rung through the chambers of his soul, and vibrated through his entire frame. "Here indeed is a man," thought he, "of rare endowments." (Douglass, 1984, p. 304–305)

It is interesting to note that this work was Douglass's only completely realized work of fiction, but here as elsewhere he showed not only the power of the Black master orator but also his own skill in using sarcasm, mockery, and irony to disarm his enemies. Exemplary of this is his subtle denigration of Mr. Auld who claimed to be both his master and superior. Forty years after his escape, Douglass visited the dying Auld and his comment on Auld's death is a caution. Who was the true great man? "We parted to meet no more. His death was soon announced in the papers, and the fact that he had once owned me as a slave was cited as rendering that event noteworthy" (Douglass, 1984, p. 219).

The argument sketched above is presented not simply as evidence of the character of Black discourse in the eighteenth and nineteenth centuries. It is an attempt to reveal those language practices of earlier periods as part of a continuum. The struggle against and the appropriation of dominant discourses marks the history of Black rhetoric. Early studies by Melville Herskovits (1958), Lorenzo Dow Turner (1949), Roger Abrahams (1963/1970), Thomas Kochman (1972), and a host of others point not only to historical but also to contemporary uses. Fragmentary notices in observers such as Frederick Law Olmsted and other early writers on culture and history reveal the depth and pervasiveness of that variety of American speech we call Black English, a mode of discourse found but not founded on the dominant discourse of the Americas—one always in a contested linguistic relationship with the privileged discourse of the "metropole." (One might contend, given recent disputes in Wayne County and Oakland, California, a tradition in *legal* contention with that discourse.) The prominence of Black linguists and scholars in both these disputes as well as their participation in the CCCC/NCTE struggle over "The Students' Right to Their Own Language" should indicate, in spite of the relative absence of their efforts in the most recent study of the CCCC document, that neither the struggle nor the problem of visibility are near resolution.

If invisibility has marked many of the male-authored texts dealt with in this discussion, silence and silencing are central tropes not only of female-authored texts but of more recent rhetorical forays. For such artists, the rhetorical struggle is to center itself on a still more inclusive rhetoric of liberation and self-fashioning than has been the norm. The new rhetorical challenge may well be what Bakari Kitwana calls the "influence of corporate elite commercialization" (Kitwana, 1994, p. 11). Langston Hughes inveighed against such influence more than sixty years ago in "Note on Commercial Theatre." The first part of the poem is a condemnation of the cultural theft of which Black America has been a victim. The poem ends with a call for resistance:

> But someday somebody'll
> Stand up and talk about me,
> And write about me—
> Black and beautiful—
> And sing about me,
> And put on plays about me!
> I reckon it'll be
> Me myself!
> Yes, it'll be me.
>
> (1934, p. 216)

It is not strange that the post–Hip Hop poet Kevin Young (2000) calls on both Phillis Wheatley and Langston Hughes, seeing them as models/exemplars, or that his anthology *Giant Steps: The New Generation of*

African American Writers includes a discography of top records (1960–1990), a list of forty Hip Hop albums of all time, and a list of seventy-five top Hip Hop singles (K. Young, 2000, pp. 353–357). Young, by doing so, points to the continuity in African American language and literature. His selections for the anthology demonstrate the continuity "with a difference" of the Hip Hop generation with its forbears and a refusal to draw a clear line between music and poetry—no generation gap here. Like Kitwana's, his is a struggle to rescue the cultural products of Black America from the destructive influence of external forces bent on warping Black achievement in such a way as to render it valuable not as the cultural expression of a people but as conformable to the price-tag mentality of those who can only hear what they want to hear: not as cultural shibboleth but as reinscription of destructive racist values and practices.

Such commercialization, while making possible a kind of cross-over appeal, has had the effect of shaping the art (rap music, for Kitwana) not according to the needs and practices of a people whose expression it was created to be but, rather, according to the desire of those without the cultural experience to appreciate an art form that realized Black assertion of both community and self. "In a society where the public is programmed (from education and politics to mass media) to seek quick-fix, easy answers, it is much less threatening to the status quo (as well as jobs, positions, and conditional friendship) to place the blame on Blacks" (Kitwana, 1994, p. 7). Black artists and Black people must reject such blame and must resist those commercial forces that have been and continue to corrupt our words. The silence must be broken.

To the invisibility tropes of *Invisible Man, Native Son, Another Country,* and their by now canonical brothers must be added a thematics central to Black women's rhetoric: the movement from silence into sound. Zora Neale Hurston's Janie is silenced by the big voice of Mr. Starks but she reached back to the dozens to triumph over her foe.

Author bell hooks strikes the exact note for this discussion of silencing and marginalizing discourses:

> Moving from silence into speech is for the oppressed, the colonized, the exploited, and those who stand and struggle side by side a gesture of defiance that heals, that makes new life and new growth possible. It is that act of speech, of talking back that is no mere gesture of empty words, that is the expression of our movement from object to subject—the liberated voice. (1989, p. 9)

This movement is clearly dramatized in the following scene from Hurston's *Their Eyes Were Watching God*. Janie, silenced and condemned to the edge of things, pressed to defiance and indignation, realizes the righteousness and the power of her own voice.

> "Whut's de matter wid you, nohow? You ain't no young girl to be getting' all insulted 'bout yo' looks. You ain't no courtin' gal. You'se uh ole woman, nearly forty."
>
> "Yeah, Ah'm nearly forty and you'se already fifty. How come you can't talk about dat sometimes instead of always pointin' at me?"
>
> "'Tain't no use in getting'all mad, Janie, 'cause Ah mention you ain't no young gal no mo'. Nobody in heah ain't lookin' for no wife outa yuh. Old as you is."
>
> "Naw, Ah ain't no young gal no mo' but den Ah ain't no old woman neither. Ah reckon ah looks mah age too. But ah'm uh woman every inch of me, and Ah know it. Dat's a whole lot more'n you kin say. You big-bellies round here and put out a lot of brag, but 'tain't nothin' to it but yo' big voice. Humph! Talkin' 'bout me lookin' old! When you pull down yo' britches, you look lak de change uh life."
>
> "Great god from Zion!" Sam Watson gasped. "Y'all really playin' de dozens tunight."
>
> . . . His vanity bled like a flood. (Hurston, 1978, p. 122–23)

Alice Walker addresses her poem "Lost My Voice? Of Course" to Beanie, a childhood bully. Maya Angelou's heroine is traumatized into silence as is Toni Morrison's Pecola. Lutie Johnson in Ann Petry's *The Street* has no voice to assail her enemies and assert herself. Celie in *The Color Purple* is silenced and enslaved until she follows Wheatley and "snatches a laurel" from that very rhetoric which is the weapon of her oppressor. bell hooks learns the nature of those forces oppressing her and determines that she will talk back.

> In the world of the southern black community I grew up in, "back talk" and "talking back" meant speaking as an equal to an authority figure . . . to speak then when one was not spoken to was a courageous act—an act of risk and daring . . . the craving to speak, to have a voice, and not just any voice but one that could be identified as belonging to me. To make my voice, I had to speak, to hear myself talk—and talk

I did—darting in and out of grown folks conversations and dialogues, answering questions that were not directed at me . . . the punishments for these acts of speech seemed endless. They were intended to silence me . . . the girl child. . . . There was no calling for talking girls, no legitimized rewarded speech. The punishments I received for "talking back" were intended to suppress all possibility that I would create my own speech. That speech was to be suppressed so that the "right speech of womanhood" would emerge. (hooks, 1989, p. 5–6)

For good reason, Smitherman (1977/1986) titles chapter five of *Talkin and Testifyin* "The Form of Things Unknown," for these forms offer an inexhaustible store to those who, feeling silenced by the discourses around them, are engaged in a struggle to readjust and redefine the very norms of language making under and within which they suffer. Such forms as Smitherman discusses are not the creation of an elite; rather, they are a part of an African and a folk heritage so all-pervasive that it is frequently evoked without conscious effort or intellection. She describes this heritage as

[c]omprising the formulaic structure of these contributions are verbal strategies, rhetorical devices and folk expressive rituals which derive from a mutually understood notion of modes of discourse, which in turn is part of the "rich inheritance" of the African background. (Smitherman, 1977/1986, p. 103)

Since this rich store of materials and strategies is not the sole property of any one individual or group of individuals, it represents a resource for resistance and creativity open to all. It constitutes a source of revision of those very negative uses to which it is sometimes put. It is, moreover, an inheritance not always apparent in surface lexical features, although Holloway and Vass (1993) and others, building on the work of Lorenzo Dow Turner, have shown that such surface features coexist with the less obvious modes of discourse and rituals which shape Black discourse.

The resistance and return to the source described here is very much a part of the postmodernist reading that Russell A. Potter makes of Hip Hop. In doing so, he argues against a number of supposed dichotomies that have dominated our consideration of Hip Hop and of rap. Central to our consideration of the rhetoric of resistance/rhetoric of creation here is R. Potter's convincing argument that Teresa L. Ebert made in her 1990 conference paper "Rewriting the Postmodern: (Post)Colonial/feminisms/ Late Capitalism" (Potter, 1995, p. 2). It is Potter's contention that "ludic post modernism," with its focus on play, freefall, parody, irresolution and satire, must be considered as serious and effective a mode of resistance as what Ebert calls "resistance postmodernism." "Play certainly can be an idle distraction, but it can also be the mask for a potent mode of subversion. . . . hip-hop culture in particular and African American culture in general, is precisely such a form" (p. 2). Potter sees no need for chronological divisions like modern and postmodern.

> It could be said that *all* black aesthetic movements are modern [his emphasis] . . . not only the history of the structures of resistance, from spiritual songs to Calypso stick-dances to Public Enemy's S1W security force, but the already double(d) history of "white" appropriation/commodification, and dilution of black artistic expression. (p. 4)

This claim for a seamless postmodernism is borne out in Baraka's 1996 discussion of *The Last Poets*. He positions them not at the end or the beginning of any movement but as part of a continuum. In their work, we certainly see much that qualifies as "ludic" and as "resistant," as undifferentiated modes of creation and cultural warfare. Works such as "OD" and "Related to What" may be outrageously funny, but they are neither trivial nor silly. Here and in all their work, they abandon a commodified Black art and return to earlier (more "Africanized") and not yet Top-40 commercialized rhetorical and performance modes:

> The Last Poets are the prototype rappers, the transmitters of the mass poetry style of the Black Arts sixties, through the whatever of WA and ourselves inside the wailing for light, with hard rhythm of What Is brought into the Now. A jazz-linked rhythm and Blues feeling the Rappers copped forms a direct connection with content. (Baraka, 1996, p. xiv)

They are the griots of the ancestral land speaking into the rhetoric of the future. Theirs is a form that "came out of the revolutionary sixties Black Arts movement, from way back beyond sorrow songs and chattel wails" (p. xvi). That form, like all commodified art, is subject to the corruption of the market place and those who see themselves as its agents. Note one aspect of that corruption: "The Word Music we make,

Poetry-Jazz, Rap is a sharp weapon needing to be held in our hands and kept sharp and pointed at the enemy (not at our sisters and wives and mothers)" (p. xvi). We get a clear sense of the result of such abuse of the griot function in the story Potter relates of the emergence of Roxanne Shanté. The band UTFO in 1984 released "Roxanne, Roxanne" in which they diss a fictional woman named Roxanne. The recorded response to this release was amazing, two dozen response raps, according to Potter. The most interesting of these was the recording debut of the female rapper Roxanne Shanté. One wonders, given her name, if she is playing with the Sanskrit "shanti" or echoing Ntozake Shange whose "For Colored Girls . . ." remains a model of ludic and resistant rhetoric. We certainly hear echoes of Shange's "Somebody Almos Walked Off with Alla My Stuff" in Shanté's lines. Shanté's "Have a Nice Day" is tied not to the denigrating images in "Roxanne, Roxanne" but, self-realizing and self-affirming, it plays the dozens with the UTFO text. Shanté names names.

No conclusion needed. The end is not in sight. Of making new rhetorical sallies, there is no end.

References

Abel, E. (1993). Black Writing/White Reading: Race and the Politics of Feminist Interpretation. *Critical Inquiry,* 19, 470–498.

Abrahams, R. (1970). *Deep Down in the Jungle: Negro Narrative Folklore from the Streets of Philadelphia.* New York: Aldine De Gruyter. (Originally published 1963).

Abrahams, R. D. (1976). *Talking Black.* Rowley, MA: Newbury House.

Adams, J. Q. (1962). *Lectures on Rhetoric and Oratory.* Vols. 1–2. New York: Russell and Russell. (Originally published 1810).

Alkalimat, A. (2001a). Technological Revolution and Prospects for Black Liberation in the 21st Century. *CyRev* [on-line]. Accessed August 30, 2001, from *http://www.cyrev.net/Issues/Issue4/TechnologicalRevolutionAndProspectsforBlackLiberation.htm.*

———. (2001b). eBlack Studies: A 21st Century Challenge. *eBlackStudies.* [on-line]. Accessed August 24, 2001, from *http://eblackstudies.net/eblack.html.*

Allen, W. G. (1998). Orators and Oratory. In P. S. Foner & R. J. Branham (Eds.), *Lift Every Voice: African American Oratory, 1787–1900* (pp. 229–246). Tuscaloosa: University of Alabama Press. (Originally published 1852).

Ampadu, L. M. (1999). *The Effects of Instruction in the Imitation of Repetition on College Students' Persuasive Writing Style.* (Doctoral dissertation, University of Maryland, 1999). *Dissertation Abstracts International,* 61, 3868.

Anderson, J. D. (1995). Literacy and Education in the African American Experience, In V. L. Gadsden & D. A. Wagner (Eds.), *Literacy among African American Youth: Issues in Learning, Teaching, and Schooling* (pp. 19–37). Cresskill, NJ: Hampton Press.

Andrews, W. L. (1988). *To Tell a Free Story: The First Century of Afro-American Autobiography, 1760–1865.* Urbana: University of Illinois Press.

Ani, M. (1994). *Yurugu: An African-Centered Critique of European Thought and Behavior.* Trenton, NJ: Africa World Press.

Anokye, A. K. (1997). A Case for Orality in the Classroom. *Clearing House,* 70, 229–31.

Anthony, E. (1990). *Spitting in the Wind: The True Story Behind the Violent Legacy of the Black Panther Party.* Malibu, CA: Roundtable.

Appiah, K. A., & Gates, H. L. (Eds.). (1999). *Africana: The Encyclopedia of the African and African American Experience.* New York: Basic Books.

Asante, M. K. (Arthur Smith). (1974, April). A Metatheory for Black Communication. Paper presented at the annual meeting of the New York State Speech Association, Loch Sheldrake. Eric document ED099945.

———. (1987). *The Afrocentric Idea.* Philadelphia: Temple University Press.

———. (1990a). African Elements in African American English. In J. Holloway (Ed.), *Africanisms in African American Culture* (19–33). Bloomington: Indiana University Press.

———. (1990b). The African Essence in African American Language, In K.

Welsh-Asante & M. Asante (Eds.), *African Culture: The Rhythms of Unity* (pp. 47–81). Trenton, NJ: Africa World Press.

———. (1990c). *Kemet, Afrocentricity, and Knowledge*. Trenton, NJ: Africa World Press.

———. (1993). Location Theory and African Aesthetics. In K. Welsh-Asante (Ed.), *The African Aesthetic: Keeper of the Traditions* (pp. 53–62). Westport, CT: Greenwood Press.

Asante, M., & Gudykunst, W. B. (1989). *Handbook of International Intercultural Communication*. Newbury Park, CA: Sage Publications.

Atwater, D. F. (1995). Political and Social Messages in the Music of Stevie Wonder. In L. A. Niles (Ed.), *African American Rhetoric: A Reader*. Dubuque, IA: Kendall Hunt Publishing.

Bahri, D. (1998). "Terms of Engagement": Postcolonialism, Transnationalism, and Composition Studies. *JAC: A Journal of Composition Theory, 18*(1), 29–44.

Baker, H. (1984). *Blues, Ideology, and Afro-American Literature: A Vernacular Theory*. Chicago: University of Chicago Press.

———. (1995). Critical Memory and the Black Public Sphere. In The Black Public Sphere Collective (Eds.), *The Black Public Sphere: A Public Culture Book* (pp. 7–37). Chicago: University of Chicago Press.

Bakhtin, M. (1981). *The Dialogic Imagination. Four Essays by M. M. Bakhtin*. M. Holquist (Ed.). Austin: University of Texas Press.

Balester, V. (1993). *Cultural Divide: A Study of African-American College Writers*. Portsmouth, NH: Boynton/Cook.

Ball, A. (1992). Cultural Preference and the Expository Writing of African-American Adolescents. *Written Communication, 9*(4), 501–532.

Bambgbose, A. (1970). On Serial Verbs and Verbal Status. Paper read at the Tenth West African Language Congress, Ibaden.

Baraka, A. (aka LeRoi Jones) (1963). *Blues People: Negro Music in White America*. New York: W. Morrow.

———. (1996). Foreword. In A. Oyewole & U. Ben Hassen (Eds.), *On a Mission: Selected Poetry and a History of the Last Poets*. New York: Henry Holt and Co.

Barns, S. (1996). Yoruba Political Representations in Old States and New Nations. In M. Ember, C. Ember, & D. Levinson (Eds.), *Portraits of Culture* (pp. 45–47). Englewood, NJ: Prentice Hall,

Bartholomae, D. (1987). Writing on the Margins: The Concept of Literacy in Higher Education. *A Sourcebook for Basic Writing Teachers*. Theresa Enos (Ed.) New York: Random House, 66–83.

The Basic Afro-American Reprint Library. (1968). *The "Amistad" Case: The Most Celebrated Slave Mutiny of the Nineteenth Century*. New York: Johnson Reprint Corporation.

Baugh, J. (1983). *Black Street Speech: Its History, Structure, and Survival*. Austin: University of Texas Press.

———. (1999). *Out of the Mouths of Slaves: African American Language and Educational Malpractice*. Austin: University of Texas Press.

Bauman, Z. (1998). *Globalization: The Human Consequences.* New York: Columbia University Press.

Béhar, H. (1995). "Dead Presidents" Press Conference at the New York Film Festival. *Film Scouts* [On-line]. Accessed from *http://www. filmscouts.com/ scripts/interview.cfm?Article Code=2760.*

Bell, D. (1987). *And We Are Not Saved: The Elusive Quest for Racial Justice.* New York: Basic Books, Inc.

Bendor-Samuel, J. T. (1971). Niger-Cong, Guur. In T. A. Sebeok (Ed.), *Linguistics in Sub-Saharan Africa* (pp. 141–178). Vol. 7: Current Trends in Linguistics. The Hague: Mouton.

ben-Jochannan, Y. A. A. (1970). *Blackman of the Nile and His Family.* New York: Alkebu-lan Books.

Berlin, I., Favreau, M., & Miller, S. F. (Eds.). (1998). *In Remembering Slavery: African Americans Talk about Their Personal Experiences of Slavery and Emancipation.* New York: New Press.

———. (1999). *Many Thousands Gone: The First Two Centuries of Slavery in North America.* Cambridge, MA: Belknap Press.

Berlin, J. (1993). Composition Studies and Cultural Studies: Collapsing Boundaries. In Anne Ruggles Gere (Ed.), *Into the Field: Sites of Composition Studies* (pp. 99–116). New York: Modern Language Association.

———. (1997). Contemporary Composition: The Major Pedagogical Theories. In V. Villanueva Jr. (Ed.), *Cross-Talk in Comp Theory: A Reader* (pp. 233–248). Urbana, IL: National Council of Teachers of English.

Bingham, C. (1998). *The Columbian Orator: Bicentennial Edition.* New York: New York University Press.

Blassingame, J. W. (1972). *The Slave Community.* New York: Oxford University Press.

———. (1977). *Slave Testimony: Two Centuries of Letters, Speeches, Interviews, and Autobiographies.* Baton Rouge: Louisiana State University Press.

Bodine, J. J. (1996). Taos Pueblo: Maintaining Tradition. In M. Ember et al. (Eds.), *Portraits of Culture.* Englewood Cliffs, NJ: Prentice Hall.

Bosmajian, H. A., & Bosmajian, H. (Eds.). (1969). *The Rhetoric of the Civil-Rights Movement.* New York: Random House.

Boulware, M. H. (1969). *The Oratory of Negro Leaders: 1900–1968.* Westport, CT: Negro Universities Press.

Bourdieu, P., & Thompson, J. B. (1991). *Language and Symbolic Power.* Cambridge: Polity Press.

Brawley, E. M. (Ed.). (1890). *The Negro Baptist Pulpit.* Philadelphia: American Baptist Publication Society.

Brewer, J. (1970). Possible Relationships Between African Languages and Black English Dialect. Paper presented at the annual meeting of the Speech Communications Association, New Orleans.

Brodkey, L. (1996). *Writing Permitted in Designated Areas Only.* Minneapolis: University of Minnesota Press.

Brown, B. G. (1996). Elocution. In T. Enos (Ed.), *Encyclopedia of Rhetoric and Composition* (pp. 211–214). New York: Garland Press.

Brown, E. (1992). *A Taste of Power: A Black Woman's Story*. New York: Pantheon.

Brown, E. B. (1989). African American Women's Quilting: A Framework For Conceptualizing And Teaching African American Women's History. In M. Malson (Ed.), *Black Women in America: Social Science Perspectives*. Chicago: University of Chicago Press.

Budge, W. A. (Trans.). (1960). *The Book of the Dead*. New York: Citadel Books.

Burke, K. (1945). *Grammar of Motives*. New York: Prentice Hall.

Bynum, E. (1999). *The African Unconscious: Roots of African Mysticism and Modern Psychology*. New York: Teachers College, Columbia University.

Cable, M. (1977). *Black Odyssey: The Case of the Slave Ship "Amistad."* New York: Penguin Books.

Cadava, E. (Ed.). (1991). *Who Comes after the Subject?* New York: Routledge.

Camitta, M. (1993). Vernacular Writing: Varieties of Literacy among Philadelphia High School Students. In B. V. Street (Ed.), *Cross-Cultural Approaches to Literacy* (pp. 156–175). Cambridge, England: Cambridge University Press.

Campbell, K. K. (1986). Style and Content in the Rhetoric of Early Afro-American Feminists. *Quarterly Journal of Speech 72*, 434–445.

Canagarajah, A. S. (1990). *Negotiating Competing Discourses and Identities: A Sociolinguistic Analysis of Challenges in Academic Writing for Minority Students*. Unpublished doctoral dissertation, University of Texas at Austin.

———. (1997). Safe Houses in the Contact Zone: Coping Strategies of African-American Students in the Academy. *College Composition and Communication*, 48(2), 173–196.

Carby, H. (1987). *Reconstructing Womanhood: The Emergence of the Afro-American Woman Novelist*. New York: Oxford University Press.

———. (1999). The Multicultural War. In M. Wallace (Ed.), *Black Popular Culture*. New York: New Press.

Carruthers, Jacob. (1986). The Wisdom of Governance in Kemet. In M. Karenga & J. Carruthers (Eds.), *Kemet and the African World View* (pp. 131–148). Los Angeles: University of Sankore Press.

———. (1995). *Divine Speech: A Historiographical Reflection of African Deep Thought from the Time of the Pharaohs to the Present*. London: Karnak House.

Carson, A. (1995). The Gender of Sound. In *Glass, Irony, and God* (pp. 119–142). New York: New Directions.

Chafe, W. (1993). Integration and Involvement in Speaking, Writing, and Oral Literature. In D. L. Tannen (Ed.), *Exploring Orality and Literacy* (pp. 35–52). Washington, DC: Georgetown University Press.

Chandler, W. (1989). Of Gods and Men: Egypt's Old Kingdom. In I. Van Sertima (Ed.), *Egypt Revisited* (pp. 117–182). New Brunswick: Transaction Books.

———. (1999). *Ancient Future: The Teachings and Prophetic Wisdom of the Seven Hermetic Laws of Ancient Egypt*. Baltimore: Black Classic Press.

Christensen, P., James, A., & Jenks, C. (2000). Home and Movement: Children Constructing "Family Time." In S. L. Holloway & G. Valentine (Eds.), *Children's Geographies: Playing, Living, Learning* (pp. 139–154). New York: Routledge.

Churchill, W., & Vander Wall, J. (1988). *Agents of Repression*. Boston: South End Press.

Cicero. (1989). *Rhetorica Ad Herennium*. H. Caplan (Trans.). Cambridge, MA: Harvard University Press.

———. (1990). Of Oratory. In P. Bizzell & B. Herzberg (Eds.), *The Rhetorical Tradition: Readings from Classical Times to the Present* (pp. 200–250). Boston: Bedford Books of St. Martin's Press.

Clark, G., & Halloran, S. M. (Eds.). (1993). *Oratorical Culture in Nineteenth-Century America: Transformations in the Theory and Practice of Rhetoric*. Carbondale: Southern Illinois University Press.

Collins, P. (2000). *Black Feminist Thought: Knowledge, Consciousness, and the Politics of Empowerment*. (2d ed.). New York: Routledge.

Columbia, B. (1992). The Split Wall. In J. Rendell, B. Penner, & L. Borden (Eds.), *Gender, Space, Architecture: An Interdisciplinary Introduction* (pp. 314–320). New York: Routledge.

Cook, W. W. (1993). Writing in the Spaces Left. *College Composition and Communication, 44*(1), 9–25.

Cook-Gumperz, J. (1993). Dilemmas of Identity: Oral and Written Literacies in the Making of a Basic Writing Student. *Anthropology and Education Quarterly, 24*(4), 336–356.

Cook-Gumperz, J., & Keller-Cohen, D. (1993). *Alternative Literacies: In School And Beyond*. Arlington, VA: Council on Anthropology and Education.

Corbett, E. P. J. (1990). *Classical Rhetoric for the Modern Student*. (3rd ed.). New York: Oxford University Press.

Corbett, E. P. J., & Connors, R. J. (1998). *Classical Rhetoric for the Modern Student*. (4th ed.). New York: Oxford University Press.

Corliss, R. P (1995, May 15). Power to the People. *Time,* 145.

Corwin, M. (1996, May 29). *Los Angeles Times*.

Crawford, C. (1996). *Recasting Ancient Egypt in the African Context: Toward a Model Curriculum Using Art and Language*. Trenton, NJ: Africa World Press.

Crenshaw, C. (1997). Resisting Whiteness' Rhetorical Silence. *Western Journal of Communication, 61*(3), 253–278.

Crichlow, W., & McCarthy, C. (Eds.). (1993). *Race, Identity, and Representation in Education*. New York: Routledge Press.

Cross, T. (Ed.). (1997/1998). The Antislavery Views of President John Quincy Adams. *Journal of Blacks in Higher Education,* (Winter), 18.

Crowley, S. (1994). *Ancient Rhetorics for Contemporary Students*. New York: MacMillan College Publishing Co., Inc.

Cummings, M. S., & Daniel, J. L. (1995). A Comprehensive Assessment of Scholarly Writings in Black Rhetoric. In L. A. Niles (Ed.), *African American Rhetoric: A Reader*. Dubuque, IA: Kendall Hunt.

Cutter, M. J. (1996). Dismantling "The Master's House": Critical Literacy in Harriet Jacobs' Incidents in the Life of a Slave Girl. *Callaloo, 19,* 209–225.

Dadie, B. (1967). Dry Your Tears, Africa! In D. I. Nwoga (Ed.), *West African Verse: An Anthology*. London: Longmans.

Dalby, D. (1972). The African Element in Black American English. In T. Kochman (Ed.), *Rappin and Stylin' Out*. Urbana: University of Illinois Press.

Daniels, Y. (2000). Black Bodies, Black Space: A Waiting Spectacle. In L. N. Lokko (Ed.), *White Papers, Black Marks: Architecture, Race, Culture* (pp. 194–217). Minneapolis: University of Minnesota Press.

Davis, A. (1994). Afro Images: Politics, Fashion and Nostalgia. *Critical Inquiry, 21,* 37–45.

———. (1999). Black Nationalism: The Sixties and the Nineties. In M. Wallace (Ed.), *Black Popular Culture.* New York: New Press.

Dawson, M. (1995). A Black Counterpublic? In the Black Public Sphere Collective (Ed.), *The Black Public Sphere Collective: A Public Culture Book.* Chicago: University of Chicago Press.

———. (2001). *Black Visions: The Roots of Contemporary African-American Political Ideologies.* Chicago: University of Chicago Press.

Deskins, D. R., & Bettinger, C. (2002). *Geographical Identities of Ethnic America: Race, Space, and Place.* Las Vegas: University of Nevada Press.

Diedrich, M. (1999). *Love Across Color Lines: Ottilie Assing and Frederick Douglass.* New York: Hill & Wang.

Dillard, J. L. (1973). *Black English: Its History and Usage in the United States.* New York: Vintage Books.

Diop, C. A. (1974). *The African Origin of Civilization: Myth or Reality.* Chicago: Lawrence Hill Books.

———. (1978). *The Cultural Unity of Black Africa: The Domains of Patriarchy and Matriarchy in Classical Antiquity.* Chicago: Third World Press.

Dixon, M. (1987). *Ride Out the Wilderness.* Urbana: University of Illinois Press.

Donawerth, J. (1984). *Shakespeare and the Sixteenth-Century Study of Language.* Urbana: University of Illinois Press.

———. (1997). Textbooks for New Audiences: Women's Revisions of Rhetorical Theory at the Turn of the Century. In M. M. Wertheimer (Ed.), *Listening to Their Voices: The Rhetorical Activities of Historical Women* (pp. 337–356). Columbia: University of South Carolina Press.

Doriani, B. M. (1991). Black Womanhood in Nineteenth-Century America: Subversion and Self-Construction in Two Women's Autobiographies. *American Quarterly, 43,* 199–222.

Douglass, F. (1969). *My Bondage and My Freedom.* New York: Arno Press. (Originally published 1855).

———. (1984). *The Narrative and Selected Writings.* New York: Modern Library.

———. (1997a). *Narrative of the Life of Frederick Douglass, an American Slave, Written by Himself.* In H. L. Gates & N. McKay, (Eds.), *The Norton Anthology of African American Literature* (pp. 302–378). New York: W. W. Norton. (Originally published 1845).

———. (1997b). What to the Slave Is the Fourth of July?, Rochester, July 5, 1852. In H. L. Gates & N. McKay, (Eds.), *The Norton Anthology of African American Literature* (pp. 379–391). New York: W. W. Norton. (Originally published 1852).

Dowd, M. (1999, September 12). Liberties: Sure I Would. *New York Times,* p. 19.

Du Bois, W. E. B. (1903). *The Negro Church: Report of a Social Study Made under the Director of Atlanta University; Together with the Proceedings of the Eighth Conference for the Study of the Negro Problems, Held at Atlanta University, May 26th, 1903*. Atlanta: Atlanta University Press.

———. (1989). *The Souls of Black Folk*. New York: Penguin. (Originally published 1903).

du Cille, A. (1994). The Occult of True Black Womanhood: Critical Demeanor and Black Feminist Studies. *Signs, 19,* 591–629.

Dunbar, P. L. (1980). *The Complete Poems of Paul Laurence Dunbar*. New York: Dodd, Mead and Co.

Elbow, P. (1985). The Shifting Relationships Between Speech and Writing. *College Composition and Communication, 36,* 283–303.

Ellison, R. W. (1958). Change the Joke and Slip the Yoke. In H. L. Gates et al. (Eds.), *The Norton Anthology of African American Literature* (pp. 1541–1549). New York: Oxford University Press.

———. (1986). "What America Would Be Without Blacks." In R. Ellison. *Going to the Territory* (pp. 110-111). New York: Vintage Books. (Originally published 1970).

———. (1995). *Invisible Man*. New York: Vintage International Books. (Originally published 1952).

Epps, J. (1985). Killing Them Softly: Why Willie Can't Write. In C. Brooks (Ed.), *Tapping Potential: English and Language Arts for the Black Learner* (pp. 154–159). Urbana, IL: National Council of Teachers of English.

Farmer, F. (1991). *Dialogic Imitation: Vygotsky, Bakhtin, and the Internalization of Voice*. (Doctoral dissertation, University of Louisville, 1991). *Dissertation Abstracts International, 53,* 0486.

Faludi, S. (1999, September 13). Glamour in the 'Hood. *Newsweek, 134,* 52–53.

Fields, D. W. (2000). *Architecture in Black*. New Brunswick: Athlone Press.

Fliegelman, J. (1993). *Declaring Independence: Jefferson, Natural Language, and the Culture of Performance*. Stanford, CA: Stanford University Press.

Flower, L., & Hayes, J. (1980). The Cognition of Discovery: Defining a Rhetorical Problem. *College Composition and Communication, 31,* 21–32.

Foner, P. S. (1995). *The Black Panthers Speak*. New York: Da Capo.

Foner, P. S., & Branham, R. J. (Eds.). (1998). *Lift Every Voice: African American Oratory, 1787–1900*. Tuscaloosa: University of Alabama Press.

Forbes, E. (2003). Every Man Fights for His Freedom: The Rhetoric of African American Resistance in the Mid-Nineteenth Century. In R. L. Jackson & E. B. Richardson, (Eds.), *Understanding African American Rhetoric: Classical Origins to Contemporary Innovations*. New York: Routledge.

Fordham, S. (1996). *Blacked Out: Dilemmas of Race, Identity, and Success at Capitol High*. Chicago: University of Chicago Press.

Forman, M. (2002). *The Hood Comes First: Race, Space, and Place in Rap and Hip-Hop*. Middletown, CT: Wesleyan University Press.

Foster, F. S. (Ed.). (1990). *A Brighter Coming Day: A Frances Ellen Watkins Harper Reader*. New York: Feminist Press.

———. (1997). Gender, Genre, and Vulgar Secularism: The Case of Frances Ellen Watkins Harper and the AME Press. In D. Hubbard (Ed.), *Recovered Writers/Recovered Texts: Race, Class, and Gender in Black Women's Literature* (pp. 46–59). Knoxville: University of Tennessee Press.

Fox, T. (1994). Repositioning the Profession: Teaching Writing to African American Students. In G. Olson & S. Dobrin (Eds.), *Composition Theory for the Postmodern Classroom,* (pp. 105–117). Albany: State University of New York Press.

Fraser, N. (1990). Rethinking the Public Sphere: A Contribution to the Critique of an Actually Existing Democracy. In *Social Text, 25/26,* 56–80.

———. (1993). Rethinking the Public Sphere: A Contribution to the Critique of an Actually Existing Democracy. In B. Robbins (Ed.), *The Phantom Public Sphere* (pp. 1–32). Minneapolis: University of Minnesota Press.

Freire, P. (1994). *Pedagogy of the Oppressed.* M. B. Ramos (Trans.). New York: Continuum.

Fuchs, C. (1996). Bearing Arms Legitimately: *The Walking Dead* and *Panther. Viet Nam Generation, 7*(1–2), 108.

Gall, M. D., Borg, W. R., & Gall, J. P. (1996). *Educational Research: An Introduction.* (6th ed.). New York: Longman.

Gandy, O. (1995). It's Discrimination, Stupid! In J. Brock & I. Boal (Eds.), *Resisting the Virtual Life: The Culture and Politics of Information.* San Francisco: City Lights Books.

Garnet, H. H. (1997). An Address to the Slaves of The United States Of America. In H. L. Gates & N. McKay, (Eds.), *The Norton Anthology of African American Literature* (pp. 280–285). New York: W. W. Norton. (Originally published 1848).

Gates, H. L. (1985, April 21). A Negro Way of Saying [Review of the books *Dust Tracks on a Road* and *Moses: Man of the Mountain*]. *New York Times,* sec. 6, pp. 1, 43, 45.

———. (1988). *The Signifying Monkey: A Theory of Afro-American Literary Criticism.* New York: Oxford University Press.

Gee, J. P. (1996). *Social Linguistics and Literacies.* (2d ed.). London: Taylor & Francis, Inc.

Gilyard, K. (1991). *Voices of the Self: A Study of Language Competence.* Detroit: Wayne State University Press.

———. (1996). *Let's Flip the Script: An African American Discourse on Language, Literature, and Learning.* Detroit: Wayne State University Press.

Gilroy, P. (1993). *The Black Atlantic: Modernity and Double Consciousness.* Cambridge, MA: Harvard University Press.

Giroux, H. A. (1993). *Border Crossings: Cultural Workers and the Politics of Education.* New York: Routledge.

———. (1997). Rewriting the Discourse of Racial Identity: Towards a Pedagogy and Politics of Whiteness. *Harvard Educational Review, 67,* 285–320.

Golden, J. L., & Rieke, R. D. (Eds.). (1971). *The Rhetoric of Black Americans.* Columbus, OH: Charles E. Merrill.

Gordon, C., et al. (Eds.). (1980). *Power/Knowledge: Selected Interviews and Other Writings by Michel Foucault.* New York: Pantheon Books.

Grant, B. C. (1996). Accommodation and Resistance: The Built Environment and the African American Experience. In T. A. Dutton & L. H. Mann (Eds.), *Reconstructing Architecture: Critical Discourses and Social Practices* (pp. 202–233). Minneapolis: University of Minnesota Press.

Griffin, F. (1995). *"Who Set You Flowin'?": The African American Migration Narrative.* New York: Oxford University Press.

Gundaker, G. (1998). *Signs of Diaspora/Diaspora of Signs: Literacies, Creolization, and Vernacular Practice In African America.* New York: Oxford University Press.

Gwin, M. (1985). *Black and White Women of the Old South: The Peculiar Sisterhood in American Literature.* Knoxville: University of Tennessee Press.

Hanaford, P. A. (1882). *Daughters of America.* Augusta, ME: True & Co.

[Harper] Watkins, F. (1858, May 22). Speech of Miss Frances Ellen Watkins. *National AntiSlavery Standard,* 1.

———. (1860, September 29). Letter to Elizabeth Jones. *Anti-Slavery Bugle* (n.p.). Black Abolitionist Papers Microfilm Edition. Reel 12, 1022.

———. (1864, May 21). Lecture on the Mission of the War. *Christian Recorder.* Black Abolitionist Papers Microfilm Edition. Reel 15, 0356.

———. (1995). Woman's Political Future. In S. W. Logan (Ed.), *With Pen and Voice* (pp. 32–35). Carbondale: Southern Illinois University Press.

Havelock, E. (1978). *The Greek Concept of Justice: From Its Shadow in Homer to Its Substance in Plato.* Princeton, NJ: Princeton University Press.

———. (1986). Orality, Literacy, and Star Wars. *Pre/Text, 7,* 123–132.

Hays, J. N., Brandt, K. M., & Chantry, K. H. (1988). The Impact of Friendly and Hostile Audiences on the Argumentative Writing of High School and College Students. *Research in the Teaching of English, 22*(4), 391–416.

Heath, L. G. (1976). *Off the Pigs!: The History and Literature of the Black Panther Party.* Metuchan, NY: Scarecrow.

Hecht, M., Collier, M. J., & Ribeau, S. A. (Eds.). (1993). *African American Communication: Ethnic Identity and Cultural Interpretation.* Newbury Park: Sage.

Hegel, G. W. F. (1964). *The Philosophy of History.* Vols. 1, 2. New York: Wiley Book. (Originally published 1832).

———. (1983). *Lectures on the History of Philosophy.* Vols. 1, 2. Atlantic Highlands, N.J.: Humanities Press. (Originally published 1833).

Herodotus. (1928). *The History of Herodotus.* G. Rawlinson (Trans.). New York: Tudor Publishing Co.

———. (1956). *The Histories.* G. Rawlinson (Trans.). New York: Tudor Publishing Company.

Herskovits, M. (1958). *The Myth of the Negro Past.* Boston: Beacon Press. (Originally published 1941).

Hiatt, M. P. (1975). *Artful Balance: The Parallel Structures of Style.* New York: Teachers College Press.

Higginbotham, A. L., Jr. (1978). *In the Matter of Color: Race and the American Legal Process: The Colonial Period.* New York: Oxford University Press.

Higginbotham, E. B. (1993). *Righteous Discontent: The Women's Movement in the Black Baptist Church, 1880–1920.* Cambridge, MA: Harvard University Press.

Hill, W. B., Jr. (1997/1998). Federal Historical Records on the *Amistad* Case. *Journal of Blacks in Higher Education,* (Winter), 18.

Hilliard, A., III. (1986). Pedagogy in Ancient Kemet. In M. Karenga & J.

Carruthers (Eds.), *Kemet and the African World View* (pp. 131–148). Los Angeles: University of Sankore Press.

———. (1995). *SBA: The Reawakening of the African Mind*. Gainesville, FL: Makare Publishing Co.

Hilliard, A., III, Williams, L., & Damali, N. (1987). (Eds.). *The Teachings of Ptahhotep: The Oldest Book in the World*. Atlanta: Blackwood Press.

Hilliard, D., & Cole, L. (1993). *This Side of Glory: The Autobiography of David Hilliard and the Story of the Black Panther Party*. Boston: Little, Brown, and Co.

Hillocks, G., Jr. (1986). *Research on Written Composition: New Directions for Teaching*. Urbana, IL: National Council of Teachers of English.

Hinks, P. (1997). *To Awaken My Afflicted Brethren: David Walker and the Problem of Antebellum Slave Resistance*. University Park: Pennsylvania State University Press.

Hirschberg, L. (2000, September 3). How Black Comedy Got the Last Laugh. *New York Times Magazine, 34*–39.

Holloway, J. E., (1991). The Origins of African American Culture. In J. E. Holloway (Ed.), *Africanisms in African American Culture* (pp. 1–18). Bloomington: Indiana University Press.

Holloway, J., & Vass, W. K. (1993). *The African Heritage of American English*. Bloomington: Indiana University Press.

Holloway, K. (1995). *Codes of Conduct: Race, Ethics, and the Color of Our Character*. New Brunswick, NJ: Rutgers University Press.

Hoobler, D., & Hoobler, T. (1995). *The African American Family Album*. New York: Oxford University Press.

hooks, b. (1989). *Talking Back*. Boston: South End Press.

Horowitz, R. (1995). Orality in Literacy: The Uses of Speech in Written Language by Bi-Lingual and Bicultural Writers. In D. L. Rubin (Ed.), *Composing Social Identity in Written Language* (pp. 47–63). Hillsdale, NJ: Lawrence Erlbaum.

Howard-Pitney, D. 1990. *The Afro-American Jeremiad: Appeals for Justice in America*. Philadelphia: Temple University Press.

Howe, D. (1995, October 6). Review of "Panther." *Washington Post*, B1, C1.

Hughes, L. (1934). *The Ways of White Folks*. New York: A. A. Knopf.

Hughes Brothers' "Dead Presidents" Captures Lives of Black Soldiers in Vietnam War and Their Return Home (Allen and Albert Hughes' New Movie). (1995, October). *Jet, 88*, 60–62.

Hurston, Z. N. (1978). *Their Eyes Were Watching God*. Chicago: University of Illinois Press. (Originally published 1937).

———. (1981). Characteristics of Negro Expression. In *The Sanctified Church* (pp. 41–78). Berkeley, CA: Turtle Island Press. (Originally published 1934).

———. (1990). *Jonah's Gourd Vine*. Foreword by R. Dove. New York: Harpers-Collins Publishers. (Originally published 1937).

———. (1999). *Go Gator and Muddy the Water: Writing by Zora Neale Hurston from the Federal Writer's Project*. P. Bordelon (Ed.). New York: W. W. Norton.

———. (2001). *Every Tongue Got to Confess: Negro Folk-Tales from the Gulf States*. New York: HarperCollins.

Jacobs, H. (1987). *Incidents in the Life of A Slave Girl Written by Herself*. J. F. Yellin (Ed.). Cambridge, MA: Harvard University Press. (Originally published 1861).

Jackson, B. (1974). *Get Your Ass in the Water and Swim Like Me: Narrative Poetry from Black Oral Tradition*. Cambridge, MA: Harvard University Press.

Jackson, G. (1990). *Blood in My Eye*. New York: Black Classic Press.

———. (1994). *Soledad Brother: The Prison Letters of George Jackson*. Chicago: Lawrence Hill Books.

Jackson, J. (1994). Common Ground. In D. Tannen (Ed.), *Talking Voices: Repetition, Dialogue, and Imagery in Conversational Discourse* (pp. 174–195). New York: Cambridge University Press.

Jackson, R. (1995). Toward an Afrocentric Methodology for the Critical Assessment of Rhetoric. In L. A. Niles (Ed.), *African American Rhetoric: A Reader* (pp. 148–157). Dubuque, IA: Kendall Hunt Publishing.

Jahn, J. (1989). *Muntu: African Culture and the Western World*. New York: Grove Press.

James, C. L. R., & Pease, D. E. (2001). *Marines, Renegades, and Castaways: The Story of Herman Melville and the World We Live In (Reencounters with Colonialism—New Perspectives on the Americas)*. Hanover, N.H.: University Press of New England. (Originally published 1953).

James, G. G. M. (1954). *Stolen Legacy*. New York: Philosophical Library.

Jarratt, S. (1991). *Rereading the Sophists: Classical Rhetoric Refigured*. Carbondale: Southern Illinois University Press.

Jayne, A. (1988). *Jefferson's Declaration of Independence: Origins, Philosophy, and Theology*. Lexington: University Press of Kentucky.

Johnson, C. L. (1994). Participatory Rhetoric and the Teacher as Racial/Gendered Subject. *College English, 56*, 409–419.

Johnson, J. H. A. (1886). Rev. William H. Watkins. *African Methodist Episcopal Church Review 3*, 11–12.

Johnson, J. W. (1990). *God's Trombones: Seven Negro Sermons in Verse*. New York: Penguin. (Originally published 1927).

Johnson, N. (1991). *Nineteenth-Century Rhetoric in North America*. Carbondale: Southern Illinois University Press.

Jones, H. (1987). *Mutiny on the "Amistad": The Saga of a Slave Revolt and Its Impact on American Abolition, Law, and Diplomacy*. New York: Oxford University Press.

Jones, K. C. (1992). Folk Idiom in the Literary Expression of Two African American Authors: Rita Dove And Yusef Komunyakaa. In C. A. Blackshire-Belay (Ed.), *Language and Literature in the African American Imagination* (pp. 149–165). Westport, CT: Greenwood Press.

Jordan, B. (1976). Who Then Will Speak for the Common Good? *Vital Speeches of the Day, 42*(21), 645–646.

Jordan, J. (1985). Nobody Mean More to Me Than You and the Future Life of Willie Jordan. In *On Call: Political Essays* (pp. 123–140). Boston: South End Press.

———. (2001). The Invisible People: An Unsolicited Report on Black Rage. *Progressive, 65*, 24–25.

Karenga, M. (1984). (Trans). *Selection from the Husia: Sacred Wisdom of Ancient Egypt*. Los Angeles: University of Sankore Press.

———. (1989). Toward a Sociology of Maatian Ethics: Literature and Context. In I. Van Sertima (Ed.). *Egypt Revisited* (pp. 352–395). New Brunswick: Transaction Books.

Karenga, M., & Carruthers, J. (Eds.). (1986). *Kemet and the African World View*. Los Angeles: University of Sankore Press.

Kennedy, G. (1998). *Comparative Rhetoric: An Historical and Cross-Cultural Introduction*. New York: Oxford University Press.

King, M. L., Jr. (1968). *Where Do We Go from Here: Chaos or Community?* Boston: Beacon.

———. (Sermon). (1996). I Have a Dream. In M. Asante & A. Abarry (Eds.), *African Intellectual Heritage*. (1996). Philadelphia: Temple University Press. (Originally given Aug. 28, 1963).

———. (1997). Letter from Birmingham Jail. In H. L. Gates & N. L. McKay, (Eds.), *The Norton Anthology of African American Literature* (pp. 1854–1866). New York: W. W. Norton. (Originally published 1963).

Kitwana, B. (1994). *The Rap on Gangsta Rap*. Chicago: Third World Press.

Kochman, T. (1972). *Rappin' and Stylin' Out: Communication In Urban Black America*. Urbana: University of Illinois Press.

Kolchin, P. (1993). *American Slavery, 1619–1877*. New York: Hill & Wang.

Kolln, M. (1991). *Rhetorical Grammar: Grammatical Choices, Rhetorical Effects*. Instructor's Manual. New York: Macmillan.

Lee, C. D. (1993). *Signifying as a Scaffold for Literary Interpretation*. Urbana, IL: National Council of Teachers of English.

Leigh, D. (2000, September 5). Shaft, the Melodrama. *Guardian* (Manchester, UK), 2, 14.

Levine, L. (1977). *Black Culture and Black Consciousness: Afro-American Folk Thought from Slavery to Freedom*. New York: Oxford University Press.

Lichtheim, Mariam. (1975). *Ancient Egyptian Literature: A Book of Readings*. Vol. 2. Berkeley: University of California Press.

Lindemann, E. (1995). *A Rhetoric for Writing Teachers*. (2d ed.). New York: Oxford University Press.

Lippi-Green, R. (1997). *English with an Accent*. London: Routledge.

Lipscomb, D. R. (1995). Sojourner Truth: A Practical Public Discourse. In A. Lunsford (Ed.), *Reclaiming Rhetorica: Women in the Rhetorical Tradition* (pp. 227–243). Pittsburgh: University of Pittsburgh Press.

Logan, S. (1996). What's Rhetoric Got to Do With It?: Frances E. W. Harper in the Writing Class. *Composition FORUM, 7*, 95–110.

———. (1998). When and Where I Enter: Race, Gender, and Composition Studies. In S. Jarrett & L. Worsham (Eds.), *In Other Words: Feminism and Composition* (pp. 45–57). New York: Modern Language Association.

Logan, S. W. (Ed.). (1995). *With Pen and Voice: A Critical Anthology of Nineteenth-Century African-American Women*. Carbondale: Southern Illinois University Press.

———. (1999). *"We Are Coming": The Persuasive Discourse of Nineteenth-Century Black Women*. Carbondale: Southern Illinois University Press.

Lubiano, W. (Ed.). (1997). *The House that Race Built*. New York: Pantheon Books.

Lyne, W. (2000). No Accident: From Black Power to the Box Office. *African American Review, 34*(39), 43.

Majors, M. A. (1893) *Noted Negro Women: Their Triumphs and Activities*. Chicago: Donohue & Henneberry.

Marable, M. (1991). *Race, Reform, and Rebellion: The Second Reconstruction in Black America, 1945–1990*. Jackson: University Press of Mississippi.

Masilela, N. (1998). Women Directors of the Los Angeles School. In J. Bobo (Ed.), *Black Women Film And Video Artists* (pp. 21–41). New York: Routledge.

Massey, D. (1994). *Space, Place, and Gender*. Minneapolis: University of Minnesota Press.

Massey, G. (1881). *A Book of the Beginnings*. London: Williams & Norgate.

Matthews, T. (1998). "No One Ever Asks, What a Man's Place in the Revolution Is": Gender and the Politics of the Black Panther Party, 1966–1971. In C. E. Jones (Ed.), *The Black Panther Party Reconsidered*. (pp. 267–304). Baltimore: Black Classic.

Mazuri, A. (1992). African Languages in the African American Experience. In C. A. Blackshire-Belay (Ed.), *Language and Literature in the African American Imagination* (pp. 75–90). Westport, CT: Greenwood Press.

Mbiti, J. (1969). *African Philosophy and Religion*. New York: Anchor Books, Doubleday Company, Inc.

Mbiti, J. S. (1970) *African Religions and Philosophy*. New York: Doubleday.

McConkey, J. (1996). *The Anatomy of Memory*. New York: Oxford University Press.

McDowell, D. E. (1995). *The Changing Same: Black Women's Literature, Criticism, and Theory*. Bloomington: Indiana University Press.

McFeely, W. S. (1991). *Frederick Douglass*. New York: W. W. Norton, 1991.

Mercer, K. (1992). "1968": Periodizing Postmodern Politics and Identity. In L. Grossberg, C. Nelson, & P. Treichler (Eds.), *Cultural Studies* (pp. 424–449). New York: Routledge. (Originally published 1968).

Middleton, J. I. (1993). Oral Memory and the Teaching of Literacy: Some Implications from Toni Morrison's *Song Of Solomon*. In F. Reynolds (Ed.), *Rhetorical Memory and Delivery*. Hillsdale, NJ: Lawrence Erlbaum.

———. (1994). Back To Basics or the Three R's: Race, Rhythm, and Rhetoric. *Teaching English in the Two-Year College, 21,* 104–112.

———. (1995). Confronting the "Master Narrative": The Privilege of Orality in Toni Morrison's *The Bluest Eye. Cultural Studies, 9,* 301–317.

———. (2000). Kris, I Hear You. *JAC: A Journal of Composition Theory, 20,* 433–441.

Miles, R., Bertonasco, M., & Karns, W. (1991). *Prose Style: A Contemporary Guide*. Englewood Cliffs, NJ: Prentice Hall.

Miller, K. (1998). *Voice of Deliverance: The Language of Martin Luther King, Jr., and Its Sources*. New York: Free Press.

Miller, W. L. (1998). *Arguing about Slavery: John Quincy Adams and the Great Battle in the United States Congress*. New York: Vintage Books. (Originally published 1995).

Mitchell, H. H. (1970). *Black Preaching*. Philadelphia: J. B. Lippincott.

Mitchell, J. L., & Hodari, C. (1996, May 3). A Wrong Turn on the Road from Hood to Hollywood. *Los Angeles Times*.

Moffett, J. (1983). *Teaching the Universe of Discourse*. Portsmouth, NJ: Boynton/Cook.

Moore, G. (1971). *A Special Rage*. New York: Harper & Row.

Morgan, M. (1993). The Africanness of Counterlanguage among Afro-Americans. In S. Mufwene & N. Condon (Eds.), *Africanisms in Afro-American Language Varieties*. Athens: University of Georgia Press.

Morrison, C. (2003). Death Narratives from the Killing Fields: Narrative Criticism and the Case of Tupac Shakur. In R. L. Jackson II & E. Richardson (Eds.), *Understanding African American Rhetoric: Classical Origins to Contemporary Innovations*. New York: Routledge.

Morrison, T. (1977). *Song of Solomon*. New York: Signet.

———. (1983). Recitatif. In A. Baraka & A. Baraka (Eds.), *Confirmation: An Anthology Of African-American Women*. New York: Morrow.

———. (1984a). Memory, Creation, and Writing. *Thought, 59*, 385–390.

———. (1984b). Rootedness: The Ancestor as Foundation. In M. Evans (Ed.), *Black Women Writers, 1950–1980* (pp. 339–345). New York: Anchor Press/Doubleday.

———. (1987). *Beloved*. New York: Penguin Books.

———. (1989). Unspeakable Things Unspoken: The Afro-American Presence in American Literature. *Michigan Quarterly Review, 28*, 281–334.

———. (1992a). *Playing in the Dark: Whiteness and the Literary Imagination*. Cambridge, MA: Harvard University Press.

———. (Ed.). (1992b). *Race-Ing Justice, En-Gendering Power: Essays on Anita Hill, Clarence Thomas and the Construction of Social Reality*. New York: Pantheon Books.

———. (1995). Nobel Lecture, (7 December 1993). *Georgia Review, 49*, 318–323.

———. (1996). *The Dancing Mind*. New York: Alfred A. Knopf.

———. (1997). Home. In W. Lubiano (Ed.), *The House that Race Built*. New York: Pantheon Books.

Morton, D., and Zavarzedeh, A. (1991). *Theory/Pedagogy/Politics; Texts for Change*. Urbana: University of Illinois Press.

Moseberry, L. T. (1955). *An Historical Study of Negro Oratory in the United States to 1915*. University of Southern California.

Moses, W. (1982). *Black Messiahs and Uncle Toms*. University Park: Pennsylvania State University Press.

———. (1990). *The Ways of Ethiopia: Studies in African American Life and Letters*. (1st ed.). Ames: Iowa State University Press.

Moss, B. J. (1994). Creating a Community: Literacy Events in African American Churches. In B. J. Moss (Ed.), *Literacy Across Communities* (pp. 147–178). Cresskill, NJ: Hampton Press.

Mountford, R. (2001). On Gender and Rhetorical Space. *Rhetoric Society Quarterly, 31*(1), 41–71.

Murray, D. (1985). *A Writer Teaches Writing*. Boston: Houghton Mifflin.

Nakamura, L. (2000). Where Do You Want to Go Today? Cybernetic Tourism, the Internet, and Transnationality. In B. Kolko, L. Nakamura, & B. Rodman (Eds.), *Race in Cyberspace*. New York: Routledge.

Neal, M. A. (1999). *What the Music Said: Black Popular Music and Black Popular Culture*. New York: Routledge Press.

Neustadt, K. (1997). The Visits of the Writers Toni Morrison and Eudora Welty. In D. Taylor-Guthrie (Ed.), *Conversations with Toni Morrison* (p. 90). Jackson: University of Mississippi Press.

Newton, F. (1996). Foreword. In H. P. Newton, *War Against the Panthers: A Study of Repression in America* (p. vii). New York: Harlem River.

Newton, H. P. (1971). Letter to Ho Chi Minh. In A. Davis (Ed.), *If They Come in the Morning* (pp. 78). New York: Third Press.

———. (1995). *To Die for the People*. New York: Writers and Readers.

———. (1996). *War Against the Panthers: A Study of Repression in America*. New York: Harlem River.

Niles, L. A. (Ed.). (1995a). *African American Rhetoric: A Reader*. Dubuque, IA: Kendall Hunt.

———. (1995b). Rhetorical Characteristics of Traditional Black Preaching. In L. A. Niles (Ed.), *African American Rhetoric: A Reader*. Dubuque, IA: Kendall Hunt.

Noonan-Wagner, D. (1981). Possible Effects of Cultural Differences on the Rhetoric of Black Basic Skills Writers. Unpublished master's thesis, University of Houston, Texas.

Obenga, T. (1989). The Universe Before the Present Universe. In I. Van Sertima (Ed.), *Egypt Revisited* (pp. 291–324). New Brunswick: Transaction Publishers.

———. (1992). *Ancient Egypt and Black Africa*. London: Karnak House.

Ogbu, J. (1986). Literacy And Schooling in Subordinate Cultures: The Case of Black Americans. In U. Neisser (Ed.), *The School Achievement Of Minority Children: New Perspectives*. Hillsdale, NJ: L. Erlbaum Associates.

Ong, W. (1982). *Orality and Literacy: The Technologizing of the Word*. London: Methuen.

Onyewuenyi, I. (1993). *The African Origin of Greek Philosophy*. Nsukka: University of Nigeria Press.

Oregonian. [Article]. May 5, 1996, A30.

Owens, W. A. (1968). *Black Mutiny: The Revolt on the Schooner Amistad*. New York: Plume. (Originally published 1953).

Oyewole, A., & Ben Hassen, U. (with Green, K.). (Eds.). (1996). *On a Mission: Selected Poems and a History of The Last Poets*. New York: Henry Holt and Co.

Pate, A. (1997). *Amistad*. New York: DreamWorks.

Payne, J. C. (1982). *The Anatomy of Black Rhetoric*. Tallahassee, FL: Graphics Communications Associates.

Pearson, H. (1994). *The Shadow of the Panther: Huey Newton and the Price of Black Power in America*. New York: Addison-Wesley.

Peterson, C. (1995). *Doers of the Word: African-American Women Speakers and Writers in the North, 1830–1880*. New York: Oxford University Press.

Phelps, L., & S. Mano (1986). Imitation and Originality in the Work and Consciousness of an Adolescent Writer. In J. Niles (Ed.), *Solving Problems In Literacy Learners, Teachers, and Researchers Yearbook of the National Reading Conference* (pp. 290–293). Rochester, NY: National Reading Conference, Inc.

Pipes, W. H. 1992. *Say Amen, Brother! Old-Time Negro Preaching: A Study in American Frustration.* Detroit: Wayne State University Press. (Originally published 1951).

Plato. (1992). *Plato's Republic.* G. M. Grube (Trans.). Revised by C. D. C. Reeve. Indianapolis: Hackett.

Potter, R. (1995). *Spectacular Vernaculars: Hip Hop and the Politics of Postmodernism.* Albany: State University of New York Press.

Pratt, M. L. (1992). *Imperial Eyes: Travel Writing and Transculturation.* New York: Routledge.

Price, S. (1993). *Co-Wives and Calabashes.* Ann Arbor: University of Michigan Press.

Putnam, R. (2000). *Bowling Alone: The Collapse and Revival of American Community.* New York: Simon & Schuster.

Rampersand, A. (Ed.). (1995). *The Collected Poems of Langston Hughes.* New York: Alfred Knopf.

Randall, A. (2001). *The Wind Done Gone.* New York: Houghton Mifflin.

Randall, D. (1971). *The Black Poets.* New York: Bantam Books.

Rashidi, R. (1989a). Middle Kingdom of Kemet: A Photo Esssay. In I. Van Sertima (Ed.), *Egypt Revisited* (pp. 184–185). New Brunswick: Transaction Books.

———. (1989b). A Working Chronology of the Royal Kemetic Dynasties. In I. Van Sertima (Ed.), *Egypt Revisited* (pp. 105–116). New Brunswick: Transaction Books.

Ratcliffe, K. (2000). Eavesdropping as Rhetorical Tactic: History, Whiteness, and Rhetoric. *JAC: A Journal of Composition Theory, 20,* 87–119.

Reay, D., & Mirza, H. S. (2001). Black Supplementary Schools: Spaces of Radical Blackness. In R. Majors (Ed.), *Educating Our Black Children: New Directions and Radical Approaches.* (pp. 90–101). New York: Routledge.

Redd, T. (1995). Untapped Resources: "Styling" in Black Students' Writing for Black Audiences. In D. L. Rubin (Ed.), *Composing Social Identity In Written Language* (pp. 221–240). Hillsdale, NJ: L. Erlbaum.

Redd-Boyd, T. M., & Slater, W. H. (1989). The Effects of Audience Specification on Undergraduates' Attitudes, Strategies, and Writing. *Research in the Teaching of English, 23*(1), 77–108.

Reed, I. (1972). *Mumbo Jumbo.* New York: Scribners.

Reid, W. A. (1993). Literacy, Orality, and the Functions of Curriculum. In B. Green (Ed.), *The Insistence of the Letter: Literacy Studies and Curriculum Theorizing.* Pittsburgh: University of Pittsburgh Press.

Rhodes, J. (1998). *Mary Ann Shadd Cary: The Black Press and Protest in the Nineteenth Century.* Bloomington: Indiana University Press.

Richardson, E. (2003). *African American Literacies.* New York: Routledge.

Rivers, C. J. (1977). The Oral African Tradition Versus the Ocular Western

Tradition. In *This Far By Faith: American Black Worship and its African Roots* (pp. 28–37). Washington, DC: National Office of Black Catholics.

Robinson, J. L. (1983). Basic Writing and Its Basis in Talk: The Influence of Speech on Writing. In P. L. Stock (Ed.), *Forum: Essays on Theory and Practice in the Teaching of Writing* (pp. 116–128). Upper Montclair, NJ: Boynton/Cook.

Royster, J. (1996a, February). Review: New Histories of Rhetoric. *College English, 58,* 2.

———. (1996b). When the First Voice You Hear Is Not Your Own. *CCC, 47,* 29–40.

———. (1998). Sarah's Story: Making a Place for Historical Ethnography in Rhetorical Studies. Paper presented at the Thirtieth Anniversary Conference of the Rhetoric Society of America, Pittsburgh, Pennsylvania.

———. (2000). *Traces of a Stream: Literacy and Social Change among African American Women.* Pittsburgh: University of Pittsburgh Press.

Said, E. (1993). *Culture and Imperialism.* New York: Knopf.

Sale, M. (1992). Critiques from Within: Antebellum Projects of Resistance. *American Literature, 64,* 695–718.

Savona, J. L. (1984). *Jean Genet.* New York: Grove.

Scheper-Hughes, N., & Lock, M. M. (1998). The Mindful Body: A Prolegomenon to Future Work in Medical Anthropology. In P. J. Brown (Ed.), *Understanding And Applying Medical Anthropology.* Mountain View, CA: Mayfield Publishing Co.

Scott, J. (1980). *Domination and the Arts of Resistance.* New Haven, CT: Yale University Press.

Scott, R., & Brockriede, W. (Eds.). (1969). *The Rhetoric of Black Power.* New York: Harper & Row.

Seale, B. (1991). *Seize the Time: The Story of the Black Panther Party and Huey P. Newton.* Baltimore: Black Classic.

Shakur, S. (1994). *Monster: The Autobiography of an L.A. Gang Member.* New York: Penguin Books.

Shaughnessy, M. P. (1977). *Errors and Expectations: A Guide for the Teacher of Basic Writing.* New York: Oxford University Press.

Shome, R. (1999). Postcolonial Interventions in the Rhetorical Canon: An "Other" View. In J. L. Lucaites, C. M. Condit, & S. Caudill (Eds.), *Contemporary Rhetorical Theory: A Reader.* (pp. 591–608). New York: Guilford Press.

Simons, H. W. (1976) *Persuasion: Understanding, Practice, and Analysis.* Reading, MA: Addison-Wesley.

Smit, D. W. (1994). Some Difficulties with Collaborative Learning. In G. Olson & S. Dobrin (Eds.), *Composition Theory For The Postmodern Classroom* (pp. 69–81). Albany, NY: SUNY Press.

Smith, A. (1969). *Rhetoric of Black Revolution.* Boston: Allyn & Bacon.

———. (1972). *Language, Communication, and Rhetoric in Black America.* New York: Harper & Row.

Smith, A. L., & Robb, S. (Eds.). (1972). *The Voice of Black Rhetoric.* Boston: Allyn & Bacon.

Smith, V. (1987). *Self-Discovery and Authority in Afro-American Narrative.* Cambridge, MA: Harvard University Press.

Smitherman, G. (1986). *Talkin and Testifyin: The Language of Black America.* Detroit: Wayne State University Press. (Originally published 1977).

———. (1994). "The Blacker the Berry, the Sweeter the Juice": African American Student Writers. In A. H. Dyson & C. Genishi (Eds.), *The Need for Story: Cultural Diversity in Classroom and Community* (pp. 80–101). Urbana, IL: National Council of Teachers of English.

———. (2000). *Talkin that Talk: Language, Culture, and Education in African America.* New York: Routledge.

Smyth, J. F. D. (1853, April). Travels in Virginia in 1773. *Virginia Historical Register, 6,* 82.

Soja, E. (1998). *Post Modern Geographies: The Reassertion of Space in Critical Social Theory.* New York: Routledge.

Sollors, W. (1986). *Beyond Ethnicity: Consent and Descent in American Culture.* New York: Oxford University Press.

Stanley, L. (1992). *Rap: The Lyrics.* New York: Penguin.

Steele, C., & Aronson, J. (1995). Stereotype Threat and the Intellectual Test Performance of African-Americans. *Journal of Personality and Social Psychology, 69*(5), 797.

Stewart, J. (2001, April 4). Martin Luther King and the New World Order. *Martin Luther King Jr. Memorial Lecture.* Pennsylvania State University.

Stewart, M. (1995). An Address Delivered Before The Afric-American Female Intelligence Society of Boston. In S. W. Logan (Ed.), *With Pen and Voice* (pp. 11–16). Carbondale: Southern Illinois University Press. (Originally published 1832).

Still, W. (1872). *The Underground Rail Road.* Philadelphia: Porter and Coates.

Street, B. V. (Ed.). (1993). *Cambridge Studies in Oral and Literate Culture: Cross-Cultural Approaches to Literacy.* Cambridge, England: Cambridge University Press.

Strunk, W., Jr., & White, E. B. (1979). *The Elements of Style.* New York: Macmillan.

Stull, B. T. (1999). *Amid the Fall, Dreaming of Eden: Du Bois, King, Malcolm X, and Emancipatory Composition.* Carbondale: Southern Illinois University Press.

Sundquist, E. (1993). *To Wake the Nations: Race in the Making of American Literature.* Cambridge, MA: Belknap Press.

Swearingen, C. J. (1991). *Rhetoric and Irony: Western Literacy and Western Lies.* New York: Oxford University Press.

Taborn, T. (2001). The Art of Tricknology. *US Black Engineer, Information Technology,* p. 8.

Tannen, D. (1994). *Talking Voices: Repetition, Dialogue, and Imagery in Conversational Discourse.* New York: Cambridge University Press.

Tate, C. (1993). *Domestic Allegories of Political Desire: The Black Heroine's Text at the Turn of the Century.* New York: Oxford University Press.

Tomlin, C. (1999). *Black Language Style in Sacred and Secular Contexts.* Brooklyn, NY: Caribbean Diaspora Press, Inc. (Medgar Evers College).

Truth, S. (1988). *Narrative of Sojourner Truth; A Bondswoman of Olden Time, with a History of Her Labors and Correspondence Drawn from Her "Book Of Life."* Frances W. Titus (Ed.). Salem, NH: Ayer. (Originally published 1878).

———. (1997). Arn't I a woman? In H. L. Gates & N. McKay (Eds.), *The Norton Anthology of African American Literature* (pp. 199–201). New York: W. W. Norton. (Originally published 1878).

T'Shaka, O. (1995). *Return to the African Mother Principle of Male and Female Equality.* Vol. 1. Oakland, CA: Pan African Publishers and Distributors.

Turner, L. (1949). *Africanisms in the Gullah Dialect.* Chicago: University of Chicago Press.

———. (2002). *Africanisms in the Gullah Dialect.* With a New Introduction by Katherine Wyly Mille and Michael Montgomery. Columbia: University of South Carolina Press.

US Department of Commerce/National Telecommunications and Information Administration. (1995). *Falling Through the Net: A Survey of the "Have Nots" in Urban and Rural America.* [on-line]. Accessed August 30, 2002, from *http://www.ntia.doc.gov/ntiahome/fallingthru.html.*

———. (1998). *Falling Through the Net II: New Data on the Digital Divide.* [on-line]. Accessed August 30, 2002, from *http://www.ntia.doc.gov/ntiahome/net2/.*

———. (2000). *Falling Through the Net: Toward Digital Inclusion.* [on-line]. Accessed August 30, 2002, from *http://www.ntia.doc.gov/ntiahome/fttn00/contents00.html.*

Van Sertima, I. (1989). (Ed.). *Egypt Revisited.* New Brunswick: Transaction Books.

Villanueva, V., Jr. (1993). *Bootstraps: From an American Academic of Color.* Urbana, IL: National Council of Teachers of English.

———. (Ed.). (1997). *Cross-Talk in Comp Theory: A Reader.* Urbana, IL: National Council of Teachers of English.

Visor, J. (1987). The Impact of American Black English Oral Tradition Features on Decontextualization Skills in College Writing. Unpublished doctoral dissertation, Illinois State University, Normal.

Vygotsky, L. S. (1986). *Thought and Language.* Cambridge, MA: MIT Press.

Walker, A. (1983). In Search of Our Mother's Gardens. In A. Walker (Ed.), *In Search of Our Mother's Gardens* (pp. 231–243). New York: Harcourt Brace Jovanovich.

Walker, D. (1995). *David Walker's Appeal to the Coloured Citizens of the World.* New York: Hill & Wang. (Originally published 1829).

———. (1997). Appeal in Four Articles; Together with a Preamble, to the Coloured Citizens of the World. In H. L. Gates & N. McKay (Eds.), *The Norton Anthology Of African American Literature* (pp. 179–190). New York: W. W. Norton. (Originally published 1829).

Walker, R. J. (1992). *The Rhetoric of Struggle: Public Address by African American Women.* New York: Garland.

"The Walking Dead": Movie Tells the Untold Story of the Black Experience in Vietnam. (1995, February 20). *Jet.*

Warner, M. (2002). *Publics and Counterpublics.* New York: Zone Books.

Welch, K. E. (1990). *The Contemporary Reception of Classical Rhetoric: Appropriations of Ancient Discourse.* Hillsdale, NJ: Lawrence Erlbaum Associates.

Wells, I. B. (1970). *The Autobiography of Ida B. Wells.* Chicago: University of Chicago Press.

Wheatley, P. (2001). To Maecenas. In V. Caretta (Ed.), *Phillis Wheatley: Complete Writings* (pp. 9–10). New York: Penguin Books. (Originally published 1773).

Which Way for the Negro? *Newsweek,* May 15, 1967, pp. 27–34.

White, A. B. (1998). Fragmented Souls: Call and Response with Renee Cox. In M. Guillory & C. Green (Eds.), *Soul: Black Power, Politics, And Pleasure* (pp. 45–55). New York: New York University Press.

White, E. (1993). *Genet: A Biography.* New York: Alfred A. Knopf.

Wideman, J. E. (1999). Foreword. In Z. N. Hurston, *Go Gator and Muddy the Water: Writing by Zora Neale Hurston from the Federal Writer's Project* (pp. xi–xx). P. Bordelon (Ed.). New York: W. W. Norton.

Wilentz, S. (1995). Introduction. *David Walker's Appeal to the Coloured Citizens of the World.* New York: Hill & Wang.

Williams, B. (1989a). *Essays in Western Civilization Presented to Helene J. Kantar.* Chicago: Oriental Institute of the University of Chicago.

———. (1989b). The Lost Pharoahs of Nubia. In I. Van Sertima (Ed.), *Egypt Revisited* (pp. 90–104). New Brunswick: Transaction Books.

Williams, J. M. (1997). *Style: Ten Lessons in Clarity and Grace.* (5th ed.). New York: Longman.

Williams, K. (1998). *Dog Days: The Legend of O. V. Catto.* [Play]. Philadelphia: Venture Theater.

Williams, P. (1997). *Seeing a Color-Blind Future: The Paradox of Race.* New York: Noonday Press.

Williams, P. J. (1991). *The Alchemy of Race and Rights: Diary of a Law Professor.* Cambridge, MA: Harvard University Press.

Wills, G. (1978). *Inventing America: Jefferson's Declaration of Independence.* New York: Doubleday.

Winner, L. (1986). *The Whale and the Reactor: A Search for Limits in an Age of High Technology.* Chicago: University of Chicago.

Winterowd, W. R. (1994). Rediscovering the Essay. In G. Olson & S. Dobrin (Eds.), *Composition Theory for the Postmodern Classroom* (pp. 121–131). Albany: State University of New York Press.

Woodson, C. (1925). *Negro Orators and Their Orations.* Washington, DC: Associated Publishers.

———. (1926). *The Mind of the Negro as Reflected in Letters Written During the Crisis 1800–1860.* Washington, DC: Association for the Study of Negro Life and History.

———. (1941). *Twelve Million Black Voices.* New York: Viking Press.

Wright, R., & Hughes, W. (1996). *Lay Down Body: Living History in African American Cemeteries.* Detroit: Invisible Ink Press.

X, M., & Breitman, G. (1990). *Malcolm X Speaks: Selected Speeches and Statements.* New York: Grove Weidenfeld. (Originally published 1965).

Yellin, J. F. (1985). Text and Contexts of Harriet Jacobs' *Incidents in the Life of a Slave Girl Written by Herself*. In C. T. Davis and H. L. Gates Jr. (Eds.), *The Slave's Narrative*. New York: Oxford University Press.

Yoakam, D. G. (1943). Women's Introduction to the American Platform. In William Brigance (Ed.), *A History and Criticism of American Public Address* (pp. 153–192). New York: McGraw Hill.

Young, H. A., & Young, B. H. (1977). Science and Black Studies. *Journal of Negro Education, 46*(4) 380–387.

Young, K. (Ed.). (2000). *Giant Steps: The New Generation of African American Writers*. New York: Perennial.

Zumthor, P. (1990). *Oral Poetry*. Minneapolis: University of Minnesota Press.

Contributors

LENA AMPADU is an associate professor of English at Towson University, where she teaches courses on African American literature, African women writers, and undergraduate writing. Her research interests include the rhetoric of nineteenth-century African American women and the intersections of orality and literacy in the teaching of writing.

ADAM J. BANKS is an assistant professor of writing and rhetoric at Syracuse University. His current research interests include African American rhetoric, technology, composition, and critical race theory.

JACQUELINE K. BRYANT is an associate professor of English and the chairperson of the Department of English and Speech at Chicago State University. She is the author of *The Foremother Figure in Early Black Women's Literature: "Clothed in My Right Mind"* (1999) and the editor of *Gwendolyn Brooks's Maud Martha: A Critical Collection* (2002). She recorded, transcribed, and compiled stories of Black elders in *A Jubilee Project,* edited by the Reverend Dr. Otis Moss Jr. (2002). She has also published articles in the *Journal of Black Studies, CLA Journal, and WarpLand: A Journal of Black Literature and Ideas* and currently serves on the editorial review board of the *International Journal of Africana Studies.* Her research interests include the literary works and the lives of late-nineteenth- and early-twentieth-century Black women writers.

KERMIT E. CAMPBELL is an assistant professor of rhetoric in the Interdisciplinary Writing department at Colgate University, where he teaches freshmen composition, social science writing, and African American rhetoric. With scholarly interests ranging from African oral traditions to African American formal oratory to rap music, Campbell has contributed various essays and reviews to several rhetoric and composition journals. His forthcoming book is entitled *Gettin' Our Groove On: Rhetoric, Language, and Literacy for the Hip Hop Generation.*

VICTORIA CLIETT is a learning specialist at Wayne State University. She is a recipient of the CCCC Scholars for the Dream Travel Award and a member of the CCCC Language Policy Committee.

WILLIAM W. COOK is a professor of African and African American studies and the Israel Evans Professor of Oratory and Belles Lettres at Dartmouth College. The actor and director is also the author of numerous essays, poems, and books, including the play *Flight to Canada* (1989). He has most recently published his poems in *Spiritual and Other Poems by William W. Cook* (1999). Cook is the 2001 Daniel Heftal Lecturer in the Humanities and has been acknowledged as one of the top fifty Black scholars in the arts and sciences in the 1998 *Journal of Blacks in Higher Education.*

CLINTON CRAWFORD is the director of the John Henrik Clarke–C. L. R. James *African World Research Institute* and teaches the first course on the life and works of John Henrik Clarke at Medgar Evers College, City University of New York. An associate professor in the Department of Mass Communications, he has expertise in language communications and art. Crawford is also the author of the internationally acclaimed book *Recasting Ancient Egypt in the African Context* (1996).

KEITH GILYARD is a professor of English at Pennsylvania State University. His books include *Voices of the Self: A Study of Language Competence* and *Let's Flip the Script: An African American Discourse on Language, Literature, and Learning.* He is also the editor of *Race Rhetoric and Composition* and is a coeditor of *Rhetoric and Ethnicity.* Gilyard is a former chair of the Conference on College Composition and Communication (CCCC).

RONALD L. JACKSON II is an associate professor of culture and communication theory in the Department of Communication Arts and Sciences at Pennsylvania State University. He is the author of *The Negotiation of Cultural Identity* (1999) and *African American Communication: Identity and Culture* (with Michael Hecht and Sidney Ribeau) and the editor of *Understanding African American Rhetoric: Classical Origins to Contemporary Innovations* (with Elaine B. Richardson, 2003) and *African American Communication and Identities* (2003). Forthcoming are two books: *Negotiating the Black Body: Intersections of Communication, Culture, and Identity* and *Pioneers in African American Communication Research* (with Sonja Brown-Givens). His theory work includes the development of two paradigms coined "cultural contracts theory" and "black masculine identity theory."

SHIRLEY WILSON LOGAN is an associate professor of English at the University of Maryland, College Park, where she teaches courses in writing, histories of rhetoric, and composition theory. She specializes in the public discourse of nineteenth-century Black women and is working on a critical edition of Frances Harper's nonfiction prose.

JOYCE IRENE MIDDLETON is an associate professor of English at St. John Fisher College. She is the editor of *Of Color: African American Literature* (forthcoming), and she has published essays on oral memory and literacy; on pedagogy, race, and gender; and on works by Toni Morrison and Zora Neale Hurston. Middleton was awarded a position in the 2001 NEH Summer Institute for Black Film Studies. She is completing a book on memory in Toni Morrison and is developing new rhetorical work on Black women independent filmmakers.

VORRIS L. NUNLEY is a Ph.D. candidate in English at Pennyslvania State University, with an emphasis on rhetorical theory (verbal and visual) and composition as well as African American expressive culture (literature, film, music, art, and popular culture) and pedagogy.

GWENDOLYN D. POUGH is an assistant professor of women's studies at the University of Minnesota, Twin Cities Campus. Her dissertation, "Rhetorical Disruptions: Black Public Culture and the Public Sphere," looks at the political potential and relevance of the Black Panther Party and rap music/Hip Hop culture for contemporary African Americans. Her forthcoming book is about Black womanhood, Hip Hop culture, and the public sphere.

ELAINE B. RICHARDSON is an assistant professor of English and applied linguistics at Pennyslvania State University. Her research interests include the teaching of rhetoric and composition to African American Vernacular English speakers, linguistic and cultural development, and the global diffusion of Afro-American cultures via digital technology. Richardson is the author of various articles and chapters concerning language and literacy. She is the author of *African American Literacies* in the Routledge Literacies series. She is also the co-editor, with Ronald L. Jackson II, of *Understanding African American Rhetoric: Classical Origins to Contemporary Innovations* (2003).

JACQUELINE JONES ROYSTER is a professor of English at Ohio State University. Royster won the Modern Language Association's Mina P. Shaughnessy Award for her book *Traces of a Stream: Literacy and Social Change among African American Women*. She has three complementary areas of interest: the rhetorical history of women of African descent, the development of literacy, and delivery systems for the teaching of composition. Royster has filled a variety of roles on committees, task forces, and commissions in professional organizations, including serving as chair of the Conference on College Composition and Communication (CCCC) and chair of the executive committee of the Division of Teaching Writing of the Modern Language Association.

KALÍ TAL is a professor of humanities at the University of Arizona. Relentlessly interdisciplinary, she has spent the last two decades working in African American and American studies, focusing primarily on post–World War II U.S. history, literature, and culture(s). She is the author of *Women in Particular: An Index to American Women* (1985) and *Worlds of Hurt: Reading the Literatures of Trauma* (1995), as well as many book chapters for edited collections. Her articles have appeared in many academic and popular journals. She is currently at work on a two-volume study of Afrofuturist visions, contrasting those literary, musical, and cinematic texts with White visions of Black futures.

KIMMIKA L. H. WILLIAMS is an assistant professor of theater at Temple University. She is the 2000 winner of the Pew Charitable Trust Fellowship in script writing and the 1999 winner of the Daimler Chrysler "Spirit of the Word" National Poetry Competition.

Index